LEARNING PROCESS IN PSYCHOANALYTIC SUPERVISION

Learning Process in Psychoanalytic Supervision: Complexities and Challenges

A Case Illustration

Paul A. Dewald, M.D.

with
a Contribution by
Mary M. Dick, M.D.

International Universities Press, Inc.
Madison Connecticut

Library of Congress Cataloging-in-Publication Data

Dewald, Paul A.
Learning process in psychoanalytic supervision.

Includes bibliographies and index.
1. Psychoanalysis—Study and teaching—Supervision—Case studies. I. Dick, Mary M. II. Title. [DNLM: 1. Learning. 2. Psychoanalysis—education. WM 18 D515L]
RC502.D48 1987 616.89'17'0711 86-27597
ISBN 0-8236-2965-1

Manufactured in the United States of America

To my children and grandchildren—and to their surrogates, my students and their students

Contents

Acknowledgments ix
Chapter 1 Introduction 1
Chapter 2 Aspects of the Supervisory Process 11
Chapter 3 Patient Evaluation and Routine Reports 29
Chapter 4 Supervisory Session 19 54
Chapter 5 Supervisory Session 20 75
Chapter 6 Supervisory Session 42 95
Chapter 7 Supervisory Session 43 119
Chapter 8 Supervisory Session 68 142
Chapter 9 Supervisory Session 87 167
Chapter 10 Supervisory Session 88 188
Chapter 11 Supervisory Session 91 211
Chapter 12 Supervisory Session 92 233
Chapter 13 Supervisory Session 99 257
Chapter 14 Supervisory Session 100 280
Chapter 15 Supervisory Session 109 301
Chapter 16 Supervisory Session 110 324
Chapter 17 Supervisory Session 117 349
Chapter 18 Supervisory Session 118 369
Chapter 19 Supervisory Session 122 389
Chapter 20 Supervisory Session 123 409
Chapter 21 Supervisory Session 124 426
Chapter 22 Contribution *by Mary M. Dick, M.D.* 448
Chapter 23 Synthesis and Summary 472
References 479
Index 481

Acknowledgments

I hereby express my deep appreciation to the patient whose psychoanalysis was the basis of this educational experience. Her permission for this material to be published represents a contribution to the psychoanalytic literature. To whatever degree this study adds to a deeper and different understanding of the supervisory process, its readers are in her debt.

Many psychoanalysts and psychotherapists are reluctant to have their detailed work extensively scrutinized and criticized by a public audience. The readers of this volume are therefore indebted also to Mary M. Dick, M.D. for her courage in allowing her work to be presented here.

I also want to thank the secretaries who transcribed the various versions of this material and manuscript: Janet Kiesler, Ann Patterson, Kathy Rosteck, Marie Meldrum, and Suzanne Byrne.

A project such as this inevitably impinges on the author's time and emotional availability for other activities. In addition to her help in reading and revising the manuscript, my wife contributed immensely by her cheerful understanding and acceptance of the effects the work had upon our time together.

Finally, Chapter 2, "Aspects of the Supervisory Process," appeared originally in *The Annual of Psychoanalysis*, Vol. IX (1981), and is reprinted here by the kind permission of the editors.

Chapter 1
Introduction

There is general acceptance among analytic educators that supervision of the candidate conducting the psychoanalytic treatment of his patients is one of the cornerstones of psychoanalytic education. In the traditional view, psychoanalytic education is based on the personal analysis, the didactic classroom curriculum, and the supervisory experience. By analyzing patients under supervision the candidate learns through personal experience more effectively to observe and integrate the material from the clinical situation, and to develop his technique of applying the psychoanalytic method.

In spite of the importance generally accorded supervision in the education of psychoanalysts, there have been remarkably few systematic and longitudinal studies of the supervisory process itself. There is an extensive psychoanalytic literature on supervision, but much of it has been anecdotal, narrowly focused, impressionistic, or didactic. Little has been offered which studies in depth or detail the long-term unfolding of the supervisory process itself.

There are several notable exceptions to this statement. Fleming and Benedek (1966) made audiotape recordings of supervisory sessions with several different candidates. From this material they elaborated and illustrated a number of basic concepts regarding the supervisory process and the educational issues involved. In their monograph, a milestone in the study of the supervisory process, they presented lengthy excerpts from supervisory sessions and commented on the teaching/learning situation.

Ekstein and Wallerstein (1958) wrote an important monograph on the supervisory process, particularly in relation to psychiatric training, in which they pooled their impressions of supervision and systematically attempted to delineate the nature of the experience and its role in the education of the psychiatrist. They do not, however, present extensive data from the supervision itself.

Schuster, Sandt, and Thaler (1972) describe a study of the clinical supervision of psychiatric residents, based upon transcriptions of tape-recorded conferences among supervisors. In these recordings a supervisor presents an account of the supervisory interaction between himself and the resident, and then discusses with the others the educational issues being illustrated. The primary data of the supervision itself, however, are not provided.

Wallerstein (1981) with a number of colleagues conducted an intensive study in which the supervisor of a psychoanalytic candidate tape recorded detailed process notes of the supervisory interactions between himself and the candidate for the first fifteen supervisory hours. These notes were recorded shortly after each supervisory session, and were transcribed and then distributed to members of the study group. Each participant then prepared a critique of the supervisory situation and process. The group met periodically over a number of years to discuss their impressions and rework their ideas. This eventuated in the volume *Becoming a Psychoanalyst.* The candidate being supervised also contributed his version of the experience, as did the supervisor. This study is a landmark in the consideration of psychoanalytic supervision, but it is limited by the fact that the data consist only of the supervisor's impressions as presented in his process notes, and also by the fact that it covers only the early phase of an analytic and supervisory process that extended for a number of years.

In some respects psychoanalytic supervision is a form of master-apprentice education in which the expert seeks to transmit to the novice the understanding and abilities needed to conduct a particular activity. This kind of education dates to antiquity, and for many lines of endeavor it remains a satisfactory method of instruction. In medicine it is the basis for clinical teaching on ward rounds and in the operating room. The student can observe the teacher performing the task in question, and on later occasions the teacher can observe, instruct, and offer feedback to the student. This may be done in group settings or in a one-to-one arrangement, but in either case the observation, whether by student or master, does not significantly alter the task in question or the process by which it is carried out. Another feature of elementary teaching situations (particularly those regarding technical procedures) is that often there is an accepted standard among the instructors, a relatively uniform agreement as to what counts as correct procedure.

But with psychoanalysis and other forms of intensive individual psychotherapy things are different. Like analysis itself, the supervisory experience here is never completely the same in two different situations. The multiplicity of factors existing in the candidate, the supervisor, the patient being analyzed, and the institute itself all contribute to the fact that each supervisory experience ends up as unique and nonreproducible.

On the other hand, there are certain elements common to every supervisory situation, again like analysis itself. Certain general techniques and interactions can be observed and classified that in spite of individual variations permit a general conceptualization of the supervisory process. Even supervisors with highly idiosyncratic teaching styles demonstrate some of these common elements in their teaching, just as candidates show common elements in their learning processes.

Individual talents vary. Some supervisors are more skillful in the presentation of ideas than are others, while some are more gifted in empathic experience and intuitive responsiveness but have difficulty communicating their ideas. These differences cannot be neglected, as they affect the nature of a given supervisory process.

The student's capacity to learn is influenced by a variety of factors; no two students are identical, even though all are carefully screened and have undergone the experience of a training analysis. The student's character and capacity for clinical work will have a significant and determining impact on the analytic and supervisory processes despite the skills of the supervisor.

These skills, however, and the very nature of the supervisory process will in turn have an impact on the way the candidate presents himself in supervision; they will in all likelihood also affect the way in which the candidate functions and reacts in his analytic position vis-à-vis the patient. The suitability of the patient for analysis will also profoundly affect the student and the supervisory situation. For instance, the patient who does extremely well may permit the inept or inadequate candidate to appear more competent than in fact he is, making it much more difficult for the supervisor to demonstrate that the candidate is not doing well in the analytic role. By contrast, the relatively skilled candidate confronted with an unanalyzable patient may have great difficulty demonstrating his capacities in the supervision, and the supervisor, for lack of progress in the analysis, may not be able to identify where the difficulties lie. These idiosyncrasies could be multiplied over and over and require caution regarding generalizations drawn from a single supervisory experience on a single analytic case.

The relationship between the patient and the therapist is a crucial element in the therapeutic enterprise, and issues of trust, confidentiality, and privacy are extremely important in carrying out the procedure. Kubie (1958) argued that the educational benefits to students from listening to audiotape recordings of their work outweigh the possible adverse effects on treatment, at least in work with psychiatric residents.

In the psychoanalytic situation, the introduction of an observer into the treatment setting (whether in person or through audio or video taping) has a significant effect on the process being observed. Such observation has been done on a research basis, and in certain cases the effects it produces can be reasonably well dealt with as an element in the treatment process.

For the student learning to do psychoanalysis the task is already complicated enough, and the presence of an observer would only compound the difficulties. The usual approach is for the student to present to the observer (the individual supervisor or a case conference) an account from notes of the interactions between therapist and patient. Even the mere awareness that the case will later be presented may have an effect on the process between the student and the patient.

In this type of reporting the presenting supervisee is also a participant in the drama that unfolds between analyst and patient, and therefore as a reporter will inevitably experience (consciously and unconsciously) biases and limitations in the extent to which his report accurately reflects what has occurred. Effective psychoanalytic listening requires the capacity for evenly hovering unfocused attention and subjective imagery and association. This is in contrast to the secondary process recall and organization involved in recording data. Furthermore, distortion and decay tends to vary directly with the time that elapses before material is recorded.

The student who takes detailed notes during analytic sessions may be hampered in his analytic function; preoccupation with recording the material may interfere with relating more emotionally and directly to the patient, or may disrupt the evenly hovering attention to his own associations that analytic posture and technique require. The record may be more accurate in terms of sequence and detail, but it may distract the student from the more important task of functioning comfortably as an analyst. However, if such a recording process becomes relatively ego-syntonic and the student is capable of secondary autonomy without interfering with his associational flow, it may bypass some of the limitations of writing notes after the session.

Wallerstein and Sampson (1971) have demonstrated that valuable understanding of the psychoanalytic process and the unfolding interaction between analyst and patient may be had from the study of summarized process notes. On the other hand, Knapp and Dahl (see Dorpat, 1973), Gill and Hoffman (1982), Luborsky and Auerback (1969), and other researchers, who study transcriptions of psychoanalytic material in great detail, have demonstrated that only accurate and extensive recovery of the material of the analytic session permits certain levels of study of the analytic process.

At the present time, most candidate-supervisor pairs base their work on the student's oral or written presentation of process notes taken either during or after analytic sessions. For better or worse, this is the record with which the supervisor must work in his efforts to help the candidate better understand

and appreciate the analytic process and his own role in it. A great deal has been written about the occurrence of a "parallel process" between the behavior of the patient toward the candidate and that of the candidate toward the supervisor. The presumption is that the supervisor can use this parallel process as another source of information about the analytic work being done. Such understanding, however, is likely to be intermittent and limited at best.

Some supervisors attempt to gain as accurate a record as possible of the events and interactions in the analytic sessions, and they encourage the candidate to present detailed material in a systematic and chronological fashion. The rationale for this is that lack of experience and analytic sophistication may render the candidate unable to judge which are the most important and revealing communications from the patient and which events in the treatment interaction are likely to evoke the most meaningful responses. The candidate may in fact miss some of the patient's communications altogether, communications the more experienced supervisor, attuned to latent meanings and implications, can pick up from the candidate's presentation if sufficiently detailed.

Other supervisors prefer the candidate to present clinical material for the most part without referring to notes; instead they prefer an associative account, assuming that from this material they will be capable of piecing together the basic themes of the case and that the student registers significant material from the patient even if not fully aware of it. In a manner analogous to listening in the therapeutic situation, these supervisors use their analytic skills to understand latent meanings as the candidate presents material and unstructured associations to it. In addition to content and narrative, the supervisor listens for blind spots, omissions, or other kinds of difficulties the candidate may have in re-creating and presenting the material without notes.

Neither of these alternatives, however, is entirely effective, and many supervisors develop a technique in which the candidate presents material from both perspectives at different times.

The study presented here evolved during a burst of creative energy that occurred seven months after this particular supervision began. The plan was to provide data, as accurate and complete as possible, of a psychoanalytic supervisory experience in the hope of demonstrating over a prolonged period the unfolding of a supervisory process and the changes that occur in the patient, the candidate, the supervisor, and the process itself during that time. Since it is impossible to present all the data in printed form, and since changes in slowly evolving functions are more readily apparent through interrupted observations (analogous to time-lapse photography showing biological growth), audio-recorded transcriptions of two successive psychoanalytic supervisory sessions were made at random intervals, some as short as a few months, others as long as a year. The hope was to demonstrate the developing capacities and sophistication of the candidate, as well as shifts in the technique and function of the supervisor in response to changes in the supervisee or patient. If such changes are not manifest, one might draw the conclusion that effective supervision was not provided.

Another advantage to this method is that it permits others access to the raw data of the supervisory situation and relationship, and thereby to draw conclusions other than those reached by the reporting supervisor.

There are of course disadvantages in this design as well. One is that the material may be skewed, as not every supervisory hour was recorded. It is possible also that supervisor and candidate were sensitive to the recording and might have altered their behavior in perceptible if often unconscious ways. The intermittence of the recording may also create problems. By virtue of its randomness, some of the more crucial or significant interactions, in either the supervisory or the therapeutic process, may be omitted. But though there may be times in either situation when specific behaviors or interactions are crucial to understanding, the more usual pattern tends to be a gradual, repetitive process in which no single session or particular interaction or interpretation stands out as the dramatic focus of shifts or changes. Furthermore, even when such crucial events do occur they are frequently alluded to or reactivated by subsequent experience or material in the analysis or supervision. The net effect is that reference to unrecorded "dramatic" events would likely be discernible in the recorded material, though this is not guaranteed.

Another issue regarding transcripts of audio recordings is that although the verbalizations may be complete, there is no way of recapturing tone of voice, timbre, tempo, volume, or pitch, let alone such nonvocal accompaniments as facial expression, gesture, and posture, all of which serve to convey (among other things) the speaker's affective states. In addition, the associative patterns and processes in the minds of candidate and supervisor as they interact (those which are not put into verbal form) are missing and cannot be retrieved in their full extent or detail; and subsequent study of the transcriptions by the candidate or supervisor is inevitably contaminated by the knowledge of what is to come, in contrast to the original situation, where only knowledge of what had already transpired was available. But these shortcomings notwithstanding, the method does permit access to a kind of data both about the supervisory process and the psychoanalytic process that is unavailable in most other forms of data collection.

The philosophical position of the supervisor will significantly influence how he proceeds in his educational role. Some take the position that the supervisor's main task is to encourage candidates to recognize and observe their intuitive responses to patients and their affective emotional interaction with them; these supervisors place great emphasis on countertransference interpretation and observation in the candidate. Other supervisors place greater emphasis upon encouraging the candidate's initiative and independent learning by experience. They tend at times to be rather silent, sparse in their interactions and communications, and to emphasize the candidate's experiential learning and active mastery through minimal interventions in the supervisory experience and process.

Others see themselves predominantly as teachers and instructors, with emphasis not only on affective responsiveness but also on cognitive expression of technique, and on conceptualization of the process the candidate is engaged in with the patient. These supervisors tend to be more active, instructional, and directive, and often show the candidate what can or should be done in a given situation.

There are also differences with regard to the relative weighting of responsibility for the clinical progress and well-being of the patient, as contrasted with the educational needs of the student. At times these interests may be in conflict with each other and may pose a problem of role responsibility for the supervisor.

My own personal position is to see myself in the supervisory role as predominantly an educator who follows general educational principles in trying to impart to the candidate various aspects of the analyst's role that must be mastered. I seek to achieve a balance among a number of educational principles: cognitive didactic instruction; demonstration of the thinking processes of an analyst (myself); listening to clinical material and illustrating the process of clinical inference; advising an inexperienced therapist about various technical options; encouraging active participation and observation in the student; providing prompt and unambiguous feedback regarding progress in learning; and demonstrating sensitivity to the various affective nuances involved both in the patient's material and in the candidate's presentation during supervision. I also take the position that the candidate (particularly in an early case) is not as yet in an optimal position to understand the latent meanings of the material and therefore in no position to select which of the many issues the patient presents during the course of an hour are the most suitable for scrutiny during supervision. I therefore prefer to stay reasonably close to the recorded process material and to the sequence in which it emerged during the sessions. In that way the flow and pattern of associations are more readily apparent both to me and, through me, to the candidate. As the supervision continues and experience with the candidate dictates, I encourage more and more active summary by the candidate, with decreased reliance on presentation of the process material.

The material being presented here is from a woman candidate's first case. The patient likewise is a woman. The case had been in analysis approximately seven months at the time the first recording was initiated, so that the very beginning of this supervisory experience will be presented in the more traditional form of summarized process notes by the supervisor (Chapter 3).

In order that the reader may more easily follow the flow of the material, the transcripts have been edited for grammatical errors, incomplete or run-on sentences, irrelevant redundancies, hesitations, etc. Other than that they present a complete and accurate account of the sessions.

It is hoped that the data presented here will permit at least some degree of extrapolation and generalization in regard to the teaching and learning that takes place in the supervisory process, as well as the type of therapeutic experience that takes place in an analysis. Other educators may compare and contrast their experience with that presented here, and perhaps will begin to elaborate their own data so that a more accessible library of experience with supervision will permit increasingly effective generalizations with regard to analytic education.

Chapter 2

Aspects of the Supervisory Process

It is my thesis that psychoanalytic supervision can best be conceptualized as a process of interaction in which each participant is acutely sensitive to the input and responses of the other. There is an unfolding sequence of experience in any single case of candidate-supervisor pairing, and also a progressive development within the candidate involved with a variety of cases and supervisors.

Although there are a number of similarities between the supervisory and the psychoanalytic process, there are also significant differences which must be respected if supervision is to be effective.

The Goals of Supervision

If the goals of supervision are well understood, experiences to maximize the possibility of achieving them can more readily be designed, and checkpoints to help us evaluate whether and when we have reached them will be available.

From a more narrow perspective, the goals of the supervisory process are to impart to the candidate a minimum core of psychoanalytic technique as applied to the particular patient under study. We seek to help the candidate integrate an awareness of psychoanalytic theory with the data base of the particular clinical situation, and to develop a capacity to shift back and forth from microscopic to macroscopic perspectives with regard to clinical material. The specific requirements of the institute and of the American Psychoanalytic Association must of course also be met.

In addition, however, the goals of psychoanalytic supervision may be conceptualized in a broader context. Subsidiary goals then include the candidate's increasing sense of personal identity as a psychoanalyst, a process involving unconscious ramifications for the candidate, the supervisor, and the training analyst (to be discussed below). Establishing such an identity should allow integration by the candidate of various identifications and professional role models.

It is hoped that supervision will also foster a sense of pleasure and creativity within the candidate about the role and function of a psychoanalyst, along with an increasing capacity for curiosity as well as surprise, and appreciation of the sense of discovery and rediscovery that occurs in psychoanalytic clinical work. The capacity to appreciate and enjoy these aspects of the analyst's role is one of the elements that distinguish the education of a psychoanalyst from the training of a psychoanalytic technician, and that ultimately may be translated into professional and scientific productivity and skills.

An increasing capacity for self-analysis, allowing recognition and acceptance of countertransference factors should evolve, along with a capacity to use these in understanding the patient's behavior as well as one's own recurrent patterns of psychopathology. Another broad goal is the candidate's capacity to work independently, free of reliance on the supervisory relationship but tempered by an appreciation of the opportunities and advantages of consultation with a senior colleague.

The distinction between the broad and the narrow goals of supervision is similar to that between the treatment goals of psychoanalysis and those of more limited, symptom-oriented forms of psychotherapy. Narrow therapeutic undertakings usually mean that the patient will not achieve the sense of personality enrichment, new experience, sensitivity, capacity for empathy and understanding (of both self and others), and discovery and development of personal abilities that can occur in a successful psychoanalytic treatment experience.

Not everyone is capable of achieving these benefits of a full psychoanalysis. For many patients, varying levels of compromise are required. A significant number of our candidates do not experience in their training analysis the intrapsychic reorganization, growth, and development that are possible. As a result, some of these candidates can become effective psychoanalytic technicians, but they do not experience that sense of enrichment and pleasure in personal development that occurs in others.

If there are significant limitations within the candidate, or limitations within the vision, educational technique, or capacities of the supervisor, the supervisory process will be defined in terms of the narrower set of goals. These goals can frequently be achieved through techniques or learning experiences that are more focal and more limited in time and scope, and that are based on active exhortation, didactic information, and procedures directed by the instructor. By contrast, other candidates will be able to experience and strive toward the broader goals of a psychoanalytic supervisory situation, particularly if the supervisor shares some of these goals and uses supervisory techniques appropriate to achieve them. In any individual instance, evaluation of the goals appropriate to a specific candidate must await observation in the supervisory situation and should not be made prematurely.

Unconscious Aspects of the Unfolding Process

The concept of a supervisory process suggests that ideally there should be a steady progression within the candidate from the first through subsequent supervised cases, and that learning from earlier cases should be carried into experience with later cases and should modify the way in which the candidate approaches, understands, and works with them. However, actual experience in the supervisory setting suggests that often this does not occur as completely or effectively as we would like. Candidates approaching their third or fourth supervised case may demonstrate many of the same cognitive and conceptual difficulties, countertransference problems, technical deficiencies, and characterological idiosyncrasies and restrictions that they experienced with their first case. Not only has this been my own personal experience, but it has often been observed in supervisory conferences at our institute, conferences in which several supervisors discuss the progress of a candidate. When I attended meetings of the American Psychoanalytic Association Membership Committee, where a survey of a candidate's cases would repetitively demonstrate the same difficulties (at least transiently) in later as well as earlier ones, similar observations were made.

It strikes me that this should be expected in view of our clinical theory and formulations. In any process of maturation and change it is inevitable that phases of progression and regression will occur. New stimuli tend to evoke the regressive reactivation of earlier modes of adaptation, followed by awareness, insight, working through, and mastery. New levels of organization and change involve grief and mourning for the abandonment of previously cathected levels, as well as pleasure in the achievement of new and more effective forms of adaptation.

This observation has been made repeatedly for individuals and for groups and organizations (e.g., Pollock, 1977). It also conforms with Schlesinger's model of therapy (personal communication, 1978), in which the same conflict cycles are observed again and again, but are dealt with more rapidly and more effectively as the therapeutic process unfolds and progresses. The same is demonstrated by various follow-up studies of successful psychoanalytic treatment (Pfeffer, 1961; Hurn, 1973; Schlesinger and Robbins, 1974) showing that core issues recur again and again and need to be worked through more than once. Conflicts previously considered reasonably mastered and resolved tend to be reactivated by the transference-stimulating experience of a new object. But they are mastered and worked through much more rapidly than before.

The psychoanalytic educational process is designed to activate a capacity for analytic therapeutic regression which promotes access to deeper levels of psychic experience and conflict. Control of this process and the ability to initiate and recover from it at will is not easily mastered. It should therefore come as no surprise that having induced such a psychic process in our candidates, we would then stimulate in them a variety of regressive behavior patterns in response to each of the intense interpersonal relationships that occur during the course of psychoanalytic education.

Each new supervisor is a potential transference object for our candidates. The candidate approaches a new supervisory experience with both conscious and unconscious information and expectations, some of which relate to the reputation, demeanor, previous experience, professional activities, etc., of the new supervisor, and some of which relate to the ways such information and experience resonate with the still unconscious intrapsychic levels of conflict within the candidate. Although these issues may be highlighted when the candidate is still in personal analysis, even the candidate who has successfully terminated training analysis manifests a potential for regression and reactivation of neurotic difficulties.

The new supervisor inevitably activates conflicting loyalties and identifications, not only with the candidate's training analyst but also with previous supervisors as well as other meaningful faculty members. The candidate may experience the new relationship angrily, as a challenge to identifications with previous analytic role models; or the new supervisory relationship may offer hopes of fulfillment of regressively reactivated infantile and childhood fantasies. Given the activation of significant personal and professional conflicts, the candidate may resort to preexisting patterns of adaptation and defense.

Progress in the candidate's development is marked by a decrease in the duration and intensity of activated conflicts and a lessening of their interference with the supervisory process. The effective supervisor must be aware of the complexity of these issues in beginning a supervision, in observing the candidate's work, and in determining interventions in the teaching-learning process.

Educational Principles

Discussing the learning that is required of a psychoanalyst, Tyler (1974) said,

> He builds a cognitive map that he finds helpful in explaining phenomena that he encounters in his professional work and learns how to use the map in dealing with the problems he faces. He must also learn how to study these problems, that is how to analyze them, how to make observations and obtain data, how to organize the observations and other information, how to interpret the data and how to verify the interpretations by additional observations and manipulations, and when initial interpretations are not verified, how to attack the problem. Such learning is far more complex than rote memorization. [p. 89]

To some extent the supervisory relationship follows the model of the master craftsman instructing an apprentice; here the correct practice of the master is emulated by the apprentice in order to achieve proficiency. But in analysis, Tyler continues,

> these techniques cannot be learned by watching and imitating the "master." They are usually based on a set of principles that form a coherent body of doctrine and problem-solving procedures. These essentials to a professional role are at least two-thirds within the professional's mind and only a small fraction is overt where a novice could follow it effectively. [p. 91]

In considering the supervisory situation it is essential to remind ourselves of the distinctions between teaching (the activity and interventions carried out by the supervisor) and learning (the activities carried out by the candidate and the changes that occur). It is the latter (learning) that must ultimately be the goal of our efforts. Unfortunately, for many supervisors the idea that they have done the teaching is enough.

Tyler reminds us also that the student needs a clear notion of what is to be learned—skills, habits, cognitive maps, ways of attacking problems, understandings, attitudes, and the like. The student must also have a role model for the kind of behavior to be developed. To show the student how one analyzes a complex situation or goes about solving a problem, the supervisor must think out loud.

Another element in effective learning is the opportunity to

practice the behavior to be mastered. As adequate practice requires that the student have a feeling of confidence, an initial level should be one that is appropriate to the student's present abilities. Then, in a series of steps, the learner goes beyond earlier levels; each step should present a new element to which the learner must respond, or should set higher standards of performance for a skill. Each new problem to be solved should require something more, by involving more factors that must be taken into account, or by demanding greater complexity or precision in the solution.

Another major element of effective learning is rewards for success. Satisfaction is necessary to reinforce behavior and encourage continued practice. The superior student finds learning enjoyable in itself; the joys of knowing, of solving problems, of understanding complex matters, of exercising one's skills, etc. are intrinsic rewards independent of applause of others. Another kind of satisfaction may be had when, for example, the presentation of a case to a conference brings the approval of friends or others whose opinions are important to the student.

Effective learning requires feedback. It is essential that learners be helped to discover when attempts to carry out the desired behavior are inadequate, to analyze their efforts to identify where the difficulties lie, and to see more clearly what behavior may now be appropriate. The feedback system should provide quick information about the adequacy of the performance, both positive and negative, and a constructive analysis of the ways in which it was inadequate.

As analysts in a therapeutic situation, we deliberately abstain from manifest praise or criticism of our patient's behavior or performance in the analysis. Some supervisors carry this abstinence over into their supervision, and the shift to active judgment and response may be difficult. The hesitation of many supervisors to have candidates read their evaluation reports, coupled in some cases by threats that if the candidate is to read the report it will be written differently, attests this failure to provide constructive criticism.

Phases of the Supervisory Process

The following schematic description of phases in the supervisory process is intended only as a general guide. There will be significant variation from one supervisor to another, and within any one phase there will be oscillations in the intensity of particular characteristics and behaviors.

The Beginning Phase

In the beginning phase, student and supervisor come to know each other's style, talents, and abilities. Frequently each has a reputation known to the other, and this of course gives rise to expectations. The supervisor may have heard about the student in positive, negative, or neutral terms, particularly in the case of a so-called gifted student. The supervisor may have various personal motivations regarding the student, or regarding faculty colleagues, and may tend to use the student as a "messenger." The supervisor may wish to serve as the student's rescuer, or as the student's critical evaluator, determined to put "more balance" into the overall institute assessment. Some supervisors may have problems with their own self-image; they may need to assemble a group of disciples, to be perceived by the student as omniscient, or to be popular and well liked.

Similarly, the student may experience and anticipate a variety of conscious or unconscious wishes in relation to the supervisor. The supervisor is bound to have a reputation within the institute that will turn some students away and attract others. Students have various ways of adapting to the perceived or fantasied demands and expectations of the supervisor. Some seek consciously to please and cooperate; others may use passive-aggressive, competitive, or masochistically self-defeating methods; and some can make reality-based use of the learning opportunity.

In the beginning phase, many of these expectations become manifest, can be tested, and may become significant factors in establishing the supervisory situation. Fleming and Benedek (1966), in describing the nature and vicissitudes of the supervisory relationship, observe that the beginning phase is frequently used by the supervisor to establish an effective learning alliance with the candidate. As in a therapeutic situation, solid establishment of the alliance generally takes precedence over other interactions.

The student must gradually come to feel comfortable in the supervisory situation, particularly with regard to exposing doubts, mistakes, countertransferences, and difficulties. Although students are aware that supervision includes evaluation by the supervisor, they must learn from experience that such evaluation tends to be objective, reasonable, and constructive. Only when students feel comfortably secure in the learning alliance and recognize the essential good will of the supervisor will they dare to expose technical and countertransference issues that evoke shame or guilt. And only when such exposure occurs can the supervisor have full access to the material of the analytic process.

It is important that the supervisor set a constructive tone in the supervisory situation; the candidate's needs and vulnerabilities should be assessed as soon as possible as a guide for interventions. A comfortable learning alliance may at times require that the supervisor delay criticism, confrontation of countertransference, correction of therapeutic style or technique, prediction regarding a particular interchange, etc. until the candidate is deemed ready for such interventions. As in the therapeutic situation, the learning alliance evolves slowly and in a spiral fashion based on the candidate's growing experience.

In other words, the candidate whose revelation of errors or countertransference problems receives an empathic and constructive response from the supervisor will be more willing and able to reveal other, perhaps more difficult, mistakes and countertransferences. If, however, such revelations are met with condemnation, criticism, guilt induction, or punitive or contemptuous reactions in the supervisor, the candidate will anticipate similar responses in the future. This may result in a form of learning in which the candidate comes to recognize what the supervisor wants, learns the supervisor's style, and then presents, distorts, or withholds material in such a way as to fit these observations, thereby pleasing the supervisor but restricting the learning process. It is frequently in the beginning phase of a supervisory relationship that these interactions are sorted out by both participants and the stage for the subsequent evolution of the supervisory process becomes set.

During the beginning phase of supervision, particularly in a first or second case, the student's major motivation is the desire to learn the therapeutic techniques necessary for effective work with the patient, and the supervisor will usually want to focus interventions at this level. Such periods are usually not propitious for discussion of abstract theoretical issues and do not favor intellectual curiosity or discovery.

This need for focusing on the basic technical aspects of the analytic situation may involve repeated exposition at levels significantly more elementary than what the supervisor is accustomed to. To be an effective teacher, however, the supervisor must retain a willingness to observe the situation through the eyes of the student, who comes to it new and fresh, and must be willing to subordinate the pursuit of more sophisticated interests to the needs of the student.

During this beginning phase, recommendations by the supervisor that are at odds with procedures used by the candidate's personal analyst or prior supervisors are likely to activate significant conflict requiring patient and sensitive handling. For example, one student used his own analyst's technique of leaving a typed notice in his waiting room in regard to the dates of several canceled sessions. The supervisor's questions about this procedure were met with anxiety, anger, and defensiveness. The supervisor, instead of insisting on a particular course of action, presented the candidate with the pros and cons of several possible procedures and encouraged the student to try different methods before deciding which to use. Several months later, the student reported that he had tried several methods and had found from his own experience that a procedure different from his own analyst's had evoked more useful and significant clinical material. By avoiding a dogmatic or demanding tone and by presenting different perspectives, the supervisor had encouraged an experiential form of learning that was considerably more effective than passive mimicking or active opposition. This approach also fostered the student's independence from his analyst in the development of technical and professional functions.

The Middle Phase

Once the learning alliance is well established, the candidate is reasonably secure in the day-to-day management of the patient, and the patient has established a sustained psychoanalytic involvement, the supervisory process moves into the middle phase. At this point, the supervisor can systematically increase the challenge to the candidate, expecting a capacity to function in increasingly more sophisticated ways. The supervisor will increasingly demonstrate the correlation of theory and clinical observation; there will be less need to "cover all the material" from the previous week; the supervisor will more actively focus attention in an alternating fashion between microscopic and macroscopic issues in the analytic process; the student will become more open and candid in presenting clinical material; the student who earlier clung defensively to process notes becomes more spontaneous; and the student who was once reluctant to have the supervisor scrutinize material now shows a greater willingness to present detailed, sequential, and organized process notes.

During this phase the supervisor may more actively point out the occurrence and impact of countertransference forces, as well as transference factors within the supervisory relationship. Such confrontations or interpretations may require preparatory interventions with the candidate, similar to the preparation for an important interpretation that occurs in analysis. In the supervisory situation the presence of a strong learning alliance and the candidate's previous experience with constructive interventions in supervision allow considerable latitude and leeway. For the candidate still in personal analysis it may be sufficient simply to point out the existence of a countertransference response or reaction and to suggest that it be taken up there. Having done this, however, the supervisor must observe whether there is evidence that the candidate has followed this advice or whether the countertransference behavior has changed. With the candidate no longer in personal analysis it may be necessary for the supervisor to point out, specifically, systematically, and repeatedly, the specific area of difficulty in the countertransference and then to observe whether the candidate's self-analysis results in behavioral change.

One candidate repetitively avoided the patient's deepening erotic transference. On several occasions the supervisor pointed out instances of this evasion—changing the subject, interpreting "upward," intellectualization, and other defensive operations—but the behavior persisted. The next step was to point out firmly to the candidate that a countertransference response must be occurring, as the issue had been repeatedly discussed with no modification of the behavior. It was suggested that the candidate do some sustained self-analysis on the issue. The supervisor had also indicated on several occasions that this is a common difficulty for students in dealing with deep sexual transference material, and openly acknowledged his own countertransference responses as a student. Eventually the supervisor interpreted directly that the candidate was sexually stimulated by the patient's intense erotic fantasies and was anxious about possible acting out but ashamed of such a response. By this time the material had been dealt with often enough, from several angles, that the candidate was capable of responding to interventions in an active and confirmatory way. Almost immediately the situation with the patient improved dramatically. From then on, throughout the course of supervision the candidate was capable of openly discussing the various forms and manifestations of countertransference as they occurred. Although the supervisor's interpretation could have been supported earlier by the clinical material, waiting until preparatory work was completed allowed the intervention to be more effective and to be generalized to other instances of countertransference.

In observing such issues we should realize that some of the candidate's behavior may involve regressive transferences to the supervisor rather than countertransferences to the patient. As a student I had a supervisor whom I idealized and wished to impress. I had observed in the material a very obvious oedipal reference, but when my supervisor asked what I thought was going on, my reaction was to feel that the oedipal reference was too elementary for him to have commented on and that I must have missed something much deeper and more elaborate. I launched into a lengthy free association on preoedipal factors, only to have my supervisor look at me incredulously, point out the oedipal theme, and interpret that I was having a countertransference response to the patient, inasmuch as I could not see her oedipal transference. I did not at that time have the courage to correct him, but instead I listened quietly to his interpretation.

Transferences to the supervisor may also involve competitive, aggressive, fearful, passive, or dependent reactions that may affect how the candidate reports the work or uses the supervisory situation. It is during the middle phase of supervision that such issues are most likely to arise as obstacles to learning.

In our work as analysts in therapeutic settings, our techniques are designed to promote regression and the evolution of a transference neurosis while maintaining a stance of transference abstinence. In the supervisory situation, where our aim is to avoid regression and instead to promote progressive integration and learning, some of the techniques useful in therapeutic analysis tend to be counterproductive. The special needs of the supervisory situation must be understood and met: the correction (or, better still, the avoidance) of transference distortions; active feedback and evaluative response to the candidate's work; active praise and reinforcement of the student's successes.

Frequently in a therapeutic situation the analyst silently and preconsciously goes through a variety of mental processes that may finally result in a terse and highly condensed interpretation. Such a model is of little help in developing a student's awareness of how an analyst thinks and of the mental processes involved in listening and responding to analytic material. It is not appropriate for the supervisory situation. It tends to promote ideas of magic, or to encourage slavish imitation, and may stimulate a feeling of discouragement in the student about reaching such conclusions alone. An active model in which the supervisor attempts systematically to express in words the various thought processes in sequence, the various options and alternatives considered as well as the reasons for selecting one, will facilitate dynamic understanding of the material and insight into the nature of technical interventions.

The student should be permitted to glimpse the thought processes and even the affective responses of the supervisor, including instances when the supervisor is uncertain, confused, or unable to understand the material. The supervisor thereby presents a model of tolerance of ambiguity and doubt without need for premature closure or omniscience.

For the supervising analyst problems may arise if too much personal opinion and feeling are revealed to supervisees; institute gossip may carry this information to candidates for whom the supervisor serves as training analyst. It should be recognized, however, that all candidate analysands will have sources of information regarding their training analyst. Such issues must be looked for and then raised in the training analysis of all candidates.

In a therapeutic situation the analyst may at times experience concern and be tempted to intervene actively with regard to the patient's spouse, children, parents, or in other important relationships. An analytic perspective, of course, dictates restraint. In a similar way the supervisor may at times be tempted to intervene in ways that would enhance the welfare of the patient at the expense of the candidate's need for learning. In my opinion, unless grossly unethical practices are occurring, the supervisor, too, must restrain this impulse; the primary focus must be the educational needs of the student.

During this middle phase of the supervisory process, working through occurs somewhat as it does in the therapeutic situation; gradually, over time, new elements in the work identity and capacities of the student begin to emerge. The supervisor must evaluate whether these represent the genuine growth of analytic functions within the student, or are merely an artifact of the student's recognition of the supervisor's expectations.

During this phase, problems may arise both for the good student with a difficult or possibly unanalyzable patient whose analysis is therefore moving poorly, and for the poor student whose patient is highly suitable and persists successfully in the analytic process despite the ineptitude of the candidate. Such situations not only create a problem in evaluation, but also make it important for the supervisor to help maintain the morale, motivation, and encouragement of the good student.

Throughout supervision, but particularly during the middle phase, a philosophical issue arises with regard to the teaching-learning situation. Should the student be expected to adapt to the supervisor's teaching methods and style? Or should the supervisor be expected to adapt to the learning needs and limitations of the student? This is an unsettled issue that cannot be resolved in a general way, but it must be considered in every supervision.

The Final Phase

The final phase of the supervisory process involves a continuing shift and change in the respective roles of candidate and supervisor. It is ushered in as the candidate manifests an enhanced capacity to work independently and effectively, with less intervention by the supervisor. The candidate manifests increasing self-confidence and demonstrates a capacity to sustain and further the analytic process with the patient; is increasingly capable of more sophisticated observations, formulations, and technical interventions; and is comfortable initiating discussion and expressing differences of opinion with the supervisor.

The supervisor comes increasingly to recognize the candidate as a junior colleague whose opinions, interventions, activities, and formulations are more and more independent. The supervisor responds by gradually withdrawing from an active supervisory role, and increasingly responding as consultant and advisor to the candidate. During the first or second case, the supervisor may have to become more active again as the patient enters the termination phase of analysis, inasmuch as the candidate will not have had prior experience in the termination technique and process, and for the time being the preexisting instructional model of supervision may have to be reinstituted. However, the general model during the last phase of the supervisory process is one of increasing independence in the candidate, with support from attitudes and activities of the supervisor that promote such emancipation.

This phase usually involves a weaning process in which supervisory sessions are increasingly less frequent and eventually discontinued altogether. Although there may or may not be an explicit statement of the supervisor's availability for subsequent consultation when and if the candidate needs or requests it, both participants should be aware of the advantages of consultation and neither should consider it a sign of incomplete education if the candidate resumes consultation with the supervisor at some future point.

It must be remembered that the termination phase, like other periods in the supervisory process, may entail a variety of conscious as well as unconscious affective responses in either or both participants. For the student, it means increasing emancipation, independence, freedom from the apprenticeship role, and recognition of the attainment of collegial status. For some students such freedom permits the emergence of previously latent creativity and effectiveness, which not infrequently have been stifled in the supervisory situation by the various conflicts that had been activated. For other candidates, this new status may be the source of conflict and anxiety, and may at times lead to conscious or unconscious reluctance to terminate the supervisory relationship and accept the independence and status such a step entails. Such candidates may find various rationalizations for continuing the supervisory relationship, and a recognition of such conflict by the supervisor will be helpful in its management.

The importance and frequently long duration of the supervisory experience in the educational and personal development of the student often mean that the candidate may undergo a response of grief and mourning as the relationship terminates.

For the supervisor, relinquishing such a role and responsibility may likewise be a source of ambivalence and conflict, particularly if the supervisory work has been gratifying and enriching, or if the supervisor has residual unconscious needs to maintain the master-apprentice status and relationship.

As part of the termination process, it may at times be helpful for the supervisor to help the student gain an overall general perspective on the case and the work that has been done between them, as well as to express in a clear and constructive way the supervisor's perceptions of the strengths as well as residual limitations in the candidate. This can be useful to the student in synthesizing experience with the case in question, as well as in preparing for further self-educational experiences. Another step the supervisor might consider at this time is the suggestion to the candidate of which elements in the case material might be effectively considered worthy of further scientific investigation and perhaps publication. In this way the supervisor may effectively stimulate scientific creativity and inquiry in the student.

Relationship to the Institute

Throughout the case, dependent on the requirements of different institutes, the candidate is expected to prepare summaries of the analysis. In this situation, the supervisor serves as a representative of the institute's educational committee, one of whose functions may be to suggest or insist that the candidate prepare the necessary summaries. Here the supervisor's willingness to take the time and energy to read, evaluate, and comment upon such summaries is of course crucial. If the student prepares a summary which is never read, studied, or commented on by the supervisor, little feedback, motivation, or realization of the importance of such an activity results.

Both candidate and supervisor are aware that periodic reports about the student's work and progress must be submitted to the education committee. Frequently these have a major impact on decisions regarding the candidate's progress through the institute. For some supervisors and candidates the supervisor's dual role may pose a problem.

However, as described earlier, if throughout the supervisory process a pattern of constructive, objective, and useful feedback by the supervisor to the student has been in evidence, these evaluative reports may actually be a further stimulus to the learning process. Instances in which the supervisor's assessment involves observations or opinions the candidate is not yet ready to be confronted with may pose other dilemmas for the supervisor.

Like the training analyst, the supervisor may also be concerned with the way colleagues will evaluate the work with a candidate, and this factor must be recognized and not allowed to interfere with evaluation of the student.

Chapter 3

Patient Evaluation and Routine Reports

To give the reader a background for the case, this chapter will include the patient's initial history taken by the clinic social worker. A further diagnostic evaluation, conducted by the attending psychoanalyst, is also presented.

Candidates are required to submit a summary of the case after six months. Since the recording of supervisory sessions did not begin until after the first six months, that summary is also presented here.

Case supervisors submit summary evaluations every six months on the candidate's progress in supervision. These are highly condensed reports which are used by the Progression Committee to assess the candidate's educational status. Because they offer an interesting contrast to the actual supervisory data, they too are included here in the form in which they were submitted.

Description of Patient

The patient is a single Jewish woman, twenty-three years of age. She is a tall, large, heavy woman, appropriately dressed, with a soft friendly voice. She was very apologetic for being two or three minutes late for our first interview. She complimented me on my "cute shoes." She was very friendly.

She is not a very pretty woman but has an engaging personality. She talked openly and honestly, although I had the impression she was trying to present a careful image that conflicts with her own self-image. The second time I saw her she was a little calmer and was saying she felt relieved after having seen me the one time. It seemed as if a load was off her mind and also she had sensed she was finally doing something about her trouble. Also, that what we had discussed clicked in her mind. Particularly her patterns with men. She realized that she was doing something self-destructive.

Presenting Problems

1. Patient has always been overweight. Her mother is overweight and seemed to emphasize this in the family. In fact, as a child the patient was not overweight, but her mother put her on a diet that the patient rebelled against. She started eating and has been heavy ever since then.

She lost thirty pounds between her junior and senior years in college, something that pleased her, but then she was surprised that when she went back to school she kept eating until she had put all the weight back on. Three weeks ago she started Weight Watchers and lost twelve pounds in one week. But then she started eating everything and only stopped the Friday before. At the time of the evaluation, she put herself back on the Weight Watchers diet. Patient sees how she will eat when she's depressed, as if there's something inside telling her to be fat. This is very depressing for her. She usually is a happy person, she says. She can't deal with depression well.

Her weight plus other feelings have caused her to feel very unattractive and incompetent. Upon graduation from the University of California, she came to St. Louis and after working in a department store she recently took an interior design job in an architectural firm. She has not yet made a lot of friends in St. Louis and has not dated many men, associated to her feelings of being unattractive.

2. Another significant problem in the patient's life is her troubled relations with men. There seems to be a pattern of choosing men who are a challenge to her. She then pursues them and ends up feeling rejected.

She dated a boy in high school. They were close friends. The night after the senior prom, he said he did not want to see her anymore. She was very hurt. She tried to explain that he was going to college in the fall and may have not wanted to be tied down with a girl friend.

Another significant relationship in her life was with Frank, a man she met at college. She saw him when she was a junior and fell instantly in love with him. She pursued him for six months and they became good friends. He told her he wasn't physically attracted to her because she was twenty pounds overweight. She refused to lose the weight. She thought he should like her for herself. He dated other women, which he would discuss with her. She said she would have done anything for him. She loved him so much.

His mother was ill and was going into surgery, which was upsetting for him; the patient offered to drive Frank to his home in Iowa. She drove him home and stayed for one week, taking care of the family, doing the laundry, cleaning, cooking, etc. He was cold and aloof with her. She finally decided she couldn't take any more from him and told him off. He got frightened and apologized. They made up until a couple of weeks later, when he laughed at her and said they could never get physically involved. She was furious with him and broke off the relationship. She feels that his final rejection cured her of any romantic feelings for him. But they did become friends again. When she went home that summer and returned thirty pounds lighter, he said he was physically attracted to her. She refused him. She felt she couldn't ever love him again.

A similar relationship is with a high school friend she's recently become more romantically involved with. He works in Peoria. They had had a couple of dates, but he seems to be inconsistent and moody. For example, after the first date, on which they had had a very nice time and also had become sexually involved, excluding intercourse (which she's frightened of because of her fear of pregnancy), he seemed to feel guilty and irritable. Another time he was cold and aloof with her and another time he lied to her. But she continued to pursue him and she felt he was challenging. She has had intercourse only a couple of times, with a boy early in college. She says, "Men are such pigs. They won't use a rubber. Women have to take care of it all."

The only satisfying mutual relationship for the patient was when she was a freshman in college. She dated a boy for a long time and it was with him that she first had sexual intercourse. But they had intercourse only two times because she became terrified of pregnancy, and feared that her parents might find out and she would be in trouble. The patient felt that this boy wasn't bright, ambitious, or good enough for her, and her parents didn't like him either, so she broke off her relationship with him.

3. Another problem area for the patient is her present job. This is her second job after college and she feels she has a lot to learn. She feels she's a very creative person who is not being used properly at her present job. They only need a draftsman, and she feels she could handle the whole creative process. Evidently, she has done quite well in her field. She won national contests in design while at college, and since being at this job she's had a couple of job offers from other firms.

Three weeks ago another woman came into the office. This woman was very talented and immediately got a better job than the patient, for which the patient was a bit jealous. It also created an imbalance in the office. The patient had been very close with her boss up until the new arrival, but since then they have been less friendly. The patient sees it as her boss becoming threatening and turning on her.

The patient has felt incompetent and angry. She believes her boss is unstable, and she is particularly frustrated now in the office. Even though she has had two job offers, she feels obligated to stay at least six months before taking a new job. She is very ambitious and would like to leave her mark on the world.

Background Information

The patient has one sibling, her brother Harold. She was three when he was born. Her earliest memory is being in an apartment in Clayton, a St. Louis suburb, and getting ready to go to kindergarten. She was afraid and cried in kindergarten.

When she recovered in a couple of weeks, she started loving school and has always done well academically. Socially, however, she's had troubles. She has always been too tall or too fat and has not had the right clothes, partly due to her mother's poor taste. In the eighth grade, the patient started picking out her own clothes and started feeling better dressed.

The patient says that her parents have always had a poor marriage. Both were very insecure and unhappy people, and the patient seemed to be cast in the role of the strong, together person. She also seems to have identified with her father, whom she described as an insecure man. Up until her young adulthood she really admired him, but now she's become disillusioned. She says he is "a bullshitter." His parents were social climbers, and the father is also a social climber. He says you can get everywhere by the people you use and know. She finds him obnoxious and she's embarrassed by him now. She feels she knows her father better than anybody, and as a child she could have married him. It would have been a lot of fun, she thought, because he was so outgoing and her mother was so introverted. The patient felt she would have been just the right balance for her father. But now she sees that he has not really done anything worthwhile in life. He works as a bureaucrat for the government and seems to take no pride in his work, doing only enough to get by.

He calls her two or three times a week to complain about his wife. The patient says she's disgusted with her father's behavior and feels unhappy because she still loves him. Also, she has been so strongly identified with him that now she's worried about insecurities in herself.

Her father had a heart attack about two or three years ago which was quite frightening for the patient. It also pointed out how poor the parents' marriage was. Her mother did not even go to the hospital to see him.

The mother works as a saleswoman. The patient says her mother is very insecure and has no friends. In fact, the patient is her mother's best friend. They are more like sisters. The patient says her parents both confide too much in her. They tell her things that she would rather not know. For example, the mother told the patient that she hasn't slept with the father for three years. This was upsetting for the patient. It seems as though the mother-daughter roles have been reversed. The patient feels that she can't talk openly to her mother, that she gets too upset and can't tolerate any unhappiness, although she will pour out her unhappiness to the patient. The parents seem to have the image of the patient as pure, and virginal, and the patient doesn't know how to live up to this.

The patient felt that both her parents' parents were the root of their problem. Both sets of grandparents seemed to be insecure, frightened people in one way or another.

The patient sees her parents as two kids, constantly bickering and fighting. She wondered how it was that she turned out so well despite her parents' insecurities.

She has a very close relationship with her bother Harold. He is totally aloof from the rest of the family and seems to exploit the parents. He's lazy, doesn't do well in school, doesn't seem to have ambition or career plans, which is disappointing for the patient.

She talks about herself as being very ambitious, something she's proud of and also a little worried about because she finds she is never satisfied with what she does. She feels guilty constantly. She's afraid of disappointing people and is concerned with their reactions. She said, "I'm most people's best friend, but nobody is mine." She feels she is a good friend because she gives herself totally to people. Also, that people have an image of her as being strong, friendly, and together. They can't really see that she has problems because she has always been the peacemaker in the family. The successful, strong, and competent person. In fact, she seems to have been the boy in the family, the one her father identified with. Her brother was always jealous of her and was always considered the weaker one.

Sexual Information

She recalls masturbating as a child, but she was always afraid her parents would find out. In the third grade, she recalls, a girl friend came to school and told her how people get pregnant. "A man sticks his thing into a woman." The patient was horrified. She went home screaming. Her mother told her that the girl friend should be quiet, but no further explanation was given.

The patient started menstruating when she was eleven years old. She had looked forward to it, as a girl friend had already started and her mother had prepared her.

She recalls asking her father if she could go steady in the seventh grade. He said it was okay, but there was to be no kissing. She was confused, as she had thought kissing was okay. It had taken her father two weeks to come to this decision, and there was no further discussion. The patient said her parents were very shy and inhibited about sex.

Her first experience with sexual intercourse was when she was a freshman in college. After two times with this boy, she was terrified of becoming pregnant. Even after she started her period, she was afraid that somehow she still might be. This scared her so much that she has refused to have intercourse without birth control ever since.

This patient talks of feelings of inadequacy, depression, anxiety, and tension.

Initial Psychoanalytic Evaluation

I interviewed this single Jewish woman after I had read the write-up which had already been done for the Treatment Service. Since that evaluation is rather complete, I determined to emphasize two kinds of information that I find important in the conduct of any analysis. First, I wanted to know about this patient's capacity to form lasting relationships; second, I wanted to know about her ability to tolerate the anxiety that goes with interpretation.

1. The patient states that her main problem is a weight gain that makes her lose confidence and feel less outgoing, less in control of herself. She correlates her weight with her ability to relate to people around her. She feels that she has never had

an adequate social life, not even when she has been thin. There has never been a dating life that was differentiated from "good friends" getting together. She always had lots of different kinds of friends in high school, but when she went to college she joined a sorority that was characterized by an attitude of exclusiveness and condescension toward outsiders. This was important to the patient because she has a history of feeling left out, of not being a member of her group. Her "Jewishness" is important in this regard. She feels that she was never Jewish enough, that is, "I was never loud enough or overbearing enough or Jewish enough in my appearance." In the patient's eyes, her father was rigidly and vigorously anti-Semitic. She feels that their religion is beautiful but that the way it is practiced leaves much to be desired. At any rate, she feels she has never made the grade in the Jewish community and has never felt accepted by Jewish people as a Jew. Her younger brother seems to have solved his problem with the family by becoming very passive. This is an avenue that is unacceptable to the patient, and so she continues to feel like an outcast, unrelated to her family. There is only one incident of a long friendship with a marriageable man. This ended in her feeling rejected by him because he could not be "physically attracted to me." Interestingly enough, the man was unable to be close to the patient when she was physically desirous of him, but when he changed his attitude she was repulsed by him. "He made me sick to my stomach. I was shocked at my response to his slobbering sickness."

These historical facts were highlighted by her relationship, or lack of it, with me during the interview. She approached my office with a timidity and cautiousness that I have not seen in other patients. She knocked on the door so gently I could hardly hear it, and when I opened the door all the way so that she could come in, she approached the office as if she were frightened. This was in striking contrast to her physical appearance. Physically, she is a large and prepossessing woman who gives the impression of great adequacy. She was open and expressive with me but not really personal in a way which made it possible to identify her as an individual. Some of this, of course, was due to the interview situation; nevertheless, I felt it interesting that she would come off looking a little distant and difficult to contact in an interview in which she was perfectly aware that it was important for her to demonstrate her ability to express herself.

2. During the interview I tried to make a couple of superficial interpretations which would give her something to react to. When she talked about the shock she felt at her repulsion toward her boyfriend, I stated that it was interesting that she should feel so much for him when he was unresponsive and feel such repulsion when he was in fact responsive. She was not in the least bit taken aback by this statement, and went right on describing herself in terms that made the problem more available. She said it was like other relationships in which she enjoyed the challenge of "maneuvering people" into responding to her. In this regard, she found herself constantly apologizing for her existence. She had no insight as to why she should feel guilty so much of the time. Her next association had to do with her father's "terrible temper" and *his* need to apologize all the time. She said, "I think sometimes I should just say I'm sorry I was born." From this I have to conclude that the interpretive statement that I made was not unduly anxiety-provoking and that it did, in fact, permit her to reveal a great deal more of herself.

In closing the interview she told me that she has felt a lot better since she has sought help. This is in spite of the fact that she has no ongoing relationship with either men or women, no love life, and no outstanding satisfaction in her work.

My conclusion about this patient is that she will very rapidly become involved in a transference relationship which will be characterized by maneuvering and teasing on the one hand, and outright rejection on the other. The patient's contempt and rage and anger, particularly at men, is right beneath the surface and will be elaborated upon the therapist very quickly. I think that the transference relationship will be so intense that it will take a considerable amount of skill and foresight on the therapist's part to make sure that the patient does not terminate or move into a very intense but nontherapeutic transference relationship. By and large, I think the patient is analyzable and is a good case for an analytic student; but that student should be forewarned about the patient's intensity.

Disposition

The patient was accepted for psychoanalysis. The case worker met with her to discuss the recommendations. The patient was worried she would not be accepted because of Dr. B.'s comment to her concerning her trouble with relationships. She feels she needs analysis and is quite ready to make the commitment, pointing out that she always sticks by her commitments. The patient was pleased and ready to begin analysis.

Candidate's First Six-Month Summary

This is a twenty-three-year-old single Jewish female who is the elder of two children with a brother three years younger than she. She came requesting treatment for periods of depression characterized by overeating, crying, and decreased ability to work effectively. She has had no previous psychiatric treatment and learned of the Psychoanalytic Institute from a girl friend who was in analysis with a candidate for several years.

The patient is an interior designer for an architectural firm in St. Louis. She lives alone. Although successful and effective in her career, she complained of rarely feeling adequate or successful, never being able to rest on her laurels or to feel pleased with herself and her success, always having to strive for more achievements. Although she has many friends, old and new, male and female, her dating life has always been stormy. She described a series of three men, the first in high school, the second in college, and the third most recently, each of whom she has liked and pursued and each of whom has ultimately rejected her. At the beginning of treatment, her current boyfriend was living with another woman while seeing her. She described becoming intensely involved with these men to the point that nothing else mattered except gaining their love. She also described intense sexual wishes and desires, accompanied by guilt and the feeling that such wishes are not appropriate for a woman. Her periods of depression last anywhere from a couple of days to a couple of weeks, frequently correlated with feeling rejected or unwanted by a man, or that she would never be truly accepted as adequate in her job, which she feels has always been a man's job. Her other stated problem has been her being overweight. She is currently, by her own calculation, thirty pounds overweight; at the beginning of therapy she was fifty pounds overweight. She has been even heavier. According to her, she did not have significant problems with her weight until puberty. She is a binge eater. She describes eating when she is extremely anxious or has feelings or thoughts she doesn't want to deal with. She then thinks obsessively what a failure she is at dieting and what a fat slob she is; she thinks of nothing else. In the very beginning of treatment she said at times she felt that if she could just lose weight all her problems would be solved. However, when she was a junior in college she lost all the weight she wanted to and was still unhappy, felt inadequate, and was subject to periods of depression characterized by feeling unloved, unwanted, and inadequate—a failure.

She relates she was the firstborn child of her family. According to family mythology, her father was so sure he would have only sons that they had no names picked out for a baby girl; when she was born it took them some time to name her, and then she was named Toni. Three years later her brother Harold was born. Her father had a job that involved a great deal of traveling away from home, but her most vivid memories of childhood involve her father or his absence. She relates a long and arduous struggle to gain her father's attention, with many examples of times when he would interrupt business trips to come home and attend her brother's Little League baseball games but would not attend functions in which she was involved, even if he was in town. She did everything she could think of to please him, including learning to do things that he complained her mother did terribly, like cooking. She describes photograph albums filled with pictures of Harold's accomplishments and very few pictures of her as she grew up. Members of the family comment that they would never have known that her father had a daughter if they hadn't met her. She described numerous frightening experiences as a child in which her father would become enraged by some small infraction; his eyes would "bug out," his face would quiver, and she would be sure that he would never love her again and cry herself to sleep.

At school she was a good student and social organizer. She describes her junior high school and high school years as an all-out campaign to become the most popular girl in the school and to have a good social life. She succeeded in becoming president of the class and of many other organizations and being the equivalent of homecoming queen, but none of it gave her any satisfaction or netted her an active social life with boys. She dated one boy in high school for an extended period, but he dated other girls as well and broke up with her before he went to college. She went on to college, which she describes as another all-out campaign to have the most friends and be the most popular person on campus. However, she gained little satisfaction from her successes or comfort from her friendships. She constantly brought gifts for her friends and acquaintances, took them for coffee and lunch, listened to all of their problems, helped them with their papers, and in general did everything she could to be liked. Although apparently she was, she continued to be plagued by feelings of not being adequate, of missing something. She dated a boy for several years in college who would have nothing to do with her physically because of her weight. She lost weight and he was then interested in her physically, but she was disgusted. They have remained friends over the years and the relationship continues to perplex her. She graduated from college and got a job at a department store in St. Louis, where she was happy for approximately six months, became seriously disillusioned with her boss, whom she had at first thought was brilliant and innovative. She ultimately found another job, as interior design director at the firm where she currently works. She was very young to be design director, and female design directors are apparently not common in St. Louis. She was not entirely sure whether she was taken seriously or treated as "just a girl."

She describes her parents' marriage as having always been unhappy. She remembers her parents sleeping together only one time, and that was when she was sixteen or seventeen. Otherwise, when her father was home he always slept in the chair in the living room. She was aware for many years that she thought her father had affairs. He was frequently bringing home gifts that "friends" gave him—sweaters, belts, etc.—and talked often about a woman friend who had a nice dog in another town. When she was in junior high school and most of her friends were going steady, the patient asked her father if she could go steady with a boy she knew; he had to think about it for a week and when he finally decided to let her, he said that it was all right as long as there was "none of that kissing stuff." She found that very confusing. She relates that when her brother became an adolescent her father put a double bed in the basement of their home for Harold's social use. The father would stand at the head of the stairs and "gleefully" listen to the bed springs squeak when the brother and his girl friend went downstairs. Her father is described by his brothers, the patient's uncles, as being the kind of guy who would "screw every girl he got his hands on—he would tell the ugliest girl in the drugstore she was the most beautiful just so he could lay her." The patient described one of the most hurtful events of her adolescence as follows: She had begun to be overweight and was walking around the house in the summer in a short terrycloth robe when her father began to laugh uproariously at her about her fat legs. She was mortified, ran out of the room, and cried for a very long time.

The patient dated off and on and engaged in heavy petting; at the age of seventeen she had intercourse for the first time. She has always enjoyed sex and feels that she has overly strong sexual desires. Her sexual activities are accompanied by such intense guilt and fears that she will become a loose woman that she is somewhat inhibited as to frequency. According to her, her parents still believe she is a virgin, and her mother occasionally talks with her about how she understands that the patient is frigid and would be terrified to have a man touch her.

For many years, both parents have confided to the patient. In early adolescence she knew that they had not had sex for years. Her mother told her that her father was impotent, but she didn't believe it; she believed he was having affairs and that's why her parents didn't sleep together. Her father complained bitterly about her mother's lack of understanding and cruelty to him, etc. After the patient went away to college, the father began to call her; in the past two years he has developed a habit of calling her at least once a day on his WATS line from work. She said he discusses his most personal concerns and problems with her, frequently telling her he could not talk with anyone but her about his concerns. He says she understands him more than anybody in the world. He calls her to discuss Harold, what to do about his marriage, how unhappy and unloved he feels, how inadequate he has felt for various reasons, and how he's never been able to discuss this with anyone but her. He tells her that he loves her more than anyone in the world and that she knows him better than anyone.

The patient relates that her father was the most important person in her life, and that she did everything she could to get his attention as a child. She remembers feeling that she would be a better wife to him than her mother and telling him that she wanted to be married to him, that she would be better than her mother because she understood him so well. She remembers feeling jealous when she was sixteen or seventeen when her parents went into the bedroom together and shut the door. She remembers thinking "They're having sex" and feeling jealous. She said that until two or three years ago she felt her father was the most wonderful, intelligent man in the world, and then she suddenly realized that he wasn't all that smart or all that special and she was devastated and cried for days. When he comes to visit her he comes without her mother and stays at her apartment; she is uncomfortable and restless and finds him disgusting. When he sits around in the armchair in her apartment, with his shirt unbuttoned and sometimes the top button of his pants loosened, he seems fat and repulsive. She remembers thinking him handsome and attractive until a couple of years ago.

The patient describes strong sexual interests, desires, and fantasies. She is most intensely frightened of these feelings when they are reciprocated, when a man she finds attractive finds her attractive. She has recently been involved in several triangular relationships. For instance, a coworker of hers, whom she has known and liked for some time and who is married, recently asked her if they could have an affair, as he was terribly attracted to her. She was interested, wanted to have sex with him, was frightened by her feelings, became very anxious, and went to visit her grandmother in Peoria. There she looked up an old boyfriend, who is living with a woman, and seduced him. She felt sexy and satisfied and desirable until the next day, when she had to confront her married friend and was coming to see me and tell me about the event, with some anxiety about how I would react. She has had a long and intense but intermittent relationship with this old boyfriend, whom she describes as in many ways very similar to her father. She has found the intensity of her desires for this man perplexing and overwhelming; the intensity of her feelings of humiliation and degradation when he goes back to the other woman are similarly overwhelming.

This young woman began analysis terribly eager to please and anxious to be accepted. She had persistent anxiety that I would find her unacceptable and stop seeing her. In the very first evaluation session she described her girl friend, who was in analysis with a candidate as being extremely dependent on her analyst, being miserable when he was out of town, and unable to run her life without him, and stated that she had no intention of being like that. During the first four months of analysis, resistance to dependency was a major theme, one which came to a head when I took some days off over the Christmas holidays. During this break she was anxious, depressed, sad, tearful—she missed me terribly. After this break she began to deal with her dependency wishes more openly. For example, she could begin to see how she would skip appointments not just because of work pressures but in order to titrate the intensity of her feelings of need for me. Toward the end of the sixth month of her analysis she was able to explore her fantasies at the beginning of the analysis that this would be a six-month analysis. She would not become dependent on me; it would be just a simple little thing that she would get over quickly. She saw this as her initial attempt to protect herself from becoming as intensely involved as she had already become. She also expressed a deep-seated belief, which she had had from the beginning of even thinking about therapy, that when all was said and done and the therapy was completed, no matter how long it would take, there would be some way in which she would not be changed, something that would not be done; and no matter how happy she was, she would be disappointed.

The therapeutic alliance with this patient was relatively strong from the very beginning, due partially, I believe, to her intense wishes to please and her resulting compliance with the task at hand. The transference shifts between a safe, regressive maternal transference and a father transference in which I am suspected of being unreliable and unappreciative but at the same time the most important person in her life, from whom she craves love, attention, and appreciation. She expresses intense feelings of love for me and gratefulness that I continue to treat her and accept her no matter what she tells me, and that I do not judge her, no matter how she judges herself. She has some difficulty expressing disappointment with me or anger at me when I cancel an appointment. Her fantasy in this regard is that if she is angry with me, I will not see her anymore. In association with this, she always remembers vividly her father's rages and her belief that he would never ever love her again or forgive her for whatever she had done to make him so angry.

In my countertransference, I like this patient, and feel she is an appealing person who seems to me to be struggling hard to face and master her troubles.

Her major defenses include intellectualization, reaction formation, repression, and denial. Diagnosis: I believe this woman is struggling at a phallic oedipal level with feelings of inferiority and inadequacy related both to penis envy and oedipal conflicts. Her oedipal struggles are intense and evident, and were complicated by her parents' unhappy marriage, her father's reported infidelity and consequent availability in fantasy, and his apparently intense involvement with her from late adolescence on. She regresses from these intensely conflictual stages to a preoedipal, regressive, maternal dependency state in the analytic situation. Outside of the analytic situation she has until recently maintained a rather persistent cute-little-girl image which I believe to be a similarly regressive defense against her strong heterosexual drives, as well as against oedipal conflicts.

Supervisor's Routine Institute Reports

Months 1–12

This is the candidate's first supervised psychoanalytic case, the patient having been selected by the Clinic Committee and referred to the candidate. The patient seems eminently suitable for analysis, with symptoms of depression, difficulty in interpersonal relationships, particularly with men, problems of self-esteem, feelings of inadequacy and inferiority in spite of superior performance and records, problems with weight, and a generalized sense of being unhappy. She rather quickly and easily moved into a psychoanalytic situation, accepting the structure of the treatment setting without undue anxiety or distress, progressively developing a capacity for free association and self-observation, and achieving understanding, insight, and the ability to use them in modifying her behavior. She has entered into a significant and well-established transference neurosis in which both maternal and paternal transferences are manifest and consciously experienced, and in which the analyst is increasingly becoming the major figure in her life. There have been significant changes in her behavior as a result of the analytic process, and the analysis is moving very well.

For her part, the candidate has demonstrated a good capacity to function in the role of analyst. She is perceptive and sensitive to conscious as well as unconscious implications and meanings in the patient's communication, and is capable of recognizing and dealing with the patient's transference manifestations. She is capable also of observing some of her own countertransference responses, and of controlling her analytic behavior when under the impact of countertransference feelings, to the point that they do not unduly disrupt the analytic process. She has made some of the usual mistakes that a beginning candidate makes, but these are in no way major nor have they been particularly difficult to modify. She is capable of framing appropriate interpretations that turn out to be useful to the patient, but is capable also of appropriate levels of abstinence in the analytic situation, thereby fostering further regression and transference development.

In the supervisory situation she is eager to learn and is perhaps somewhat unduly anxious and concerned about errors or not performing up to her own expectations. However, she is eager to improve, asks appropriate, effective, and intelligent questions about herself, her role, the process, etc. and seems to take genuine pleasure in both the analytic procedure and the supervisory learning situation.

During my two-and-a-half-month illness this past winter, she continued to work with the patient on her own, with apparent continuation of effective analytic progress and further development of the analytic situation.

All and all, I would rate her performance as superior and would strongly recommend that she be approved for a second case.

Months 13–18

The case continues to progress very satisfactorily. The patient is involved in a deeply regressive and fully developed transference neurosis, in which the preoedipal as well as oedipal transferences are repetitively present, oscillating defensively from one position to another and accompanied by significant affect, regressive experience, developing insight, and a capacity for recognition of neurotic disturbances. In all, a generally progressive analytic process is occurring. This translates in her behavior into an improved recognition of her capacities and talents, with change in her ability to maintain self-esteem and appropriate assertiveness in her work. In her relationships with men there is an increased recognition of the neurotic meanings of a long-term relationship with one particular man and a realization that this relationship cannot be a permanent one. There was some attempt to move into a healthier relationship with a less neurotic individual, but this has been rather tentative and unsustained, accompanied by a variety of defenses involving regressive behavior and a failure to move further.

A major theme has been the analyst's pregnancy, which the patient has consciously denied for a long time, but which was unconsciously present in many preoedipal associations, particularly a conflict over sibling rivalry with her younger brother, an increased sense of anticipation of rejection, a sense of phallic inferiority as the reason for the rejection, and feelings of rage and resentment in regard to the brother's birth and position in the family. The candidate handled this extremely well, waiting to confront the patient's denial in regard to the pregnancy until an appropriate intensity of experience and associated material was present. When the interpretation was finally made by the candidate, it resulted in a significant elaboration by the patient, a recognition of the previous denial patterns, and a continuing and intensifying regressive conflict of rage, wishes to harm and destroy the candidate's baby, feelings of being displaced, and anticipations of defensive patterns to confront such rejection.

The candidate's capacity to understand the flow of analytic material and to respond appropriately in an analytic way is improving steadily and significantly. Countertransference issues arise occasionally, but she recognizes most of them and their effects both on herself and on her analytic posture or technique. When she does fail to recognize countertransference, calling it to her attention is usually sufficient. She is capable of further self-analysis and is usually able to correct the difficulty. An example of this is the fact that recently she met the patient in the women's restroom following a session, and then avoided exploring and interpreting the patient's reactions. When this was pointed out to her, the candidate recognized her rationalizations and made plans to reintroduce this material.

One issue still unresolved is that the candidate has decided to take four months off following the birth of her child this spring, a decision she made and informed her patient of without discussing it in supervision. I suspect that she anticipated—correctly—that I would feel that four months was too long, that

I might point out the deleterious impact this might have on the analysis of her patient. She therefore chose to close the issue before I was in a position to voice any objections. Up to this point I have elected to say nothing about this, and instead to observe what happens in the analysis as a result. Other than this, the teaching-learning situation continues at a high level. She seems to experience pleasure both in her analytic role and in the learning process. Overall, her performance continues at a superior level.

Months 19–30

Since the last supervisory report, this candidate interrupted her work with the patient in order to give birth to her child and spend her first few months at home with the infant. When she resumed the analysis, the patient was able to return with a minimum of disruption of the ongoing analysis. She reentered the transference neurosis, which is now again active, and the candidate is once again handling this fairly well.

The material seems to have shifted somewhat, from a preoedipal to an oedipal focus; the patient is increasingly able to recover childhood experiences and memories, along with current transference reenactments. She continues to progress and change, both in her character structure and in her current capacities and self-image; she has become significantly less masochistic in her external life and relationships.

The candidate does well in the supervisory situation and maintains an openness and curiosity about the material. She is able to ask cogent and penetrating questions, at theoretical, technical and immediate clinical levels, and to correlate the material from one session to another, as well as from one phase of the analysis to another. Generally speaking, her performance is superior.

Months 31–36

The candidate and her case continued to move along in an effective and appropriate fashion. The patient is once again fully immersed in the analysis and the analytic process, and is making significant use of her analytic experience as regards her career and effectiveness at work, her interpersonal relationships, her self-image, and her general freedom from psychological inhibition. Continuing structural change as a result of working through in the transference neurosis has brought about improvement in all of these areas. In recent months she changed jobs, a major career advancement which, however, made it difficult for her to make her analytic sessions. This has resulted in a significant transference-countertransference conflict in which the candidate is able to maintain the analytic situation without granting the change of hour the patient is requesting, and in which the patient is using the realities of this scheduling problem as a means of acting out preoedipal conflicts of a defiant and aggressive nature. Additionally, she manifests in the transference neurosis anxiety about her competitive oedipal constellation, with guilt and inhibition as regards reporting and enjoying her successes, and anticipation of hatred, rejection, and destruction of the oedipal mother as their consequence. The patient's progress is such that within the next year or so I would anticipate she will be well into the termination phase.

The candidate is increasingly comfortable in the analytic role and is able to follow the ebb and flow of the case material with reasonable understanding and ease. She is able to intervene effectively, and her interpretations are for the most part well timed and well phrased; there are very few countertransference disruptions. From time to time she herself becomes aware of a countertransference response and takes appropriate self-analytic action to deal with it. She has made excellent clinical progress over the course of her work with this patient.

In the supevisory situation she is functioning with increasing independence. She has in fact been somewhat erratic and irregular in her attendance at supervisory hours. However, her cancelations are usually announced well in advance and seem to be a function of other pressures or activities in her life. She seems increasingly capable of working independently, and I therefore have no compunctions regarding the relative paucity of supervision over the past six months. On the other hand, I suspect these will have to be increased when the patient enters the termination phase. The supervisory sessions themselves now take the form of general discussion rather than detailed process notes, although from time to time, when she is in doubt about some aspect of the patient's material, she will again present detailed process material. At other times she will come in with a question for us to discuss in general terms as senior-junior colleagues. Generally speaking, I feel she is functioning well above average.

Months 37–42

The patient continues to make analytic progress, though she still uses job difficulties as a defensive rationalization regarding the frequency with which she attends her analytic sessions. The patient is working at both oedipal and preoedipal levels and seems increasingly capable of self-analytic awareness. Continuing improvement in her overall capacity to function interpersonally and in her work situation is also evident. The transference neurosis continues to be the central focus of therapeutic attention and there is some beginning awareness that the neurosis is being resolved in favor of a less regressive and more integrated self-image, reaction to sexuality, response to other people, and capacity for affective behavior.

The candidate is capable of independent work and is able to understand and follow the material. She makes appropriate interventions, is capable of tolerating some of the patient's provocations, particularly with regard to the patient's irregular attendance, and is able to appropriately interpret the patient's transference experience and behavior.

In the supervision the candidate is increasingly interested in how the clinical material from her patient relates to various theoretical issues that have arisen in her classwork, and she is increasingly spontaneous in her ability to interact with the supervisor in an appropriate fashion.

All in all, the case is going very well, as is the supervision, and I would anticipate that this patient will be entering the termination phase in another few months.

Months 43–54

The patient's analysis is progressing very rapidly. Marked changes are occurring in her sense of self and in her sense of feminine identity. There is a growing ability to integrate previously conflicted functions related to her being a woman. These elements of change occurred first as a result of the patient's becoming capable of reexperiencing the psychic trauma of urethral dilatations for stricture in early childhood. This had resulted in castration fears, in masochistic images of the role of women, and in manifest distortions in her fantasies of self and in her relationship with her parents. The patient was then able to accept and elaborate the candidate's intepretation of her phallic conflicts, which had as their central organizing fantasy the body as phallus, and of the multiple effects this has had upon her. A large number of behaviors and subjective states resulting from this core conflict were modified following effective interpretation of this material. The patient is now heading toward a natural termination probably sometime next year.

The candidate is doing extremely well in her work. She is capable of following the flow of the material, of maintaining an appropriate and effective analytic stance, of recognizing some of her countertransference processes and of modifying others when they are pointed out to her. Her interpretations tend to be effective and well timed, and she appears to derive genuine pleasure and professional fulfillment in her role and function as an analyst. Her technique is now significantly improved, and she is capable of assessing the effects of her technical interventions with minimal need for direct suggestion or technical confrontation by the supervisor.

The supervisory relationship remains at a high level, and increasingly the sessions are devoted to general concepts and theoretical abstractions from the immediate clinical data, with a mutual sense of enjoyable interchange between candidate and supervisor.

All in all, she is an excellent analyst and this first case has been an extremely effective analytic experience and learning process.

Months 55–60

Both candidate and patient continue to do very well. A termination date has been set and will be met. The patient continues to consolidate her previously described analytic gains and is increasingly capable of self-analytic awareness and resolution of conflict. Renunciation of transference demands and wishes is occurring in an appropriate and satisfactory way. The patient has undergone major intrapsychic change, which is manifested behaviorally—in her capacity for controlling some of her neurotic and masochistic behavior, and in an increasing sense of personal achievement and gratification. There is increased acceptance of herself as a woman and resolution of some of the phallic and urethral fixations that previously had interfered with this series of functions. Her interpersonal relationships seem more fulfilling and satisfying and she is increasingly capable of pleasure and fulfillment. Much of her innate talent in her chosen field has been released, and she is now on the threshold of major professional success and further responsibility and development.

The candidate has continued to do an excellent job and is able to follow the material comfortably, with only minimal help from the supervisor. She has been able to sustain the analytic process during the termination phase (three months of which have elapsed, with four yet to go) and is capable of recognizing termination process and dynamics. She continues to develop her sense of identity as an analyst and enjoys functioning in that role.

In the supervisory situation she continues to be an active participant, and though she now needs less direct advice from the supervisor, she nevertheless requires some help in recognizing some aspects of the termination process, particularly as this is her first terminated analytic case. She is able to combine the status of student and learner with that of junior colleague, and the supervisory sessions tend to be lively and enjoyable.

All told, this has been an excellent case and a fine learning experience for the candidate.

Months 61–64

This is the last supervisory report, for candidate and patient have brought the analysis to a successful conclusion. The termination process was well conducted and the patient underwent a significant degree of resolution of the transference neurosis. At the same time she demonstrated major intrapsychic structural change, and showed considerable satisfaction with the results of her analysis. These changes are reflected in her external behavior, and there has been significant resolution of some of the deeper core conflicts.

The candidate has continued to function at an extremely high level of sophistication and effectiveness, and she conducted the termination phase successfully, with only modest help from the supervisor. She was capable of recognizing some of her own countertransference responses to the termination process and of then correcting her technical interventions and responses appropriately.

The learning alliance of supervision continued solid and strong throughout the termination phase, and in general the candidate has had a very positive educational experience. She is now a sensitive, articulate, effective, and superior psychoanalyst.

Chapter 4

Supervisory Session 19

Candidate: I gave this patient the bill on February first, also telling when I'd be going away. She didn't say anything about it, and I commented that she didn't say anything.

Supervisor: She didn't say anything about it right then?

Candidate: She didn't say anything about it *ever.* About two-thirds of the way through the next session, I had given her a little bit of time and that's when I commented that she hadn't said anything about it. She said that she didn't have any thoughts about it, she hadn't had, and then when she thought of it she said her initial reaction was that she was disappointed, and then she cut it off and didn't have any more thoughts about it. In retrospect, when I think about what happened later, I think that the next six weeks had to do with that. It had to do with her struggles about my going away, but it only *seemed* to be brought out more into the open the week before I left. Actually, I think it was apparent even earlier. So originally I thought I would start today with the week before I left.

Supervisor: So it was in the background the whole time.

Candidate: Well, she kept saying—let's see, there was one phrase she kept saying. She didn't want to think about something. She didn't want to think about it. She was impatient. In the six weeks' time a lot of rather upsetting things happened, but they didn't have to do with my going away. But she didn't want to think about that.

Supervisor: What kind of things?

Candidate: Well, I haven't gone back over those notes. About four weeks before I went away—if my timing is right—she started working more and she already works a lot. She started working more, and feeling that she didn't have enough time, wasn't going to have enough time to get everything done. Those themes kept coming back again. There wasn't enough time, she couldn't manage to get everything done. The other thing was her feeling, which doesn't have to do specifically with my leaving, but another theme that has become more apparent since I saw you last, was the feeling that she is missing something, that no matter how she succeeds, and she has had rather dramatic professional success in the last three months, it is unfulfilling to her and she doesn't really understand why. She has begun to talk about being terribly jealous of her brother Harold, and she had never thought in the world that she might be jealous of him. She had a girl friend who came to visit her out of the blue and who had brought her married older boyfriend. The patient was terribly disgusted and thought about it and kept saying there is no excuse to do that to a wife and children.

Supervisor: For the girl friend to have seduced this man.

Candidate: Whom she was disgusted at.

Supervisor: She was disgusted with men.

Candidate: She wanted to burn the sheets. She wanted to burn the bed they were in. She wanted them to get out. She could hardly tolerate the amount of her disgust. Then she started to talk about her father's presumed affairs in more detail. Gifts that he brought home. A man who apparently doesn't buy himself very many clothes, but he would come home with an alligator belt a friend had given him. He talked a lot about a woman with a dog who lived in another town somewhere. Had sweaters, hand-knitted sweaters, and other things like that. And he bought her brother Harold a double bed and put it up in the basement when he was sixteen and told him it was for him to use. He would get all excited whenever he could hear the bed. It was a bed with bed springs. And she was disgusted by this. That all came up around Phyllis's visit.

Supervisor: She also heard Harold down in—

Candidate: She talked about it as if she were there. She would have been nineteen or twenty at the time—no, she would have been eighteen. She talked about being disgusted that her parents were standing at the top of the stairs with the door shut, being all excited.

Supervisor: Uh-huh.

Candidate: So that's another major theme that has been rumbling and coming up. And I think in conjunction with that she has talked some about her own feeling of asexuality. She doesn't feel feminine in anything but a little girl kind of way. In a cute, cuddly kind of way. She doesn't feel masculine. She feels real uncomfortable with anything that reminds her of there being men and women. Anything. She can have boyfriends, but the minute they make a sexual overture. . . . It is not sex per se, at least not as she described it. It is having it rubbed in that there are men and there are women and that she is a woman. She's not quite sure what that's all about. And she just doesn't feel sexual.

A week before I left was Monday, March third. I had, the week before this, said several things about her reacting to my impending absence. In fact, at one point I had said something about it and she came in the next day thinking I was leaving, that that Thursday was her last day. But she had another whole week. I remember that at Christmastime she had not come on the Thursday before I was to take some time off. She hadn't realized that that was the last day and then had been bereft. And now the same thing happened, except it was a week ahead of time. And she talked about how she hadn't realized, that she forgot I was going until the day before and here she only had one day left and she was bound and determined she was going to get here today because at Christmastime she hadn't. Two-thirds of the way through the session I commented that there was another week and I wondered about it, and she talked about wanting me to get back, to go ahead and get it over with and get back. And that was the end of it.

The patient comes in and says she wants to cry. She talked about the pressures at work. She didn't work all weekend. She didn't think about anything all weekend. Now she is at work and she doesn't want to deal with anything. She doesn't want to do anything. She expanded in detail about how she didn't want to think about or deal with anything. I asked her about that, what it was she didn't want to think about and deal with. She described pressure, deadlines, can't get it all in, there isn't enough time, can't get everything done. She was crying some, and I asked her if she was feeling pressure about our work and my impending vacation. She said there is so much inside her that she's frightened. She feels like there are a great number of serious things on her mind that she doesn't want to become conscious of. She doesn't want to think about anything, and she doesn't want to think about anything when I'm gone. She didn't want anything to become conscious while I'm gone. She expanded on this some and said that a lot of things have come to her awareness in the past four weeks, and I detailed some of the things: her need to achieve; her uncomfortableness with being female; her uncomfortableness in social situations with men; some of the ways in which she presents herself. That's another piece of the little girl female thing. And the way she drives herself. Maybe she feels it is hard for her to have me go away with so much bubbling up—those are words she has used herself on previous occasions. She said she was afraid to let any of it come to her mind without my being here. She needs me. She is scared without me. She catches herself stopping thoughts, like holding her breath. She talked about how that has increased in the last week and how she has worked frantically, the feeling of holding her breath. She talked about how her work has been a refuge, but it isn't anymore. But it is somehow involved in what we have been talking about. She needs to be liked. She has a lot of concerns about being liked. She had a sudden thought at that moment that if she disappointed her father it would be the worst thing in the world, because he was disappointed in the very beginning because he had wanted a son. She was silent. I don't know if this is the first time this has come up—if it is, we'll hear more about it this session. She said, sometime during the past four weeks, that her father had only male names picked out before her birth and they hadn't been able to name her right away. It never occurred to him that he might have a daughter. And that's the story that's told in her family. She was silent and wept softly. Why is she always disappointed in herself? Even when she succeeds it's not enough. She described recent successes and how she was pleased but went immediately to the next proving ground. She feels that she will get really upset and eat herself into oblivion for the two weeks that I'm gone. That's a comfortable habit, one she indulges instead of dealing with her real feelings and problems. It's like holding her breath until I get back. She described how she eats when she doesn't want to think about anything. She only thinks about what she's going to eat next, and then she eats it and thinks about what she's going to eat next after that. And then she feels bad because she's eating, but it effectively focuses all of her anxiety. She talked about being obsessed about not being able to stand people being disappointed in her. It's easier to be disappointed in herself than to disappoint someone else. For the first four to five months that she came, she thought ahead and worked real hard to prove some things to me, but now it's a refuge. There is no other place that she can come and be herself. She'll really miss me and miss the refuge. She just wants to be sick and stay home the whole time I'm gone. Coming here helps her to hate herself less. She's afraid that she will slip all the way back into the old habits and hate herself and eat and cry and be depressed. And that was the end of that session.

Supervisor: How do you understand this feeling? "As long as you're here I can face and think about these things; if you're gone, I'll just hold my breath and not think about anything."

Candidate: I don't know what to say, except that it seems to make some kind of sense to me. It seems to make a lot of sense to me. It seems to be what she's been fighting, this kind of strong need to have me. It's kind of a protective—I wonder what she's—the association that I've stopped on is it reminded me of the phobic people who take somebody with them, who have to have, it's not called a protector, but the person that they take with them is often the person they have ambivalent feelings about, like little Hans and his father.

Supervisor: Well, one can look at it from several different perspectives. It could be looked at, let's say, as the phase of separation-individuation a la Margaret Mahler. Remember some of her studies on the child who needs to know that the parent is there in order to function, and who can't tolerate, at this point, too much in the way of prolonged separation from the mothering figure? What you have here could be seen as data supporting Mahler's conceptualizations about the separation-individuation phase in the mother transference, the need for the mother to be there in order to facilitate refueling. It can also be looked at, a la Kohut, in terms of the mirroring transference, in terms of your presence, being there, smiling at her, telling her she is all right, and mirroring to her a sense that whatever has been going on, you approve. And when you're gone that means that you don't approve. That means that her self-esteem can't tolerate the separation, the absence of a positive, benign mirroring figure. It could also be that you are a superego to her and that your presence, your listening to this, and your not reacting, permits a modification, or at least the experience that "Maybe what I am doing, thinking, feeling, saying, et cetera, is not so horrible. But when I'm by myself I feel terrible, I feel guilty, I feel I am bad, I feel I am worthless, I feel I can't allow these thoughts to occur, because it means I'm bad." So it could be a fixation at varying levels. It could be any one of these.

Candidate: One of the troubles that I have with the Mahler and the Kohut is that they seem like two different ways of talking about the same thing. It seems like the mirroring phase is—when I watch children, anyway—the mirroring phase seems to coincide with the separation-individuation phase.

Supervisor: Yes, the phenomena are the same. What differ are the theoretical formulations derived from them. However, in the Mahler situation this is part of an object relationship. In the Kohut situation, it's part of a narcissistic developmental stream which is not related to objects, or at least it's not predominantly an object-related kind of developmental stage, but rather a stage in the evolution and development of the individual's self-esteem along narcissistic lines.

Candidate: Why can't it be both?

Supervisor: It could. It doesn't have to be an either-or proposition.

Candidate: Because it seems like—I'm using you to ask questions about these theories—we don't develop, a person doesn't develop, without object relations or without narcissistic evolution, and that both things have to be going on at the same time and that neither one, well maybe one of them is predominant, but if one of them is I certainly don't know which one. I can't separate them, yet.

Supervisor: Okay, let's go ahead with it, from Monday on.

Candidate: At five o'clock the morning on the fifth she called my answering service and said she'd be unable to make the appointment. That's Tuesday, that's an eight a.m. appointment—oh no, Tuesday she made it. Monday, not Tuesday. She said she feels a lot better after yesterday, not so bottled up, anxious, and driven. She didn't overeat, she went out with friends, she slept, she woke up and went to work early without the anxious, driven, panicky feelings. She felt really open to thinking about things for the first time in several weeks. That's a reference to the "I don't want to think about anything" that I've been hearing off and on for a while. She has felt the best that she has in six weeks. This cycle of eating started with Phyllis's surprise visit, and she doesn't want to be friends with her anymore.

Supervisor: Phyllis is the girl who has the older boyfriend?

Candidate: Yeah.

Supervisor: Which adds an additional formulation to what we've been talking about. If the real concern, if this is valid that this—

Candidate: They did coincide, my giving her the bill—

Supervisor: Coincides with Phyllis's visit, it could be that she is pushing and displacing everything onto Phyllis, in order to get away from the idea that it was your separation, your going away, that's caused all of this. It may also be that the oedipal conflicts stirred up by Phyllis's visit have evoked in her a regression to a preoedipal fixation or a preoedipal phase of conflict, as a defense against the anxiety, the disgust, the erotic stimulation, and the activation of all the fantasies triggered by the visit. But the real elements of conflict are still at the oedipal level, from which this current business is partly a regression. We have to listen to the material with these formulae in mind, and look for validation in the patient's spontaneous material as to which seems most reasonable.

Candidate: She says she doesn't want to be friends with Phyllis anymore. She's felt like this before. She described her relationship with Phyllis and then with Frances, a woman at work whom she doesn't like but whom she's friends with. She emphasized how much they both disappoint her and how it seems so strange to her that she has to prove to them what a good friend she is. She emphasized how she has to prove she's a really giving person. She wondered why it is so hard for her to accept anything. She describes gift-giving in her family, how hard it is for her father to accept gifts from her, and reviewed the incident on his birthday in October when he gave her gift to him back to her, to return to the store because he didn't like it. He didn't even try to camouflage his disappointment with the gift. She took the gift back and didn't feel like buying him anything else, so she didn't. She and her brother used to spend a fortune on each other. She described that the gifts had to be really big to please. It's really hard for her to accept things. I said something here; I commented on her uncomfortableness accepting things. She remembers growing up that Christmas lasted all year round. She was never told, "No, you can't have something." But then her parents didn't buy gifts for special occasions. She always wanted a present to be all wrapped up on her birthday, a surprise. She described growing up feeling very jealous of other kids and wanting holidays terribly, wanting birthday gifts terribly, feeling guilty because she had so much already. She expanded on this, and I said that she was describing her wants, and earlier in the hour she had described her need to prove that she was really a giving person, and I wondered if that is in opposition to a wanting or taking person, a camouflage to herself and to other people that she wants to take things she doesn't have. She said yes, she'd admit that, but she felt selfish and guilty whenever she wanted something. She had said ten minutes ago that she was never denied anything, but she has been. That's a storybook image. She can't stand to be said no to. She talked about the unacceptability of the slights and disappointments of the past, she pretends that they happened to another person. She has always maintained that you can get just as much pleasure out of giving as taking. It makes her feel really curious about why, why she feels this way. Sometimes she thinks it boils down to a fear of asking for something and not getting it. I wondered—

Supervisor: What did you have in mind with your interpretation? What were you hoping was the need or what it would do?

Candidate: I was hoping that it would . . . I felt that she wanted something and couldn't say it. Like at Christmas she couldn't call me and ask for anything. Giving things to people is her defense against wanting or taking things from people, which is a derivative of her wanting to steal a penis or take a penis, I think. And I wanted to interpret that defensiveness against this all-giving gift in terms of her wanting it, also. I remembered that at Christmas, and later after Christmas, she had wanted to ask me for extra appointments but could talk about it only long after. It seemed like she was talking about that kind of thing, she was talking about wanting and giving and being friends with people she didn't like, and being the best person in the world, and the best patient.

Supervisor: Well, the point I'm making is this: that just before you're ready to take off and be gone for two weeks, it's probably not an optimal time to get the patient into a whole new area, or a whole new awareness, or to try to remove a particular defense when the patient is not going to be in a position to continue to work it out with you over the next couple of weeks. Follow that?

Candidate: Uh-huh.

Supervisor: And I think that one would have some concern about uncovering too much of this, and making her become aware that really all this giving is just subterfuge and camouflage, that what she really wants is to take. This might push her into a situation overladen with anxiety, in which she would not have the support of the analysis in working it through. Or there is the possibility that she will accept the interpretation, work it through, and then intellectualize it. And you may then have some difficulty getting to it.

Candidate: Getting at it again?

Supervisor: Yeah.

(Long pause)

Candidate: I was not happy with this. I wondered if there was something she would like to ask of me, and she answered very thoughtfully and slowly that she feels really satisfied here now. She says that there have been times in the past, like before Christmas, when she couldn't ask for an extra appointment but she doesn't feel that way now. She feels that maybe she could ask now, she's not sure. She feels something could be worked out, she's not sure about that. The fear of personal rejection is really very great. She knows that, that she's sure about, that she might ask for something and not get it.

And then at five in the morning she called and canceled. On Thursday she talked about how strange it is, she gets so totally frightened and panicked at not being able to get something done. She worked all Tuesday night to be able to get a project done for Ruth and she was so anxious about it. She worked and was so worked up and had such mixed emotions that she couldn't stand the pressure. There was supposed to be a noon meeting, and she knew she wouldn't be able to make it. She was a nervous wreck by five, so she just called and said she couldn't come because she was a nervous wreck. She wondered if she would be able to arrange things, but she would have to go to the noon meeting anyway. There was so much pressure. She felt very disappointed. The meeting was rescheduled for four-thirty and everything went well. Everyone was pleased with her work, but it wasn't as good as it should have been or could have been had she had more time. She felt she had been hard on herself and had not allowed herself to see me. But she couldn't handle all of the pressure. No matter how she tries or works there's always something missing or wrong. She should be happy with her successes but she's disappointed. She didn't disappoint Ruth but somehow she disappointed herself. She talked about the review coming up, and whether she'll get the raise she deserves. She wonders if they'll come through or if she'll be disappointed again. She wants to make more money, to be independent of her parents. She talked about financial ties between her parents and herself, the confused feelings she sometimes has. She talked about how materialistic her father is and how she isn't like that, but then she stopped and said she does have confused feelings and sometimes she has feelings like her father has, and she's not sure about her own. Money is a measure of everything, that's her father. She wonders if she is materialistic. She wouldn't want to find that out. Her father makes a lot of money and does nothing. She resents him. She knows she resents him because he does nothing and earns so much, and he's always bugging her to earn more. And she works her head off, but she knows that she really doesn't try to be independent of him or even try to work out a budget. She talked about the ambivalence of cutting them off. If she doesn't come here to see me she feels really lonely at night, really sad, full of all kinds of things from the day. That's why weekends are so lonely and that's why last night she was lonely and sad and disappointed, and she called her father and she heard all about her brother. She expanded on that conversation and said she just felt really lonely, so she hung up the telephone. She could never tell her mother that she's lonely. It's really hard for her to admit that she wants or needs somebody or anything. Ninety percent of the time she'll be disappointed. She doesn't want to admit that she wants her parents to be hovering, interested parents, but it's true. All her parents paid attention to was Harold. She gave many examples. Her parents used to tell her it was too bad she had to work so hard for grades when Harold could just go in and get it like a snap. She keeps cramming all her positives and successes down their throats, and then they will see her differently. And I said something, that it seemed not at all unlike the struggle to stay independent of me, not to need me. She began to cry and said yes, she fought so hard not to need me and yet she does. She tries to prove that it's not true. She tries to pretend not to have wants or needs. She feels guilty wanting something and then ends up feeling disappointed in herself. She doesn't want to feel this way anymore.

She has been talking about a six-month analysis. Her initial fantasy was that she would have a six-month analysis. And at about six months it came up that she was realizing that it wasn't going to be six months now, and then she was absent without leave for a couple of days. When she came back, she said she can't go without this. And I suggested she was disappointed that all this wasn't solved in six months. She said yes, she has feelings like that, of being disappointed here. She was so sure she would be done in six months, but she's so grateful for what she has gotten. She feels frustrated and wants to understand now what's wrong. She's a very impatient person. Yet she fears she'll find out everything and will be finished here, but that nothing will change and she'll be disappointed. She talked about changes in herself over the last six months, and how much there is still to do, and how much she wants to get started doing it right now. It's time for me to get back already, so that we can work again. She said she doesn't feel so nervous about my going anymore, not like last week, just impatient. And that was the end of the hour. She got up and smiled at me and said have a really good time and then got kind of a funny look on her face.

I wasn't particularly interested in getting to the root of all evils when I said all that about taking. I was getting at this wanting, taking me, this wanting me to stay.

Supervisor: So again it's the difference between a shotgun and a rifle in terms of making interpretations. The more the interpretation is focused on a specific element or a specific incident or a specific wish as here, a feeling, the more effective it is likely to be. So you should perhaps have said, if your intention was as you say, "I think what you're doing is trying to get away from the feelings you have about these next two weeks, about what you would like from me and are afraid you won't get." Do you see? Connect it up with those two weeks.

Candidate: Okay.

Supervisor: Or, as in this last interchange, when she talks about how she wants her parents always looking at her over her shoulder—you look at her over her shoulder, constantly. If that's what she wants. These are all references, you see, to wanting you, wanting you to be there constantly, and the feelings that entails. What she's afraid of is to allow herself to recognize the intensity of her attachment to you, her dependence on you, and of her wish to have you stay. That's one part of it. She's also afraid, of course, to recognize the intensity of the anger, the resentment that her wish is not going to be granted. That's point number one. And point number two is that she is so powerless vis-à-vis that wish. It makes her feel her helplessness. "Even if I have this wish," she must feel, "and even if I express it and even if I get angry about it, it's not going to make a damn bit of difference. You're going to go anyway." Now on the one hand that's reassuring to her, but it also activates feelings of helplessness: "There's nothing that I can do to change her mind, just the same as there's nothing I can do to change my parents' minds even though I keep trying over and over again. I'm ramming my successes down their throats but it doesn't change anything." So there is this sense then of helplessness, of feeling weak and small, and there is probably also a good deal of concern about the anger and aggression, and a fear of expressing it. These are all elements of the conflict that has been stirred up by your leaving, that you will need to listen for and begin to bring out: "In terms of what we're talking about, there's a fear of facing how angry you feel, but I'm going anyhow."

Candidate: That comes up the first session I come back.

Supervisor: You see, it's safe only after you come back, because of a magical fantasy: "If I get angry at you, you may never come back."

Candidate: Do we have time for when I come back?

Supervisor: Yes.

Candidate: Well, she came in, this was Monday, and talked about how glad she was to be here today. I didn't approach the anger before she left, and I did this on purpose. I don't know if it was appropriate or not, but it was a decision on my part because it has been so hard for her, she has such strong resistances against depending on me to begin with, and just dealing with that narrowly, and she has even, I'm not sure if they're higher, but they seem higher to me, resistances against admitting anger. And it seemed like that was too big bites for her. What happens if I go too fast for her in these things is that she says no in a real loud voice and continues saying no for the next five to—you know, it really builds it up, it intensifies it. She felt bad when she left on Thursday, the last time, because she had complained about my leaving so much, saying that she didn't want me to leave and that I should stay, but then she did want me to have a good time and was afraid, for the entire two weeks, that I wouldn't have believed her when she said, have a good time. She really did want me to have a good time and worried about whether I would believe her. She was afraid she would come here today and I wouldn't be here. She was in agony about what she would do if she couldn't come back. She couldn't stand it. Things would happen and she would get upset and not want to think about it during the two weeks, so she would eat and then feel more upset. All she did for two weeks was work. She worked thirty-one hours this past three-day weekend alone. She talked about the pressures of work, the raise, and other things. She feels emotionally and physically exhausted, with remnants of feeling that she should be able to do it herself, that she shouldn't need me. She remembered her original vow never to depend on me, like Sally never depends on her analyst, and reviewed her plans for a six-month analysis. It came back a lot in the last two weeks. Sometimes she got really mad at herself about needing me to help her. It seems like a weakness. She should be able to do it herself. She should have control over herself and her life. She feels weak making excuses for herself. She feels she should be able to be stronger, she doesn't understand why she's so hard on herself. That was in response to, well, to that whole pile of stuff she just said. Why can't she just let herself alone and let herself need me? The week after I left she described a whole series of things she was mad at. She was really angry with herself for taking on so much work. The first weekend after I left she had a great weekend. She didn't do anything all weekend but she felt guilty—she always feels guilty when she doesn't work all the time. So then she worked. She got mad at herself. At least at work she loses herself completely. She's always been happiest when she's been working all the time and pushing herself. There was an interesting phrase: she said, "I always thought that's oblivion—total happiness." She now feels it's crazy to work like that but she can't stop it yet. She had a fight with her father on the phone, screaming at him and hanging up. She got mad at a lot of people.

I wondered if the bad feelings when I left—about whether

I would believe she meant me to have a good time—and her guilty feelings might have been a reflection of her anger, as they were earlier with her parents. I reminded her that she had described being mad at a whole bunch of people over the two weeks I was gone. She said she couldn't sit here and admit that she's angry with me; she has to put it away and be angry at someone else. She has never gotten so mad that she didn't apologize in the exact same breath, and she talked about that some more. And I reminded her that it's kind of a two-part statement. I said she had told me how much she appreciated coming and that she was so glad to come and appreciated me so much, and I wondered if that was only one half of the feeling, and that—I didn't say to cover up the anger, but I did say something like that. And she said yes, it is only one half, but the guilt is worse than anything, the guilt at being angry, it's worse than covering it up. She talked about the intensity of guilt in various situations and how rarely she shows anger or any critical feelings, how hard it is to show any negative feelings at all or even to let herself feel them very often.

Supervisor: What's happening here is you're going after the content before you deal with the resistance.

Candidate: Okay, tell me.

Supervisor: The resistance is hooked up to some kind of a fantasy of what it is that makes being angry so frightening. What you're saying to her is, "You're angry at me and all this anger at these other people really belongs here." She is saying, in a kind of remote way—

Candidate: She says, "I can't do it."

Supervisor: "I can't do it, it's too scary." Now the resistance, then, is hooked to some kind of a fantasy. What is the scariness? What is she afraid of? What would happen if? What is the fantasy that holds you back, that would be hooked into the resistance? Until you get that out—

Candidate: It's still going to be too scary—

Supervisor: into conscious awareness it's still going to be too scary. She will have to use other defenses. Like she accepts the idea, "Yes, I can see I probably am angry at you, but I just can't tolerate it, can't deal with it. And so, on the affective level, the anger, the resentment, the rage, isn't experienced. Not until the fantasies connected with experiencing aggression and anger and the expectations of what this will do to the relationship with you are brought out into consciousness, where they can then be tested and set aside, can you go ahead with the content.

Candidate: Good—because this day and today she talked a lot about guilt and anger and stuff, and I didn't, well, I just mostly left it alone, like today, because I couldn't get a handle on what I needed to do to help her with it. She has to push it away and then it comes out other ways. She felt terrible when she left last time, because she didn't think I really believed she wanted me to have a good time. Even jealousy, any negative feeling, is intolerable. She described situations at work where she has been jealous in the last couple of weeks, triangular situations, and how she's told the people, uncharacteristically for her, she's started to tell people when she feels things, but only later, and then feels really guilty. She feels guilty but at least it feels better to talk about it. She talked about the pressures to have everybody like her, and that she feels that that's crazy and she doesn't understand it. It feels like the most important thing in the whole world. She worked the whole two weeks I was gone because it was an escape from facing her feelings. She talked about the reality pressures of work, but that that wasn't where it was at. She knows she has to work. But she worked till eight, and she doesn't have to face anything when she works and eats, works and eats. Then she can just feel bad about those two things. She didn't want to talk with anybody but me. A girl friend came up to her and said, "You really look terrible, what's happening, tell me about it." And she wouldn't talk to her. And that's new and different. The only person she felt she could talk to was me. And that's the end of that session.

And then today—

Supervisor: We're going to have to—

Candidate: Today was just a continuation of that, with lots of feelings of why do I feel so guilty about everything, about any negative feelings. And I listened and tried to figure out what I should do to help her.

Supervisor: That is where the experience in the transference is the source, or the way *into* this whole issue. "You must have some kind of feeling or fantasy of what would happen to our relationship if you ever allowed yourself to experience the anger here. That fantasy would be frightening to you." In that way you try to bring the resistance out, the resistance against the experience of the anger and the expression of it. Only after that fantasy has been explicated and dealt with will she be able to experience the anger.

Candidate: To take the next step: Should we go back to one-fifteen, I mean one-o-five?

Supervisor: Well, we'll do that but I'll have to call you because I have to go back in the hospital sometime very early next week, to have some teeth taken out.

Candidate: The offending teeth.

Supervisor: Yes, so I'll call you. Next Tuesday I definitely won't be available, but hopefully the Tuesday after that.

Candidate: Okay. Here, or don't you know yet?

Supervisor: I don't know. I may be able to get to my office downtown.

Candidate: I hope so.

Supervisor: I do too. Bye-bye.

Candidate: Thank you.

Supervisor's Comments

This supervisory session occurred after the supervisor's recovery from a major illness that had occasioned a two-month lapse in supervision. During this time the candidate had continued to see the patient regularly, without supervision.

The candidate begins the supervisory hour with a report of the events of the analysis and shows that she recognizes the effects of her announced cancelations; she also shows an ability to summarize the material while acknowledging that she has not thoroughly reviewed her notes. There are indications that the patient is beginning to experience and express previously unconscious material. She speaks directly of her jealousy of her brother, while in the report of her girl friend's relationship with an older, married lover, derivative oedipal material and voyeuristic fantasies begin to emerge. Despite this development, however, the patient's thinking remains organized at the secondary process level, and most of her associations avoid direct reference to her transference experience.

As noted above, the candidate is able to recognize the impact of her forthcoming vacation on the therapeutic situation and relationship, and seems capable of observing the patient's reactions while waiting for a good opportunity to point them out to the patient—"two-thirds of the way through the session." In response to the upcoming separation, the patient demonstrates a deepening attachment to the analyst with an affective response regarding her feeling about the analyst's departure.

The patient is increasingly capable of describing the depth of her need for the analyst and also demonstrates her improving capacity for free association. In the midst of her associations about being liked and her separation from the analyst, she suddenly has a series of associations regarding her father and his wish that she had been a boy. Although still operating predominantly at the secondary process level, the patient is capable of recognizing her use of eating in a defensive way, as well as connecting this to the analyst's impending absence and her own tendency to regress to old symptomatic behavior. These are all indications that the analytic process is progressing and the patient is becoming more capable of self-observation, and of reporting her associations in an increasingly free and spontaneous way.

The supervisor intervenes to ask for the candidate's understanding of the patient's response to her absence. The candidate indicates some doubt, but the quality of the learning alliance is reflected in the comment "the association that I've stopped on," which demonstrates a willingness to expose her thinking to scrutiny by the supervisor. The supervisor focuses on the theoretical significance of the patient's experience, formulating it in terms of various psychoanalytic theories (Mahler, Kohut), presumably with the intention of helping the candidate better conceptualize the analytic interaction. The candidate responds at the level of these theoretical formulations, and there ensues a give-and-take between supervisor and candidate with regard to the theoretical implications of the material. In retrospect, it seems likely that at this point the supervisor (for reasons that are unclear but related probably to his recent illness) has a need to intellectualize the process and to deal with the candidate at the level of theoretical abstraction rather than immediate clinical experience relating to separation and loss.

In any event, the supervisor recovers from this theoretical excursion and suggests a return to the description of the analytic process. Once again, however, his own defensive needs seem to initiate a return to theoretical formulation. Although this may be helpful in allowing the candidate to understand some of the dynamic processes evident in the patient's material, it nevertheless is remote from both the patient's and the candidate's personal experience, and is probably determined more by the supervisor's needs than by those of the candidate. The supervisor does, however, provide a model of waiting to observe the patient's material before reaching closure on the theoretical issues.

The candidate continues her report, describing the patient's conflicts over giving and receiving, and an interpretation to the patient regarding an underlying desire to take and receive. The supervisor's question as to the purpose of this interpretation seems intended not so much to elicit information as to set up a subsequent intervention questioning its appropriateness. When the candidate offers an explanation that includes her recognition of some of the transference implications of the patient's behavior, the supervisor fails to acknowledge the candidate's reasoning as cogent. Instead he proceeds directly to his caveat regarding the opening up of significant new areas just prior to a prolonged separation. Although this is expressed in cognitive, theoretical, and technical terms, in an instructional mode, the candidate seems to feel criticized and uncertain, as reflected in a long pause followed by her comment, "I was not happy with this." This tone of defensiveness recurs later in the supervisory session, when the candidate explains her reasoning as to why she elected not to confront the patient with regard to the issue of anger, and also in her remark that she was not interested in "getting to the root of all evils."

In response, the supervisor returns to a more effective teaching position in explaining the difference between a generalized and a specific interpretive intervention, also illustrating one form such an interpretation might take. The supervisor continues with an explanation of the transference dynamics, as well as illustrating an empathic experience of the patient's possible fantasies and affects, hoping thereby to encourage the candidate to become aware of the patient's experience with regard to the impending separation.

In her explanation of the decision not to focus on the patient's aggression, the candidate is demonstrating her capacity to observe and reflect on the patient's material and responses, as well as an understanding of the dynamic process. In reporting this material the candidate is also documenting the way in which the patient's transference responses are increasingly activated and affectively experienced; although this is still formulated in secondary process terms, there is a significant deepening and a capacity to express more directly the elements of her experience of the analyst and the analytic process. The candidate demonstrates a capacity to understand and deal with the patient's conflicts and aggression when she describes the way she interpreted this aggression to the patient and the patient's defensive responses to the interpretation.

The supervisor's intervention, distinguishing content from resistance interpretation, elicits from the candidate the response "Okay, tell me"; this reflects the candidate's eagerness to learn and desire for deeper understanding. Following this, candidate and supervisor engage in a reasonably animated dialogue concerning this issue. The candidate is able to express her uncertainty, and the supervisor is able to present some conceptual background for technical interventions that might prove effective. The candidate's response ("Good"), followed by an admission of the doubts she had had as to what was appropriate, is then followed by a resumption of the reporting of the analytic work. The patient describes a further intensification of her involvement with the analyst, whom she considers the only person she can talk to.

The session ends with the candidate indicating some uncertainty as to how to help the patient grapple with her feelings. The supervisor tries to explain the importance of coping with the resistance. In this interchange he is once again responding to the candidate's uncertainty by providing a model with which the candidate may identify, and by illustrating for the candidate the way in which an analyst begins to think about the patient's material and to plan the interventions.

The supervisory hour ends with plans and arrangements for the subsequent supervision, in the course of which the supervisor's recent illness is referred to, tangentially, for the first time.

Neither the supervisor nor the candidate has in any sustained way reflected on the supervisor's illness and unavailability to the candidate during the preceding weeks. In retrospect, this should have been done actively, but both supervisor and candidate would probably have experienced reluctance and resistance to refer to this anxiety-producing episode. Also, the candidate deserved a more direct and immediately reinforcing expression of the supervisor's approval for the way in which she carried on with her first case in the absence of supervision.

The session demonstrates how a significant personal experience in the life of the supervisor may interfere with his capacity to be helpful to the candidate; without the supervisor's conscious awareness he has responded on the basis of his own personal needs rather than of the candidate's learning needs.

However, on the basis of their previous work together the learning alliance seems strong enough to withstand this temporary disruption.

Chapter 5

Supervisory Session 20

Candidate: I made a little summary for us based on this calendar, which helps me. Those are the times she wasn't here—Jewish holidays—and this is the day I'm about to summarize.

Supervisor: Okay.

Candidate: On the Jewish holidays she went to Peoria with her mother, to visit her grandmother. She had been looking forward to that. She talks about the weekend, and how left out and misunderstood she felt. She talked about that a good bit but without a tremendous amount of affect; then she started to talk about a friend of hers, a married male friend who is one of her suppliers, one of the people she works with, who propositioned her—she did not use that word—on Friday evening. He said that he would really like to have sexual relations with her and what would she think about that? It shocked her and made her feel really confused, because she likes him. She told him no, she couldn't do that, because he was married. And then she went off to Peoria and called up a—toward the end of the weekend she just kept mulling it in her mind and toward the end of the weekend she called up an old boyfriend of hers who lives in Peoria, whom she's seen off and on for nine years and whom she had had sexual relations with, but quite a while ago. She called him up and invited him out on a date, and went out and had sex with him and had a wonderful time. But she didn't tell me that at first. She said she felt really bad. She feels really bad, guilty wanting sex. She talked a long time about how women don't want sex like she wants sex. That's okay for men. She feels her sex drive is really strong; she's afraid of being labeled loose; she's confused by what she did; she didn't feel guilty at the time; that she had a wonderful time; she continued to feel good; she felt sexy; she felt attractive. She got back on the plane to come back to St. Louis. She continued feeling good. She flirted with the man sitting next to her and felt attractive. It was Monday morning, when she saw on her calendar that she had to call the married man who had propositioned her. She had to contact him as part of her work and she started to feel really guilty, feeling that she was a bad person. I asked her to explore that some. She was able to say that she wanted sexual relations with him and that made her feel bad. That made her confused. She didn't expect that from herself. And that was that session. The next day starts a series when I think—well, the next day Ted calls. The next day she tells me that Ted, and Ted is the old boyfriend, calls and she begins to get in a terrible muddle about her feelings about this, which are probably best exemplified by today's session, and I'm not quite sure how to. . . . She thinks that it's crazy to want to have anything to do with this man. He's a crook. She thinks he's a crook.

Supervisor: This is Ted that we're talking about?

Candidate: Yes. He's a crook. He hurt her. He has used a number of women. She knows his history. He's all mixed up, but her feelings are much stronger than the intellectual part of her, feeling that she will make him happy. She needs to make him happy. He is more important than anybody in the world. This distresses her. She said today—let me find it, it's after the—this is what I want to talk about: It's been a slowly coming on muddle, in that it took a week to come on as badly as it is today for her, or yesterday, with her originally refusing to see him, her saying that he had dumped her, had been rotten to her, that she didn't intend to get hurt again. He kept calling and calling and calling, like twelve times in one day. He finally came over there that evening and she saw him. She said she felt her heart would break with love for him. She describes the—let me just use today's session and see if that works, since there are all those sessions in between.

Supervisor: And we won't have time for them.

Candidate: And they're all the same material, only it started out with her all intellectualizing and saying, "I'm not gonna see him," but being aware that she wanted to see him and not understanding why. Seeing him and feeling this terrific rush of feelings and wanting to go to bed with him and wanting to please him and wanting to make his life right and wanting him to want her—he's still living with this other woman—wanting him to get rid of the other woman, wanting to be the center of his life, and yet at the same time suspecting that she doesn't, that somehow that's not the point. Frequently she will say, "He's like my father, he's a crook like my father," "He uses people like my father," "All my life I tried to get my father's attention away from my brother." Today she said she was miserable yesterday, as miserable as she's felt since six months ago when this whole thing started. She always blames herself. That was the major intervention—well, actually I made two major interventions, only one was yesterday. One was that she was thinking in order not to feel, which she was doing; and, the other one was just a comment like "You're being awfully hard on yourself." She was really sidetracking herself, I felt, with the superego. I don't know how to say what I'm. . . . But let's go on. She always blames herself, and that doesn't get anywhere. She feels humiliated by Ted, she has fantasies of him laughing at her, thinking how stupid she is, but she doesn't want to play hard to get. She feels like she should do something else, she shouldn't just fall into his arms like this, yet she feels humiliated that she is not playing hard to get. She feels humiliated that she wants him so much. I was four minutes late, I was significantly late, this morning, and I asked her if she had had any thoughts about that while she was waiting for me, any thoughts about why I was late. She said she had had the fantasy that I wasn't going to come. That has been her fantasy for a long time, that some day she will come, she wants to come so badly, she wants to be here so badly, and I just won't be here. Then she said that it was true what I said yesterday, about thinking and understanding in order to keep from feeling. These feelings are scary, they feel like fear and sadness, those two feelings and humiliation. There's something very humiliating. Where does she fit into his life? What place does she have? That's all she can think about. She hasn't been able to work and she hasn't been able to sleep. It's a puzzle. On the one hand she feels she would do anything to get him to love her, and on the other she thinks that if he really left Mary and wanted to move in with her, she is not sure she would want him. She remembers being sick of him before, when he would be around too much. She talks about how she doesn't trust him or understand his intentions toward her. She can be rational about him when he's not around, but when he is, she just wants to believe that he cares about her, that he really has changed, that everything will be different. She talks about how badly she wants him to get help and she knows he won't. He won't change. But that doesn't faze her when he's around. She feels very caught up in this thing. That's been one of the things she's expressed since the beginning of it, it's so powerful. She feels the only way she can not be helpless is if he goes away. She feels helpless in the face of her feelings, like she'll do something she doesn't think is good for her. She said yesterday she thinks there is something unhealthy about this, that this is going to make her unhappy. But she thinks she is going to get involved in it anyway. Not when he's not around—she doesn't think she's going to get involved in it then, but when he is around, she feels in a quandary about going to bed with him. She described earlier having to sit on her hands to keep from touching him. She believes that he will just use her like he has used other women, but she really wants him badly, and she talked on about that and then said she feels really sad. She feels that if she agrees to see him, she'll feel totally humiliated and laughed at, a fool, and if she doesn't agree to see him, to get involved with him, she'll feel that she hasn't given him enough of a chance. She feels she can't step out of it, she's trapped, and that makes her feel very tired. She doesn't want to believe that he is a bad person, using and manipulating her. It will be just as upsetting if she wins the prize, if he leaves Mary and comes to her. It feels like that would be just as bad as him leaving her and going to Mary, and she doesn't understand that. There is a correlation with her father. She thought about it all weekend, and yesterday. She has worked for years and years and years for his attention and love, and in the last two to three years he has turned to her, she has become more and more important to him than she was before. She has won in a way, but it doesn't even matter. She is still caught up in the game of winning him. She won and—it's weird, she doesn't understand it. Now that she has him calling her every single day, she doesn't want it, and yet when she feels that she's not being the exact perfect daughter and he might be displeased with her, she gets real upset. She feels it's up to her to make him happy.

Supervisor: This is the father that's calling her every day?

Candidate: Uh-huh. And occasionally she has stopped that, but then she gets wracked by—at least what she reports to me is that she feels so guilty. When she yells at him he won't call her for like three days. Once she said that she missed him calling, but the other times she said she feels that she's making him miserable and that she feels guilty, but it's always been an aside. But that's the history of it. He calls her every day on the WATS line from his office, sometimes more than once a day. She goes through periods when she hangs up on him saying "I'm busy," but he calls her anyway. That's the feeling with Ted, that she should make his life better, that she would always be gay and happy and a perfect hostess with him and it nauseates her. She described that that's how she is with him, that she's not like she is in my office, that she never shows that that's how she feels, but that she is gay and lively and a perfect hostess. Right now it nauseates her, she is tired of pretending, tired of wanting something so badly that she has to mold herself into something she isn't in order to get it or keep it. She reviewed her earlier relationship with Ted, how she fit herself to his needs, and how her self-esteem plummeted. Like she offers herself on a silver platter and says take me and then she feels there's nothing there to take. This is not something new. This is something she has done again and again. She saw that this weekend. She reviewed previous relationships in which she had given up everything, including all her pride, for further attention. She talked some more about not wanting to believe he is a rat, and about how much she hasn't wanted to believe that her dad's a rat, how she hasn't been able to confront them, either of them, with how she feels or what she needs or wants, because she is so afraid of losing them. She talks about the strength of her physical desire for Ted and how afraid she is that she'll give in and do something that will make her really unhappy ultimately. That was it essentially. I hadn't said anything the whole session, because yesterday, well, there was a little bit more to the session. I'll tell you a little later. I was in a muddle and I now realize why I was, I think. I didn't do anything, but I was feeling like I wanted to rescue her and wasn't doing anything. And I *wasn't* doing anything, not in the bad sense of indulging a rescue fantasy, anyway. And so I decided that today I would sit and be quiet and see if I could figure out what was going on, either with me or with her or between us, that I felt so muddled yesterday. I felt confused. I felt distressed and so I didn't say anything, and I was comfortable but it was also a change. I had said some things yesterday toward the end of the session, and I wish I had said something a little different. She wafted away, her voice got really soft, and she seemed to get real small, and I wish I had asked her what was going on or, you know, how she was feeling, that she was getting so soft and quiet. I asked her if perhaps she was disturbed that I was saying so little, and she said yes. She knows I'll talk when I have something to say that will help her, but she feels so upset and so disturbed that she wishes I could give her the answers right now, that I could tell her what to do, and it's disappointing that I don't. She doesn't want to leave my office ever. She just wants to stay here and then she expanded on that—just wanting to stay here away from it all. And that was it, the end of the session. I think, when I started to think about this, I thought I didn't understand anything that was going on or what I was supposed to do about it, because I was so—in a muddle or however you might describe it. And then, as I kept thinking about it, it occurred to me that the muddle was that I wanted to help her in a way that I can't help her, only that I had that impulse, the impulse that most of her friends must have in that they all tell her what to do or what not to do. I was feeling uncomfortable because of that. Once that came to my mind, I stopped feeling muddled, at least in that way. I'm still not sure that I—that only came to my mind about half an hour ago. So that in straightening it out now I think part of my difficulty with this is knowing how to handle it in the analytic situation, other than listening to it and allowing it to continue to develop, knowing if I should do anything else. It doesn't feel like there's anything else I can do. Today I was listening and I was thinking: What's she doing with this material, you know, is there some way I can—is there something I should do? Like other times you and I have talked about a way she's defending herself that should be interpreted to her so she could move on, and I couldn't find anything I could do.

Supervisor: Well, let's back up. She comes in, she starts talking about Ted, how concerned she is about what she might do, and how she is upset about the possibility that she would give in to him; she wants him but she doesn't want to be too easy, but she doesn't want to play hard to get and she's all up in the air about him. After a number of minutes of that, you say to her, "Did you have any thoughts while you were waiting for me this morning when I was late?" Do you have any thoughts why you chose to say that or to point her in that direction when you did?

Candidate: Well, because what she was saying about Ted was not what she was afraid she was going to do, but that he was going to be unreliable and that she wouldn't be able to count on him and he wouldn't come back, I wondered if—see, I had also been sick and had taught the week before, and I had asked her about that, but she always pushes these things away immediately. She doesn't want to talk about them. Actually she didn't know I was sick. I just called to say I couldn't see her, and she figured I had something else to do and that it doesn't bother her when I don't come, it bothers her when she doesn't come. I think I also had been wondering in this week of listening to all this about Ted and about getting involved—I mean I know there's a reality thing happening out in the world that's distressing her, but I wondered if there was any way to bring it into the transference. See, that's where I get muddled, I think that's one of the places I get muddled. When things are ticking along in the outside world like this, I don't have so much trouble with pulling things into the transference or talking about them in terms of the transference. But whenever there seems to be an explosion in the outside world, then, well, I don't have any trouble letting it explode for a day or so, but I do have trouble then pulling it back in. Do you understand what I'm saying?

Supervisor: Uh-huh.

Candidate: And I don't know the balance there. I think that's what disturbs me. I don't know the balance.

Supervisor: At any rate, you had the feeling that when she's talking about Ted, what a rat he is, how unreliable he is, how she's going to get herself sucked into something, that he's going to take advantage of her again, what he's done before, that when she was saying all of that she was also thinking about you. You were four mintues late this morning; you were sick last week. Right? Now, what was her response?

Candidate: She said she thought I wouldn't show up.

Supervisor: Uh-huh.

Candidate: That she had the fantasy I wouldn't show up. And I thought that that confirmed what I thought.

Supervisor: Uh-huh. And then what happened?

Candidate: Well, she went on talking about Ted, because—well, I don't know why, but she did. I was aware in that pause just then that there might be a way for me to pick this up but I am not quite sure how to.

Supervisor: So what you're saying is that you—

Candidate: That's what I meant by the balance between things exploding in the outside world and bringing them in in a way that the person can—a way that's appropriate.

Supervisor: So you can't pretend that Ted doesn't exist.

Candidate: Yeah. You can't say, well I really think you're not talking about Ted. I was just going to say that an exaggerated inappropriate thing to say would be, "You're afraid of getting involved here." I mean, that's just something that would not be done. And I know that that's an exaggerated inappropriate thing to do, and I was aware this morning that I thought my being late was a way I could pick it up. I mean I didn't arrange to be late just so I could do that. I had been sick that day. And she *was* talking about me as well as about Ted. But then I didn't know how to go from there without—

Supervisor: So you would not at this point want to interpret all of the things going on with Ted as a displacing of the transference.

Candidate: No.

Supervisor: On the other hand, there is a certain parallel between what's going on with Ted and what's going on with you.

Candidate: I think so. I think there is.

Supervisor: The question then is—

Candidate: And I think there's a parallel between her levels, her two expectations from wanting that I—I mean the expectation that she tells me when she's with me and her fear when she's waiting in the waiting room. You know, I think there's a parallel. She is afraid that I'm not going to come.

Supervisor: She's afraid that—

Candidate: That I'm not going to come through, that I'm going to leave. She told me this when I asked her what her fantasy was of what would happen if she got mad at me, if she got angry. It made her too anxious to even think about it, but then after a while she said she thought it was just that I would leave, or that I wouldn't like her, that I would go away. So I do think they are parallel.

Supervisor: So how are you going to get *her* to begin to think about the possibility that they are parallel?

Candidate: Yeah. Well, I have to follow up on something like my comments. I need to say—something. Using her experience, things that *she* said in a way that will be convincing to her, and I'm not quite sure why that's hard for me to do whenever there is—it doesn't seem hard for me to do when the outside world is relatively everydayish, but it does seem hard for me to do when there is a crisis, even if it's part of the illness.

Supervisor: Well, you see the question. She suddenly has taken up with Ted again and he's called and she, in one way or another, encouraged him to continue. She could have just said no, and that would be that. If he calls twelve times, she could take the phone off the hook, she could have done something to stop him. She chooses to continue this. She has her interest in Ted suddenly reactivated, very intensely. She is very excited and very sexually stimulated by him, and by the possibility of going to bed with him. The question is whether this would have happened in the absence of anything going on in the transference. Is this just a continuation of her feelings and fantasies about Ted? Or is it in some way a displacement of the transference? Perhaps because certain things are being stirred up in her, she needs to find some object out there, some person, some situation, some relationship in which to express feelings that are unacceptable in here. To a certain extent, you can see a link here to the time a week ago when the married man made a pass at her, a sexual approach. She gets very upset and very anxious, rushes out and has to find somebody else with whom to discharge her sexual tension. Then she feels fine about it, until she comes back here and all of a sudden she feels guilty about what she's done.

Candidate: Yes, she is anxious.

Supervisor: When she gets back here, to tell *you* about it.

Candidate: Yeah, she was anxious about that and very relieved the next day.

Supervisor: And very what?

Candidate: Relieved the next day.

Supervisor: Relieved that what?

Candidate: At being able to—that she didn't feel judged, or that it was okay. That she was okay, or something was okay.

Supervisor: You see, in that piece of behavior, what she is illustrating is the tendency to act out and to seek in the external environment someone to relieve inner tensions that are being mobilized toward one person, but which she cannot express toward that person. She must discharge them on somebody else. That certainly is what she did with this married man and this old boyfriend. The question then would be, is she doing the same thing with you?

Candidate: And if so, how to point it out to her.

Supervisor: But the first thing to find out is—

Candidate: Figure out if she's doing this.

Supervisor: Yes, and if she is, I don't think you'd want to come in and say straight out, "I think you're using Ted to express feelings and fantasies that really belong here in your relationship with me." On the other hand, you have a situation in which, intuitively, you sensed the following: that what she's talking about vis-à-vis Ted and his being unreliable is really related to me and my being late, and my having missed last week because of illness, or not because of illness—she didn't know that my having missed—

Candidate: I had something better to do. (Laughs)

Supervisor: Yes, and maybe feeling you had something better to do. So you're unreliable too. Anyway, you sensed this, you intervened, and she confirmed your intervention: "I thought you weren't coming at all" and so on (just like Ted). And then she goes back and talks more about Ted.

Candidate: Uh-huh.

Supervisor: So that is, in a sense, a confirmation of an hypothesis that we have just been working on, but it is not a confirmation that is likely to be convincing to her. So it would probably be more appropriate to suggest something like this: "There seems to be a certain kind of parallel between what's going on between you and Ted and your feelings about him, and also the feelings about your dad and how Ted reminds you of your dad, and the same sorts of feelings are also coming up here with me." In other words, you're not suggesting that this is all a displacement of the transference, but simply that there are parallel feelings. You could add, "There is a similar situation and a similar set of feelings being stirred up here with me as are stirred up with Ted. But it is probably easier for you and less threatening and more comfortable to talk about it when it comes up with Ted than to talk about it directly when it comes up with me."

Candidate: That's what I was searching for, or one of them anyway, that step in between. I find one of the things that becomes more difficult the more I know about my patients as they talk, as I move further ahead of them, is to find steps in between. To find ways to say things—uh, that are palatable. Small steps, small things. When I was only an eighth of a step ahead of patients, then I didn't have trouble with that, because I could never say anything that was too, too big a bite. But with this the trouble I was having was the difference between saying nothing and having to tackle total displacement. And that seemed totally inappropriate.

Supervisor: Yeah, it would have been—I mean, to have made that interpretation.

Candidate: And so I shut up.

Supervisor: It would have made her feel that you are not really interested in what she is thinking, and it would have been to lead her too much. On the other hand, it is possible to point out that there is a parallel and eventually to make the next step, which is to point out that some of the feelings going on in here are being reenacted and displaced onto Ted.

Candidate: Okay.

Supervisor: So it would suggest that, at the moment at least, the transference is predominantly related to her father. Even though you are a woman, this is a *father* transference.

Candidate: I'll have to look back through my notes because while you were sick I had an inkling of a father transference. It was very strong and I can't remember what it was, but I had, I just remembered thinking, this is shifting and there is more—distrust is the wrong word, but I am becoming more and more unreliable in her eyes. I am becoming more manipulative and more unreliable, more like her father. Whatever it was, wasn't real loud and blaring, but it did announce itself before this.

Supervisor: You see, this is in all likelihood the reason why she got so panicky when this married man approached her; instead of just accepting it, she got very upset and concerned about it. That's the transference.

Candidate: The last one who did that, she just left. The man with the dream machine—in fact she remembered it this time. The time machine. The guy who runs the time machine competition, and she was doing designs for him, and she just canceled his contract and, because he got kind of pushy about it and she didn't know how to handle it, it made her nervous. But she talked about it that much at least, and said that he was obnoxious, you know, that she didn't want to have anything to do with him. But it was a very different kind of response from this kind of panic.

Supervisor: So the likelihood is, you see, that this kind of panic was activated by virtue of the fact that in the transference these feelings are being aroused.

Candidate: Aroused without her being articulately aware of them.

Supervisor: Right, without her being aware that these are feelings directed toward you, and through you toward her father. There seems to be some increased awareness, though, that she has had fantasies and feelings about her father, that Ted does remind her of her father, and she probably did have some conscious sexual thoughts and feelings about him, about his peccadillos and so on. So with you this is being stirred up, but she doesn't experience it toward you. Having this as the stirring up of the pot, vis-à-vis these fantasies, then with this man out here offering her the opportunity to act this out, she becomes very anxious and panicky.

Candidate: Then I would postulate this: that if Ted hadn't called on Tuesday, Wednesday—you know, he didn't have to, he could have gone off with another woman—that she would have got—you are saying then that she is ripe for this, because of what is going on in the transference.

Supervisor: Uh-huh.

Candidate: And that the weekend before, when she reacted to her friend the married man, and then found another boyfriend, that if Ted didn't call she would have found someone else.

Supervisor: Possibly.

Candidate: For her to, to—

Supervisor: Reenact this with.

Candidate: Yeah. There are several men at work who are kind of always, whom she talks about off and on, but I can now see that one of them could have become—well, there are few women, she is the only female designer, she is surrounded by men. She could have found one without much difficulty, I think.

Supervisor: Someone else on whom to displace these feelings.

Candidate: Yeah. And I think part of my confusion in this was the reemergence of an old boyfriend, you know. Well, it wasn't really confusion—that's a wrong word—but not knowing how much to trust my instinct that this has to do with me too. When I say that there was turmoil in the outside part that gave me pause, part of the difficulty had to do with the the real life situation being believable, more believable than if she had just zapped onto somebody, you know, hooked onto some new, strange person. And I'm not saying that I should think this way. I'm just trying to—there is a hole in my thinking, I sometimes get taken in by the—

Supervisor: The hole in your thinking is a failure to recognize and to really appreciate that you are the most important person in her life.

Candidate: Yeah. And I think that I don't really appreciate—

Supervisor: You don't really appreciate that yet. And you still have the feeling that these other people are real and you are just imaginary, a fantasy and therefore less important.

Candidate: Yeah, and that her life really doesn't revolve around me.

Supervisor: And the other thing is the difficulty, which can be a real difficulty, in recognizing that the transference is independent of the sex, the biological sex, of the analyst.

Candidate: Well, I've been thinking about that for the last month, and sometimes it seems to be a greater problem than other times, but I think that it feels—well, it's like the first time doing lots of things. It feels awkward until you've done it.

Supervisor: Uh-huh. Sure

Candidate: You know, like, once I've done it and I know that it's—once I know from, from experience that it's true for the other person. You know, that it *is* true. That the transference doesn't respect the biological sex of the analyst, then I won't feel awkward. And I think it is a first time. You know, I think that's where the awkwardness comes in.

Supervisor: Sure.

Candidate: And I just—when I've been thinking about it for the last month, I thought that that's probably part of the awkwardness with the first case, and that it is just something that I have to wait out and recognize as *my* awkwardness. But it feels more like awkwardness than anything else; it doesn't feel like some uncomfortablenesses that I'm having. It feels like I'm just learning.

Supervisor: Well, that brings up a question about a second case. Have you thought about a second case?

Candidate: I didn't write my summary. I can't have a second case until I do my six-month summary.

Supervisor: Well, have you thought about it? Do you want to start a second case?

Candidate: I'm ambivalent about that. But I was ambivalent about starting a first case, so I guess I just have to think about it some. I didn't—

Supervisor: Well, give it some thought.

Candidate: Nobody has asked me that, you know.

Supervisor: Give it some thought, because, for one thing, having just one case tends to promote an overcathexis, a hypervaluation of that one particular patient. Secondly, there is no opportunity to contrast analytic processes.

Candidate: That's one of the things that I would like, that contrast. It's not just a hypercathexis or overvaluation of that patient, but of not being able to use my skills in the rest of my practice; I only have one place to excercise them.

Supervisor: Well, as I say—

Candidate: And so that's, my impulse to take a new patient is kind of based on that restlessness, that I want to have another place to exercise. Because it feels like it will broaden my mind.

Supervisor: That's right. That's why, as I say, I think you are ready to, and I think you ought to give it some thought.

Candidate: Well, that might give me the—what you're saying is that this might give me the spur to write my six-month summary?

Supervisor: Get that summary written and then we'll talk about it again.

Candidate: Okay, but just tell me that that summary does not have to be the be-all and end-all.

Supervisor: No. It doesn't.

Candidate: Okay. (Laughs) Because I, I—thank you.

Supervisor: Okay. I'll see you next week. Bye-bye.

Supervisor's Comments

The candidate, having prepared a summary and calendar of dates, indicates active planning and initiative with regard to her educational experience in the supervision. She may also be reacting to the strain on the learning alliance from the supervisor's expression of his own needs in the previous supervisory session.

She continues her reporting of events in the patient's life, material that contains various derivative expressions of the patient's oedipal conflict. Her way of dealing with being propositioned by the married man and her renewing the relationship with Ted, a man she recognizes as in many ways similar to her father, are instances of this. The candidate shows she can tolerate limitations in the learning situation ("and we won't have time for them") and can summarize and present samples rather than needing to present the patient's material in its entirety. She can also observe her own interventions ("actually I made two major interventions") as well as shift conceptual gears by interjecting, "She was really sidetracking herself, I felt, with the superego." These capacities are evidence that the learning alliance and situation are well established. She is capable of shifting from one perspective to another and not only of reporting data but also of reflecting upon it, both within herself and in her interactions with the supervisor.

Subsequently the candidate demonstrates the capacity to recognize the impact of her own behavior and the importance of the transference. She asks about the patient's responses to her lateness, briefly evoking the patient's transference fantasy of being abandoned by the analyst. The patient's spontaneous shift from Ted to the father demonstrates her increasing capacity to shift from one focus to another, to associate in a more spontaneous way between current and past relationships, and to begin to recognize parallel experiences and feelings.

The candidate can begin openly to express her own concerns, countertransference uncertainties, and doubts regarding her tactical interventions, thereby reflecting both a capacity for self-observation as an analytic instrument, and trust in the safety of the supervisory relationship. She also recognized, appropriately, that given this uncertainty the best course of action was to intervene only minimally. However, she recognized also that her minimal interventions themselves had an effect on the patient. For her part, the patient demonstrates an increasing depth of transference involvement ("she doesn't want to leave my office ever") but at the same time reflects a solid therapeutic alliance in her tolerance and understanding of the analyst's silence.

The candidate recognizes her muddled state, as well as her countertransference wish, but realizes that these have occurred only in the current setting. Directly and indirectly, she is asking the supervisor's advice as to how she can promote the analytic situation. At this point the supervisor begins to formulate some of the analytic process in anticipation of helping the candidate cope with her uncertainty and confusion. By summarizing some of the process in concise form he permits the candidate to follow the material macroscopically, and then asks for her ideas. This is an attempt to avoid an authoritarian posture and to encourage the candidate's active participation in thinking through the issues. After the candidate has elaborated on the material and expressed once again her uncertainty and doubt, the supervisor resumes his synthesis and summary of the process. He confirms the candidate's intuition and continues to invite her active participation. The candidate responds and a lively dialogue ensues during which the issues are further delineated.

Believing the preparations adequate, the supervisor now begins a fairly elaborate synthesis and active demonstration of how an analyst might think about the material presented by the patient. He considers several options for understanding the material, connecting the experience with Ted to something the patient had described a week or so ago. The candidate's response is to interact with the supervisor, interspersing the dialogue with her own thoughts and opinions. The supervisor then more directly advises the candidate regarding specific interventions that might be helpful, expressing himself via identification with the analyst.

The supervisor then follows with a direct suggestion as to the kind of intervention that might permit the patient to take an intermediate step toward transference awareness. He also makes suggestions regarding the interpretation of the patient's defense of displacement away from the transference. The supervisor is deliberately responding to the candidate's expressed wish for technical guidance and instruction. He feels she has struggled valiantly on her own, has managed the analysis adequately by not intervening in this circumstance, but that she lacks the clinical experience to develop an effective intervention on her own. He therefore provides a model, along with an explanation of why it might be effective.

The candidate responds with active appreciation and recognition that the supervisor has been helpful; she also nicely demonstrates her own learning needs as separate from countertransference interferences. The supervisor continues to demonstrate how interpretation may involve a series of progressively deeper but planned interventions, illustrating through active example the technical dictum of interpreting from the surface of consciousness toward the depths.

The candidate's response ("Okay") is an indication that the immediate technical problem has been resolved, so the supervisor moves to a different conceptual level and focuses on a dynamic understanding of the patient's material and process. He focuses upon the possible existence of a cross-sex father transference response, anticipating that this might be an area of difficulty for any candidate in a first case. The candidate responds immediately with associations to the patient's material and to a preconscious awareness within herself a while back that a father transference had been emerging, though she had not fully or clearly identified it as such. Her response confirms the correctness of the supervisor's hunch, just as an analysand's response may confirm a correct interpretation.

The supervisor is now in a position to refer back to the married man who had propositioned her and to introduce the understanding that the patient's response to that experience had been stirred and initiated in her transference experience toward the analyst. Supervisor and candidate then begin an active discussion of the meaning of this behavior, and of ways in which similar feelings might have been expressed had the external situation been different. This is an attempt by the supervisor to help the candidate recognize the interrelation of intrapsychic experience, including fantasies and wishes, with the vicissitudes of interpersonal life as experienced in various reality situations, for which otherwise there might exist only superficial explanations.

The candidate returns to the problems of her learning needs (in contrast to countertransference interferences) and the supervisor responds with an active identification and explanation of the process that all candidates must go through in recognizing and experiencing the centrality of the transference once an analysis has been successfully initiated. The candidate can then further elaborate her own uncertainties, questions, and learning needs, allowing the supervisor to give repeated encouragement and reassurance, though not in an overly active way. The candidate is able to describe her own experience of awkwardness in becoming an analyst, a form of experiential learning that must be undergone if one is to master the analytic technique.

The supervisor has felt for some time that this candidate would benefit from having a second case in analysis. But not wanting to force the issue, and recognizing the impact of his illness and the hiatus in supervision it occasioned, the supervisor has been waiting for an appropriate way to introduce the idea. The candidate's reference to "awkwardness with the first case" provides this opportunity. The intervention is supported by the candidate's progress, and her ability to handle the current situation effectively. The supervisor feels that her identity as an analyst needs further positive reinforcement and would benefit from beginning a second case. The supervisor introduces the idea with a question aimed at eliciting the candidate's participation in the decision.

The candidate's response is initially one of ambivalence, and the supervisor attempts to be encouraging without applying too much direct pressure. He explains why a second case would be appropriate at this time and reinforces the candidate's motivation by saying, "I think you are ready to." Candidate and supervisor agree to discuss the issue further, but the supervisor remains encouraging. The issue of the six-month summary is dealt with in an informal, pressure-reducing fashion, but also in a way that discourages the candidate's use of it as an externalized defensive rationalization.

There are many evidences here of a solid and effective learning alliance. These include the candidate's ability to summarize the material in a lively way, while also providing sufficiently detailed process material to permit the supervisor to understand the analytic interaction as it unfolds. The supervisor's interventions tend to be responded to by the candidate in an active and animated way, and not just with passive acquiescence or acceptance. The candidate feels free to respond with her own personal experience and associations, and able to acknowledge errors, doubts, and uncertainties with a minimum of shame or expectation of hostile criticism. Intermittently there are animated and active interchanges between candidate and supervisor; these indicate that each is responsive to the other in an effective way.

Chapter 6

Supervisory Session 42

Candidate: Wednesday she talked about how she loves and also resents and hates Harold, and said she feels worse for hating him because he's such a wonderful person. She starts to describe how wonderful, or I asked her. She said he's a wonderful person. He's the most wonderful person in the world. In a characteristic tone of voice which I noticed but can't describe. I don't know what it means—it's a tone of voice that comes with that, and I asked her to describe what she meant by that. She said he seems finished; he's happy-go-lucky, he seems like nothing bothers him. She envies how he feels with their parents. He walks in and out whenever he feels like it and knows he can get away with whatever he wants. He doesn't give, he's a taker—with them especially. She gave examples. What's important to him is his life, without consideration for others or for other people's needs and wants. He is selfish, but not with the patient. He will do anything in the world for her. He's always real concerned about what she thinks of him. She recounted the incident of his smoking pot. In that sense he seems more finished than she. He doesn't have to care about the parents' approval. Those things aren't important to him. Whereas she has lived for what they think. That's how she defines finished or unfinished people. With me she's unfinished because it really matters to her what I think and how I feel about her and whether I care about her. Her brother was never like that. Sally Jones was not like that. And she went over how Sally Jones disregards her analyst.

Supervisor: Disregards what?

Candidate: Disregard for her analyst and the way Sally Jones used her analyst. She didn't go over .that particular thing. It comes up again and again. When it got inconvenient for Sally to remain in analysis, she just quit. Other patients of mine probably don't care like she does and are more finished. To her being unfinished is a real sign of weakness, feeling that her value depends on what other people think about her. On that score she compared herself unfavorably with her brother again. She has frequently said she's "too easy" with her parents, and I said that's one of the ways she tried to explain to herself why her parents seemed to pay more attention to Harold. She said yes, she could remember, and then she recounts lying in bed at night vowing not to tell them anything, to be cold and indifferent to them because then they would love her more, but never being able to keep it up for more than half a day. If she was more reserved, she felt, they would want her. And then as she talked she decided that Harold was really an unhappy, selfish, self-centered person and that she really doesn't want to be like him—he's not happy and never will be. He can't express love or any other feeling. He can't be close to people. When she looks into his eyes she sees trouble there. He's not as finished as she has always thought. It's like he's rotting from the inside out. She went on to describe how disturbed and limited she feels he is: no goals, no drive, no plans, no past, no future. He lives for the moment and for money and for anything else that he gets. She talked about how she will live up to what her father wanted in a son, or from a son, and how that's hard on both of them. He will still wish that it is Harold who is succeeding, and she will wish that she could be valued for herself. Then she talks some about how her success doesn't matter so much because it's superfluous, because she will get married and have a family. It's confusing to her because she does want to get married and have a family, but not to the exclusion of her career. When she was home recently with her family she talked with her father and he said he really wants her to find someone to take care of her and to love her. It's very confusing, because she always wanted to be a boy. She felt that she could capture her father and his love only by being as much a boy as possible. It's real confusing being a woman, because she knew when he said that that he cares about her. She talked some about Harold being a boy and her being a girl and that being confusing. I said, right at the end of the session and I didn't write it down until later in the day, I said that all these ideas are ways of trying to understand what she felt as a child and feels as an adult. But as an adult she has more capacity to understand. Oh, I know, she said: Those were stupid things to think—that it was because Harold was a boy or that she was too easily this or that. And I just said that as a child she also tried to understand and explain things and that there were many ways, I thought, that she had tried to understand—that maybe it was because she was a girl, maybe because she was too easy. And she interrupted me and said, "Yes and they are all still there in my mind and confusing." And that was the end of the session. But first she elaborated just a little bit on that and asked me a question about what I was saying and then said, "Yes, they are all there in my mind and that confuses me." And that comes up in the beginning of the next session. She said she feels more. That it felt really good to be able to ask me to clarify something I was saying so that she could feel a little bit better.

Supervisor: Now, do you want to comment on that session or do you want to go on to the next one?

Candidate: I'd rather go on.

Supervisor: Okay.

Candidate: Unless there's something glaring that you want to talk about.

Supervisor: Well, the only question I would raise is how—no, let's put it differently. Did you consider whether you wanted to bring this into the transference or not? She's using the past, Harold and her father and so on, as a defense. She says, "You know I feel the same way with you. All the rest of your patients are finished much more than I am." That's an opening to bring you into the transference; you may, for reasons of your own, have chosen not to.

Candidate: Yeah. I thought that she was doing it, but when I press it too much she shuts up. Then we must spend three weeks and three days talking about Ted, and I felt that she kept bringing it in. She kept going back and saying it's the same way here. I wanted to leave it that way.

Supervisor: Uh-huh.

Candidate: She was saying it's the same way everywhere. It's that way here too, and then, remembering or thinking about things outside, saying see it's the same. Thursday she said she felt good when she left, especially good that she had been able to ask me to clarify something she hadn't understood well. She feels more comfortable with herself, exploring things about herself more easily, not quite so ashamed. Anytime anything involves Harold and her, she feels left out, unimportant, thinks about the dinner with Ruth and her father. The discrepancy between her perceptions and Ruth's. Anytime Harold is involved, her perceptions may be all wrong; she may see what she expects to see. So I asked her to explore what she expects to see and what might be causing her to distort. She says maybe she takes it for granted. She expects her father to be that way. It seems self-destructive; it keeps her from really believing that she's okay. She has a fantasy of what it would feel like to feel positively praised by her father, instead of always—and she elaborated that a little bit and said that it seems scary. She knows how she feels when he says he wants to take *her* on vacation, which he did this weekend. Her mother and father are going on vacation, and she said, "I hope you have a good time." And he said he would have a better time if she were going instead of her mother. She knows how she feels when he says he'd rather take her on vacation. It makes her feel uncomfortable. It seems like if he really praised her, she would also be uncomfortable. He makes her feel that he loves her more than her mother, and that makes her feel really bad and disloyal. It's not anything conscious or sexual, but having her father at least on the surface favor her brother saves her. She recounted her mother saying that her brother comes first with her father, then the TV, and then us. She remembers feeling real bad about it when she was young. She remembers thinking at the same time that her mother was a horrible wife and that she could do so much better. Her father seemed so pitiful, so desperately miserable; she knew it was her mother's fault and that she—the patient, that is—could make him happier. The father made the mother into the bad guy to the kids—she did all the work and the disciplining, and he acted like the good guy except that he was always screaming. Mother and father had a competition going about who could be most popular with the kids; it still feels that way. She remembers feeling puzzled when her mother said that her father did not care about her much, that he cared about Harold first and the TV second. She remembers her father screaming the same kind of thing at her mother: "If you do not watch out you will lose her." Screaming at the mother for her to stop doing this or that, for her to stop doing something because if she did not watch out she would lose her daughter. She is saying that it seems to work both ways, that both father and mother were saying similar things and saying things to manipulate the children, vying for the attention of their kids: "Your father does not care for you, I do." That is getting back to the idea of why she thinks she must think of things negatively. It keeps her from feeling guilty about her mother, maybe. Also it feels like it protects her from her father and the real old feelings of wanting to take care of him, be his wife maybe, make him happy; keeps her angry and disgusted with him. She strived for so many years to have him think she was neat and now she cannot deal with it. She cannot see the positive—even after Ruth said what she said she still cannot see it, still cannot hear it. She just knows that is what Ruth said, and she cannot make it change the conversation, all she hears and thinks about Harold. And when he compliments her it is always in a question, anyway. He wants reassurance that she is okay.

Supervisor: Now how do you understand this material yourself?

Candidate: Well, I think she is beginning to say what you and I have postulated. Part of what we have postulated, but I am not sure it is all of it. I have not said anything because I felt she was doing a pretty good job and because it is all totally new. This way of looking at it is totally new. As of two weeks ago she perceived her father as criticizing her, because he does.

Supervisor: Because what?

Candidate: He does. It is truth—and maybe I am missing some deeper implications of it. I was pleased that she was beginning to unravel this without much road-pointing from me.

Supervisor: And you felt that she didn't need any priming?

Candidate: I felt that it was easier for her to deal with it if she was doing it than if I was. I guess what I'm saying is that I was impressed that it's easy for her to deal with now; some groundwork must have been done, because anytime in the past that—I could remember times in the past when I had to suggest things that were no more difficult. I wished that it was unfolding. So I just sat back and I wished that it was unfolding. So now I just sat back and listened. She then started to say that she was talking yesterday about being easy in all of her love affairs. She never wants anyone to be easy, she always wants them to be a challenge. She was easy and so her parents didn't appreciate her, and she saw the same situation with all her love affairs—she gives and gives and gives, and feels unappreciated and unloved. It's all over, everything; it's all around her. She always wondered why she felt her parents didn't love her, she always wonders why her lovers don't love her as much as she loves them. With her parents, it was that she was too easy, a bore; she showed them too much how much she loved them so that they felt too secure in her love. Harold always felt that too. She tried to change but couldn't. She remembers crying about it. She talked about not being able to understand the difference between Ruth's perceptions and her own. She thinks that in other situations her judgment and perception must have been off, but she can't see it, she can't. I think what she's saying is that she can't shift it, she can't see it now through Ruth's eyes. She continues to hear what she thinks she hears but thinks that there must be a distortion. I asked her and she gave some examples, examples she had given before, but wondered if she had heard all that wrong too. Maybe it's never been reality, maybe she made up her mind that she was second and that's the way it would be and she kept it that way. I asked her why she would hold onto that, to that painful frame. She has suggested that it might have had some protective value, that to be singled out and to be special in her father's eyes was too disturbing. I wasn't totally at a loss at that point. What I wanted to do was to get her to thinking about what might really be, why she might be distorting things, and changing her. She's saying now that she thinks she's insistently seeing negatively and she doesn't understand that.

Supervisor: But painful as this is, it serves a defensive function against something even more painful, frightening, or upsetting.

Candidate: That there's something under it, and could she think about that? That was essentially what I was trying, to take it down the next flight of stairs. And then she responded to that by saying she thinks of other situations where she meets people and feels rejectable, vulnerable, exposed, unfinished, and assumes they won't like her. And how so often after she ends up getting to know the people that make her feel this way, they have feet of clay; they have faults. She gave some examples. They are just people, some of them she doesn't even like, much less care whether they like her or not. It's a real conflict between the way she sees herself rationally and how she sees herself inside, and things like what Ruth said she does not hear from the inside. Like here, even where she's accepted she feels nervous and anxious and doesn't believe it. She doesn't believe that I accept her—oh, she doesn't really believe that I *don't* accept her or that I'm going to stop seeing her. But in that inner feeling she doesn't believe it, it makes her nervous, she wonders if it's true, when it's going to end. She can't relax and enjoy being accepted and cared about. And that's the end of that. Then on Monday she has a dream about me and doesn't want to talk about it. In the first half of Monday's session she feels really comfortable and good, like she has come a distance in herself. She talked with her parents, and she feels a different distance with them. She's just kind of recounting but not just to fill the time; it's more like she's taking count. Then she said the little girl feeling felt replaced by someone more perfect, feeling it would happen again and again and again. She wonders when it will ever go away, that anxiety. She can't imagine not being afraid of that, also afraid of being too positive, afraid if she feels good enough about herself something bad will happen. There still must be something she's too afraid to look at. She dreamed about me last night. It was very real. I was a teacher in a classroom situation with a lot of other people going through analysis.

Supervisor: "I" meaning you or herself?

Candidate: Me. It was like a teacher-student conference situation—you know, where it's your turn to talk to the teacher. And it was her turn, and she pushed the couch up in between all the chairs, closer and closer and wondered about the other people—why were they there and who were they and would they be able to hear what she said to me? So she pushed the couch closer so she could talk real soft. I was different, the same voice and everything, but real different, I was radical-like, not exactly a hippie but radical. I had my feet up on the desk or a chair or something and I was mad at her. She had missed a Tuesday appointment, she had got mixed up or something. I had canceled the Tuesday before and she had thought it was this Tuesday. Half way through this Tuesday she figured it out. She did not call—she was real upset and afraid that I would be angry at her.

Supervisor: Now wait a minute, was that reality or in the dream?

Candidate: The dream.

Supervisor: There *was* a canceled session—that was when, how long ago?

Candidate: Tuesday.

Supervisor: This past—

Candidate: Tuesday, two weeks ago.

Supervisor: Two weeks. But that has already come and gone—aha! Okay.

Candidate: Come and gone, but we talked about it last week.

Supervisor: Okay.

Candidate: Remember, that was the Tuesday I canceled a week ahead of time, and then she did not come Thursday or Monday and came Tuesday saying that it did not have anything to do with anything. So it took us a while to work that out, so that the talking about it is not so long ago.

Supervisor: Uh-huh, okay.

Candidate: So in the dream she got mixed up and she was real afraid I would be mad at her, and I was. I told her that I was. She came and apologized, I was real angry. I told her that I was angry with her and that I had sent her a letter telling her so. She was upset, but then it was okay and she went on talking. There were other people in the class and she did not know about them until afterward, when she realized that they were talking about things they discovered about themselves in analysis, and she realized they were in analysis too and that made it okay. It meant—now this is her talking—that I did not say anything. Her feeling was that she is going to be replaced; they were perfect people, finished, and she was embarrassed to lie on the couch. Then she realized that they were my patients too, with problems, and she was relieved they were not finished. She relaxed. Seeing me that way made me a lot more human; I was a person too. All of the fear and anticipation about missing the appointment was real, too, like it is in real life. She hadn't even called me because it was a mistake. All those times she was afraid I would be angry, and in the dream I said I was and it was over and she relaxed. Now, my notes on this are terrible. Somewhere later I asked her about the Tuesday cancelations. The fact it was Tuesday and that there had been a previous cancelation—she said she didn't feel like she was getting back. She was worried that she hadn't called. It didn't quite make sense and then she explained how it didn't make sense. The canceled Tuesday had already happened. She had already not come on the canceled day. How could she possibly get mixed up and think it was the following Tuesday, when it had already passed? Maybe she was subconsciously trying to provoke me into finding fault with her. And, in re-reading the notes today, when I read the notes right before this, that seemed to be more important than the thing that was going on. The other people, let me see, I have some things written over here: She didn't know why they were there or why I was in a classroom. She felt scared and embarrassed. She knew she had done something wrong; she didn't believe that she really could miss an appointment and not call. She didn't know if she feared being kicked out of class or was really afraid that one of those people would replace her and get on the couch. She felt shy, embarrassed at having an audience. As she walked out of the room with the other people, she realized they were all my patients, too. And then it was okay. She wasn't worried anymore about them taking her place with me. The thing that most amazed her was that once I said I was really mad at her, the anxiety, and that had been very real, went away. And she was relieved. It was a normal anger—it wasn't like her father's. She can't imagine my reacting that way. I was a lot more human in the dream. I was a character, a real person. Here I seem like a real person, but in the dream she could relate to me on a different level. In real life she has always been very good friends with all of her teachers. I was still her doctor but I was her friend too. I asked her if it was possible that it made her anxious that I didn't seem to get angry with her. And she said yes. The things she thought I would reject her for had happened, have come by, and I didn't reject her. None of the anticipated fearful things have ever happened. She wondered what *will* happen. And she talked about the fact that she can't easily express being disappointed at me or mad at me. She's afraid of offending me. Maybe that's what will make me reject her. I was getting lost.

Supervisor: All right. So how do you understand this now?

Candidate: Well, in the last session—this is kind of spotty. The last thing was having to do with being in the psychoanalytic training program. That was right at the end of the session.

Supervisor: Of this same session?

Candidate: Yes.

Supervisor: Uh-huh, okay. Now, how are you to understand that material?

Candidate: I don't think I understand it too well. My first association as she was relating the dream had to do—well I had three all at once, which was part of my perplexity. One had to do with the cancelation; one had to do with my getting angry with her, and, later when I re-read the notes, her assumption that people might be angry when they really aren't. I think there is something comfortable in that thought. And the third had to do with I wonder if this is material about being in analytic training and the analytic thing coming up again. My being in a classroom with other people, other people hearing her, her talking with me, and I just kind of hung that and waited to see if it all would come up or whether it was all artifact.

Supervisor: The issue of confidentiality?

Candidate: Yes. What is most striking to me now as I go over it is what she insistently pointed out—that I'm angry with her and that she did something that made me get angry with her and that that made her relax and made her feel more comfortable. I am not entirely sure what to do with that except in terms of her having described it as a defense against closeness with her father. Or perhaps a defense against some kind of fantasy with her father was to keep the anger going, and this was expressed with me.

Supervisor: So you have to see this, then, in the context of the emerging transference we were talking about a little while ago, which you'd been observing in the previous sessions but had not interpreted. She was talking about her fears of positive attachment to the father, and his responsiveness, when she has won the oedipal victory, when she is preferred to the mother—how threatening and dangerous that is. And you yourself, as we were talking, have been aware that she uses this as a defense—the anger, the idea of being rejected, the idea of being hated, the idea of being used defensively against a much more powerful threat of closeness, intimacy, and approval by the father. That was the context you have been thinking about and observing in the past couple of sessions but said nothing about. Now then in this dream, it's as if she is reenacting the whole thing all over again and focusing it much more specifically—

Candidate: The defense.

Supervisor: The defense against you or with you. Namely, she sets up a situation that is impossible, in which you have a whole bunch of other people in her analytic hour with her. She also sets it up in such a way that you respond in ways you do not ordinarily. She says this subsequently and even in the dream. Why am I seeing you get angry when you do not get angry? Why am I seeing you behave this way when you would not and don't? That is not my experience of you. So we have to see that she is doing the same thing with you, accusing you of something in the dream which is unrealistic and inappropriate and which does not fit the way you actually behave toward her, which is what she has done with her father.

Candidate: Which would be more comfortable for her.

Supervisor: Which she has done with the father all along. Then she has accused him or has him accusing her of all kinds of terrible things: You're no good. You're a mess. I don't love you. I prefer your brother. But all the time the father really enjoys that dinner, which confirms that he is not really saying that at all. And now she is reenacting that with you. This is why—

Candidate: That's what I hinted at, that I needed to make more clear, when I said—

Supervisor: You have to make that much more explicit.

Candidate: I said something was making her uncomfortable about my not being angry with her. I had a feel for it but not as clear as when I had gone back and read the notes.

Supervisor: So she has to be helped to see that this is explicit. Now, the next thing she does in this dream is she accuses herself of a crime she did not commit. You are mad at her and she is a bad girl and all the rest, because she missed that Tuesday appointment, which is not true. You follow?

Candidate: No, go on, because I might.

Supervisor: Well, that she is saying, "The reason that you got mad at me was my behavior, which included missing that Tuesday appointment." That is part of the manifest dream. But that was not true. She did not miss the Tuesday appointment, she missed the Wednesday, Thursday, and—

Candidate: Thursday; Tuesday was canceled.

Supervisor: Yes.

Candidate: She missed Thursday and Friday; I missed Monday. I mean, she missed Thursday, Monday; I missed Tuesday because it was canceled, and then she did not miss anymore.

Supervisor: Right, so when she says, I missed a Tuesday appointment in the dream, she is not the one who missed the Tuesday appointment, you are.

Candidate: All right.

Supervisor: She did some other things, but she did not miss the Tuesday appointment.

Candidate: Is that a reversal?

Supervisor: It may be a reversal; it may be a reversal from passive into active. But the point I am trying to make, you see, is that this whole thing, how she sets it up in such a way that you and she have this interaction and so on and in which the net effect is that once she leaves your office with these other people, then she feels very relieved that you did get angry at her, but only after she has left the office.

Candidate: No, in the office after I got mad at her with all these other people around, she felt more comfortable and relaxed, and then she talked for the rest of the session. She still did not know who the other people were.

Supervisor: But then what happened? . . .

Candidate: But it happened about—at the end.

Supervisor: And she left the hour.

Candidate: She left, and she got to talking with one of the other people, or listening to one of the other people. He was talking about his realizations about himself in analysis, and then she felt like they were all equal.

Supervisor: That made what?

Candidate: That made them being there okay.

Supervisor: And what did it do for her?

Candidate: It made her feel okay, that they were there, that's all, but that was two levels of comfort. She felt comfortable with me right after I was mad at her, all the fears of devastation that if I got mad at her the world would come to an end—none of it happened. I got mad at her and she relaxed and was comfortable.

Supervisor: Okay, but the main thrust of what I am trying to say is still valid, I think. Namely, that she is again reenacting with you a situation in this dream, and in the transference. It is a repetition of what she has done with the father.

Candidate: Oh yeah, I just don't understand—

Supervisor: And the issue you have to dig out with her now is what fantasies in the transference is she defending herself against by setting it up this way?

Candidate: By making me mad at her?

Supervisor: Making you mad at her, putting distance between you, making her do something wrong.

Candidate: We've been talking a whole lot about not being able to express negative feelings when that may be part of the defense.

Supervisor: That may be. But on the other hand I suspect it's much more likely to be fear of very intense—whether it is a father transference and an oedipal sexual fantasy with you in which you are the father, whether it is a regressive reuniting with the mother in defense against the oedipal victory, in which you, in the transference, would be the mother and it would be a homosexual impulse. It is something along those lines that she is warding off through these other mechanisms. Through having all these other people there so nothing could happen, having all the witnesses, and the whole question this brings up of the primal scene and so on, whether or not she is involved in reenacting a primal scene fantasy with you through the change, the distortion in the situation, away from what it really is through the need to depreciate herself. This she does with you just as she has done with the father. She is going to be replaced. All these other people are in the dream, all these other people are taking her place, she is no better, no different than them. So all I can see is her attempt to ward off with you some kind of threatening transference fantasy. That is what has to be made explicit for her: "We have talked about this and the way in which you protect yourself against closeness with your father through seeing him as always being critical and negative and so on. This is what you are doing with me." "What you are doing with me is you see me as ready to kick you out; you see yourself as inept, you see yourself as not a good enough patient. All these other contemptuous critical comments that you attribute to me in this situation serve the same defensive function with me as those other things we talked about serve with your father." "There must be a fantasy that goes on in your mind vis-à-vis you and me that is very threatening, even more threatening than the thought of my kicking you out." That is the conceptual model, you see, of what you want to get across to her. Now whether you do it in small pieces or whether you do it in a large bolus, that is your style and so on, but the idea is it has to be made explicit. You may or may not have been right in the first sessions not to call attention to it directly in the transference, in a sense, promoting a more and more conscious awareness. What happens then is that she moves ahead and you stay behind.

Candidate: Then I stay behind?

Supervisor: You did not help her when she did move ahead and bring it into the transference with this dream. At that point it was necessary for you to move in.

Candidate: Yes.

Supervisor: But you have to see it first before you can move in, obviously, and if you do not see it then you are best off doing what you just did, wait and see how to understand it later. You cannot start with a preconceived idea—I am like your father; or you are responding to me as if I were your father; or these feelings are the same as you had with your father. Or that she is seeing you in a male role. That may be the fantasy, but we do not know that. Nor would you want to just assume that you are a female in the transference fantasy. But you do point out that "there must be some kind of a dangerous fantasy or a fantasy that you feel would be dangerous in your mind vis-à-vis you and me, and to avoid all that you step this up this other way." Let *her* be the one to give you the material, to tell you. Is it oedipal, is it preoedipal, are you the father, are you the mother, what is going on?

Candidate: That is about as far as we got. Today she talked about being a clinic patient and that being one of the things that made her feel different from the other people in her dream. The other people in the dream could be my other patients.

Supervisor: Now you had filed away in your own mind when you first heard the dream, is this the confidentiality issue about being a clinic patient? Did you—

Candidate: Well I asked her. I am pretty sure that they know a good bit about how the clinic works when they come here. I am pretty sure that the case worker tells them that the candidates are students and that they have supervisors, but I am not entirely sure.

Supervisor: It does not matter. You see, whether the case worker tells them or does not tell them, the patient will have his or her own fantasy.

Candidate: So what I didn't want to do is make a presumption, because I didn't know what she meant. But it had come up before. You and I have talked about it.

Supervisor: Uh-huh.

Candidate: I just brought it up as a question.

Supervisor: What kind of question?

Candidate: Well, *she* brought it up, actually. I asked her about the other people in the dream and she said that—

Supervisor: Now, this is today's session?

Candidate: No, this was the end of yesterday.

Supervisor: No, let's get to today's session. Because she came back to—yeah, let's get to today's session.

Candidate: And then she came in talking about it. I didn't ask her. It wasn't necessary to ask her about the clinic, because she talked some about it.

Supervisor: What did she say about it?

Candidate: She said she thought about what I'd brought up. She feels like she had some fantasies originally, but she suppressed them. But that's what made her different in the dream from the other people. The dream has increased the fears of replaceability, of her being able to be replaced. She doesn't know how long it will last before I replace her. They didn't tell her very much about the program, and she didn't ask. Maybe she would be replaced by a full-fee patient, but then she knows she serves a purpose for me, too. She started to go on to something else. I asked her, what about that? She said that she thinks, she's not sure, but she thinks that she's part of my psychoanalytic training. She's not sure, she's not sure, she's not sure. That she's a guinea pig; she's my guinea pig in psychoanalytic training. But knowing that doesn't lessen the fear of being replaced by private patients.

Supervisor: Knowing that doesn't lessen the fear; again she's reversing. Knowing that should *enhance* the fear. If she's your guinea pig, as soon as you are finished with her she thinks you will get rid of her.

Candidate: Okay. I could think right along the lines she was thinking: I can't get rid of her because I have to finish this case. I need her. You know, she was saying that she serves a purpose—I couldn't get rid of her because she serves a purpose for me.

Supervisor: Her purpose is served whether—

Candidate: It has a tempo.

Supervisor: That's it. You don't give a damn about her, as soon as her purpose for you is served, her image is, "Goodbye kid, I'll see you."

Candidate: And then she went on and talked forever about—I let her talk about it.

Supervisor: You see, you have a countertransference problem here that you have to look at in terms of feeling guilty about using this girl. That's why you are not picking up on it, because she needs to expose and explore these fantasies much more, and the affects that go with them. I mean, what is it like to be a guinea pig? It must infuriate her, but she's passing it off as "Well, you know, that's all right. I know and I can understand. You'll replace me with a private patient." You can't let her evade those affects or the facts. She says for instance, "They didn't tell me much about the program." An appropriate response would be to point out to her, "You don't have to know much about the program in order to have a lot of fantasies and feelings about it. And, it's those that we are interested in and not the facts of the program. And the fact that this came up in a dream and it's your dream and you dreamt it just yesterday, or the night before last, whenever it was, means that even though we have talked about this a number of times before, it still is an active thing in your mind, so there must be other issues that we haven't yet touched on relating to your being a clinic patient and my being a candidate."

Candidate: And my countertransference problem is feeling bad for not being fully trained.

Supervisor: Sure.

Candidate: Feeling bad for being a novice.

Supervisor: Sure. And feeling somebody else would do a much better job with this woman than I do and so on and so on and so on. And those are typical candidate countertransference problems. You have to—

Candidate: They make it hard to explain.

Supervisor: Exactly. But you have to look at them, be aware of them, and then offset them somehow.

Candidate: Don't buy them.

Supervisor: Because it's a crucial issue that she has to come to grips with.

Candidate: I was struck by her use of the word guinea pig. It appeared to me that there had to be more behind that. But not clear enough to make me say anything.

Supervisor: Uh-huh.

Candidate: And then she talked a lot about—more or less, things that are not relevant to what we are talking about.

Supervisor: All right now, the one thing you have to be careful about is, don't drag this in by the ears the first five words she says some session. Listen for another opportunity.

Candidate: Can I wait for it to come up again?

Supervisor: That's right. That's what I am saying. Wait for it to come up again. Don't force the material, but when it comes up be sure—

Candidate: That's one of the reasons I didn't drag it in in the beginning of the dream, because it was one of the first things in the dream that came to my mind. But it's been on my mind ever since I missed it last time. I'd have clomped all over something because it's been my agenda.

Supervisor: So just take your time and wait. It will come back, but when it does, then be aware of it and its importance and it doesn't hurt anything to let the affects connected with this build up a bit. Certainly this pattern of "You're going to get rid of me. You're ready to throw me out" and so on, that's not going to go away.

Candidate: The word again she said was, "Well, maybe I'll get *tired* of being in the program. Maybe I'll get tired of being in the program and I'll get out of it and then I'll get rid of you."

Supervisor: And then what?

Candidate: I'll get rid of her. If I quit being here, then I would get rid of her, because she has to depend on my continuing to be interested in doing that.

Supervisor: Uh-huh.

Candidate: That's just an example in my mind. Those thoughts have been elaborated.

Supervisor: That's right. Okay.

Candidate: Thank you.

Supervisor's Comments

The candidate's presentation of the material flows relatively smoothly, and the supervisor has a sense of the dynamic process unfolding in the case. The patient is establishing a psychoanalytic dialogue and regressive involvement with the analyst, but most of the material is still couched in secondary process terms. However, the conflicts to which she directs her attention are significant derivatives of the patient's deeper psychopathology. The main theme seems to be the ambivalent and competitive relationship with the brother, focused at phallic levels and relating to her general feelings of inadequacy and inferiority. The increasingly conscious ambivalence toward the brother, the underlying sense of resentment and contempt, are also manifest, as well as allusions to her oedipal attachment to the father. At this point the patient has been in analysis slightly more than a year and the main technical question is how to deepen and intensify the regressive and transference elements in the analytic process.

After the candidate's initial presentation, the supervisor invites her to decide whether or not she wants to discuss the session in question. Her response that she would rather go on, the supervisor's acceptance of this and then the candidate's invitation for the supervisor to offer comments, are suggestive of a well-established teaching alliance in which both candidate and supervisor are respectful of each other's contributions.

The supervisor's intervention indicates his perception of the opportunity to encourage a focus on the transference, but the issue is introduced in a way that acknowledges the candidate's role in the decision as to whether this is appropriate. The candidate indicates that she had considered it, but on the basis of her experience with the patient had elected not to intervene. This the supervisor accepts as a valid technical decision, reassured that the candidate has clearly recognized the transference component.

The candidate resumes the presentation of the manifest case material, which indicates that the patient is feeling more comfortable exploring herself, less prone to externalize problems, and more willing to ask herself about her role in them. In that sense the analytic process is developing well. The material shifts to a triadic oedipal configuration, combining current experiences and perceptions with past memories from latency and adolescence, with the emphasis still on anxiety and defenses.

The candidate's response to the supervisor's invitation to discuss the material indicates that she is able to retain and use formulations made in previous supervisory discussions, but also that she is capable of recognizing that the material reflects a new view the patient takes of herself, that progress in the analysis is satisfactory, and that there is therefore no need to intervene. Her explanation of her technical decisions shows she recognizes her role in the treatment process and is conceptually aware of its progress. Toward the end of the rather lengthy description, the candidate manifests a sense of uncertainty ("I wasn't *totally* at a loss at that point."), indicating what she hopes to accomplish, and the supervisor responds with a conceptual intervention regarding the patient's defensive function, hoping it will allow the candidate a better perspective on the patient's manifest behavior. Once again the candidate indicates that she had herself anticipated something of the sort and that she has integrated previous supervisory discussions of interpretations proceeding in manageable sequences.

The patient's material indicates that she is becoming increasingly aware of the differences between her affective and subjective experience, as contrasted with reality, her observation of others, and her ability to recognize the experience of transference feeling and fantasy, while simultaneously observing herself in the process. This is a further sign that the analytic process and relationship are developing and that the candidate, too, is able to observe and respond appropriately to these elements ("she's just kind of recounting but not just to fill up the time; it's more like she's taking count").

In the candidate's presentation of the dream she is demonstrating a form of communication in which there are shifting levels and free access and flow between herself and her patient. The result is a degree of confusion for the supervisor, who then, with a series of questions, seeks to clarify the situation.

Later she seeks to avoid that kind of confusion by indicating to the supervisor, "now this is her talking." In presenting the material the candidate indicates that "in re-reading the notes today . . . that seemed to be more important than the thing that was going on." In other words, she can begin to recognize that she has now altered her perceptions, as well as acknowledging her difficulties directly, while still trying to work directly with the patient's transference experience. Her final comment ("I was getting lost.") is a request for assistance.

Once again the supervisor initially responds by inviting the candidate's active consideration and participation, and by now this form of intervention is recognizable as a prelude to providing active help. It encourages the candidate to indicate that she has been actively thinking and entertaining several hypotheses without having to feel either defensive or decisive about which is correct; simultaneously she is able to indicate her continuing uncertainty and confusion. These are further indicators of a well-established learning alliance in which the candidate feels confident in asking for help, while at the same time she continues to struggle actively with the material without being either defensive or embarrassed. She is also demonstrating a more comfortable sense of composure and confidence in the therapeutic situation ("I just kind of hung that and waited to see if it would all come up or whether it was all artifact.").

At this point the supervisor begins a series of lengthy interventions in which initially he connects the current issue with ideas discussed in previous supervisory sessions. He demonstrates his recognition that the candidate has already considered some of these issues, though she has not as yet interpreted them. Then, slowly building from the manifest content of the patient's material, he offers a series of formulations and progressively more inferential constructions. He is doing this deliberately in an attempt to verbalize the way his mind functions while reflecting on this kind of analytic material, so that the candidate will have a model of how problem solving occurs in clinical analysis. Throughout this series of interchanges the candidate is responding with interjections that indicate she is following and absorbing the supervisor's formulations. The supervisor concludes this series of interchanges with a direct suggestion for a technical change, but this occurs only after the candidate's own recognition of some of the issues involved.

The supervisor then takes another tack, specifically focused around the missed appointment. He alludes to this change of direction but in an obscure way; recognizing his obscurity, he asks the candidate, "You follow?" In the ensuing discussion there is clearly a good deal of confusion with regard to dates, suggesting that an unconscious conflict has been mobilized. During this phase of the supervisory session, communication between supervisor and candidate has been disrupted. The candidate is having difficulty understanding what the supervisor is saying, and the supervisor is expecting the candidate to guess what is in his mind. This pattern is finally broken by the supervisor's lengthy formulation of the dynamic meaning of the material, to which he appends model interventions in response to the material. Although he had offered his own style of interpretation as a model, he is careful to emphasize that the candidate needs to use her own style to achieve the tactical goal in question, and that ideally the candidate would have kept pace with the patient through a more appropriate intervention. He emphasizes that this is a *learning need* of the candidate, indicating to her that in the absence of understanding, she had done the best thing.

At this point the candidate returns to the issue of confidentiality, which has come up earlier in the session. The supervisor points out that she had already recognized the importance of the issue, thus indirectly offering both praise and encouragement. The candidate's response is to emphasize reality, the information the patient had received about the clinic. The supervisor challenges this by emphasizing the patient's fantasies.

In the next series of interventions, the supervisor preconsciously recognizes the candidate's reluctance to cope directly with the issue of the patient and the clinic, and his interventions initially focus on clarifying the actual analytic interchanges. In this connection the candidate shows a somewhat uncharacteristic tendency to accept at face value the manifest material presented by the patient, even though she may have recognized some of the patient's conscious experience of the issue ("I could think right along the lines she was thinking."). This uncharacteristic emphasis on manifest material and lack of awareness regarding latent meanings is further evidence that the candidate is experiencing an emotional countertransference interference.

At this juncture the supervisor points out to the candidate a specific countertransference issue, explaining that these are the factors behind her difficulty in coping with the problem with the patient, and once again providing a model for the candidate as to how such an issue might be approached. Following this, the candidate feels somewhat reassured and is capable of directly expressing some of the countertransference issues (the supervisor is aware that these manifest countertransference experiences are probably derivatives of significantly deeper issues but assumes that the candidate will refer to them in her own personal analysis; he therefore does not pursue the matter further). The supervisor offers reassurance ("and those are typical candidate countertransference problems") while at the same time directing the candidate to recognize and acknowledge her countertransference.

The supervisor follows this interchange by cautioning the candidate to avoid acting upon a typical supervisory transference response—trying too rapidly or forcefully to carry the supervisor's ideas into the treatment. When the candidate says, "Can I wait for it to come up again?" the supervisor gives explicit permission and instructions, and the candidate then is capable of further elaborating her own awareness of the issue. Her recognition, "it's been on my mind ever since I missed it the last time," is a further illustration of how the candidate's unacknowledged countertransference feelings have been impacting on the analytic interaction.

The ability of the supervisor to directly comment on the candidate's feelings in a constructive way, and of the candidate to hear it without undue defensiveness and with effective elaboration, attests the essentially positive status of the learning alliance. This is the result of similarly constructive interchanges in earlier sessions, and the candidate's final words, "Thank you," are a reflection of what seems to have been another useful teaching-learning experience.

Chapter 7

Supervisory Session 43

Candidate: Wednesday she came in and said she had been thinking about her relationship with Ted and the fact that she had made up all kinds of reasons for not talking about her feelings about what was going on with Ted, and what was going on with Ted and with me. And when she started thinking about it the night before, she began to suspect that all those reasons were just rationalizations for not looking at it and keeping it out of awareness. She said her life felt like it was split in two different compartments: one was nice with me, and then she would leave my office and all the complexities of her relationship with Ted would descend on her. She talked about the relationship, how she feels she pushes him away, feels she is scared to let anyone love her for fear that it won't last and—even scarier—that it is real and might develop into something, like with her father. The thought of her father loving her makes her want to run. She talked about her fantasies and wishes as a child to take over her mother's territory and how much it scares her, her father loving her the way he does. And that was essentially it. Somewhere in the session, in the context of her propensity for provoking trouble in order to push people away, I brought up the dream and her thought that in it she might have been provoking my anger, pushing me away. I asked her what it was—what feeling or what might lie behind feeling—that was so uncomfortable and so frightening that she has to push me away. And she said that she *is* pushing me away and confirmed that that is her problem. She then went back to Ted.

Supervisor: She went back to Ted?

Candidate: Back to *talking* about Ted. But I just waited to see what would develop, and what developed was beginning to make some connections again, connections I think she prefers to forget between the times she talks about them, between her relationship with Ted and her relationship with her father. She came in Thursday and started talking more about Ted and how she feels she concentrates on bad parts of him and bad parts of the relationship in order to escape the discomfort of his apparently accepting her and loving her. She wondered if she created the unhappiness with her father as she was growing up. She noticed that she always feels most trapped and uncomfortable with Ted right after they have had a really good evening or a really good time. Then she pushes him away. She discounts him and thinks he is a bum. I made a connection between this and her running arguments with her father about him loving Harold more and her devaluing him—he is a bum, he is an embarrassment to her—as a means of keeping him at a safe distance. And she responded by saying she doesn't know what she is afraid of with regard to her father. She has the fantasy that he will ask her to marry him or that he wants her to. She thinks she reverses; she thinks she is really afraid of how intensely she loves him for something that she wants. It was so strong as a child, she can feel it now. She really wanted her father to be happy. Her mother really pushed him away. Her mother did not know what he needed to make him happy, and she really resented her mother. "God, Mother, what are you doing to him?" She had millions of fantasies of having cocktail parties, with him and for him. She prided herself that she was like her father—confident, outgoing with friends, not cold and unfriendly and reserved like her mother. She wished she could take her mother's place, not in a sexual way, except that she did want to hug him and stroke his hair and tell him everything would be all right and make him feel comfortable. She wanted to give him someone to talk to. Her mother would never listen. She drew him out. She remembers making concerted efforts to listen to his concerns, to draw him out, to make him want her. She wanted to take care of him, and she gave more examples of that. She spent a lot of time trying to make him happy; she wonders if that is why she did not date. But maybe she wasn't so caught up in that later; she spent a lot of time away from home, driven to prove to her father how really popular she was. She used to look at it in terms of competition with her brother, but she wonders. Maybe wanting to prove to her father that she can be everything her mother was not, that she was really like him and she wanted him to share these things. Her perception was that he was not interested, but now she is not sure that it was really that way at all. She remembers telling me how really upset she was that he did not attend the Queen's Assembly, and she has gone into that at length. You probably remember. It is like being homecoming queen; there was an induction assembly, and he did not go. She has told me many times that he did not go because he didn't give a damn. She mentioned it to him years later, how disappointed she had been that he had not gone. And he said that she had not invited him, that he had wanted to go, but he felt he was not welcome. She had invited her mother, but not him. She thinks she did not invite him to a lot of things that she felt bad he did not attend. She feels like it is more her feelings, not so much something someone else was actually doing. She was afraid of falling in love with him. She felt guilty over those feelings, she feels they are wrong—that is her mother's place. She is being disloyal to her mother, she wanted to take her mother's place, she wanted him really to love her, not like a little girl. She remembers telling me not long ago that she was never her father's daughter but a confidante or something; that is scary. I asked her what about it was scary, and she said the guilt, she was disloyal to her mother, she does not know. In her fantasy she knew what she wanted to happen, but in reality it seems strange that as she got older he stopped being so important. She really started to worry about herself and panicked that she didn't date more. Her father said that he didn't understand why boys wouldn't ask her out in flocks, she was so beautiful and wonderful and warm. That's when she started to gain weight; that's when she got fat. She didn't understand. She really felt bad, there was something wrong with her. But her father didn't think there was anything wrong with her; her believing there was was some kind of distortion. But I wondered how it made her feel that her father was so concerned that she didn't date boys. Rejected and confused, she said. She remembers not allowing herself to think about it, getting very busy. She thinks she still wanted to marry him and felt something was wrong with her and felt really ashamed of those feelings.

Supervisor: Now this was as an adolescent? Was she still thinking and having direct oedipal sexual fantasies about him?

Candidate: It's the first time she's talked about it. And this would be prior to the very late disillusionment with her father. This would be her father's way of bugging her about not dating when she was fifteen or sixteen.

Supervisor: What do you think of that?

Candidate: I don't know. I don't. I just—I don't know. Perhaps she's being overly compliant.

Supervisor: Overly compliant toward you?

Candidate: Uh-huh. What she's saying, I think, or the way I understood what she was saying, was that all through her adolescence she thought that her father wasn't interested in her, that he wouldn't go to anything she was interested in. She made so many efforts to make him notice her, and he just didn't notice any of them. And that's what she's been detailing for all this time to me and to herself, and what I thought she was saying was that she doesn't know that that's true anymore, that she questions that whole thing. And I don't really hear her coming up with an answer yet, but she doesn't believe that that's true anymore. She believes that he was interested in her but that she screened him out, that she made it appear to herself that he was rejecting her because something was frightening her. What at this point she isn't saying is that her father's response to her frightened her; instead she's saying that her wishes and fantasies frightened her, the continuation of wanting to be so important to him. Now, I didn't think beyond that.

Supervisor: Well, this is my point, that fifteen or sixteen is kind of late for an adolescent girl to be having direct sexual fantasies about marrying her father and wanting to take her mother's place and how she's so deeply afraid she's going to fall in love with him. All that is usually there, but is relatively repressed. These are fantasies much likelier to be conscious during the oedipal phase and into latency, but by the time the patient enters puberty we would usually expect that these impulses and fantasies would be repressed. That they would then often, if not all the time, be replaced by a reaction formation in which she can't stand to be near her father or feels uncomfortable around him, wanting to get away from him, wanting nothing to do with him, thinking what a stupid jerk he is and so on. Or she uses a displacement. She idealizes a movie star, a teacher or a neighbor, a friend's father or somebody else as a great person. And the displacement of the oedipal wish is to some other oedipal figure. But for it to stay with the father up to and through ages fifteen, sixteen, seventeen, that's late. And that's my question. What do you think about that? Is it that for reasons that are not completely clear this was not repressed in her? Is it that she is unduly or unusually sensitive? Is it that by virtue of the whole analytic process up to now she can recover from repression fantasies and feelings that were earlier repressed but are no longer?

Candidate: I don't hear her saying to me, and maybe I'm screening what she's saying, I don't hear her saying to me that when she was an adolescent she was aware of having direct oedipal fantasies about her father. I hear her saying *now* that she was, that a lot of her agony as an adolescent, of trying to get his attention and believing that he wasn't paying any attention to her, was all a cover-up for something that then she *wasn't* aware of.

Supervisor: Well, that's what I'm trying to find out from you.

Candidate: Yes. The reason I didn't answer your question is because it seemed so clear to me that I wasn't careful to avoid ambiguity.

Supervisor: Okay.

Candidate: It seems like she's saying that that *is* how she saw it as an adolescent, that he wasn't paying any attention to her, and that he cared about Harold more. And I think what she's saying *now* is, if she pulls all that away as not true, then she's beginning to see things that were not conscious to her then.

Supervisor: Okay.

Candidate: Very guilty. She talked a very little bit at the end of the session. There were a lot of fears about how guilty she felt at her father's reciprocation and how uncomfortable she felt now when he would call her up and tell her that he would rather take her on a holiday and leave her mother at home. That was the end of Wednesday's session. At the end of Thursday's, I told her that I would not be able to see her the coming Thursday. Monday she came in and said it was a really weird day, that she had been very self-absorbed. Oh, over the last several weeks, because of her relationship, her involvement with Ted, she's been very self-absorbed and hasn't kept up with her work. Now she is more aware of her work and has to make up for her negligence. And she started to describe it, and then she stopped and said she thinks it's all mental, it's all her imagination. She said, for instance, she had a fantasy of one of the executives going to the owner of the design company and telling him that she wasn't performing up to standard and that they should throw her out. She has feelings of losing control over her life, and she feels that really nothing has changed in her life over the past year. And I asked her if she had any notion of what this might have to do with, and she said she just feels she can't plan anymore, things just happen. She feels that way with me and with Ted. She then described some of her Friday night scene with Ted. I wondered if that and the fantasy about the executive had anything to do with my having told her at the end of the last session that I wouldn't be able to see her next Thursday. She said her first impulse was to scream, "No! No! No!" but she didn't know and she didn't think about it. She thought about it this morning and was trying to be aware of her feelings, but she was very aware of a role of not letting herself feel. She had some fantasies about what I was going to do. Maybe I was going out of town, taking a long weekend, since it's a Thursday and not the middle of the week. She never really thought that I would see someone else instead of her, but maybe that's something she's avoiding. Mostly she's just very aware of very tight control over her thoughts and fantasies. She does not let her mind roam about this, even when she's alone. She catches herself doing all kinds of things. All of her thoughts about it amount to rationalizations as to why she shouldn't have feelings about it. For instance, that since she has to cancel appointments sometimes because of her work, I too have a right to cancel appointments. She feels like it's all a protective device to keep something under cover, negative feelings or something; she has to keep them suppressed. She hates it when I cancel an appointment, mostly because she knows that I'll ask her about it and she doesn't know what to say. How she feels about me doesn't square with the professional relationship. And from the way she said this, it would seem clear to me that how she feels about me is something to be kept out, like Ted is to be kept out, and the professional relationship is to be kept in. And I just commented on that, that it sounds like she's closeting a group of feelings outside the analysis.

Supervisor: Good.

Candidate: She said she does that a lot. When things are going bad or she doesn't understand her life or something on a weekend, she fantasizes about me and telling me and what I'll say and how that will make her feel better or this or that. But then she stops herself. She reminds herself that our relationship is Monday through Thursday, fifty minutes a day. Even though I don't know what she thinks about me, and she really wouldn't ever have to tell me, she feels she shouldn't do that. It's not allowed. Sometimes she has fantasies of telling me something and my reactions, but she stops herself. She stops herself because it upsets her, because she can't separate her personal feelings from the professional relationship. And I asked her about that. I just said, "What is this personal feelings/professional relationship separation? What's that all about?" And she said we have a very personal relationship, because she has shown me more of herself than she's ever shown anyone in her life. But she has a real fear, a physical fear even, in the pit of her stomach. It's really okay to tell me how much she appreciates me, but she doesn't have a right to express other things like being disappointed or wanting this or that. She doesn't have a right. Whatever my reason is for whatever I do, it should be okay. Even if it's not okay. She knows she feels rejected and cast aside and unhappy, and wondering about why I'm doing that to her when I cancel an appointment, when I canceled the one on Thursday, but she can't express that. She can hardly even allow herself to feel it. She doesn't want to show it. She thinks it goes back to being afraid I'll be angry with her. She started to cry. She can remember as a little girl wanting her father to pay attention to her, to be there with her. My canceling appointments is like him canceling plans; he always had something else to do. She always felt so rejected and dejected, but she couldn't show it, because he would just get furious and start screaming at her. If she tells me, it will be like her father if she didn't conform to the rules—and he made the rules to the game, and she had to accept them. If she didn't, she had a real fear of losing him totally, not physically, not like he would go away and never come back, but that he would just be gone for her. If she ever told him she was disappointed or had really wanted to go wherever they were going but didn't. And she gave some examples of times when she could remember being all ready, all dressed up, and he would have said in the early part of the week, "I'll take you to the zoo on Saturday," and she would get up and she'd be all ready to go and have her shoes and coat on and everything. She would then go to find him, and he'd be sitting in his chair, because he slept a lot, and he would say, "Well, I know you'll understand and you won't mind if we do it another day, but I'm too tired to do it now. I'm not going to go with you." Every weekend he found an excuse not to do whatever he'd promised to do. She remembers him saying he was too tired and she'd tell him she understood and then she'd go into her room and cry and cry. She could never verbalize her disappointment, because he would just scream at her. Her mother never disappointed her like that. Her mother always followed through. But the patient never had the feelings for her mother that she did for her father. She wanted to have a close relationship with her mother. She can remember friends when she was in grade school who did have close relationships with their mothers and who went shopping and to the hairdresser together. She felt left out because she wanted that. She wanted that with her father because they were more alike. She idolized him. Her mother could never understand her even from an early age. She remembers being in grade school and her mother not understanding. She gave a lot of examples where she would try to get her mother to understand. She wanted to dress like the other kids in school, and her mother wouldn't ever seem to hear her. Or she would have a crush on a boy in grade school and go to talk with her mother about it, and her mother would just say, "Oh, you're being silly." She always seemed so preoccupied. It wasn't you're being silly like mean or derogatory, just preoccupied and busy or something. She feels that her mother favored the brother because they were more alike. She can remember hearing her parents talk like that: she was like her father, and Harold was like her mother. The only things her mother could ever talk about with her that were of real interest were being overweight and going shopping. She related an incident again, and this is an incident she relates frequently, of coming home from college, early in college, and just being horribly upset and rejected and hopeless, and sitting on the bed with her mother and just crying and wanting her mother just to listen and hold her. Her mother didn't know what to do. Her mother just withdrew and froze and suggested that the patient go to a psychiatrist. She remembers screaming at her mother that she didn't want her to do anything, just listen. She felt so far away from her mother; she did even as a little kid. She can remember: so far away and alone she couldn't reach her. She remembers following her around and trying to reach her. She related her mother's unhappy, lonely, tortured childhood growing up alone. But no matter how hard the patient tried, the mother couldn't understand. She knows that her mother has always wanted good things for her and has tried very hard. She was very involved in Girl Scouts, she was a room mother, but she wasn't very much emotional support. The only thing she did was to comfort her and save her from her father's rages. She remembers she and Harold were both terrified when they had to be alone in the house with their father. She remembered and related again when she was little, and still there was that woman she's described before, Helen—who I think is related to her somehow but I haven't gotten it quite straight—who's her mother's age and used to be her mother's friend and lives in Peoria, and

Helen's daughter is Vicki. I think that they're similar ages, Helen and the patient's mother, and Vicki and the patient. And the patient has always felt that Helen was the kind of mother she wanted herself and was jealous of the relationship that Vicki and Helen have had. She talked about that again. She said she needed her mother to help her and tell her things were okay, because she was scared when she was a child. She lived in terror of doing something wrong and not knowing what was right and what was wrong and didn't feel very accepted when she was really young. That's part of her trouble here with me. She always feels unsure about whether she really is okay in all of her feelings and really afraid of showing all parts of herself. And I asked her if she possibly interpreted my canceling an appointment as a censor, or a threat about her feelings of disappointment, like she'd better act right and behave or else something will happen. And she said she just had a flashback when I said that. It reminds her that I make the rules and she'd better not rock the boat or she'll lose me, and she has too much at stake here. The same emotional changes she had with her father. If she was disappointed or cried, he could never put his arm around her, he would just yell. That goes on. I want to talk about the shift from father to mother and back, because I didn't quite understand what was happening. One thing she might have been saying is that one of them needed to be available to her. And I just have to say, I know that there was a shift here that makes sense, but I don't understand it.

Supervisor: Well, judging from the material in this session, the primary transference is at the oedipal level. She associates you and the canceled session with the father and all the times he disappointed her, let her down, didn't show up for things he said he'd be there for. So you're just like he is. And the expectation is, "If I tell you that I'm disappointed, that I'm hurt, that you let me down, that I feel resentful, that I feel bitter, that I'm going to miss not seeing you, then you're just going to get angry and scream at me the way he would." So that is the predominant transference at the moment. There is the feeling, "I cannot show myself as I am and I cannot be a complete person with him and can only, as with you, show the idealizing side, tell you how much I need you, tell you how wonderful you are, and so on. But I can't get mad at you. But I need somebody to talk to." So it seems as if in following the flow of the material, from this there then occurs, "Maybe I can get Mother to listen to me, maybe I can talk with her." So the mother at this point serves partly as a regressive retreat from the oedipal transference and the oedipal attachment to the father, and partly also as a substitute, a sort of parallel: "Well, I can't have this with Dad, but I can have a relationship with Mom like Vicki has with her mother."

Candidate: That's one of the things that was hard for me to understand about it, because it seemed to me like I kept hearing a younger, a regressive thing, but also something continued to be very oedipal about it. I couldn't make it one or the other, and what you're telling me is that you don't have to make it one or the other.

Supervisor: That's right. So, you see, the relationship with the mother is not so much that of a preoedipal little girl, infantile, passive, demanding. It is more like "Treat me as a peer, listen to me, take Dad's place in this. Let's you and I go shopping, get our hair done together, do things like that"—there is an identification with the mother at an oedipal level. Wanting her mother to listen to her, to be interested in her, but also wanting to be like the mother. She and her mother will share some things, which is part of the resolution of the oedipal relationship—I'll be like Mom and so on. So, there's a shift from the oedipal object, the father, and the libidinal attachment to him, and the anxiety and conflict about the aggressive component about him, across to, so to speak, an identification with the mother as another phase, another aspect, another element in the oedipal constellation. So she and Mom can sit and talk together and "We can go out and go shopping and we can do things, and maybe I can get some attention from Mom," which is another aspect of, another phase in, the resolution of and experience of the oedipal attachment. Does that seem to fit the data?

Candidate: Yeah, it does. I just never heard it so clearly. She continued to talk about my making the rules, her father making the rules and the fear of his rage. Her shred of hope was that if she did everything right and pleased them, it wouldn't happen, they wouldn't throw her out. She had the fantasy that she could push her father too far, and then even her mother wouldn't be able to save her. Then she paused a minute and said it's strange how she's evolved; now she protects them. And she described a telephone call from her father last night (I think it was last night, or maybe a couple of nights ago) when he called from Ohio and told her the details of his diet and everything he had eaten that day and how good he'd been. He was just like a little boy seeking approval, and she heaped it on him, and he was—well, he felt so good. And she was just commenting that that was such a strange turnaround, and I said she holds the power that she once felt he had over her, the power to accept or reject, the power she felt helpless in the face of. And she started to cry and said yes, that she had had the fantasy of his telling her mother the same things and her mother tearing him to shreds, and it happened in reality later that week. They both called, and her mother did tear him to shreds, and the patient defended him and was infuriated. And she described a scene where the father was again describing that he had lost eight pounds or something, and the mother belittled that, nothing is ever good enough for her. The mother did that to the patient for years. The patient thinks she was infuriated because she's sick and tired of it. Her father seems so fragile, just like she felt for years when she was a little girl. She felt fragile, and nothing ever satisfied her mother. And she gave a lot of examples. There were only about three minutes left in the session, but she had a number of examples. She was really mad, and I wondered if she was mad at me, but I kept thinking back, and I couldn't, I wondered if I had been demanding of her, so I looked back, but I couldn't find it and so I just wasn't—

Supervisor: See, that's the therapeutic task for you, to figure out, or to focus on, or begin to draw the aggression into the transference.

Candidate: All of this is the transference.

Supervisor: That's right.

Candidate: More and more of it into the transference.

Supervisor: Now you see what happened was that she says, "Well, it's interesting how it all got reversed and now I take care of them, and I'm the strong one and they're the ones that are acting like children and they're the ones that are scared and they're the ones that get torn apart. Mother tears him apart and I have to protect Dad," and so on. And she's going on and on and on about it. That's great. But it's all defensive. And the interpretation that might have brought this out is, "But you haven't reversed it here with me. You're still the same frightened little girl here. When you're afraid that if you tell me that you're angry and resentful and bitter about my canceling your hour, then I'll have a temper tantrum and therefore you have to hide that whole side of yourself from me." You see in the transference she is reenacting and repeating the defensive pattern. When she reverses it with her parents that's interesting, but it's an escape, at this particular moment, from the stimulus to this whole business, which was that you canceled her session, and she's scared to tell you that she's angry and upset. Your job, then, is to try to keep this in the transference as an active, ongoing, conflict-laden process. You wouldn't stop her from talking about her parents, but you might at the end of this say, "You know, I think it's easier to talk about how you are now the strong one with your parents and you have to protect them, than it is to feel how frightened you are of me and the thought of experiencing anger and the anticipation or fantasy that I'll attack you like your father would."

Candidate: Uh-huh.

Supervisor: In other words, you don't say "Oh, forget about all that," but you do say, "Yes, we can see that that's what's happened, but at this particular moment it serves other functions."

Candidate: Uh-huh.

Supervisor: It's not that it's irrelevant, it's not that she shouldn't talk about it, it's not that her associations don't lead in that direction, but your job is to try to help her see that in this particular moment, in this particular context, what is most important is your cancelation and her responses to it. These include, among other things, the negation of her fantasy (she says, "I don't think that you would see another patient in my place," which is a negation of the fantasy she herself has just admitted but then dropped). "If that's what you're thinking," you might say, "it must have stirred a lot of feelings in you." Or, "If that's what you're thinking, you must have some fantasies as to *why* I would put somebody else in your place." And then, you see, you can get into all the issues about why would you prefer someone else to her and how angry she would be and maybe get into the phallic issues about herself vis-à-vis Harold or some male patient or whatever. Or you could begin to get into the issues of the pregnancy, which again she must begin to be aware of by now but has not mentioned. And really behind all this may be fantasies like are you really pregnant or not, and if so, what's going to happen, and so on.

Candidate: Yeah, I heard that, some, in her saying that this time is the first time I've not seen her that it's been personal.

Supervisor: This is the first time what?

Candidate: That I've not seen her, that in her mind it's been personal. I'm not seeing her for personal reasons. It had something to do with my family, I'm doing something with my family, going away for the weekend. And when I asked her for details about that, she said that's what led into her feeling of why she can't let herself think about it.

Supervisor: I wouldn't hook that into the pregnancy directly, because that can also be just a function of an increasing freedom as a result of analytic process.

Candidate: Okay.

Supervisor: That will happen also, whether you're pregnant or not. As the patient moves into the analytic process, the capacity for free association is enhanced, the willingness to express fantasies that would otherwise be repressed or suppressed is increased, and the freedom to fantasy becomes greater. Add to this the awareness of the intensity of the relationship. When the patient says, "Well you probably have a very good reason to go, it's probably a professional reason, you probably have a meeting or you're delivering a paper, you're doing something else," that in a sense is "all right." But to do it because you'd rather be with somebody else or because you're going to go off with your family or because you're going to do something that's fun, that's impossible to tolerate. Well, as the patient moves into the analysis, those kinds of fantasies will increasingly be available for expression.

Candidate: Uh-huh.

Supervisor: So, as I say, I wouldn't necessarily think of her as linking that to the pregnancy but rather would look for ways to specifically bring this in. "You must have some fantasies as to why, if that's your thought, I'm going to be seeing somebody else instead of you, even though you at the same time say you don't believe it. Nevertheless, the fantasy occurred to you. Let's take the fantasy a step further. What would be the reasons for that?" You're looking for ways to get her to begin to recognize that something's going on here between you and her.

Candidate: My choice at that point, and it was a thought actually, was that the last time we went through this it seemed like the defenses against having that fantasy were very strong, and it seemed again, to me, like there was a smooth wall in her mind. At that point I made a thought-out choice to see if I could get clearer what this was all about, and thereby make it clearer to her why it was so forbidden to think about what I was doing.

Supervisor: Uh-huh.

Candidate: Why it was so forbidden to have feelings, even in private, of being mad at me for, or disappointed in me, for canceling an appointment. Why she felt so controlled even in private, why she could not, not just tell me but even have the feelings. What that was all about. Because I felt like I was badgering her before, earlier, because she kept saying, "I don't know, I don't, I can't let myself think about that."

Supervisor: So what you're saying is that you need to zero in on and focus on the resistance, which in this instance is the inability to even permit the awareness of her fantasies, before you can get into the transference interaction?

Candidate: Out of that came, I thought, her remembering that her father makes the rules and her father's cancelations and how disappointed she was feeling that she just better keep her mouth shut, that he couldn't tolerate it and I couldn't tolerate it, her expressing those feelings, being disappointed and really wanting him to go to the zoo with her or whatever, and being disappointed. She said she felt I would behave the same way and that she was expecting me to.

Supervisor: Well, in that case, then, if that is the thrust of what you're thinking, this might have been an appropriate time to hook that into the transference. "This may be why it's hard for you to fantasy about me and my motivations and your feelings about it, because of the fears that if you would fantasize and think about them and have to express them, I'll react like your father did."

Candidate: When she says that she thinks she's behaving with me as if I'll react like her father, I need to say that again.

Supervisor: Oh no, you don't say that precisely, but you hook it in: "This is why it's hard for you to even have fantasies about why I'm canceling your session." Yes, you have to make that explicit. You can frequently follow the train of this because you're standing off at a distance.

Candidate: Yes, because then I feel like what I'm saying is super-self-evident.

Supervisor: Yeah, but it's not super-self-evident to her.

Candidate: And I forget that.

Supervisor: And she is the one who needs to recognize. Although you may be in a position to follow this, partly because you're more distant from it, you're observing the ebb and flow of it and also are not experiencing it at the moment. The other reason you can follow it is that you have a whole theoretical conceptual background that this is important. Whereas for her the two things you're linking up may just be coincidental. She has to begin to see the repetition with you, and how the defense that she used with her father, of not allowing herself to think anything or to say anything, is the same defense she's using with you. After a while she stopped thinking about him and that's what she's doing with you. She doesn't think about it because she doesn't want to say it.

Candidate: Okay. Where are we?

Supervisor: We have only a couple of minutes.

Candidate: Okay, then I'm not going to get into today's session, in which she makes a lot of connections. She brings up Ted again. She starts to talk about him, and again it's all separated off from the rest of her life, as if this is the first time it's ever happened. It's like nothing else in her life, and she kept saying she doesn't understand it. And I—actually it's interesting, it only took two words. She was saying, "Oh yes, it did happen before, all these men in my life have been the same way. I've done the same thing." And I said, "Starting with Father." And she started to talk about how maybe not wanting to have sex with Ted had something to do with the fact that this was a repetition of the relationship with her father. She remembered my saying that this relationship with Ted was a place she could act out her fantasy or live out a fantasy rather than look at it, and she thinks that that's one of the reasons she hasn't wanted to talk with me about it, because she didn't want to look at it, and that some of the—well, she just drew a lot of parallels, which from her tone of voice sounded like they were new to her, and talked about her feelings and the way she sees the relationships and some of her anxieties about the relationship with Ted, which didn't make any sense to her and was separated off. And I listened to this. Well, I did more than listen; I made her make some of those connections, because she would just have talked on for the next three weeks about Ted as if it were just a first. And she ended the session with, "It's the same goddamn thing." And she made some—I think, although I have to look at the notes again right now—she made some connections that she expects the same things from me, the same kinds of behavior. Toward the end of the session, then, she pushes me away or she has to think, she has to distort some things that I say. And she ended the session with, "It's the same goddamn thing repeating itself over and over again, or I'm doing the same thing."

Supervisor: See, this is an illustration of what we've just been talking about. This material about Ted equals Father, and the relationship with Ted equals what happened with her father, the repetitions, the transference—none of it is new. Yet she comes to it *as if* it were new.

Candidate: Yes, she really does.

Supervisor: As if she hadn't seen the connections before.

Candidate: Yes, she really does.

Supervisor: And that's the point I'm making, you see. You cannot take for granted that because you've made the interpretation once it has—

Candidate: Sunk in!

Supervisor: Sunk in or, putting it differently, it goes to a certain level but increases as the patient goes on in the process. Frequently they will come up with, "Now I finally understand what we've been talking about all of this time."

Candidate: Uh-huh.

Supervisor: In other words, it becomes increasingly a more personalized, more meaningful connection. You cannot be sure, you can't just assume, "Well, I made that interpretation once, so I don't have to make it again." You don't want to just reiterate the same words, but you take different material and you help the patient see it—

Candidate: Again.

Supervisor: Again and again. You hook it again and again into the transference as well as into the past history.

Candidate: Uh-huh.

Supervisor: You help her recognize that these are the defenses that she's been using. And this patient's tendency to compartmentalize, which you're seeing now, is another kind of defensive style, one you'll have to listen for and interpret again, because it will be her tendency to use this as a characteristic defensive posture.

Supervisor: Okay.

Supervisor's Comments

The candidate starts with an organized and relatively detailed presentation of the process notes of each session and indicates that the patient has begun to recognize her own defensive pattern of distancing herself from objects she is dependent on or toward whom she experiences positive attachments. The candidate was able without difficulty to recognize that much of the material manifestly about Ted was in actuality a displacement of the transference. In the previous supervisory hour last week the supervisor had specifically cautioned the candidate not to push too intensely the formulations developed by the supervisor at that time. In spite of the warning the candidate did seek to direct the patient back to that material ("I brought up the dream."). The candidate demonstrates, however, that she is capable of waiting for the patient, inasmuch as she does not pursue that line; instead she "just waited to see what would develop."

As the patient's material progresses several manifestations and derivatives of her triadic oedipal organization and conflict emerge. She is capable of expressing (and the candidate of following and reporting) both the oedipal wishes and the defenses against them, as well as the various manifestations of conflict that the patient had experienced since early childhood. The manifest material is organized in terms of secondary process derivatives of core issues, but the patient is manifesting a significantly increasing capacity for new regressive experience, self-observation, and movement back and forth between past and present. She is capable also of recovering and expressing new memories and feelings as well as of recognizing some of her defenses against earlier conflicts. With apparent spontaneity, she begins to modify her projective defenses and recognizes her own active role in arranging for her father to reject her and to be unable to express his interest. Most of the material is from her early and middle adolescence, and includes manifestly conscious and blatantly direct references to oedipal fantasies toward the father, accompanied by guilt, fear, and a sense of disloyalty and competition toward the mother.

As this material is unfolding, the supervisor begins to wonder how effectively the patient's ego defenses had been operative during her development. He is particularly concerned about the apparently manifest incestuous fantasies and their implications. He approaches the issue by asking when these fantasies had occurred, and then inviting the candidate to consider the issues. In some respects this is similar to the therapeutic process, where the focus of interest and attention begins at the surface of what is conscious and leads toward deeper, less conscious material. The candidate offers a well-organized explanation of how this is new material to the analysis and how the patient is spontaneously recognizing her prior distortions and is beginning to attribute her sense of rejection to her own defensive needs. The supervisor then offers a lengthy discussion of the normal adolescent ego and sexual developmental models, which will serve as background for a series of questions, an attempt to clarify the dynamic and potentially psychopathological implications of the patient's adolescent behavior.

The candidate's response is that the recovery of these memories and feelings is the result of the analytic process and the undoing of resistance and defense, thereby reassuring the supervisor with regard to the patient's ego organization. The supervisor accepts this explanation without further comment.

The candidate's observations and explanations are indications of the patient's progress in the analysis, and also demonstrate the candidate's increasing independence and capacity for observation and integration of primary clinical material.

The same issues are demonstrated in the way both candidate and patient handle the patient's response to the candidate's having canceled a session. The candidate's increasing technical skill is illustrated by a recognition of the displacement from the transference and her capacity to invite the patient's associations as a preliminary intervention. Following an initial displacement, the candidate makes a more direct interpretation of the response to the cancelation. The patient's response is an indication of her development in the analytic process, inasmuch as her initial reaction is an intensely affective no, followed by her own spontaneous overcoming of her resistance. She begins to associate more directly and immediately into the transference and into the various fantasies and experiences surrounding the cancelation. She recognizes her resistances, and the candidate is able to follow this and to focus on the resistance in her intervention prior to addressing the content.

The supervisor's response ("Good") offers immediate reinforcement and approval for the way in which the candidate handled this issue. This success is the result of a number of previous discussions in supervision with regard to interpreting resistance before content. The patient elaborates further on the nature of her patterns of defense, and the candidate follows up the resistance, focusing on the patient's tendency to separate the various elements of the transference relationship. Following this, the patient is capable of an even more sustained focus on her defensive and resistive patterns of behavior, and begins to recall and express memories of similar experiences with her father, together with her reactions to it and defenses against it, all of which were being reenacted in the transference.

Having dealt with these resistances, the patient now is able to present a variety of new memories, experiences, associations, and feeling states toward both parents in the triadic oedipal organization. The candidate follows up by interpreting into the transference with regard to censorship and feelings activated by the canceled session. As a result the patient suddenly experiences a "flashback" in which she eventually combines both the transference and the earlier experience. All of this indicates how very well the analytic process is unfolding.

The learning alliance is again documented by the candidate's ability to ask for help in understanding a phenomenon she had observed but had herself not been able to integrate. The supervisor's response is an alternation between theoretical formulations about transference and overt empathic identification with the patient. This an attempt to illustrate to the candidate how empathic experience of the patient's psychic processes can permit a form of understanding which is then integrated from the posture of a listening analyst into a theoretical and clinical framework. The candidate's response reveals her ability to use the supervisor's explanation ("I couldn't make it one or the other, and what you're telling me is that you don't have to make it one or the other."). The supervisor supports the candidate's understanding and provides a further basis for integration through again combining empathic experience of the patient's position with general clinical psychoanalytic theory. The supervisor's return to the basic observable clinical data ("Does that seem to fit the data?") is a deliberate attempt to provide a model for using the clinical material as the ultimate guide for checking formulations. The candidate's response is an illustration of how an analyst's clinical and theoretical understanding influence the perception of the primary data.

The candidate's increasing sophistication and capacity to use an interpretive stance are illustrated in her interpretation in regard to power and the reversal from passive to active. This is followed by a significant and sustained affective response from the patient ("and she started to cry") which the candidate can appreciate and observe from an empathic position. At the same time she can check her own analytic responses to see whether or not there had been a distortion.

The supervisor then begins to focus on technical issues, seeking to help the candidate not only to recognize the dynamic line of the material but also to formulate strategies and tactics for effective intervention. The candidate has recognized the transference elements, and the supervisor once again uses the same model of shifting back and forth, a mixture of empathy and clinical theory, as well as a further elaboration how an analyst develops plans to approach certain conflict-laden material in the treatment setting. As part of this discussion the supervisor brings up the issue of the candidate's pregnancy (the candidate is several months pregnant, is beginning to show, and the issues of how to listen for or encourage the patient's observation and responses to the pregnancy have been discussed in previous supervisory sessions). The emphasis is on the resistance manifested by the patient in not mentioning the preconsciously perceived pregnancy, and the candidate indicates that she has been listening for derivatives and has associated to the pregnancy in the patient's comments about the cancelation being for personal reasons. As a further indication of her clinical development she waits for more clear and definitive evidence from the patient. The supervisor encourages this by pointing out that there might be connections other than the pregnancy, once again directing it toward the candidate's further understanding of the patient's progress in the analysis, as manifested by an increased sense of freedom in associations.

Candidate and supervisor next exchange ideas about the material, with the candidate explaining in well-organized form her various decisions regarding her responses to the patient and her material. In these interchanges there is essential agreement between them, but the supervisor is emphasizing the need for interpretation of resistance and repetitive interventions, which the candidate acknowledges as a learning need rather than a countertransference issue. The supervisor presents some of the theoretical background for these issues through emphasizing the position of the analyst and the theoretical guidelines an analyst uses, in contrast to the position and needs of the patient when focusing on the clinical material.

As the end of the supervisory hour approaches, the candidate demonstrates a capacity for effective summary and synthesis away from her process notes. And the supervisor uses the last material to illustrate his previous point of reworking psychological material and the varying levels of insight, acceptance, and affective awareness that are part of the process of working through. In this last material the candidate's remarks indicate that she is engaged in an active and effective listening and learning process.

Chapter 8

Supervisory Session 68

Candidate: She canceled a Wednesday session and this was a Thursday. I don't remember what went on Tuesday. (The candidate is breathless and apparently tense at the beginning of this session.)

Supervisor: She took a week off for—

Candidate: She told me a month in advance she was going to go and visit her family over Thanksgiving. She put in for her vacation. She gave me all the dates and stuff.

Supervisor: Okay.

Candidate: I think this is the session in which there is a dream I want to talk to you about. Yeah—had a dream last night. I saw her Tuesday, and the content of the Monday and Thursday sessions had to do with what we were talking about last time—her rage at me, her wish to take from me, her fear that that would kill me and her not wanting to kill me, and I got sick and my coughing meant that she had taken too much, and her fantasy of wanting to deplete me and being afraid to deplete me too much—that only one of us can be happy or alive—is part of that. And if she's happy, then I'm sad; and if she's sad, the reverse. Well, on this day, I saw her when I was coming in. I was running up the stairs, and she came into the stairwell on the first floor. I had run up a flight of stairs already and I was singing, humming, or something. She said "Hi" and I kept going. She saw me in the elevator three weeks ago, and that's why, I'm sure, she was walking up the stairs—because she hates running into me. She saw me in the elevator and I said "Hi" and she said "Hi" and then I didn't say anything else and she felt excluded. She felt I didn't want to talk to her, and then she felt that she had made up that whole group of feelings because she felt so uncomfortable when I was so close to her in the elevator. As she drove over she was thinking how good she felt. She hasn't felt this good for a long time. When she saw me in the stairwell she felt really good, and it really threw her for a loop that I seemed happy, that I was humming. She wanted to suppress her good feelings and lock them up, not show me. She thought I did not understand why she missed her appointment yesterday. She knows that I do; she knew that I would, but she thought that I would get mad. No, *she* got mad—why wouldn't I understand, why wouldn't I believe her that she had a reason to miss an appointment? She felt at my mercy, like it's in my power whether she is happy or not. I control her destiny. She feels like she has the fantasy that she has been feeling so good, on top of things, yesterday and today. She has a real sense of power, everything is under control. She described getting her life and her work in order prior to vacation, getting her desk cleared off, getting everything done that needs to be done. Last night when she finally sat down, she had real mixed emotions about not coming here. At first she was just frustrated and mad. Then she decided she simply didn't have time to deal with all the complicated feelings, and she called me and canceled and figured she would deal with them today. It makes her crazy. She has a fantasy that I have the power to take everything away and that I will get mad at her. She was wondering if my cough was better. Then when she saw me, she worried about my cough. When she saw me on the stairs and knew I felt good, she got anxious. She wanted so bad to tell me the good things, and that made her worry about my cough. Then she saw me feeling healthy and good, and it threw her and now her insides are tight. I don't really, I mean we've heard this before and I really don't understand. I understand what she is saying, but I don't understand what's behind it. There is just something I don't know yet, either that or I'm not putting something together. The pieces of it are that she gets real anxious when she wants to tell me something good; when things are going well for her and she wants to come in and tell me that they are going well, she can't. This is another piece of it, that she can't tolerate it if both of us are happy at the same time. It clashes with something.

Supervisor: Uh-huh.

Candidate: I ask her what's going on, she doesn't know. She wants to tell me bad things, make me feel bad, or something. She wants me to feel bad and it gives her power in her fantasy if I feel bad, if she makes me feel bad. If I feel okay despite all the injustices, she is powerless and left out. If she doesn't make me feel bad, she feels ignored. If she is not thinking about me in some way, if she gets preoccupied with something else, then she feels guilty. She is not taking care of me, she is not being concerned with me, she is being selfish, living her own life. She felt like that this morning. She felt good, accomplished, that sort of thing. And for the past week, she has felt terrible, coming down on herself. That was to punish me. She has felt so free today, she got her hair cut, wants to come out of her shell, have that sense of power. That's what she wants from me, that's what she wants me to give her. I have it, the power. I said something about I think she is caught in a vise and she wants to come out of her shell and be herself, powerful, but at the same time she wants something desperately from me that she feels she can only have if she is little and powerless. She thinks she wants to be loved by me, like she sees me loving my husband and my son. If she is vibrant, attractive, an adult woman, she can't have it ever. She can have it only if she is a man with a penis or if she is a depressed baby. I could never understand that she couldn't come yesterday because of job pressures, because she has never shown me that person, the person who works and is accomplished. I could never believe that that downtrodden, depressed baby would ever let job pressures overcome her need to come and see me; that doesn't fit her fantasy here, the part of her that she has projected here. She is in control at work and in her life, but she has never brought that person here. She isn't comfortable anymore with the image of herself that she has projected onto me. Something clashed. I can't read what I said. It looks like, why does she bring that, why does she have to be that baby here? She says guiltily that she made me sick. She once had the power of being okay, healthy and happy. She made me sick, and she has to pay for it. If she is happy and in control, she can't have me and may even make me sick again, may even make me die—and that scares her. What she wants from me is a continuous thing. That's important. My body, the ability to have a baby, everything, but she also wants me to be with her, in her, happy with her, together, sharing. She doesn't want me gone ever. She is afraid of being happy in herself here. This goes on for a long time, and then she says that she feels something like—well, that she wants to take everything away from me. It feels like she already did somehow take everything from me, and that's why I'm depressed. She has taken everything—my breasts and body—away, and hides them under her fat. That's what she has done with her whole life; she hides it, and she brings in this depressed person who is really not her. The other fantasy she had when she was sitting in the waiting room, after she saw that I was happy and that my cough wasn't worse, was that I would be disinterested in her and preoccupied. That's just another variation on being downtrodden and unloved. It really makes her anxious, both of us being happy at the same time. She sees me and she has needed to see me as an old-fashioned ogre. She has built up this image of how rotten I would be to her, that I would always punish her. Today in the waiting room she began to feel the old person that she knows she is, with just little bits of thoughts of our both being happy at the same time and nothing terrible happening. Then she went on about something else that made me say that she has a lot of rage against me, and she said yes, a whole lot, it feels like she is waiting for permission from me, for me to say that I can handle it, for me to say it is not too much for me, that it won't kill me, that she can go ahead and be herself, that it would make me happy in fact. She is aware of feelings she had in the last ten years, ways to punish herself. Then I have a big blank, so she must have said something. And then I said she wants to be fed and held, and if she can't have that she wants to bite. She said, "Yes, I had a strange dream last night." She was in San Francisco with Ted. It was exciting being there because she had such a terrible visit last time she was there. She felt left out and alone the last time. Anyway, she was there and

Ted got sick so they couldn't go out, and she was very upset because it was going to be a repeat of the first trip. If she wanted to go do anything, she would have to go do it alone. She was out walking around and feeling so depressed, and she ran into two girls from work who asked her to join them, but she really didn't want to, it wasn't good enough. But she went back to the room to take a shower, and there were all these trays of food. She sat down and started stuffing her mouth, angrily eating everything in sight. Then she felt sick and opened the door to where Ted was; it was a cold room. There was a man sitting in a chair holding Ted like you would hold a baby, and she felt really bad and angry that this man was taking care of him and holding him, and she felt jealous because she wanted to take care of him. She ran into the bathroom. Ted had obviously been sick. The toilet was on wheels and was suspended in the air. There was a stack of pillows near the door. She knew Ted had really been sick and she had gone out. She felt very guilty because *she* wanted to be taken care of and *she* had been feeling mad and bad and *she* wanted to be shown a good time. She was angry that he got sick. Why should she have to take care of him? He should be taking care of her. The same feelings as with me. Then she went and bit some more food. She wants to be fed and held and nurtured by me, and I get sick, and I don't do that. And I get sick and then she is really angry. And then she is frightened and feels guilty that she has deserted me. She gets angry when I get sick because I desert her too. She wants to hit me, hit me back. In the dream Ted was really sick, and she felt really guilty. She felt her anger made him sick. The two girls represented the fact that it is me she wants and no one else, no one else will do, just me. It is all so very intense. That's the end of the session. The dream came up pretty close to the end, and that was the last session before I didn't see her for over a week. I don't know, I don't really have much to say, except what's in that session, I think, except what I said to her, which I think is—I think of it as oral incorporative and oral aggressive.

Supervisor: Then nothing came up about her trip home for Thanksgiving?

Candidate: No, that came up the last session, the session before this one. She talked some about it, or I brought it up. I brought up that what she was talking about, also how she was feeling, was about being gone for a week, and she said yes that was on her mind. She was going to miss me and she was very ambivalent about being gone. She talked a whole lot in the first two sessions that week about how she was going to, she *knew* she was going to get into these fights with her mother about her weight and eating. Then I didn't bring it up again.

Supervisor: Uh-huh. Well, I think you have to see that the forthcoming separation and all that it means is the context in which this session occurred. And the whole question is, what it means to her. She comes in and says how angry you were that she missed a session on Wednesday; she doesn't say anything about how angry you are that she is going to be gone for a week.

Candidate: Uh-huh.

Supervisor: And of the two, the latter is certainly the more significant.

Candidate: The week is longer, yeah.

Supervisor: Not only that. For the Wednesday session she had a "good reason"—pressure at work.

Candidate: Yeah, and for the other one she has no reason at all.

Supervisor: Except that she wants to go.

Candidate: She is just going because she wants to.

Supervisor: She is going because she prefers being with somebody else to being with you. So the whole context, you see, of the session is what will determine how you then understand some of the material, which includes the dream business of being on vacation and having a good time in San Francisco, and then it turns out rotten because Ted gets sick—just how she sees her taking off as influencing you.

Candidate: And when she comes back she is convinced—you see, I canceled Monday's session.

Supervisor: Uh-huh.

Candidate: And on Thursday she—well, when she was at her parents' home, she had a great time until Thursday. Then she got in a fight with somebody and got unhappy and started to think about me and realized that she hadn't thought about me the whole time. Then she felt intensely guilty that she hadn't thought about me, maybe something terrible had happened to me. Then when I canceled Monday's session, she was sure she had killed me; something terrible *had* happened to me by her neglect. If she is not thinking about me, then I'm not thinking about her. But worse than that, I will dwindle away and become sick if she doesn't feed me with her attention and think of me. So that's a confirmation of what you are saying.

Supervisor: Uh-huh. You see she is trapped, not trapped, but she is involved here in an oscillation between a positive oedipal attachment, in which she and you are rivals and in which only one of you can be happy or can be effective or feminine or womanly or successful or anything else, because you are competing with each other for the same man in the positive oedipal constellation. She is oscillating between a positive oedipal constellation and a negative oedipal constellation, where she is the man and she makes love to you and that's the thing that would make you happy and she would be a better man and a better husband to you than your husband is and her father was. So that's the second position that she oscillates back and forth between. The positive oedipal where she is a rival with you; the negative oedipal where she is the man and is making love to you. Now, in part because of the inability to resolve that conflict, she then seems to undergo a regression to an oral—

Candidate: Okay, that's where the oral comes in.

Supervisor: An oral incorporative fantasy. But that, in this context, is probably regressive and defensive in the sense that it takes it away from either of the other two more advanced oedipal constellations. Then she goes back to being the poor, helpless, weak baby whom you as the mother will love, appreciate, take care of. And in that sense then she can hopefully avoid that other conflict, go back to be the infantile, orally incorporative child who incorporates either through love or through aggression. But one way or the other she is taking you in orally.

Candidate: And it's a dyadic—

Supervisor: Yes, a dyadic, in contrast to a triadic, relationship.

Candidate: Uh-huh, and she retreats from the triadic conflicts.

Supervisor: Exactly. So at that point—

Candidate: That's why I sometimes get confused, because the material seems to go from dyadic to triadic in a span of three or four minutes; it seems to shift. Just as I get a handle on it, it shifts.

Supervisor: Well—

Candidate: Not always, but sometimes it will.

Supervisor: So that seems to be, then, the meaning of this oral material at this point.

Candidate: Uh-huh, whereas a while ago it was more primary.

Supervisor: Uh-huh, plus at this point she is in the context that she is going to be leaving you. All right, she is going to be leaving you, and she has this dream that she is going to San Francisco to have a real ball and a blast and a sexual relationship with whatever his name is.

Candidate: Ted.

Supervisor: Ted. But then he gets sick and so on. The context of the dream is that she was having a good time with you but then she made you sick. She is going to hurt, castrate, take, destroy, do something damaging to the man. In that context, then, you see, again we see some of that in this dream. But she is also going back home. She is hoping to have a good time, but she is also going home for a big family Thanksgiving feast. So there is a regressive reactivation of the regressive trend there as well.

Candidate: Uh-huh.

Supervisor: So with all that going on then—

Candidate: Well, she also does have, which we haven't gotten to yet, but I just see little edges of real—well, fantasies of wishes to castrate her brother and her father, and get a penis that way.

Supervisor: Sure, sure.

Candidate: Not just from me, but then there is another whole—

Supervisor: No, you represent—

Candidate: To kill them and make them sick that way.

Supervisor: Right, and you represent, you see, in the transference you are not just the mother, you are also the father, you are also the brother.

Candidate: Uh-huh, uh-huh.

Supervisor: You are the one who has the penis, and only one of the two of you can have one. So if you've got it, then she wants it and she is going to steal it from you. If she grabs it from you, if she grabs it from you and steals it from you, then you shrivel up and die. You are sick or she destroys you in getting it. If she grabs it and puts it on herself, then she can use it with you when you are the woman.

Candidate: Uh-huh.

Supervisor: And this is where the difficulty comes in following the material. Keep in mind that you can be male as well as female in the transference, and the fact that you are a woman doesn't mean that you are a feminine figure in the transference.

Candidate: Well, and to also figure out where she is at, what I am at the moment for her, is not always real easy.

Supervisor: That's right.

Candidate: Even if I keep that in mind, it is not real easy to find out where she's at in all this shifting. When she stays in one position for a long time—you know, for a week or two—then it's—

Supervisor: But now, you see, when you then take up with her the idea that she wants to bite you or devour you, take you in and so on—

Candidate: Then I'm, I'm supporting the regressive.

Supervisor: Right. Rather than interpreting the conflict from which the regression occurred, which is: "I'm a woman, I'm going home to my dad, I'm going home to have a good time, I'm not going to think about you," and so on.

Candidate: Uh-huh, uh-huh.

Supervisor: "Because I want to have fun."

Candidate: "And you are going to be here working."

Supervisor: That's right.

Candidate: It gets confusing to me because sometimes, because she has oral—there's an oral mode that goes through all of it, in that when she is competing with me, wanting to take things from me, she often wants to bite them from me. I mean not always, but there is an orality about the triadic material, too, that—

Supervisor: Yeah, she is going to use her vagina like a mouth.

Candidate: Uh-huh.

Supervisor: As an incorporative, destructive organ. You see, this is kind of a—

Candidate: Yes, it was last week that I was using bite in terms of a way to get things from me, as opposed to a way to pay me back for not holding her.

Supervisor: Uh-huh. But you see, the biting and the fantasy of oral incorporation can also then be part of the oedipal sexual configuration, particularly in the fantasies of fellatio and a wish to bite the penis and get it that way, castrate the man by biting his penis off, or fantasies of displacing all of that to the vagina from above to below, the incorporative vagina as a grasping incorporative organ.

Candidate: Uh-huh, and getting it in.

Supervisor: That gets him in and then snaps him off and keeps it.

Candidate: So where does her vaginismus then fit into this?

Supervisor: It is a defense against the fantasy of castrating the man. The fantasy is, "I get the man's penis inside of me, then I can keep it, then I'll acquire it, then I'll castrate him." But there is also, simultaneously, guilt and shame for these wishes, and so vaginismus is one way of avoiding the expression and fulfillment of that fantasy. It is the defensive side of the incorporative wish. (Long pause)

Candidate: How do you make an oral interpretation, not diadic, not—how do you? You just did. You did it with more explicit material than we had in the session.

Supervisor: When she says, "You know, I can either be the boy and have you that way, or I can be the—"

Candidate: Depressed baby.

Supervisor: The depressed baby. Yes. "Let's look at this fantasy of being the boy. How are you going to get the penis?" And get her to elaborate on her fantasies or her feeling, "I don't know what I'd do." You might say, "I think in some ways the fantasies that you have about devouring, about eating, are a way of getting things. I think in some ways you feel that your vagina is like something that will grasp and grab the penis and not let go. And because that wish frightens you and because you feel scared about it, that's why you have that vaginismus trouble."

Candidate: And it still comes back from time to time.

Supervisor: Well, the next time it comes back, what—

Candidate: And she will bring it in, and I've never been able to get a handle on what—

Supervisor: That's the point. You try to get at it through the details of the material that she presents. So the next time she presents it, say, "Wait a minute, let's go back. What was going through your mind when you and Ted decided to make love that night? Let's trace it from there. What was the—"

Candidate: And she is often the initiator. She wants to make love, she feels—

Supervisor: "When you were the initiator, what did you fantasy, what was going through your mind?" Then you look for the omission, because she won't have a conscious recollection of "I want to grab his penis." She might, but the likelihood is she won't. "Wait a minute. There is something left out there. You were doing this and suddenly this. What went in between?" In that way you deal with her resistances against recall. Eventually you make the interpretation: "I think you have a wish that when Ted's penis is inside of you, you can use your vagina like a mouth and bite it off and keep it." And at that point, she can confirm it or negate it. But eventually you follow that up with the interpretation: "That's why at times when you have the vaginismus it is just a way of avoiding this fantasy and of saying, 'No I don't want to do this.' " But you try to hook these theoretical constructs of more clinical constructs into the specifics of her material, which will be experienced, expressed, through mostly her fantasy life in connection with some of these incidents with Ted or somebody else—masturbation fantasies or what have you. That's where you then have to interpret them and then the resistances: "You are avoiding the details of the fantasy. I think there is a fantasy there that you are frightened to look at." Something along those lines which indicates and encourages her to fill in the gap. And then when you feel she is ready, you don't have to wait for her to come up with the fantasy; you can pose or present it as an interpretation, a reconstruction of the fantasy, which you offer tentatively and to which she can then say, "Well, no, that's not quite right, but what I did think—"

Candidate: And then perfect it.

Supervisor: "What I did think was x-y-z," and she modifies it in accordance with her specific fantasies.

Candidate: Uh-huh. I have terrible notes on this last session. I canceled; I called her late Sunday afternoon, and I canceled all my Monday patients. She came in on Tuesday and said she feels so much love and appreciation for me, and she expanded on that. Then she started crying. Strong feelings today. I thought that was a response to my canceling the appointment. That has happened before. I didn't ask her about it. She has strong feelings today, feels equal to me today for the first time and real appreciative; believes I care about her, just as she believes her parents and brother do. It's strange. Something is strange. She felt fine all week until Thursday and then she fell apart. She cried at the drop of a hat. She and her grandmother had a fight, and she told me about it. She didn't tell her grandmother that she was going to visit her parents. Her grandmother lives here, and she doesn't like her. So she doesn't call her, doesn't do any of the things that anybody thinks she ought to do about her grandmother. So she didn't tell her that she was going home, and her grandmother found out and was real mad—very snotty. The patient was mad and felt guilty and felt in the middle between her parents and her grandmother. In the middle, but I don't know who between, actually. Then she paused and said she really thinks—that was Thursday—that it started with her brother coming home from Europe on Wednesday. He called Ted to pick him up at the airport, but he told him not to tell anyone, not even the patient, that he was back in the United States. But Ted, of course, called her and told her and then told her not to tell her parents. She didn't tell her parents but she felt very much in the middle. It is always like that. She called, finally; she waited all day Thursday for her brother to call her parents and surprise them or make them happy or show up. Finally she called Ted late on Thursday, called him and asked him what the hell was going on. She was real disappointed that he didn't go to Ohio, where they'd once lived. The whole beginning of the week she might as well have been an only child; it was very nice. Then Harold came back. Her parents were so looking forward to Harold coming back around Wednesday or so, that she was very disappointed when he didn't come home and make their Thanksgiving. But at the same time she hated him, because she felt they would rather he be there than her. When her mother said to her that she wished she wouldn't get so upset about the grandmother, that the grandmother is just an old snot and just don't pay attention, the patient's response was that never in her whole life has she ever felt like anybody's favorite. Then she said she didn't know what's wrong with her here today. She doesn't understand what's going on. Something is going on that she doesn't understand. I asked about her feelings or fantasies about my canceling our appointment yesterday, and she said she was worried about me, she was grateful it was only one day. She was afraid I would cancel the whole week, afraid I would call again this morning and cancel the rest of the week. She felt some premonition that something bad happened to me, something in my family, somebody had died or was sick. She didn't want to come today and be like this, in tears, be upset. I said, "You wanted to come today and cheer me up." She said yes, be a good girl. I said, and if she is not? She said I won't be available to her, she feels an intense need to grab hold of how she sees me being with her right now, right before, right now—warm, receptive, supportive. She had all kinds of fantasies about how I would be today—desolate, upset, gone. Maybe showing it, maybe not showing it, but being very desolate and preoccupied, feeling that I would be lost to her, that it would be over, and this really scares her, for a variety of reasons. One, that she would feel to blame, she had done it to me; and two, that it makes her feel that I am fading away, that she will lose me. When things are really good she wants to run away. She expects them not to stay that way and it won't last, it never does. She feels afraid and resigned to it. Yet it feels good to be here. Yet she is afraid to spill all that's inside of her. Maybe I. . . . She wanted to come in here and be happy and positive, as if telling me she is okay, she doesn't need too much. The strongest feeling around my canceling the appointment yesterday was real fear—and then, today, fear that what she would want and would take from me would do the rest, would do me in. Going home made her want me even more. She feels like she playacts. She is the parent with her parents. The only way she can escape from that mold is to feel really bad, even though it is the mold she made herself. I asked if what happened here just now was a little piece of the mold? Taking care of me, so that she doesn't lose me? And she said, hmm, she started to feel bad last week. Oh, when she started to feel bad last week she had the fantasy of killing herself, just floating away from it all. She feels like she can't escape from this mold. She can't ever ever be herself. Instead of just being herself and saying, "This is the way I am, that's it," she makes herself miserable. Then she made a long list of the ways she is capable of making herself miserable that we know about and she knows about. She can eat too much or she can say she is a bad person or she can feel guilty or she can ride herself mercilessly about things she hasn't done. She is tired of her mother looking at her like she is some kind of pathetic person, even though that is the exact picture she has painted of herself for her mother. She doesn't want to be like this anymore, but she is afraid to be anything else. She is really afraid to just need me for me, not because she is a depressed, pathetic baby, or unhappy, but just because she is a human being and needs to be loved. She is afraid of taking too much. She thinks she felt guilty for not being here last week. She thinks she has the fantasy that she takes care of me; she felt guilty leaving me, felt she was selfish. I asked her about that, about the fantasy of taking care of me and what happened when she left me, what I was doing.

Supervisor: She has in the past had fantasies that she had to take care of her father.

Candidate: Both of them. Both of them. She had to take care of her mother to keep her mother from being depressed. And when her mother had back problems and her father would go out of town, she was the one, even though she was only four years old, five years old, and it was obvious that she couldn't have been the one who took care of everything, in her memory, in her fantasy, she took care of everything. She was the man of the house. And then, at a different stage of her life, she had to take care of her father so that her father's feelings wouldn't get hurt, so that he wouldn't get injured and upset and unhappy and give everybody a hard time. She had to keep him so that—

Supervisor: Uh-huh, so that, technically, you want to orient yourself at a moment like this.

Candidate: Help me, because I have trouble orienting myself!

Supervisor: You can ask, "Well, who am I right now?"

Candidate: Oh, okay. That never dawned on me.

Supervisor: "Are you taking care of me as Mommy or taking care of me as Dad?"

Candidate: Uh-huh. She took care of them in different ways.

Supervisor: Yes, so that's, you see, the point.

Candidate: So that's another key to how—

Supervisor: Each, she takes care of them in different ways, so that you could say to her, for instance, "In what way are you taking care of me? What kind of care are you taking of me right now? In this image what's the detail of your taking care of me, what exactly are you doing for me?" And then you can make the interpretation. If she is saying, "Well, I'm protecting your feelings" and so on, "You are hurt and disappointed," and so on, then you interpret, "You are seeing me as your dad."

Candidate: Uh-huh.

Supervisor: Or if she is saying, "Well, you are all alone and you know your husband has left you out, and he is off on a trip or off with his girl friend," you say, "So you are seeing me as your mom, right?" But that again is the way in which you orient yourself to where she is in the transference, through that kind of intervention which doesn't discourage the fantasy but encourages her to reenact it even more.

Candidate: Uh-huh.

Supervisor: You see, in that sense you are participating in the fantasy with the patient. You are not standing off and saying,

"Wait a minute, this is a fantasy, how come you think that?" Rather you are saying, "Yes, this is the fantasy and who am I?"

Candidate: You are taking a role.

Supervisor: You are taking a role in the fantasy and fostering the patient's reexperience or reliving of this as part of a fantasy system.

Candidate: Uh-huh. Because I do have trouble. And her picture of me as an ogre is the paternal, the father transference.

Supervisor: Well, in contrast to the interpretation that stands off and essentially points out a fantasy as something irrational, which essentially says, correct this fantasy—

Candidate: Or stop it.

Supervisor: Or stop thinking this way, which may actually be appropriate at a particular time. I mean, this is part of a fantasy system that I am thus and thus and thus. That's the corrective, reality-orienting, adultomorphic kind of—

Candidate: Well, you have to have an observing ego—

Supervisor: Yes.

Candidate: To get through this. (Laughs)

Supervisor: That's right, but, at the same time, at this particular point if you are confused as to where the transference is, you would participate in the fantasy and foster the patient's further—

Candidate: Elaboration.

Supervisor: Elaboration of it, and *then* stand off and say, "I think that what we can see is that in this set of feelings you are reenacting with me the feelings that you had about your father" and this, that, and the other circumstance.

Candidate: Uh-huh.

Supervisor: Which then orients her into the adult self-observing ego, in contrast to participation in the fantasy that promotes the regression.

Candidate: Uh-huh.

Supervisor: You oscillate from one position to the other, and then she follows suit. Well we have to stop here, but this is the way you can begin to follow this material. You sort of ask yourself what's going on, and then if you don't know you follow into the fantasy to find out, and then you back off into the self-observing ego.

Candidate: Because I often find myself asking what's going on. And then I ask her for more details but I haven't done anything like that because I, I don't get massively confused like I used to, but in a session I'll get lost as to where the transference is, what is going on.

Supervisor: Yeah.

Candidate: And often I won't say anything for a long time, because it's just not clear to me what's going on.

Supervisor: Uh-huh, but you've got two options. One is to wait, as you sometimes can, and the other is to intervene along the lines—

Candidate: Yeah, to do something to help get it clarified.

Supervisor: That's right.

Candidate: Thank you.

Supervisor: Okay. Oh, listen, two weeks from today I won't be here, so our next scheduled time would be—

Candidate: Four weeks from today.

Supervisor: Four weeks from today. Let's see, that would be, I think, December thirtieth. I have the second, ninth, sixteenth—yeah, the thirtieth.

Candidate: Okay, I may be taking that week off, but if I'm not I will let you know.

Supervisor: If you need to see me in the meantime, give me a call.

Candidate: Okay, thank you.

Supervisor: Uh-huh. All right, bye-bye.

Supervisor's Comments

Since the last supervisory recording thirteen months ago, a number of things have happened. The candidate's pregnancy was finally acknowledged consciously by the patient, and her aggressive, envious, competitive, and depressive transference responses were extensively analyzed. This represented a reliving in the transference of the patient's experiences around the time her brother was born, when she was about three years old. Late in her pregnancy the candidate interrupted the analysis for a planned and previously announced maternity leave of five months, during which time she gave birth to a healthy baby girl. During the interruption the patient made no attempt to contact the analyst or the person covering for her. When the candidate contacted the patient at the previously arranged time, the patient returned and resumed the analysis without delay. This supervisory session occurred three months after the analysis was resumed.

Despite her anxiety, expressed chiefly through heavy breathing during the early part of the supervisory session, the candidate launches immediately into a detailed, animated, and affectively responsive account of the patient's material. Compared to the last recorded session, thirteen months ago, the patient demonstrates that a significantly deepened and intensified regressive transference neurosis has evolved. The material includes numerous manifestations of primary process fantasy and affect, directly experienced and reported by the patient as part of the transference process without undue resistance or anxiety to the expression of such thoughts.

The candidate is capable of accepting the patient's experience, distortion, and affective range without undue concern or defensiveness, and is equally capable of vividly reporting these phenomena to the supervisor. She appears comfortable both in the analytic process and in the supervisory process. The candidate also demonstrates her capacity to observe herself and her role, as shown by her recognition that the patient's having seen her running up the stairs was an important interactional stimulus. While reporting this, the candidate is able to associate to a previous occasion, some weeks earlier, on which the patient had seen her in the building elevator; she remembered how this experience had modified the patient's behavior. This form of reporting demonstrates the candidate's growing capacity for free-floating attention and easy shifts in the level and focus of her awareness.

For her part, the patient demonstrates that as the transference neurosis has evolved into its current regressive form and experience, her capacities to function effectively in her job and in the outside world have been enhanced. She is developing a sense of capability and good feeling, while simultaneously focusing the increased affective experience and primitive fantasies onto the analyst as part of the therapeutic transference neurosis. All of these are important positive indicators of a significant and extensive deepening of the analytic process.

The transference experience centers around the patient's responses and distortions regarding the candidate's cough, as contrasted with her perception of the candidate's feeling well at the present time. The candidate then indicates she is having difficulty understanding the material, a request for the supervisor's help. Earlier on, the supervisor responded promptly to such requests, but by now the candidate's experience and progress suggest that the request is not an urgent one. As a pedagogical tactic, the supervisor does not respond but allows the candidate to struggle on her own and formulate the material without his help. The candidate tries to explain the various "pieces," and the supervisor responds with a noncommittal uh-huh, thereby presenting a model of tolerance of ambiguity—there is no need always and at every moment to fully understand the patient's material.

The candidate reports the patient's transference experiences, particularly her aggressive and competitive fantasies, which the candidate demonstrates she can tolerate comfortably and interpret more deeply in terms of the patient's conflict between being herself and being the powerless little girl. The patient can then respond to the candidate's deepening transference intervention with fantasies of being either a man with a penis or else a depressed baby. The fact that the patient's performance outside the analysis has improved as the regression in the transference neurosis has deepened and been focused within the analysis is an indicator of significant development in the analytic process.

This deepening of the analytic process is itself the result of internal psychological change due to previous work in the analysis. The patient's capacity to tolerate her own intrapsychic processes without undue anxiety reflects a shift in the superego toward accepting fantasies and wishes without the intense guilt and shame that had once accompanied them. It also reflects an improved ability to separate thought and fantasy from action, an enhanced sense of confidence in her own adaptive capacities, and an identification with the analytic function of the analyst. She is also increasingly able to express transference wishes and fantasies directed toward the analyst, while at the same time she is able to tolerate and accept the inevitable frustration of these wishes. As a matter of fact, it is the patient's recognition, through her own experience, of the candidate's capacity to appreciate the transference and its meanings (while at the same time maintaining an abstinent posture toward gratification of the transference wishes) that permits her to experience and more deeply express these wishes.

The patient's fantasy of taking everything from the analyst, including her breasts and body, and hiding them under her own body fat is an illustration of the degree to which the patient is now capable of experiencing her own primitive psychic thought content in a direct and therapeutically useful form. The patient demonstrates her synthetic self-observation by recognizing that these have been lifelong patterns, and the candidate, through quietly accepting and listening, encourages the elaboration of such fantasies. A somewhat parallel process is seen in the supervisor, who listens quietly without intervening as the candidate elaborates the patient's transference experience.

The patient begins to demonstrate, through an immediate experience, a transient and spontaneous correction of the primitive transference distortions: she experiences herself and the analyst as happy at the same time, with "nothing terrible happening." The candidate's interpretation of the patient's transference rage moves the process forward and is followed by the patient's expression of defenses against these affects. The candidate demonstrates developing analytic sophistication in that she abstains from directly responding to the patient's requests for reassurance with regard to her aggression, thereby allowing the transference neurosis to deepen even further.

The candidate's direct transference interpretation regarding the patient's wish to be fed and her aggressive wish to bite in response to its frustration demonstrates her capacity to interpret in a nonintellectualized, affectively appropriate way, which then leads to the patient's association to the dream. This sequence also demonstrates the patient's enhanced capacity to participate effectively in the analytic process and to associate without need for explanation of the shifts in her ideation.

Although the dream is not fully analyzed, the candidate has recognized its importance; since it came up toward the end of the session, she can accept being unable to explore it further.

The supervisor's question about the Thanksgiving trip is intended to bring the material back to the current adaptive context, which had not been manifest in the report by the candidate. Her explanation that she had previously attempted to deal with it, although apparently not fully effectively, allows the supervisor to see that she was aware of the issue. Even so, the supervisor uses the concept of the context as stimulus to the patient's material in the current interaction to try to demonstrate to the candidate the importance of the separation process and the patient's responses to it. This leads to an active interchange between candidate and supervisor in regard to the patient's vacation. The candidate responds to the supervisor's comments with additional confirmatory material while illustrating once again the depth of the patient's transference distortions and neurotic process.

At this point the supervisor attempts to help the candidate formulate a macroscopic view of the analytic process and the dynamic oscillation between positive and negative oedipal positions, as well as the defensive regression which the candidate then spontaneously recognizes herself ("and it's a dyadic"). The supervisor attempts to explain to the candidate the concept of a regressive and defensive retreat from the more advanced oedipal level of conflict to which the candidate is able to respond appropriately and actively, recognizing the shift to a dyadic relationship, and also to express her own doubts at the rapidity of the shifts she can observe in the treatment situation.

The supervisor's temporary block in regard to the name of the patient's boyfriend (Ted) is an indication of the supervisor's affective and intense participation in the analytic experience and process through identifying with the candidate in the transference experience, from which he recovers and returns to a more cognitive pedagogical position.

There follows an active interaction in which the supervisor once again explains the patient's perception of the candidate as a male with a penis she wants to acquire, about which she feels guilty, once again repeating the point made previously in supervision that a woman analyst can represent a male transference role. The supervisor here is responding on the basis of the educational principle of repetition, very like the process of working through in a therapeutic situation. The candidate acknowledges difficulties in following the material from time to time. When the supervisor begins to point out to the candidate the meaning of the patient's wish to bite and devour her, the candidate immediately (and correctly) observes, "I'm supporting the regressive," and candidate and supervisor then participate in an exchange which helps clarify their dynamic understanding of the material. In this exchange the supervisor illustrates the principle of distinguishing between manifest form or content and unconscious dynamic meaning, though he does not identify it as such. During the course of a prolonged supervisory relationship a great deal of teaching and learning of basic principles occurs without their being specifically labeled or acknowledged.

This leads the candidate to introduce a question about a specific symptom—vaginismus—which is new and unfamiliar to the supervisor. This is a process similar to what occurs in correct interpretation in treatment—namely, the subsequent emergence of related but previously unacknowledged material. The supervisor's explanation of the dynamic meaning demonstrates the concept that a correct formulation lends meaning to a variety of manifestly different phenomena.

The candidate then seeks explicit suggestions in regard to technical handling, expressing her wish for an appropriate model of therapeutic technique. The supervisor responds by providing an illustrative, interpretive approach, allowing the candidate to observe the model intervention. He shifts between specific technical interventions and conceptual explanations of the steps involved in the interpretive and therapeutic process. There is an attempt to differentiate interpretation of resistance from interpretation of content, and to shift back and forth between the two modes of teaching, thereby providing the candidate a model of how the supervisor's mind functions in regard to this material. Another important element in this interchange is the supervisor's emphasis on reconstruction or interpretation of fantasy as tentative, and on permitting and encouraging the patient to modify or correct it, which elicits the candidate's active recognition ("and then perfect it").

The candidate at this point returns spontaneously to her reporting of the process material, taking the initiative in directing the supervisory session but also demonstrating that she has grasped the previous issue, feels satisfied, and is ready to proceed. These are all indicators of the state of the learning alliance. The patient gives a brief glimpse of her capacity to correct her transference experience, in which today she feels equal to the candidate for the first time.

The candidate had previously recognized the patient's response to the cancelation as a transference reaction, but had elected to permit the material to unfold further before interpreting this issue, thereby allowing the process to be less interrupted and more spontaneous in its evolution. The patient again indicates her capacity to associate, her involvement in the transference neurosis, and her capacity to respond to the candidate's interpretation with a deepening elaboration of the transference experience.

She also demonstrates a growing capacity for the achievement of insight through self-observation, recognizing her own participation in her distress and the fact that she herself has been responsible for presenting the picture of an unhappy and miserable individual to the world. When the supervisor points out that some of the current material is a reference to previously expressed needs to care for her father, the candidate responds with further details of how the patient has experienced a need to care for *both* parents. In this material the candidate demonstrates a capacity to accept the patient's experience of psychic reality in the caring for her parents, while at the same time maintaining a sense of actuality and objectivity ("it was obvious that she couldn't have been the one who took care of everything").

The supervisor, pointing out the need to orient oneself at moments like this, elicits from the candidate a direct request for help, and the supervisor's suggestion elicits an appreciative response. This is followed by both a specific model of intervention and interpretation, as well as a shift to the conceptual understanding of how and why such interventions influence the process. The supervisor also emphasizes the need to participate empathically in the patient's fantasy as a psychic reality in the transference experience, using this as a technique to orient and understand oneself in regard to the material the patient is presenting. The emphasis here is on the need to accept and tolerate the patient's psychic reality without undue pressure to resolve or correct the fantasies or experiences, thereby encouraging an empathic immersion while at the same time retaining the capacity to move on to the more objective observing, interpretive position of an analyst. Such behavior by the analyst tends to foster the patient's abilities to observe and experientially correct distorted fantasy systems. Once again the teaching of these concepts is occurring at the level of supervisor as role model, and the specific issues are left tacit. The candidate's learning process includes a preconscious identification with the supervisor and his modes of thought and experience.

This results in an active interchange between candidate and supervisor in which the supervisor shows how the analyst's functions in the patient's experience of the transference neurosis lead ultimately toward resolution and renunciation of the more distorted transference attitudes and images. The candidate voices some of her learning needs and doubts, and the supervisor supports her in accepting the option of waiting, which the candidate has used, as being one appropriate choice among several to which the process would lend itself.

On several occasions toward the end of the supervisory session, the candidate expresses her thanks for what seems to have been an active, effective, and significant supervisory session. In arranging for the next session because of possible cancelations, the supervisor indicates his confidence in the candidate's ability to carry on in spite of the fairly prolonged interval till the next supervisory hour, but at the same time offers his support and willingness to see her sooner if she needs him.

The long lapse of time since the last supervisory transcript highlights even more dramatically the changes that are occurring. From one therapeutic or supervisory session to the next such changes tend to be very subtle, brief, and often transitory; not infrequently they are followed by a retreat to previous forms of experience and function. The cumulative effects of these changes can be of sufficient magnitude, intensity, and persistence over time to allow their recognition both by the participants and by an outside observer. The present session demonstrates just such a process.

Chapter 9

Supervisory Session 87

Candidate: Are you taping again?
Supervisor: Uh-huh.
Candidate: Does it pick up good at that distance?
Supervisor: Yes.
Candidate: I started taping the supervisory sessions with my other case because I find I organize everything I think and I say it, and I think, "Gee, I should write this down and it would make it easier for me," but I never write it down. I have not done much for today. This is a bad time. My father-in-law is dying and there are just a lot of demands right now that I attend to first.
Supervisor: Sure.
Candidate: We are the only family.
Supervisor: Is this something that was expected?
Candidate: It is now. He's eighty years old. He was really relatively hale and hearty until mid-August, and then he had a stroke, and then he had another one, and then another one and another one, and now he is—well, there's really not much we can do. But his wife, my mother-in-law, just had her seventy-fifth birthday. She sits by his bed twelve hours a day and talks to him. So it's just, you know.
Supervisor: Sure.
Candidate: So I'm kind of unprepared. There are a couple of things I wanted to talk about that I think are interconnected. I made a nonstrategic defense interpretation. There's a global defensive style. I don't know what you call that kind of defense in that article that I read so long ago (Dewald, 1980). I don't think it was strategic. I made an interpretation of her vagueness

that we have been noticing and interpreting in ninety-five different ways for a long time. This glossing over things and glossing over things and glossing over things and not being able to get any details, and this is after a couple of weeks of interpreting, withholding, and her withholding herself and getting vengeance on me, and that kind of passed. She was talking about how disappointing her family was to her and how she was so dissatisfied and she always wanted more, always wanted more. She felt there was something wrong with her because she always wanted more. It wasn't clear to her what she wanted more of, but she's just always wanted more. She wanted to be a Roman Catholic because some friends of hers were Roman Catholic and there were four or five daughters and they had a tight-knit little family. She thought it would be nice to be a Catholic because then you could be part of a Catholic family. But she always wanted more. In the context of that, I believe, she started to talk about how she made it appear to her family that everything was fine and about the feeling, which she still has, that she has to make it appear to her family that everything is fine. Now, that's a major distortion because she doesn't actually succeed at that. But I knew what she was talking about, this making it appear that everything's fine. It's kind of what you do at a cocktail party, you know: "How are you doing?" "Oh, fine." "What's going on?" Well, you know, you never get into the nitty-gritty of whatever is going on in your life. That seemed to be what she was describing, feeling that she had to do it with her parents to keep them from knowing that she was so dissatisfied and also to keep from recognizing herself how terribly disappointing something was to her, how terribly disappointing her family, her life, everything was. I interpreted her inability to bring details into the analysis as that, as doing that here.

Supervisor: Good.

Candidate: The next day she was far more—well, the interpretation seemed to make sense to her, though I don't remember what she talked about. It was two-thirds of the way through a session.

Supervisor: That's an illustration, you see, of the transference of a defense and of a defensive style into the analysis.

Candidate: Uh-huh, and throughout, forever, coloring the entire nature of the analysis. I don't know quite what word to use—the characteristics of the analysis.

Supervisor: Uh-huh.

Candidate: It is true that some of her nonspecificness is withholding. It is true that she sometimes doesn't tell me things in order that I might think she is more miserable than she really is, so that she can make me miserable, so she can get back at me. All of these other ways in which I have interpreted this globalness are true of it, but this is a more—

Supervisor: They are narrow elements of meaning.

Candidate: That's what I'm trying to say.

Supervisor: And in addition to that, there is a supraordinate meaning of this repetition with you of her style of relating to her parents. In that sense, you see, it's what I would call a tactical resistance, in contrast to a strategic one. Tactical in the sense that it keeps you at a distance. Tactical in a sense that it keeps her from recognizing and letting you know how miserable she is.

Candidate: And not strategic in the sense that it doesn't deal with a specific thing but deals with a whole. The statement I'm trying to understand—

Supervisor: No, the strategic resistances are a little bit different, at least as I conceptualized them in my article. The strategic resistances are the wish to reenact and repeat and get satisfaction *now* for the things missed when you were growing up.

Candidate: Okay.

Supervisor: In that sense, yes and no. In that sense she wants you to—

Candidate: A repetition compulsion.

Supervisor: It's a repetition, that's right. The strategic resistances are the manifestations of the repetition compulsion, the desire to gain satisfaction now.

Candidate: In the context of this particular stylistic maneuver or style of relation, she talked about her father's rages and remembered being very little and her father raging and her being terrified, hiding under her bed, hiding in her room, thinking, "What am I going to do? My father hates me. He's going to get rid of me. He'll kill me. He'll kill my brother. He'll kill my mother," not having any idea why the rage was precipitated and from her description it could be anything from the color socks you have on to really doing something bad, you know, naughty. And then her discovery—she could remember the day, she thinks, either preschool or early grade school—her discovery that she was in terror in her bedroom and went back out and apologized to her father. She didn't know what it was about, but she apologized. Oh, and he would always in these rages say he would die and then she'd be happy, she'd get the money. Or the mother and this girl. She went out and apologized to him and discovered that she could wheedle and cajole him, and that if she behaved in certain ways she could keep these things from happening so often, and she could get him back in a less volcanic frame of mind. That buttressed—in addition to the disappointment, whatever that's about—that was another buttress to this glossing-over behavior, that she could behave in certain ways to keep things, as she says, on the up and up. Keep things moving along in this nonexplosive way.

Supervisor: And to keep her father from knowing about her, so he wouldn't get angry when he knew. So what you're saying, then, is that this becomes, as part of a complete interpretation, the origin of a particular defensive style. The transference is the expectation of your knowing what she really thinks or what really goes on or if she gives you something specific, it will give you an excuse to blow. If she is vague and chitchatty and everything is going fine and you don't know what is going on, then you are not going to blow the way her father did. And that's the interpretation I would make to her. It's the origin of a pattern now being reenacted with you.

Candidate: In the transference.

Supervisor: In the transference. That's right.

Candidate: The session after I made that interpretation—and I don't remember how completely I made it—she was—well, even when I looked over the process notes, I couldn't come up with anything specific that tells you how or why I felt she was less glossing-over, but I did. I don't really think the facts were any different; she just felt more focused and was talking more directly.

Supervisor: Uh-huh.

Candidate: This was the last day before our Thanksgiving break, so I don't really have much after that because I took some time off. And at that time she remembered feeling always frightened and wondered why she felt so frightened as a kid. She remembered lots of surface things, as in false self things. I've never talked with you about false self and don't really know what you think about the concept, or even what I think about it yet. She talked first of all about the fear and the emptiness inside her, and the disappointment from the feeling that there was something wrong with her because she was never satisfied. And then this acting as if everything's fine—this glossing over and keeping everything fine—and then keeping grandmother happy, and who you had to kiss, and when you had to kiss them, and be sure you do this and that, and a lot of support for clean-looking surfaces or untroubled-looking surfaces and her perfection, with the exception of her weight problem, I think, of an acceptable surface in doing things right and keeping things on the up and up. Then when she was an early adolescent they moved to Ohio. I don't know where they lived before that, but they made a major move to another city. And she said she felt like being by herself. She was in school. She wanted to come home from school and read in her room; she didn't remember it as a depressed period. She just remembered it as new things were happening to her body; new things were happening to her. She was in a new place. She just was feeling her way pretty slowly, and she overheard her parents, some conversation they were having wondering why and worrying about the fact that she didn't have more friends. And she got frightened—I think this is strange, this relating of this in this way—she got frightened and went out and made friends with everybody, anybody who would talk to her she would be friends with so that the surface would look right again. Her father wondered with her why she didn't have more dates and she couldn't really *do* much about that. But she tried. It was in that period that she determined to become homecoming queen, and she did. And again, the surface was always fine, and she had a storybook family and everything was perfect and just like *I* have a storybook family now. I have a boy and a girl and everything is perfect, glossy perfect. I don't think she is withholding details; I think she doesn't *think* details about it. There's a fireplace and chestnuts roasting on the fire like out of *Better Homes & Gardens* or one of those old Christmas books. And everything. And I had supportive mommies and daddies and I'm a wonderful mommy and my kids are very self-assured, and she kind of constructed this fantasy about herself too, and seems to express horrible disappointment that it might not be true. That has been a theme throughout the whole analysis, that she wanted a storybook family and she can't abide the possibility that it's not true. Just like that. You know, she loved her brother; they were a wonderful brother-sister team. And how horrible it was for her to have to admit that she hated his guts and she was jealous and wished he would die and was afraid she was killing him. So I don't know if this is more an extension of this defensive style or if it's—I wrote in the margin to talk with you about false self and that whole thing.

Supervisor: Well, this would be an illustration of the strategic resistance: "I want to believe that I had an ideal family and that's what I still want today, and that's what I want to have had today, and that's what I want with you today."

Candidate: To avoid the affect, to avoid the feelings of anger and disappointment and need?

Supervisor: Partly that, partly that, but also to *get* it.

Candidate: Okay, to make it for yourself, like an imaginary playmate.

Supervisor: Exactly. To not have to accept the fact that it wasn't that way, and there's still time to get it. "I can still go back and re-create that image. I can still hold onto it and draw pleasure from it."

Candidate: Uh-huh, uh-huh. That *is* like an imaginary playmate, because you go there in your head and play there with the playmate. She can go into this family, no specifics, and have everything be like the night before Christmas.

Supervisor: That's right. Now, this concept of false self/true self is an illustration of, say in the terminology of structural metapsychology, of an intrasystemic conflict in contrast to intersystemic. It's not a conflict between id and ego; it's a conflict within the ego of two different images of herself that are in conflict with each other.

Candidate: Uh-huh.

Supervisor: One has a greater sense of validity, and one is used to conceal the distress or the affective disonance produced by the other. So that one sees multiple images, multiple images of one's self.

Candidate: Well, then when she is projecting this thing that I'll call false self she feels, she expresses many—it's not comfortable for her.

Supervisor: It feels empty.

Candidate: It feels empty and she feels very needy and hollow.

Supervisor: And lonely.

Candidate: And very lonely. When she's able to be with me not as her false self, she doesn't feel those dissatisfactions, but she has lots of conflictive feelings that she's not used to dealing with.

Supervisor: Right. The issue, you see, is that she knows that it's a false self. No matter what anybody else says, she knows that "if they knew what I was really like, they wouldn't love me." So no matter what anybody said, no matter how attractive or pleasant or enjoyable or how nice to her or wanting to love her or wanting to have sex with her they were, none of that has any lasting impact because she herself knows—

Candidate: That it's just a phony—

Supervisor: That it's an "as if" quality. And she therefore projects this "If they knew what I know, they wouldn't like me. So whatever they say that shows they like me means nothing."

Candidate: Well, she herself expresses it, similarly, I think, but with a little different tinge to it. She says that in her real fear, she has never been satisfied.

Supervisor: Uh-huh.

Candidate: She could never get enough. When she would say I want, I want, I want with her parents in her behavior, she would get things, nice things, but feel dissatisfied with them. Not feel held. She wants to be held, and lots of other feeling-tone things, so she would never feel satisfied and she felt empty inside. She describes also the erection of this false self part of her as a defense against the emptiness and to fill the emptiness, although it fills it unsatisfactorily; then she had an experience—she was at Ted's adoptive parents' house. They were over there for dinner and that's apparently, in her experience, kind of an open and free, accepting, loving family that may cuss at you but likes you anyway. I think it was there, but anyway somewhere she was in a family situation. There was a little girl who sounds like she was about six or seven, and the patient was talking to this little girl and listening to her. The little girl was telling her and they were listening to each other. Then the little girl, a little later in the evening, came and pressed her body right up against the patient. "Pressed her whole body," she just kept saying, "her whole body right up against me." And she felt so uncomfortable that she wondered if she would be able to tolerate having a child. It was stirring something up in her and that wasn't right, it was wrong. And I referred that into her fantasy. She has said all along that any wishes for physical intimacy that she might have with me are not, are just, are *wrong*. You don't get *touched* by women and that feeling of wrongness hasn't given way to, you're bad because you're afraid. That means you're homosexual. It's just this kind of pervasive feeling along with the pervasive feeling that it's wrong to touch yourself. It's wrong to want to be held by a woman. Then she also remembers that in her family nobody touched anybody. There was never any lap-sitting that she remembers. She remembers body hungers in bed at night and holding herself or wanting to go be someplace, except when she would sleep with her mother that was how she would get held. But like everyday sitting in somebody's lap or getting—there just didn't seem to be any. It's an uncomfortable area for her. I don't get it all yet. I don't know what it's all about, except when this little girl pressed up against her it made her uncomfortable inside, and it was in this context of making things appear right and the confused feelings inside.

Supervisor: It is also, you see, a contrast; the little girl is expressing herself directly, openly, and is directly in touch with what she wants.

Candidate: And saying so.

Supervisor: The patient cannot tolerate that in herself, can't allow herself to be aware of that.

Candidate: Okay, so it's a challenge of that specific defense, not just a challenge of her early yearning, a stirring up of her early yearnings. Not just a stirring up of her early yearnings, but a challenge of this.

Supervisor: That's right. And the little girl, you see, is getting from her what she, the patient, wants from you but can't admit to wanting from you. But to see somebody else admit that they want it and go after it makes her feel all the more her inhibition, her isolation, her loneliness. Her wish that she could have been and still could be like that little girl and press herself up against you.

Candidate: And get.

Supervisor: And get. And that is, again, a strategic resistance, the yearning to still get, which today she's going to have to renounce because she can't have it. She's going to want it and yearn for it and have to cry about never having had it. But eventually she's going to have to give it up.

Candidate: She's going to have to stop this glossing over for a significant period of time.

Supervisor: That's right. She's going to have to realize and let you know that "that's what I want from you and I'm never going to get it."

Candidate: This has been of interest to me all along, it's just been nagging at me since the beginning of this analysis. I swear in the first week of it she said—she didn't use these words, at the moment I can't remember her exact words—that she is a real and authentic person way in there somewhere in her fat and behind her fat.

Supervisor: Uh-huh.

Candidate: Inside her and behind this other person that the world sees. If she could just get out. And off and on she would refer to—it's as if she will say, it's as if she created this complicated—hiding is the wrong word, it's not a word she would use—this complicated camouflage game and then got trapped in it and can't get out. But the sense of two experiences of her has been expressed from the very beginning.

Supervisor: I don't know if I have ever recommended it to you, but a very, very practical, very useful paper is "Rivalry with the Product."

Candidate: It's an interesting title.

Supervisor: It's by a man by the name of Nathaniel Ross (1960) in the *Journal of the American Psychoanalytic Association* about twenty years ago. It focuses essentially on anal productivity and the child's rivalry with, jealousy of, resentment of, what it produces.

Candidate: What the child produces.

Supervisor: What the child produces. Because the child wants to be loved for himself and thinks he's being loved for what he produces, so he hates the very thing that he produces.

Candidate: And sabotages.

Supervisor: He sabotages it and also feels empty and feels he can't ever accept anything because he never knows, "Is it for me or is it for my feces? Is it for me or is it because I'm submissive?" Now to some extent, you see, she's manifesting that same process. "Is it me or is it my false self? Is it me or is it this illusion that people care for?" So that on the one hand—

Candidate: "Love me fat and then I will lose weight."

Supervisor: So that on the one hand she wants to be loved, but she hates the fact that they love her for this illusion that she's created.

Candidate: Oh, yes, intense.

Supervisor: And therefore she can't take any satisfaction from the love that is offered.

Candidate: Because it's not her.

Supervisor: Because it's not her, exactly. I would look up that article because it might be applicable in this particular constellation as a direct interpretation to her.

Candidate: Uh-huh.

Supervisor: And what she needs, you see, is to experience with you—and this is where you are beginning to challenge this defense as important—that you *can* see her as she is and not as this illusion, and still accept her. She can be the authentic person she is in here, in a transference experience for you.

Candidate: And I won't blow up and I won't dwindle and get depressed. Like the first day back from the time I took off, I think I probably did look awful. (Laughs) I mean I tried not to, but I'm sure I did, and she's real good at picking up those cues.

Supervisor: Uh-huh.

Candidate: And she wanted to come so badly. She had missed me a whole lot, and the minute she saw me, she then had to struggle against this false self, because her fantasy then, that if she wants me with those real wantings, she'll dwindle me down.

Supervisor: Uh-huh.

Candidate: So those are two different ages, I think, of that experience. One that she dried her mother up and ate her up and then dwindled her and withered her, and the other that she explodes her father.

Supervisor: Now, I have a patient, I *had* a patient, who expressed the same set of processes in the image of a balloon. He and I were balloons. Either I blew him up, but then as he blows up I shrink, or he blows me up, in which case *he* shrinks. It's always this same exchange of air back and forth, where one of us is big and the other is shrunk. And that's what she's doing. So she has to have the experience—

Candidate: But in addition to her needing it, she said last week before the break and during the period of time that all of this was coming out, she has only felt that she's too much for everybody. She definitely feels like she's too much for herself, her real self is too much for herself. She's always felt she's too much for everybody, and the only way people can tolerate her really is if she keeps things on the up and up. And if she really dumps on me, I will either blow up and get crazy or I will dwindle and wither and get depressed and have to take time off to rest up from her. That's one of her fantasies about weekends and time off, that I need them because she's just so too much.

Supervisor: That's an area that you again and again have to interpret—her defenses against showing you what her real self, her authentic person, really wants and needs. And she's going to have to run the risk that she's going to destroy you in the process, and then live through the realization that it isn't so.

That's where she, in a sense, can have a second chance to relive this conflicted childhood configuration, and have it come out different, because you are not going to respond the way the transference figures did, either by pushing her away or by being the person who can't tolerate what she really is.

Candidate: Just as a passing, aside kind of thing, I'm curious about the fact that I have gone from having a son to a daughter. I think that that's interesting. I asked her for more specifics about it, and she said that she's recently become aware that she's no longer sure that I have a son, that she thinks I have two other children, a boy and a girl. And it was abundantly clear from the phrasing of that sentence that it was two other children besides her.

Supervisor: Uh-huh.

Candidate: And that the most recent one, the one a year and a half ago, was a girl. And then it all takes over, this kind of everything-is-rosy, chestnuts-roasting-on-a-fire quality to it, which has to mean something. A shift in her use of me? Or she is giving me now the family that she fantasized for herself?

Supervisor: Right.

Candidate: Which is very different from my having a son or her hating his guts. And my loving him more than I love her.

Supervisor: But, you see, it's also a step in the direction of an authentic, if you want to call it that, self. It's possible to be a girl and be loved.

Candidate: That's the part I noticed first as she said it: I could love a girl? You know.

Supervisor: Uh-huh.

Candidate: A girl would be enough.

Supervisor: And you see, as primitive as it sounds, there are patients who in this transference experience will say, "If you ever saw me naked and knew that I was a girl, you'd get rid of me; you wouldn't love me. You would be disgusted with me. It's only because you don't know what I am." Fantasies then of an illusory, hidden penis, aren't really a boy, that sort of thing, but a defense against or an expression of this fantasy and the conflict connected with it—"If I'm a girl I'm unlovable, so I hide from the fact that I am a girl or that I can be an attractive girl."

Candidate: Uh-huh.

Supervisor: You see again, "If I am fat, then it is not surprising that you don't love me. But if I make myself as attractive as I can—"

Candidate: Now she has something to blame the emptiness on.

Supervisor: Right.

Candidate: All she has—it puts it within the realm of her control—all she has to do is go on a diet and this beautiful person will emerge. Which she does not believe in anymore, and that makes her nervous. She does not believe anymore that there is this perfectly formed beautiful glamour model underneath all this fat. She believes that it is more likely that there is an attractive, ordinary woman underneath there.

Supervisor: Uh-huh.

Candidate: But it's always put within the realm of her control. She's remembered feeling the same way she feels about her body now even before she gained weight, but feeling at odds with it. Like what do you do about it? Not what you do about her body, but what do you do about the feelings—how does she fix it? And it got easier after she got fat. Then the way that you fix it is that you go on a diet, and the way you fix that is that you never go on a diet, you just think about going on a diet.

Supervisor: Yeah, obviously there is this rivalry, "Do you love me, or do you love my thin attractive body?" But there is also another element here. If she attempts to be as attractive as she can, goes on a diet, loses the weight, wears attractive clothing, thinks of herself as all right, she still cannot force you to love her. So she gives you the power to say yes or no. If she is all within herself and the reason you do not love me is because I am fat, then it gives her the illusion of control.

Candidate: She's got it all. She had an interesting series of events happen to her—I have seen her once since I came back—and she related them. On Monday she went home to her parents' house and came back; it was great to have Ted there, he's a stabilizing influence for her. She came back—I think this is the order in which it took place. She got interested, she began to feel sexual and got interested in him sexually in a playful kind of way. She got up to go to the bathroom, and it hurt when she urinated. She went back, he was real interested in sex and "came on to me hard" and she got *furious* and upset and got out of bed, just like that, and spent the whole next day puking, spent the whole night puking. She came to her appointment the next day, which is a real step in the right direction for this young lady. She came to her appointment, looking like she just dragged herself off the bathroom floor, and related this series of events. So somehow sex, somehow the sexual fantasies and the urethral stricture are wound into here in a way that I am sure will get clearer in time. I just kind of leave this in for right now.

Supervisor: But also, you see, the fact that she came looking the way she did is a movement in the direction of allowing you to see what she is really like.

Candidate: She came; she would usually cancel that appointment and come a couple of days later.

Supervisor: When everything is okay.

Candidate: Yeah, and, you know, just more or less okay. But she came in jeans, and she lay down on the couch. It did not look like, well, like sometimes she does. Like she says that this false self she created for herself was either unrealistically horrible or unrealistically beautiful, but it never was real. She would either come in and be all upset and terribly depressed, and even her depression did not have a sturdy ring of her real feelings to her, and she would either present me one and the rest of the world one or the other of these poles. But the upset that she brought in on Tuesday was her, I thought.

Supervisor: See, again, in terms of needs to establish control in this way she maintains a sense of control—

Candidate: The illusion.

Supervisor: Of control of the situation. It is an illusion but in the sense, "I am in charge and whatever happens is because of me." What she cannot tolerate and what is most threatening to her is to allow you the choice of loving her or not loving her.

Candidate: And allow that she cannot do anything about it.

Supervisor: Right, that is in some ways the most threatening and devastating position to be in. And it is another reason that she keeps up this artificial game.

Candidate: Another reason why she wants to make me need her. And that is another piece in her illusion of control, that she runs around and makes people need her. And she has insinuated herself into her parents' relationship in such a way that they are very dependent on her—they *do* need her.

Supervisor: And they follow her all the time—

Candidate: And they call her all the time—

Supervisor: And ask her advice—

Candidate: And blah blah blah, because it's that extra piece of safety.

Supervisor: That's right. So these are the issues she emanates. It's not so much that this is going to be a new and revolutionary insight, it's a matter of repetitively getting into it, working it over—

Candidate: It's been very helpful to me, because it's been helpful to see this global glossiness in some way other than withholding or, you know, the various ways in which I was able to see it before. It gives me another way to interpret it and another way to understand what she has been telling me.

Supervisor: But this then is another illustration of how an analyst thinks and works; you can use your interpretive processes like you have about the specific narrow meanings that the behavior might have had. Keep bringing it up and you find new ones, another one and another one. If the behavior persists, you sort of stand back and say to yourself, "What meaning am I missing? What *else* does this thing mean?" And this is where you then oscillate between the microscopic, the specific thing, and standing back and looking at the trees, the whole forest away from the trees, at the macroscopic, and you begin to come up with new configurations or new meanings that the behavior may have. Add those interpretations and wait to see whether the interpretation changes the behavior. If it does, fine; if it doesn't, then you have to say to yourself, "All right, why hasn't it changed? Where am I missing something?" And you look for some other meaning.

Candidate: Well, I feel like things are going okay in this.

Supervisor: Okay. Yes.

Candidate: Are you going to the meetings?

Supervisor: Yes. So two weeks from today I won't be here.

Candidate: And I'll not be working for the two weeks or so around Christmas.

Supervisor: So our next time will be six weeks from now.

Candidate: Thank you very much.

Supervisor: Have a nice holiday.

Candidate: You too. (Here the candidate shows the supervisor a picture of her daughter.) There's the youngest family member. I just picked up the pictures on my way here.

Supervisor: Oh! Interesting. Very sweet, very nice. How old is she now?

Candidate: Nineteen months. A good age.

Supervisor: Bye-bye.

Supervisor's Comments

There is an increased sense of informality and interchange, illustrated by the remarks about tape recording, as well as her comments about the illness of her father-in-law and the supervisor's acceptance and response to this information. This suggests that candidate and supervisor are comfortable in their interactions, and an increasingly collegial atmosphere has evolved.

The candidate spontaneously initiates the case material, expressing herself in a style which is focused not on detailed process notes but on synthetic and summarizing comments. By this time the supervisor has confidence in her and is no longer concerned that the candidate provide immediate and direct primary data. In describing her intervention, the candidate alludes to a paper written by the supervisor (Dewald, 1980) on different varieties of resistance and defense; she nevertheless continues (without comment from the supervisor) to present the material in a summarizing fashion. In describing the patient's defensive style, the candidate is able to make use of her own experience and associations, as illustrated by her comparing it with behavior observed at a cocktail party. This leads to an interpretation of the defensive style as similar to the patient's guarded behavior with her parents. The supervisor's immediate praise—"good"—serves to reinforce what the candidate had spontaneously done.

The candidate is able to describe the effect of that interpretation, as well as admit that she no longer clearly recalls the detailed material. The supervisor follows with a conceptual explanation of clinical theory with regard to the transference of defenses into the analytic process and experience. The candidate demonstrates her capacity to recognize and synthesize the patient's defensive behavior patterns, and to recognize that there is more than the patient has yet been able to express.

The candidate responds to the supervisor's explanation of the "narrow elements of meaning" with a recognition that this had been her own idea. The supervisor continues his explanation of the style of interaction with the parents that is being reenacted in the transference, and distinguishes tactical and strategic resistances. The candidate has some confusion at this conceptual level, and the supervisor repeats his attempt to clarify the issues, alluding to the paper mentioned earlier (Dewald, 1980).

Returning to the case material, the candidate describes the patient's interpersonal and intrapsychic responses to her father's behavior, which serve to clarify the genetic origins of the specific defense discussed earlier. The supervisor elaborates on the patient's earlier experience as it relates to the development of a particular defensive style, and suggests a transference interpretation that might be appropriate. The candidate recognizes the transference experience, and the supervisor immediately supports and reinforces her understanding ("That's right").

The candidate reports the patient's positive response to the resistance interpretation, also demonstrating her sensitivity to the patient's nonverbal, affectively toned behavioral shifts. The patient's capacity to shift her behavior in response to the candidate's interpretation has a number of implications with regard to the analytic process. The therapeutic alliance is well established, permitting the patient to tolerate the candidate's comments without feeling unduly criticized; there is a tacit invitation from the candidate to the patient, to which the latter responds positively, to be more open and direct and to reduce the intensity of her defenses. In other words, there is further identification with the analyst's function in the therapeutic alliance, as well as a capacity to correct the transference expectation of criticism or attack in response to self-revelation.

The candidate then shifts levels to mention a theoretical issue—the "false self"—but continues with the patient's material in regard to character structure, style, and the way in which she related to other figures in her family. Apparently the patient was capable of significantly modifying her behavior in order to achieve gratification and praise from her parents, in spite of unresolved and unmodified intrapsychic self-experience and self-images; as a result, though her external behavior was significantly modified in adolescence, her intrapsychic state remained relatively unchanged. The candidate can recognize without undue anxiety how the patient idealizes her and can accept the patient's needs for positive fantasies of a family background and how these are reenacted in the transference. These are all evidence of the analyst's increasing capacity to function in a sensitive and therapeutically appropriate fashion. She is capable of sophisticated observation as well as of moving from primary data to theoretical concepts; the latter is illustrated by her apparent interest, even as she is in the analytic situation, in the concept of "false self."

The supervisor begins a series of explanatory interventions in regard to the nature of resistances and the patient's wish to reenact, repeat, and achieve gratification. The candidate has an animated and affective response, as seen in the analogy she draws to the imaginary playmate. At that point the supervisor returns to the theoretical issue of the false self, raised earlier by the candidate, and discusses it at the level of metapsychological theory—intrasystemic and intersystemic conflict. Candidate and supervisor then enter a give-and-take in which both oscillate between experience-near clinical data and more experience-distant theoretical abstraction. The participation by both candidate and supervisor is indicative of an active and animated learning process.

Returning to the description of the patient's material, the

candidate demonstrates a capacity to understand, recognize, and accept the patient's early homosexual transference fantasies, as well as the anxiety the patient is experiencing in regard to such wishes, and a capacity to elicit further elaborations by direct interpretation of this material. Here the candidate demonstrates her tolerance of the patient's transference impulses, thereby providing the patient a model of comfortable acceptance and willingness to elaborate and explore such material. The supervisor supports this by explaining the patient's transference wish in a slightly more conceptual way, thereby encouraging the candidate to further understand and accept the patient's homosexual transference. At the same time, the supervisor is explaining how in the treatment process transference activation must ultimately be replaced by tolerance of the transference wishes but renunciation of their gratification.

The candidate then uses the supervisor's explanation to synthesize material from early in the analysis, thereby further consolidating her understanding of how analytic material can be understood later, whereas at the beginning of analysis it may appear remotely derivative and therefore cannot be used.

As part of this interchange and the associations it evokes in the supervisor, he recommends an article to the candidate (Ross, 1960), discussing in general terms its relevance to the current clinical material. As part of this, the supervisor once again attempts an empathic description of what the patient may be experiencing, correlating this with the literature he has just recommended, and there is an interchange between candidate and supervisor elaborating the points just made. This leads to an explanation of how the patient is reliving earlier development and experiences as a result of transference regression. But in the current version the patient is able to relive in a different manner issues that originally had resulted in developmental arrest or distortion, thereby arriving at an emotionally new experience and a resolution of the issue.

The candidate acknowledges this and appreciates how the patient's transference experience and expectations are part of this reliving. The supervisor uses his own clinical experience to elaborate the point, thereby generalizing the issues beyond the immediate case. The patient's transference distortions are addressed, and the supervisor explains how the patient needs to reexperience conflicted childhood configurations with the analyst and to find, through her own experience, how to correct these distortions.

The candidate demonstrates her learning and development through a recognition of a transference shift in which the patient experiences her having had a daughter *in contrast to a son,* and the candidate expresses the attendant feelings by means of a metaphor—chestnuts roasting on a fire. The supervisor points out how this shift in the transference experience represents the beginning of an authentic expression of the internal self, thereby returning to the false self issue raised earlier by the candidate. The supervisor seeks to generalize from the regressive transference experience by emphasizing variations on the same theme from other cases. The candidate responds in an affective way with regard to her own patient's experience.

Candidate and supervisor participate in active dialogue in regard to the patient's dynamic processes, in the course of which the candidate alludes to a central traumatic experience of repeated medical treatment for a urethral stricture during early childhood. This had come up many times in the past, in derivatives as well as conscious memories. The candidate can appreciate the patient's increasing sense of authenticity, inasmuch as she came to her session even though disheveled and unhappy. The candidate recognizes the shift on her own: earlier the patient would have canceled her session until the issues were under active control.

Once again candidate and supervisor engage in active dialogue, the candidate developing a deeper appreciation of the patient's defensive behavior. The supervisor takes this opportunity to show how an analyst oscillates between microscopic and macroscopic observation of the patient's material, and needs continually to search for new and previously unconscious meanings.

The session ends, as it began, on a collegial, personal, and informal note, relating to the arrangement for the next supervisory hour and absences around the Christmas holidays and

American Psychoanalytic Association meetings. Before leaving, the candidate shows the supervisor a picture of her daughter, to which he responds with personal interest.

Chapter 10
Supervisory Session 88

Candidate: I am unprepared for this, but I did do my case summary for the site visit. I think I just want to let off steam about how frustrating this lady is. She is so withholding that at times she could incite me to riot if I didn't do it outside of sessions. She and my twenty-month-old daughter have a lot in common. I can't decide if she's teasing me. I don't think she's doing any of this consciously, but the effect on me is telling me something. I can't decide if she's teasing me. She'll come and she'll get into something and really start to work. There's one particular session I could read you that would illustrate this, but in short there was a lot of affect and it wasn't phony. But then she won't come until it's all cooled down. And I know that part of that is diluting, and that part of it is her reaction to one of the things she's real mad about. She came in once, one particular session was a real—well, I should preface this by saying I haven't seen her very much since I saw you last. She'll come two sessions and skip two sessions and come two sessions and skip another two. I think she skipped on a Thursday and a Monday, and then came on Tuesday and was enraged. She was so mad at me. I just am a cold tit. Then it got around to—she went on for thirty minutes—how I was just like her mother. Then, with a lot of other things thrown in, it came around to when it was time to come today, to this session, she received a luncheon invitation she really wanted to accept—a big, important client. But she wanted to come to her session more than to go to this luncheon, and that enraged her. The whole thrust of it up until then was that she had to come and take care of me. And when she said that, she could see what she had done with it, that it was making her mad that she needed me, that she was dependent on me. On the weekends she doesn't want to come—one of the things that's making her mad is that it feels to her like it's on my terms. It felt to her like with her mother—it was on her mother's terms. Her mother was not available to her when she needed her. She had to catch her when her mother wasn't depressed or when her mother was available. With me, if she has a client lunch, if she has this, if she has that—for instance, one day she was preparing for something and couldn't come, but by four o'clock that afternoon she was ready to talk to me. And it just infuriated her that I wasn't ready to talk to her then. And, of course, she can't call me if she can't ask for anything, because my husband will get mad at her. My husband doesn't like my working, he's resentful, or he would be furious with her just like she pictures her father. All that's good work. And then she doesn't come. At least it seems to me like good work.

Supervisor: Now what meanings have you and she worked out as to what it means that she doesn't come?

Candidate: Well, diluting the intensity of her feelings and being able to generalize them. Diffuse, transfer the transference, hate somebody at work. For instance, she was starting to do that a little bit in this session where she was so mad at me, and it was just like a tiny sideline that I caught when I read it. But I know it goes on all the time. For instance, she wanted to go to lunch with her client because there's this new bitch who works in her office who's a real man-eater. She wanted to be able to go and successfully compete with this lady, which is a splitting of a piece of the transference. She does that and that's been interpreted again and again, without nagging her about it, and she recognizes that she does it, but more or less after the fact. So diffusing the intensity of the transference—I don't know what to call this in psychoanalysis, but I think it makes her more comfortable to deal with part of the transference in the analysis and part of it outside the analysis than to have it all in one place. It has something to do, I think, with ambivalence. It simplifies it somehow to have only one set of feelings about me.

Supervisor: So she splits the transference.

Candidate: So in order to split the transference she is withholding. Doing it at her convenience proves to me she doesn't need me, that she can—and proves to herself that she doesn't need me, that she can do things when she needs to do them. Right now, in the last month, she's in the midst of being really incensed to discover that she does need, on a really deep level, me, Ted, relationships with people in general. The breakdown of the defense that she would never again let herself be in a position where she ever needed anybody has incensed her. Every time she comes up against anything that tells her again that she does have these needs, it infuriates her. Sometimes she reacts against that recognition and does things to prove she doesn't. So about withholding: she'll give me herself when she wants to. It's been a while since those interpretations have been made, an interpretation I haven't figured out how to make yet because I'm not sure what it is. Is it some sense of control over me? Because if she only comes at the rate she's been coming, and it coincided with—she was coming more frequently and I pointed this out to her. She was coming more frequently until—I used her words for this, though I can't remember what they were. Whenever she started to deal again with her fantasies of castration and oedipal fantasies and the urethral stricture, suddenly she got very busy at work and stopped being able to come so regularly. When she comes infrequently and brings tons of material when she does come, I think she knows I can't catch it all. How do I say this?

Supervisor: And this pattern occurred after she'd begun to talk about the urethral stricture?

Candidate: After she'd begun to talk about it *again*.

Supervisor: Again. Oh, all right.

Candidate: The last time you and I met she had just reapproached—remember she said, "I don't want to talk about it?" She had the dream of the tiny baby. It wouldn't hurt to have that baby. She walked around in her associations and I said, "The size of the penis," and she said, "Yes," that was her initial association but she didn't want to think about it. She didn't want to talk about it. Then we spent a session or two on how she's not sure how much of the initial interpretations that were made of that she just complied with and she doesn't want to talk about it. I accepted that but also interpreted her resistance to get into it, to explore it. It's not just that she doesn't want to talk about it because I may cram something down her throat. She doesn't want to talk about it because she doesn't want to explore something new. That happened one week and that was it. Then she started skipping.

Supervisor: You see, when you run up against a pattern like this and it seems to be this stubborn, you've got to ask yourself: What other potential meanings does it have?

Candidate: That's why I'm blowing off steam here.

Supervisor: What's it say? One of the things you've described is that she doesn't come for quite a while and then she gives you everything.

Candidate: She *floods* me.

Supervisor: And floods you.

Candidate: And I *feel* flooded.

Supervisor: Do you think perhaps she is reenacting the urethral stricture?

Candidate: Is she doing it to me?

Supervisor: No, no.

Candidate: Is she—okay, go ahead.

Supervisor: Was it painful for her every time she urinated? Does she therefore wait and hold her urine as long as she could and then get it all out and just have it once? And then a long period of time in between?

Candidate: She did do that. She's described that.

Supervisor: So, is this her reenactment of that pattern?

Candidate: And, in the sessions that she does come, the predominant material, besides her frustration at the dependency which is kind of a clumsy thing, the predominant material *is* the urethral stricture. Not directly, but her associations will be she dreamed about—remember some time ago she used to have a girl friend that was a displacement of a transference? This girl friend got married and then got pregnant and had a baby and shut her out and the patient was enraged at her. She hasn't talked about or thought about that girl friend for a long time.

But the other night she had a dream in which that girl friend was married and being very nice to her, on the surface very sweet, and everything was okay except there was this peculiar thing: the patient was married to this girl friend's husband and the girl friend somehow didn't know it. And she knew that all hell would break loose if the girl friend found out. She associated—I didn't even have to ask her, that was the session in which I said very little—she just—whooo!—She wanted to have her father, marry her father, that her mother found out, that she even thinks her mother thought she was pregnant. Because she had the urethral stricture in conjunction with her mother having this baby. That's just come up recently, that she doesn't know whether it was right after or right before Harold was born and maybe she thought *she* was pregnant and her mother had her aborted or broke her. Then an association to her terror when she had intercourse for the first time. But her major terrors have always been that she would get pregnant, and she has stopped menstruating now. She is not pregnant. She's been to a doctor; she's not pregnant, she's just not menstruating. And she feels like a eunuch.

Supervisor: I see. So what she's doing, she's reenacting then, and shifting this from her thoughts to her actions.

Candidate: To her, kind of, whole experience.

Supervisor: To the whole experience of the analysis, where she would come and let it all out—

Candidate: And it hurts terribly—

Supervisor: Floods you and it hurts terribly for a short time, but then you wait and try to make it as long as possible before you have to go again.

Candidate: And you hate that you have to go.

Supervisor: So are you beginning to think along those lines, as to what kind of meaning this has?

Candidate: Uh-huh.

Supervisor: So you see the whole analytic process involves a stream of associations.

Candidate: That's beautiful, because I've been looking for that.

Supervisor: A stream of words, communication, verbal things, letting it all hang out. You name it, these are all imagery by which this can have a urethral meaning for her and be a reenactment of both the trauma and the defense against it.

Candidate: A defense against being an avoidance of it until it's absolutely necessary.

Supervisor: So she can't help it.

Candidate: And that gives me new—I've been looking for this in the material with respect to what I'm going to write my paper on. And I think from time to time about this. I think there has to be a way in which this—if it is an organizer in some way for this girl, not the thing that made her neurotic but an organizer—then there has to be a kind of *big picture* pattern like that. I just started looking for that or thinking about it on Friday, and that's what I was looking for. To some extent it makes her rage at my unavailability make more sense, because one of the things in her thinking my husband would be mad or I would be mad if she called me that she's been able to describe to me so far, is the notion, around the experience of the urethral stricture, that she couldn't tell her mother that it hurt because she was sure she had done something wrong. She felt her mother wasn't available to her, either because she pushed her away or her mother was involved in this new baby or whatever, but she couldn't tell her. She had to bear it all herself until she stopped being able to urinate. And then she had to tell her mother because it was a crisis. On the weekends the pain builds upward and she can't reach me, reach out to me. It's not that she can't reach me, that she calls me and I'm not there. She can't call me for some unspecified reason, because she will feel guilty and because I would be disappointed. She can never quite get to a specified reason. But I think the reason is similar to whatever reasons she couldn't tell her mother when it first started to hurt when she was urinating.

Supervisor: Because, among other things, her mother can't stop the pain. You see, this way she has the fantasy, "If I could tell mother, then she would stop the pain." But to tell her mother, and her mother still can't stop the pain, means either mother hates me or wants me to suffer, or that she is as helpless as I am.

Candidate: So one of the turning-around things is a kind of defensive maneuver that's pervasive in this lady. I need her, her seeing that I need her, and what she's mad at is that she needs me. So that perhaps the feeling that if she calls me on the weekends I would be disappointed in her is that *she* would be disappointed in *me.* If she begged her mother or told her mother it was hurting and her mother couldn't fix it, the disappointment would be too much because—

Supervisor: That's it.

Candidate: Another thread through this is that her parents and I have been disappointing in our lack of omnipotence.

Supervisor: I see. If she tells Mother that it hurts and Mother is omnipotent, then she will stop the pain. She tells Mother it hurts and Mother can't stop or doesn't stop the pain, or Mother get more and more uptight—because you see, what you're feeling now is how frustrated, how on edge, how angry you feel at her, how you want her to get on with this thing. You must think what the mother must have felt when this girl would scream and scream and scream. The mother is trying her best to stop the pain, feeling upset, increasingly uptight, and the child can't be soothed and the mother feels increasingly helpless.

Candidate: And they had been through that once before. This is the second time. Not with the urethral stricture, but with her bowel habits. They had been through the pain of elimination and her mother saying, "If you eat more you'll be able to go to the bathroom." Then the kid trying, supposedly, and withholding at the same time. So she has a base of experience before she even gets to the urethral stricture.

Supervisor: Right. So all of this, you see, is what this behavior pattern is all about, and it serves several functions simultaneously. Among other things, it frustrates you and gets even with you; it creates a situation of distance and tension between you. It also, however, preserves her hope that you could stop the pain if you knew. But she is never going to ask, so therefore "if you don't stop the pain, it's not because you're not omnipotent; it's because you don't know. And if I ever did ask you, *then* you could do it." It preserves that image. But it also serves getting back at you, serves to frustrate you; it serves to make you suffer with her.

Candidate: Why does she have the fantasy (maybe I know this) why does she have the fantasy that if she calls me, she knows I would not see her? Like if she calls me on Friday and says, "I have to see you tomorrow." She knows I'm not going to see her. That's why she doesn't call me. I'd be mad at her. But then she says that it would really scare her to death if I did see her. And I think she's right. I mean I don't think that that's all fantasy. A long time ago I changed an appointment because she wanted it changed and it was no skin off my nose—in fact, I think it was more convenient. And there was trouble. I can remember thinking, I'm never going to do that again. And you and I talked about it, but maybe that has meaning in another frame, in terms of getting what she wants and how far will I go to give her what she wants, a kind of ultimate seduction.

Supervisor: Yeah, I think you can see a relationship. As you listen to this girl and observe what she does, try to keep in mind the picture of a little girl in chronic pain, helpless to do anything about it herself, and with a mother also helpless to do anything about it. What must the little girl feel and what must the mother feel and what must the little girl then think about what the mother feels? Many people who are actual child abusers, for example, tell you that what happens is they got increasingly uptight because the kid wouldn't stop crying. They had to shut the kid up at all costs because to hear the kid go on crying and screaming made them too uncomfortable. I would suspect that something like that happened between your patient and her mother.

Candidate: And that, then, may be the basis of some of this, *some* of her sense that her mother kept going away.

Supervisor: Yeah, but it may also be partly a sense of, "I don't want my mother to come." If she asks you to come and see her on Saturday, it's like Mother being called into the bathroom one more time, or Mother being called into the bedroom one more time because the girl is still screaming, and the mother getting furious and saying, "Now stop it," and slapping her or doing some other horrible thing. "So don't come in. I don't want you to come because that's what I'll get if you come."

Candidate: Well, and that's her experience, but it's not those details yet, but that's the experience of her memory, the way she relates it. When she did tell her mother, her mother called the pediatrician and took her to a urologist, who then hurt her with the mother watching. So he was the mother's arm.

Supervisor: So "I want Mother to be there to do something for me, and when Mother is here, it makes it worse. It just hurts more." But also, I would suspect, as I say, the mother must have been at the end of her tether with this kind of pain and inability to do anything about it and the child screaming and hurting and dribbling a little urine and having enormous pain. The mother finally getting furious. I'm basing this, you see, on your *own* feeling that you're ready to blow off steam at this girl; this is what she's induced in you, and that must be what happened when she was a child.

Candidate: Well, and I think it's—if I base it on my feelings, what I think happened when she was a child is that her mother got furious with her for not telling her.

Supervisor: Uh-huh, that's possible.

Candidate: For not giving her the chance to help her.

Supervisor: Exactly.

Candidate: For letting it get so bad that it was an emergency, not in the sense of her not wanting to take care of an emergency, but not having been able to take care of the child because the child didn't tell her, because that's how *I* feel. Here is a girl who's in trouble, she's hurting, she's got a lot of things going in a lot of different directions, she brings it in, she splurts it all over the office and I feel like I could help her. You know, like the process would help her.

Supervisor: If she only would let you.

Candidate: If she would let me. But then she goes beyond my reach and she doesn't bring it to me anymore and I have no—I'm powerless.

Supervisor: Yeah. You see, this is what I think of as the creative use of the countertransference, where feelings get evoked in you and you ask yourself: Is this part of what the patient is seeking to do? Is this part of an early constellation of interaction and experience being reenacted here? And if so, from what? This is an illustration of how you can use these feelings that are engendered in you constructively, to reconstruct what it must have been like when she was growing up. Then you use that as the basis of your—

Candidate: How do you use it technically?

Supervisor: Well, by grasping it—

Candidate: As the basis of my understanding?

Supervisor: That's how you use it. And from there on you interpret in that framework.

Candidate: Okay. You wait for data then and use that framework of understanding—

Supervisor: To frame your interpretation: "I think at times you must have the feeling," when she says, "You know I can't call you at home." "I think at times there must be a fear that if I get upset, it's like what happened with your mother. She was unable to help," or, "I think at times the feeling you have that you're in this all by yourself must have been the way you felt as a child when nobody could do anything that would relieve your pain." When she says, "It will just make it worse for you to be around."

Candidate: Or that I will get mad when she tells me she needs something.

Supervisor: Then you would use this as a form—

Candidate: Maybe, like a kid running out in the street. You know, if they don't get run over, your impulse is to knock their block off. That's the kind of feeling—it's different, but it's the kind of feeling I think might have gone on with her mother, of "Why didn't you tell me before?"

Supervisor: So this is the way you use this material or this understanding as the framework within which you can begin to interpret from a more objective position. "Could it be that this is what you want me to feel?" "Could it be that this is a reenactment of what happened to you as a child?" "I wonder if maybe pain that you are experiencing now, that you feel nobody can help you with, was like the pain that you had when you were a little girl." "I wonder if coming here only very intermittently is like holding back the urine so that you wouldn't have such hurt over and over again each time, and waiting as long as you can and then coming here to get it over with would be like urinating and then waiting as long as you could." "You told me how you used to hold it back, and in some ways you're doing the same thing with your thoughts." These are ways you can use it to frame the interpretation.

Candidate: What do you call that? Let me see if I can formulate this question. When you're talking about that kind of reexperiencing or repeating or reliving in the patient, that kind of—my impulse is to say global—what do you call it? Or do you just have to describe it?

Supervisor: Well, it's a transference reenactment or reenactment in the transference and countertransference, and then using that you reconstruct what the original situation must have been. If you want to read about that, read Greenacre's paper on constructions and reconstructions in analysis (1975). This would be using the current transference experience and how it makes you feel in the countertransference and how she's behaving in the transference, and you're using that observation of this reenactment. You're using the assumption she's reenacting something here, and then on the basis of your observation you reconstruct what she must have reenacted or what she experienced as a child. A patient of mine whose father committed suicide when she was a little girl, and who was not allowed to go to the funeral, comes in one day in the midst of a significant transference and says (I had been away on a week's vacation), "I knew you were on vacation. I knew very clearly; somebody told me where you were going, but I still kept looking for you all around town. Every place I went I was sure you were going to be there. And I kept looking and looking and looking, but I obviously never saw you and I'm glad you're back." Well, this was the transference experience. Now, the reconstruction from that experience was: "Because you didn't go to the funeral to see your father, you weren't ever sure that he was dead." This then led to a whole host of material that had never come up before about how every time she saw an older man she'd look into his eyes to see if it was her father. She couldn't believe that he was dead, and she kept looking for him, waiting for him to return. The transference experience was the manifest current reenactment, which led then to a reconstruction of what must have happened as a child, which in turn led to the uncovering and working through of that whole experience and process and new material.

Candidate: It's easy for me to see transference reenactment there, because it's almost a direct translation. The thing I am curious about at the moment and must be learning about because I'm looking for it in other cases, too, is this: nondirect translation and a structuring of experience around a more concrete experience. Like coming to sessions, peeing in my office only occasionally, is a less direct translation and almost verges on being a stylistic way of handling emotional experience. If that's not going too far. The development, somehow the taking, of something concrete, a specific experience, and making it into a style of—

Supervisor: It becomes a paradigm for her living experience.

Candidate: Yes, yes, and not just for dealing with similar things.

Supervisor: Uh-huh.

Candidate: But that's what I guess I mean by global. It is something that becomes stylistic. And this is a girl who works like that. She will work for a hundred and twenty hours, sleeping, you know, only when she just falls off her chair, and she will then—

Supervisor: Then what?

Candidate: Then she won't work for a while. She will just—well, she'll work. It's like there's a level of work she has to keep up in order to stay good and to do her job, but then she also has these incredible spurts. You know, she spurts in lots of directions.

Supervisor: Uh-huh.

Candidate: I guess that's a reenactment, but it's a reenactment in a more pervasive way.

Supervisor: Well, you see, this is the central—

Candidate: It's fascinating to me.

Supervisor: One of the central, organizing, core conflicts and fantasies. And the more central and the more traumatic or the more conflicted the original experience and the original set of feelings and the fantasies connected with them, the more pervasively will they be experienced in each and every element in the patient's life experience.

Candidate: And the more they become organizers or prisms or ways in which you experience all things or deal with them.

Supervisor: There is then developed a coherent, consistent, and persistent defensive style. This is a defensive style. In the original it was a defensive way of coping with—let's call it very intense traumatic, unbearable physical pain—which now gets broadened to coping with psychological pain or any other kind of situation. In that sense then, you see, it becomes a coherent ego style of how to adapt to or integrate with a particular set of conflicts.

Candidate: It's finding those things in a patient that makes it all make sense.

Supervisor: Another patient of mine, for example, who from the time he was about three or three and a half years old, was obsessional, very prissy about his clothing, very rigid in his behavior. He has pictures of himself from that age on, standing with virtually no expression and so on, memories and family myths about how he couldn't do this or couldn't do that, always standing on the outside, never could get dirty at recess, never could play with the other kids.

Candidate: Because of his own prohibitions.

Supervisor: Never athletic, because of all his inhibitions. Now in his current adult life he can't participate in sex, is constantly rigid in his behavior, very controlled, and in the analysis can't regress in service of the ego. He lies on the couch in a motionless way, never moves, the same rigidity, as a character style reenacted from the time he was a child right on through. Most patients, when they're on the couch they move or they turn over or they cross their legs and uncross them. This man lies flat, arms at his sides, and never moves.

Candidate: And from your description people can lie still and yet be relaxed. But it doesn't sound like he's—

Supervisor: Even psychologically, you see, he can't let himself go. He's got to have everything under control. Well, that's the kind of style, a major defensive ego organization, he uses now, partly because it was successful then and persists unchanged.

But it incorporates wider and wider segments of his behavior. Now, when a defensive style like this is unsuccessful, it wouldn't be adopted. Some other style would be used instead. Let's assume or say that this patient had been able—I'm trying to think how to hypothesize this. I'm thinking, for example, of my patient. Let's assume his "good" behavior fits in with the family constellation and they issue a reward for it. But let's assume he had a parent who wouldn't reward him for that kind of behavior. Then he'd have to adopt something else. With your patient, let's assume that the mother was somehow able to comfort or relieve her or would not get angry at her or in some other way handle this situation so that some other kind of interaction would take place; this style would be changed and some other style would have been adopted.

Candidate: In terms of the predominant defensive style.

Supervisor: Right. Or let's assume that the urethral stricture had been cleared up fairly promptly with topical anesthetics or whatever and it wasn't so painful to urinate; this would not have become her style.

Candidate: Uh-huh. Something else.

Supervisor: Something else would have taken its place.

Candidate: Maybe this also: Do you suppose this also is a source of her sense that if she lets herself go emotionally there will be these terrible outbursts which she has always associated with her father's outbursts?

Supervisor: Uh-huh.

Candidate: But that has never been enough. I mean, I understand these associations, but lots of people have explosive fathers and don't get it as deeply ingrained in them as she has, the sense that if she gets angry or if she lets her emotions out it will hurt terribly. It will be terrible, and so she had better just hold it all in.

Supervisor: So it might be the translation of her urinary problem into the area of her affective life.

Candidate: It's very exciting to see these things. All weekend I found that I was working on my other case, the summary. I was thinking there's something going on in this case that I can understand the whole case in terms of and has to do with the urethral stricture. Seems like, and I think I've been through this set of thoughts before, I think it's because I'm still learning, going through an analysis for the first time. This level of understanding makes everything, not everything but a lot of things, in the case make a lot more sense and have coherence for me. That then circles around and gives me more tolerance and I think I've been pretty tolerant of lacks of understanding. But this makes me feel even more tolerant of the myriad of loose ends earlier in a case, because of some sense that unless you reach the central organizers—I mean, everybody has a defensive style, and you must in a successful analysis come to understand the defensive style or you haven't gotten there. I'm still working. And this is a piece of her defensive style and I presume there's more to it but—

Supervisor: I've used before, I think, the metaphor of a tree. Any leaf in the tree, you can begin to trace it back; all the manifest behavior patterns or experiences or thoughts or feelings or affects or dreams or whatever can be equated to the leaves out there on the peripheral branches and twigs—any one of them will lead you eventually to the roots.

Candidate: Uh-huh.

Supervisor: But as you get in closer you come to grasp more and more but still there are, you know, various levels of branches—major branches, minor branches. You get into the trunk or the roots of the tree and then from there you can go back into any one of the others and it becomes a coherent structure.

Candidate: Yeah, and you don't have to worry about forgetting stuff.

Supervisor: That's right. Exactly.

Candidate: You know, things that have been said, that you have said and that have been written in the literature, the ways in which I've watched Jule Miller work—I ask him a question and he'll say, "Ehh, I don't know, you'll have to wait and see." All of that I have understood on one level, and now I think it's just the process of learning to be an analyst. It's gratifying to say this is how, this is why it's possible to tolerate, it's why you don't have to take notes forever, it's why, unless you want to for some specific reason, because—when I was doing my case summary for this, I didn't read my process notes. I thought all along that I was going to have to read all the process notes to do a case summary and I couldn't do case summaries because I was going to have to read, because I might forget something. But as the sense of, as my understanding gets greater, in the sense of this coherence the cases take on, that becomes unnecessary. I remember key dreams, or if I don't remember the details I remember enough, and if I feel particularly obsessive I can go look it up.

Supervisor: And if it isn't in one dream, you look in another.

Candidate: Yeah, yeah.

Supervisor: If it isn't one experience or symptom, it'll be another one.

Candidate: It comes up and comes up and the frantic feeling of being a beginning analyst three years ago, that of missing something or not, it just goes, and that sense of how it works out develops and I'm beginning to be convinced that nobody can tell you that. That's just something you have to experience. I mean it's been good to have people tell me that, it's been reassuring, but there is nothing like experiencing it.

Supervisor: What it also tells you is that there's a certain kind of unfolding that has to occur and you can't rush this process. You can sometimes get in its way or you sometimes accelerate it a little, but you can't rush through it to get to the point. Following any of these twigs, any one of these peripheral branches, you begin to get into the roots. And once you're there, then the whole thing maintains a kind of coherence. But until you get there, it seems fragmented or may at times seem random or incoherent.

Candidate: And that all of the little clues you have—my other patient is extremely obsessive. I mean, there is material from the end of the analysis presented on the first day. He is just so obsessive that his dreams are very detailed and full of very intellectual—or they used to be—full of stuff a beginning psych student could write tomes on. All of which is passingly interesting. It's never been *terribly* interesting to me, but passingly interesting in that it gives clues about what might come later.

But all along I've gone on the assumption that it's not important to understand all that, don't worry about it, just wait and when it's important it'll come up and you will understand it. But now I know that it's not important to understand it. That those are all clues, and that as it develops in the transference it will develop and become clear. I think the same kind of thing happened in this case, but I didn't feel as relaxed about it as I did in my second case. In my second case I just let all that stuff go by and worked purely at the level of the transference from the beginning. I didn't worry about the piranha fish biting off his finger when that wasn't where the transference was. Anyway, I'm just telling you something you already know about.

Supervisor: Uh-huh.

Candidate: I've done my second—do I just tell the Education Committee that I've done my second six-month summary? I'm going to ask to be cleared for a third case.

Supervisor: Okay.

Candidate: I have one that might become a third case, but I don't want to be counting my chickens.

Supervisor: You mean a patient you now have in therapy?

Candidate: I have a patient I have been seeing very cleanly, because from the first time I saw her I thought she needed analysis and I've just seen her since early November twice a week, and I've been very careful to keep it pure. I spoke to Nate Simon about it, and he said he didn't see any problem, considering I started out with that notion. I don't know if she will. Just as I say, I'm not counting my chickens, you know? And if you come across somebody else—

Supervisor: I'll let you know, sure. Okay, I'll see you then in a couple of weeks.

Candidate: Yeah. Now the week of the—I don't know if you meet that week anyway, the week of the site visit, if we do meet; we don't, right?

Supervisor: Yeah, right. Uh-huh.

Candidate: I haven't looked that far ahead.

Supervisor: Yeah. Okay, bye-bye.

Candidate: Thank you very much.

Supervisor: Uh-huh.

Supervisor's Comments

The candidate arrives in a state of affective arousal planning to use the supervisory session to "let off steam" in response to frustration experienced as part of the analytic process with the patient. Her capacity to announce her intention to use the session in this way indicates that the learning alliance is well established and that she feels free to use the situation as her needs dictate. The supervisor recognizes the intense countertransference and her need to express feelings. He makes no particular comment but listens attentively as the candidate presents and summarizes her experiences in the analysis. Although not recognized at the time, the question can be raised in retrospect as to whether there is a parallel process occurring between the patient's affective rush with the candidate analyst, and the candidate's affective rush with the supervisor.

The candidate spontaneously compares the patient's behavior with that of her twenty-month-old daughter and recognizes that "the effect on me is telling me something." Intermittently, as she describes the patient's behavior and associations, the candidate is capable of her own synthetic formulations, and she recognizes and tolerates the patient's transference experience of her in critical, contemptuous, and hostile terms. She is capable of recognizing when the patient is using, and reenacting patterns of behavior from the relationship with her mother. Throughout this early portion of the case material the supervisor is aware of the intensity of the candidate's affect and her continuing needs to express her reactions directly.

Eventually the supervisor begins to reflect back to the candidate and to encourage a more cognitive focus on the material. The candidate attempts her own formulations, recognizing the manifestations of the transference process and a shift in the patient's defensive posture and organization, as well as the patient's provocations. The supervisor's summary in regard to splitting the transference is an attempt to afford the candidate a more objective and cognitively organized opportunity to formulate her perceptions of the analytic process.

As part of the candidate's efforts at formulation and understanding, she mentions that some of the patient's behavior seems to have evolved after the patient brought back material about the experience of her urethral stricture and the severe trauma it occasioned. This material had previously been worked on.

At this point the supervisor begins silently to develop an understanding of the material in terms of the urethral stricture and its consequences and begins to call attention to the topic. The candidate responds by reminding the supervisor of the ideas previously connected to the stricture, once again synthesizing the material and recognizing that the patient started skipping sessions after the issue began to come up again. The supervisor's initial teaching activity is an attempt to prepare the background for the idea he will be offering, a process analogous to the preparation for an interpretation in the treatment situation. The supervisor deliberately wants to demonstrate the sequence of his thought processes, so that the final interpretation will not seem magical or too abruptly intuitive to the candidate.

The supervisor then begins to suggest to the candidate ways of thinking about the process when intense resistances such as the one described begin to occur. The candidate admits, "That's why I'm blowing off steam here." She has been unable effectively to integrate the experience, and is observing her affective state while asking for help.

The supervisor reflects to the candidate a way of summarizing the patient's behavior, again similar to the therapeutic situation in which an analyst prepares the patient for an interpretation. The candidate's response, "She *floods* me," indicates that the maneuver by the supervisor is successful. The candidate is more observant and can now recognize her affective and cognitive responses. The supervisor then presents a formulation in which the patient's behavior is seen as a transference reenactment, but the candidate is initially confused.

As the supervisor rephrases his formulation and shifts from an abstract conceptual statement to more immediate clinical description the candidate begins to respond in an animated way. She becomes increasingly capable of producing and correlating further material, rather than merely reacting to what the supervisor has said. As part of this she is able now to describe and correlate the patient's primitive thinking and fantasy, and begins to recall further material relevant to the issue in question. The supervisor, responding to the candidate's elaboration of the data, once again interacts, attempting empathically to reconstruct the patient's childhood experience currently being reenacted in her nonverbal behavior. The candidate identifies with the supervisor's immediate style and mode of communication, empathically recognizing the patient's childhood experience—"and you hate that you have to go." The supervisor continues to elaborate the theme, and as he suggests that the analytic process and the stream of urine are symbolically equated, the candidate's response, "That's beautiful, because I've been looking for that," indicates the candidate's capacity to use the supervisor's formulation to reach a new level of understanding.

This bit of teaching and learning illustrates the collaborative nature of the process. Each participant is engaged in a mutually enjoyable effort at discovery, and responds with further elaboration and new insights to the input from the other. It is likely that without this input neither supervisor nor candidate would have arrived at so clear a formulation.

The candidate transiently shifts the focus away from the immediate clinical situation to the more strictly cognitive realm of a paper she is writing; in it she is attempting to use her current understanding to develop concepts about psychic organizers and a general clinical construct. But spontaneously she returns to the clinical material, indicating that "it makes her rage at my unavailability make more sense." She thereby demonstrates further active mastery and the ability to integrate the material as an organized process. She elaborates the admixture of original experience and current transference in a clear and lively way.

The candidate's elaboration stimulates the supervisor to encourage the candidate's empathic identification with the mother in hopes of encouraging the candidate to use her countertransference experience as a source of awareness of what the mother-child interaction may have been, and how the analysis is repeating that earlier pattern. The candidate's response, that the interaction around the urethral stricture was itself a repetition of a pattern evident in the patient's toilet training, opens channels of association and communication of material not previously expressed or correlated by the candidate.

The supervisor shifts to a more cognitive and conceptual level in demonstrating the principle of multiple function without specifically naming it, thereby encouraging the candidate to generalize this clinical experience. The candidate responds with active attempts at learning, beginning with her question about the motivation behind the patient's fantasies. At the same time, she demonstrates that she has been able to use her own earlier experience with the patient to shape her interventions and can appreciate the importance of abstinence in the transference.

This is followed by an interchange in which each builds upon the contributions of the other toward a deeper empathic understanding, appreciation, and reconstruction of what had been an important and recurrent traumatic experience for the patient in childhood. The supervisor returns to the candidate's original countertransference experience of frustration and tension, using it to illustrate how an analyst can appreciate the meanings and basis of behavior by being sensitive to countertransference feelings. The candidate partially accepts the supervisor's suggestion, but corrects it, based on a more accurate and detailed description of her own countertransference experience.

The candidate's curiosity about how countertransference can be used technically allows the supervisor to describe the framing of interpretations based upon this type of understanding and gives the supervisor the opportunity to model potential interventions so that the candidate can once again observe how an analyst thinks while responding to the patient's behavior and material.

In this material the supervisor is careful to provide several models of intervention. The candidate asks broader questions as to how this can be conceptually understood, to which the supervisor responds first at the clinical level and then by referring the candidate to a paper on reconstruction by Phyllis

Greenacre (1975). As part of the elaboration the supervisor refers to material from his own clinical experience, primarily to illustrate the idea that such processes and phenomena are common, but also to enlarge the candidate's store of clinical phenomenology and experience.

The candidate returns to her struggle at the level of conceptual understanding and begins eagerly to inquire about defensive and adaptive style and organization. She demonstrates her increasing ability to move from specific clinical data to clinical concepts and theoretical formulations and back again. In this interaction the candidate shows an increasing identification with analysis and the excitement of discovery ("it's fascinating to me"), and candidate and supervisor again engage in an active give-and-take around the conceptual issue of the choice and origins of defensive style. The supervisor includes a developmental perspective, further demonstrating to the candidate the concept of genetic and sequential antecedents, as well as the effects of reality and the vicissitudes of life. As part of this, the supervisor goes beyond the clinical data to hypothetical modifications that might have occurred had circumstances been different. He thereby attempts to broaden the candidate's appreciation of the multiple issues determining these complex developments.

The candidate's excitement in the learning process is shown by her capacity to apply the concepts of the discussion not only to the current case but also to her other clinical experiences. She describes how this level of understanding allows comfortable comprehension and tolerance of loose ends while listening to a patient's material. The candidate is capable of reflecting on her analytic development and educational progress over the past three years, and notes that she is now capable of moving away from mere reporting to a greater comprehension and understanding of the material. She also shows an appreciation that this must be learned through experience rather than through purely didactic and cognitive instruction. The supervisor supports this awareness by referring to "a certain kind of unfolding that has to occur."

This supervisory session effectively illustrates various aspects of the teaching-learning experience. There is a balance here between affective experiential elements and those in a more cognitive style. The process oscillates from one mode of learning to the other. There is also a mutual interaction between candidate and supervisor, a shared experience of creative discovery and deepened awareness.

Chapter 11
Supervisory Session 91

Candidate: Sorry about misjudging the time. I'm out of breath. I have it all summarized, leading up to a real recent session, starting with the last time I saw you, which was a month ago. That's a Wednesday. The major thing that came up that Wednesday with respect to the things I want to talk about is that she can't draw bodies. She has mentioned a lot that she can't draw. She's a decorating artist, and it's a handicap that she can't draw people. She told about how she had to leave a class one time when she took a figure drawing class where they had live models. She had to drop it. She had to leave the first class because she couldn't look at a naked body.

Supervisor: Male or female or both?

Candidate: She never tested it. She thinks the first. Basic confusion about bodies centers on the genitals, how the penis is put together. It fascinates her; it scares her. Had a fleeting memory of her father standing naked, seeing his penis was interesting looking, don't touch. Seeing an image of Harold. Don't touch. Didn't come Thursday. Monday she says she had a wonderful weekend. Didn't even feel like eating fattening things. Hasn't had a period in three months. Scared to go to a gynecologist. Couldn't be pregnant. Getting pregnant means getting caught. Fantasies of running away with her father, little girl fantasies. Have a baby. Mother always told her she would never be able to have a baby naturally. She was too small down there. That's bizarre coming from this lady. This lady is tall, broad-shouldered, and even if she gets down to optimal weight she's still going to be broad-hipped. She's the kind of woman you would look at and say, "That woman is built to have babies."

Supervisor: So what do you make of that?

Candidate: I think it has to do with her perplexities about the urethral stricture, being too small down there.

Supervisor: Right, she was being dilated at the time because she was too small down there.

Candidate: Uh-huh. Once was enough. She must be malformed, confused. She feels out of touch with her body, disconnected. She's always been in control. She doesn't feel sexual with Ted. This weekend she felt she loved him, and that's the first time in a long time. She's been out of touch with those feelings, and yet she wants to have an affair, a secret affair, to win a person over and have a secret affair. She thinks it has to do with her father, that it must be secret. In a funny kind of way she's confused about her body. She's been wishing recently that she weren't a woman. She does everything as well as a man does, and yet they keep treating her as less. She's less well than Harold. I made a statement toward the end of that session about the birth of her brother, the urethral stricture, the difference between her body and Harold's. Somehow making some kind of sense out of this, that *she* had to make some kind of sense out of this, out of her feelings that Harold was very special. Why was he so special? And conclusions and fantasies that helped her make sense out of this were coming out. But then she didn't come the next session. That would be Tuesday she didn't come. Wednesday there were themes of competition with competitor males. She's enraged. These must be feelings from work. She works with a lot of men. She had a dream last night of a man with a penis hanging out of his pants like a tulip. This was the man she was supposed to be getting married to, the man her parents picked out. She was supposed to marry him, but she wasn't sure if she wanted to or not. She was supposed to get married. All the other women were married. And he was walking around with his penis hanging out of his pants like a tulip. Everybody thought it was okay. They thought it was wonderful. She wanted him to zip his pants. He was hurt by it. She's always been fascinated by flowers. She remembered studying Mendelian genetics. She described in detail to me about stamens and pistils and how one fertilizes. It gave her something, some way to understand penises. Then more about incompetent men who succeed because they are men. She described emasculated men who are pitiful, and herself. The next bit had to do with herself and how they treat her badly. And then she said she feels she got castrated. It was humiliating lying there with her legs up in the air having men look at her. She knows she had a penis. She knows she had a fantasy that she had a little penis and it would grow, and one of her notions about what happened with the dilation is that they made it so it wouldn't grow. Everyone in the dream thought the penis was so wonderful. Harold was wonderful because he had one. The mother and the doctor did something to make hers not grow. She had a fantasy—it's almost like she had a fantasy she was really a boy. She hated women; she hated the slutty behavior that they would go through. They'd do anything to get a man. She was always there, but her mother never appreciated that. Her mother would always take her father back. Tuesday she didn't come. I had previously canceled Monday. And she hadn't come Thursday. I had canceled Monday; she didn't come Tuesday and Wednesday or Thursday this week. So that is a week and a half. This is wonderful. It does all begin to make more sense. This is Monday the twenty-eighth, her next session. She felt comfortable the last time she was here and then work got crazy and there were babies everywhere. She felt strange. All these women had something she didn't have. She missed coming to treatment last week, yet she felt queasy and sick on the way here. She doesn't understand. Babies are everywhere, even in her dreams. She got her period last night, yet she's still anxious about being pregnant. For the first time in a long time she's attracted to babies. She has always been afraid of them; they seem so fragile. She knows she hated Harold and wanted to kill him and to protect him from that. She is envious of women with babies. She feels she can't have one. She wants one real bad. Strange feelings about her mother right now. She thinks this is from when she was little. She's upset with her mother when her mother is nice to her. She has been the same here at times with me. She missed me terribly last week. I listen to her. She even got along with my answering service. I take her seriously. She feels lonely with her feelings without me. She has felt that way before. And then—this came entirely from her—not being able to get here last week represents something else. It's something more. She couldn't get here but that's not important. She always wanted to approach her mother and felt she couldn't. She felt lonely with her feelings, the same way she felt last week. Her mother seemed cold and unapproachable. Then she was rawer. She had a lot of troubles. Sometimes when she—sometimes she's okay and sometimes she wasn't available to the patient. I made an interpretation that by making herself unavailable by not coming she would avoid the disappointment of coming and finding me distracted and not available, and she started to cry. She turned everything around and took the stance of taking care of her mother. But it was a very distant stance, a protective stance. It didn't allow any closeness. Her mother does love her and wants to be close with her. Being fat keeps a barrier between them, a fight, a distance. Her father gets so jealous when her mother buys the patient presents. (Boy, what a jump that was!) She sees herself and her mother walking down the street arm in arm. She's thin, they're both very happy. She thinks she's afraid of wanting something very close with her mother. The fantasy that her father would find her attractive is just a cover-up. Somewhere in this I reminded her of her fear of calling me on the weekends. She said my husband would be enraged because she caused her parents' bad marriage; she could make her husband jealous. She wanted her father to never come home again. My husband is a barrier to getting to me. They have to be pacified, these men. Strange how much she wants to have a baby, a little boy just like Ted. She thinks she's afraid that my husband would get mad and leave me, and then she'd never be free again. It's Monday. We don't have many more sessions. Tuesday. She didn't want to come today, no particular reason. She was happy when she left yesterday. She thinks we hit a nerve. Staying fat is protective against closeness with her mother, and today she wanted to keep her distance with me. She's afraid she'll be disappointed, expect too much from me. She can say she needs me but when she really starts to feel it, how badly it really scares her. She realized just how much she missed me last week. She cried at M*A*S*H. She described the final episode of M*A*S*H: people working with each other a long time and then having to leave each other. Now she's worried about her grandmother dying, she's getting old. She feels she didn't live up to her end of the bargain when she was little; she didn't give back what she was taking. She wanted her mother all to herself, she wanted her father to go away. She wanted her father all to herself, she wanted her mother to go away. It's most intense right now with her mother, with me. She hated her father for coming home. Her mother always took him back because he was a grown-up and because he had a penis. Always got real anxious. Also got real anxious yesterday because of her period. No period for so long, and then just spots, unsure, a torment. She feels I don't want to listen to her, and I said, "It's easier to fight than to be close." She said yes, she never really fought, she just made up all these distances inside of herself, these phantom fights. She talked about her grandmother getting old and dying. She was crying. She decided she'd never need anybody anymore, and I asked if this really seemed at all related to her getting her period. She said three months she went, almost seeing herself as a man, big and strong. She didn't even think about getting her period for three months, much less worry about being pregnant; it never crossed her mind. It didn't exist. And then wham, she started to worry. She feels so vulnerable and strange. It reminds her of losing her virginity. She was so anxious about having been penetrated that she never even thought about getting pregnant for three or four weeks, until she was late for her period, and then—panic. And then she was standing in Bloomingdale's and swish. She was so relieved. She has some fantasy that she can control all things, that her period is not a body function. She didn't have it for a time and then she got the fear that she might never get it back again even if she willed it. She wanted it; she wanted to menstruate but it didn't happen. She lost control. I made some association with the urinary stream, associating urinary stream and menstrual flow. She said it's humiliating not having control. Great anxiety at the loss of control when she finally had to urinate. Last Thursday she got absolutely hysterical when she decided she would have to go to a doctor because she didn't have her period. Even I couldn't do anything, she told me, I couldn't tell her, I couldn't fix it. She had to go to a doctor, just like her mother; her mother couldn't fix it. Now her period is starting and stopping, spotty. Her body plays tricks on her. Why did her body do that? Sometimes she doesn't want to take care of herself, to punish her body. She has been out of touch with her body for so long, she feels it doesn't go with her. She doesn't want me to think she's a candidate for a sex change operation or anything, because it's not just a penis. That's bad enough. Her whole body has disappointed her in so many ways. She didn't understand things her body did to her. I said something. She said something about withdrawing, and I said something about withdrawing from her mother to protect herself, withdrawing from me in the last week to protect her from unknowns, from surprises, from disappointments, withdrawing from her body. She said yes, it also helps to maintain some fantasies like she isn't heavy. Even when she could have sex and could have orgasm, she never let go; she must have control. Wednesday she was twenty minutes late, out of control, enraged, furious, stomping, screaming about some situation at work, which later in the session she realized she had made up. Always being chosen over men or always chosen first. She was just *enraged.* The patient interpreted this. She began to say she's making this up, she's making much ado about nothing. She interpreted it in terms of her family, the feeling that Harold was chosen first, always wanting to be first with me, wanting me always to be available to her when she needs me, not to go home to my husband, not to have other patients. It was very hard yesterday talking about being out of touch with her body. She had a dream. She's had bathroom dreams for many years. (I had two patients who had bathroom dreams in the same week.) I'll think she's weird or there's something wrong with her. She had a dream last night—bathroom dreams for many years. She's never mentioned them in this analysis. She has had them forever. A big locker-type of bathroom with lots of stalls without doors or sometimes no stalls at all, just toilets. You have to go in front of other people, and she can't. She's real uncomfortable. She can't go, others can. She doesn't have enough time. She can't relax enough to have a bowel movement. She can remember being chased through bathrooms, hiding in bathrooms, always a lot of stainless steel. She remembers how she felt when she was first in gym in high school and had to take communal showers; she never wanted to take her clothes off and had to pretend it didn't bother her. She woke up at five a.m. and thought about it. When she first started to develop breasts, she had stretch marks, and her mother got all worried and said, "I hope they go away, I hope those ugly purple marks go away." She felt so uncomfortable, totally disconnected from her body. She's envious of women who are connected. This was all in the last four minutes of the session. I said to her, "I didn't write it." It's obvious that this is a real important dream and a real important series of dreams and that it's something general, but we were out of time. "That it is significant and is probably significant that it comes out at this point in the session. It needs to be looked at." Then she didn't come Thursday.

Supervisor: So that was last Wednesday's session, and then she doesn't come in Thursday.

Candidate: She didn't come Monday either. However, she came yesterday. Oh, at the end of that session she got up and looked at me. I gave her a bill, and she looked at me and said thank you and asked if she could wait to pay me till the fifteenth of the month. Now, this girl has almost always, except recently—this has been an issue, but it's been an unaddressed issue. At the beginning of every treatment I always tell patients that they have until the end of the month to pay, that they should pay the bill before I make up the next one, I don't carry any balances. But she asked if she could pay me on the fifteenth, and I said that as long as she paid me before the end of the month, and that we need to talk about it. Then she came in and gave me the check and apologized for being late on Tuesday. Now that she's here, she's not sure what to say. I asked her about paying me and about asking me about the delay, about delaying it until the fifteenth of the month. She explained her financial situation and then said she always felt really funny, she always felt she had to bring it in the very next day. She didn't realize she had any time at all. She always paid the next day but doesn't feel so caught up in it anymore. She feels uncomfortable today because she hasn't been here since last Wednesday. There aren't enough hours in the day, not enough time. Thursday when she couldn't come, Ted couldn't bring her. She got crazy. She couldn't afford a cab. The car isn't done yet. They bought a second car, so she's going to have her own car. The main purpose that they bought it is so that she can get to her sessions without having to depend on Ted. She had had so much feeling, so much inside her, and nowhere to go with it. Yesterday she woke up and worked until ten p.m. She wavers between being happy that she's getting the experience she needs at work and feeling that her work is unappreciated. I made a statement about not having enough time here to get it out and about the bathroom dreams, not being able to relax and let it go. She said she had a triangle dream last—Thursday, maybe. Ted and Mother and Father and a man she works for, whom she likes but isn't attracted to. But there's a big celebration to celebrate the patient's losing weight—dinner. This man had four daughters, and he came up after dinner and told her that he really loved her and wanted to leave his wife and four kids for her. She wanted to go off with him, but she didn't know what to do with Ted. She kept thinking, "Why is he telling me this? If I hadn't lost weight, he wouldn't be telling me this." It was like Frank; she was crazy about him and heavy, then she lost weight and he wanted her. She felt despair in the dream. The next night she had a dream that she was in a shopping mall with her mother and her mother was buying her clothes. She was shocked, because her mother never buys her clothes when she's heavy. Mother was picking out all these clothes that the patient didn't like, but the patient was going to let her buy them anyway. Aunt Susan was there. Susie's been fat all her life. She was saying the clothes really look nice, but the patient didn't know why. The store closed, so the patient couldn't get anything. Then she saw a beautiful sweater on her way out the door and said, "Mother, you work here. Can't you just get me this sweater?" But her mother said no. A lot of temptation, but nothing, never getting anything. There was a key line in the dream that she forgets. She went to see her grandmother this weekend, and then she talked a lot about how close she feels to her grandmother. Her grandmother is like me, she listens to her, she validates her, she takes her seriously. She feels that as a child, in many ways, she wasn't taken seriously. How afraid she is that her grandmother will die. Her grandmother is really getting old. She can remember being afraid that her grandmother would die for as long as she has lived, because after her grandfather died, when the patient was a year old, the grandmother had been saying, "Well, now I'm going to die. I'm not going to last much longer." It's scary to her, especially now since her other grandmother just died. Her grandmother is—she started talking again about her body. She envies women who are in touch with themselves, who are concerned about their bodies. For a long time she has blurred all these feelings. She wants to be concerned about how she really looks. She talked about how she rationalizes, keeping those wishes away. She will focus all of her creative energies on making nice designs and arrangements with pretty people. And now they're going to get a new apartment, and she's going to decorate the apartment. And if she's going to do these things, she doesn't have time to worry about her nails, to look in a mirror, to go on a diet. She was telling me that in the tone she knows is a rationalization, because she said she rationalized it. And now she doesn't have time to do these things. I said, "Again?" She said yes, she envies women who make the time. She wonders why she drives herself so much and then doesn't feel appreciated for what she does. She doesn't feel acknowledged. Why doesn't she allow herself to appreciate herself? Right now she feels real relaxed, like she has time. But then she finds herself thinking, "Well, we're almost out of time here now." She will have to get all revved up and go out to combat this afternoon. She doesn't want to be busy all the time. I said that if she relaxes here, she feels like she doesn't have any time, time is almost up, and she must—as if she can't take the time that she has. She said that is why she got upset last Thursday; that's why she didn't come. I mean there were other reasons, but really she didn't come because of this. She wanted to come, but it was Thursday, so why bother?

There's never enough time. She used to come four days a week every time. She never missed one for a long time, but she still didn't have enough time. She was afraid about going to her new job at Barlow, that she would ruin our work, and in some ways she had. She longs for a time when her life had a focus, me. Now, there are lots of things that are important to her. I am very important to her, but others are important too. She talked about how upset she gets—last week when she lost control, the day she came when she was so furious. I made a statement about the analysis and other things in her life now having to do with time and controls in the bathroom dreams, and not having her work appreciated. She said it all fits. It was really not a very specific statement but a statement that was about as generalized as that. She said it all fit but that it seems like it's too easy, too simple. She said we probably don't have enough time to go into it, and then she laughed. She said she feels like she has to go, right now, to the bathroom. She wants to talk but feels rushed, like she has to get up and leave. So she is stifled. She can't go. She feels both things at once: She can't go; she has to go; she can't go on. She doesn't have any thoughts. The same thing happens with sex. She never really feels there's enough time. She doesn't want to be interrupted. She would go to the bathroom to escape the dinner table. It was so awful at the dinner table. She would stay up there forever, and her mother would always wait for her to come down to do the dishes. She hated it. She thought that if she waited up there long enough, her mother would go ahead and do them. And then there's something—she also mentioned the distant past and some of the other things she has mentioned before about her bowel controls, about having to eat more so you could go and you can't ever go and feeling constipated, not being able to go and wanting to go. That's all. It's not fleshed out. I am interested in—I, too, think her skipping sessions is in the transference, and I'm interested in it. I'm interested in the withholding and in—I guess I can't see yet, but it seems like I will eventually be able to see how this more anal phase affected her experience with the urethral stricture. It seems like she's talking about body products now and being appreciated and giving me things and having enough, you know, but also about—I can't translate having enough time into other words, besides having control. Part of it also is that I have a daughter who is almost two, who spends a lot of time on the pot, who decided to do this of her own volition. She comes and goes and wants to sit on the pot and can sit on it forever. And it seems real important for her to be doing this at her own pace. I realize that that's my experience, but that experience comes to me as I listen to her talk. So that something about control over your body-self, not just over your bowels; but that seems to be the place where the battle first starts to get fought. And I guess I call that anality. It certainly focused on body products and control issues.

Supervisor: Well, last time we talked—it was two times ago—you had come up with the idea that her coming and not coming and her flooding you with material—

Candidate: Was the urethral stricture—

Supervisor: The urethral stricture, avoiding the pain of urination as long as she could and then letting it all out to try to get through it in a hurry.

Candidate: And that made a lot of sense to her, and then it seemed like we moved on to the next, to another level.

Supervisor: It made a lot of sense to her, except that you canceled another session shortly after that because your child had been injured—I don't recall what the details were—and she canceled the following session. Now, did you ever connect your cancelation—

Candidate: With her cancelation.

Supervisor: Not only with her cancelation, but with this meaning that made so much sense to her? When you hit home, that interpretation that you offered, when you hit home, when she came in for a week in succession and then you canceled at the last minute because your child had been injured and then she canceled the following day, and since then she has been very spotty.

Candidate: And she said it was humiliating.

Supervisor: She said what was humiliating?

Candidate: To come the next day after she felt I was—

Supervisor: How did she interpret your cancelation? That's what I'm trying to get at. Or maybe you didn't analyze or you didn't—

Candidate: No, I think it was analyzed and I think you and I went over it last time, the last time I was here, but I have to go back over my notes, because it seems like she was saying that it was humiliating to come and she felt like I was testing her, that I was saying—go on, I might be able to reconstruct it.

Supervisor: What I'm trying to get at is that the pattern is again resumed of intermittently coming and then not coming, coming a couple of sessions or maybe every other session. One session in particular, which you were reporting just now, you mentioned that in the last four minutes of the session she just flooded you with material again—the dream and all the other things connected with it and the fantasies, the fantasy that she once had a small penis which she was sure was going to grow but never did, the basic defect in herself, the flower and all these other things, these are very phallic in their orientation. On the other hand, she talks about boys and their penises and she can't tolerate drawing bodies and sexual differences. Does she see herself as unable to control her sphincter *because* she doesn't have a penis? That a boy has a kind of spigot, a faucet, something he can turn on and off but she can't? Passive and out of control, she's been castrated. She is now deficient. She can't tolerate her own genitals. She can't look at them or other people and their bodies. All of this, it seems to me, relates or seems to relate to a reenactment in the transference and in her associations of this fundamental traumatic experience.

Candidate: But see, I think that *prior* to that fundamental traumatic experience was a previous concept and experience which colored how she experienced the urethral stricture.

Supervisor: It's possible.

Candidate: And I think that it's coloring it now. In the bathroom dreams it's always bowel movements and not being able to move her bowels, not having enough time to move her bowels. There's a whole lot of—producing *tons* of material that is not appreciated.

Supervisor: The question would be, does the anal—

Candidate: She is filled with anal problems prior to—It's a girl who's constipated, so constipated she had a hemorrhoid before she was a year old, and lots and lots of bowel struggles with her mother, and a hemorrhoidectomy when she was eighteen because it started to bleed. And she was terrified and thought she was going to die.

Supervisor: Well, the question would be, Did the anal conflict precede and therefore make the urethral issues more traumatic?

Candidate: That's one of the questions I'm asking in this material.

Supervisor: Or did the urethral stricture and the fantasies connected with phallic comparison—the pain of urination, the fantasy of having a penis which was then cut off, castration anxiety, and connected with that is humiliation but mainly the pain of it—did all that evoke or provoke or induce a regression to the anal material and reactivate it? Of this I'm not sure. I suspect the latter, but I'm not certain. She doesn't have the traits of an obsessional character fixated at the anal phase.

Candidate: She's far more phallic.

Supervisor: She's much more phallic. She's much more hysterical. She's much more affective. She's much looser, less rigid, more creative.

Candidate: Uh-huh.

Supervisor: She's less restricted than the usual person who has an anal fixation which then influences their phallic-oedipal development. So my hunch would be the latter, that yes she may have had some anal struggles with her mother, but these tend to be exaggerated now by virtue of the fact that moving ahead in the phallic phase she runs into this stress and then moves back to an anal phase, in a regressive way, to try to cope with the conflict at the phallic level.

Candidate: Well, also she had a lot of pain. There's associated pain again with body products—is her body working? She had a lot of pain defecating, a lot of sitting on the toilet praying. It's like instead of sitting on the toilet praying she'd never have to pee, she'd sit on the toilet to pray that she could poop. Lots of pain, which she can't date, but she sounds really little, using little potties, not sitting on the toilet. And she was at least two with the urethral stricture, if not three. So that the pain about which her mother could do nothing already preceded it. And her body doing bad things to her, which is one way she put it, her body doing bad things to her also preceded the urethral stricture. What she said in one of these sessions is, it's as if the urethral stricture cemented something (I don't know the exact word she used) something that was already going on.

Supervisor: But the point I would make is that it may be that she has belatedly, after the fact, reactivated some preoedipal anal memories or exaggerated her recall of them to cope with the later conflict. And that can sometimes happen. The analogue of this would be Freud's interpretation of the Wolf Man's dream as a primal scene, which was flipped back when the child got into the four-year-old phase and then the old experience was reactivated.

Candidate: Made a new kind of sense.

Supervisor: Right, it made a new kind of sense. My question with this patient would be: How much does her anal fixation, her anal conflict—because I don't really see her as anally fixated—how much does her anal conflict express the feces-penis equation, her reaction to the penis she never had or thinks she's lost but that she's not reproducing though she tries and tries and tries. But it never stays and it never comes out.

Candidate: Well, that makes sense in terms of the session where she goes from the bathroom to *wanting* a baby. I can't remember all of those things: competition to males and how they always win even though they're incompetent asses, to—

Supervisor: And the only reason they're admired is because they have a penis and she doesn't.

Candidate: To feeling castrated, to wanting a baby, to bathroom dreams. And that seemed to be all in one five-minute period.

Supervisor: So there's another element there, you see. Sitting on the pot waiting to go, waiting for it to come out, can also be a pregnancy fantasy, a delivery fantasy, in which the anal, the fecal mass is the baby which is to compensate for phallic inferiority, in which she then has to wait to go into labor, so to speak, to allow it to come out, the pain of labor, whatever. And whatever her mother may have told her about having a baby and her seeing her mother with her belly out when she was carrying her brother and then Harold being born and all of the fantasies connected with that—how much of that is in part re-created in a regressive way at the anal level? And the sequences you're describing in just a five-minute period go from one to the other and puts all of them together. And you said to her, these are all hooked up together, and from there she misses the next four sessions, the next session and almost a whole week following.

Candidate: The whole week.

Supervisor: And also, if you think about it, in that dream there were at least four, maybe five, references to the number four. The number four equals her four sessions a week.

Candidate: Uh-huh.

Supervisor: So this is being repeated and reenacted in the transference.

Candidate: Four daughters.

Supervisor: What?

Candidate: Four daughters.

Supervisor: Four daughters. There are a couple of other references there that I made a note of as they went by.

Candidate: I was impressed with the four daughters: Why *four* daughters? Why not seven or two?

Supervisor: Four is the four scheduled sessions each week that she's supposed to be here. So I think that that is where the action is. Now the point I'm trying to make, if I can get there, is: Don't use *your* fantasies to force or steer this material. Let her experience and express it in the transference, and keep interpreting or try to bring it into the transference. I would again repeat with her the idea that this skipping of sessions has to do with the pain of the urethral stricture and the wish to avoid it, whatever it is, the flooding of material occasionally and then stopping, the idea that she lets a little of it out and then retains it.

Candidate: In her affect in intercourse.

Supervisor: That she cannot lose, that in intercourse she can't let herself have orgasm even though she actually could, because to her that means a loss of sphincter control, a loss of containment, flooding.

Candidate: I feel like that scene hasn't been lost. It keeps coming back. She brings it back or I bring it back. It is everywhere, and I don't think it's just everywhere that I see it. She also will bring it up again from a new stance or just from a different stance.

Supervisor: Don't you see? She's manifesting in this material all the positive and negative oedipal conflict.

Candidate: Not exactly all at once, but real close together.

Supervisor: And she'll flip-flop.

Candidate: Real fluid.

Supervisor: She wants Father out of the way so she can have Mother; she wants Mother out of the way so she can have Father. She sees you—

Candidate: Or one day she wants me intensely and wants to get rid of my husband. Then the next day, flip-flop or the next day she comes.

Supervisor: Yes.

Candidate: But I don't think the heat right now is oedipal heat.

Supervisor: No, it's phallic.

Candidate: I wanted to make sure you weren't saying that.

Supervisor: And it's relating, I think, still to this unmastered traumatic situation. You have to go back to it and try to help her.

Candidate: And all the ways in which she tried to, all the ways in which she fantasized or understood it.

Supervisor: Right. Okay.

Supervisor's Comments

The candidate initiates the session by outlining how she wants to use the time. Following this she launches into her summary of the past month's material. In this summary the candidate indicates her awareness of a theme in the patient's material and her wish to focus on it. The supervisor's response, "Right," suggests that his previous question inviting the candidate's opinion was really a wish to have the candidate guess what was in his mind. The candidate continues her summary, including her interpretation to the patient focused around phallic issues and fantasies related to the urethral stricture.

The patient's subsequent material seems to focus around issues of sexuality and phallic competitiveness, with fantasies of castration and her own spontaneous return to the humiliating procedure of being examined for the stricture. This includes the patient's direct regressive expression of her unconscious fantasy of having been castrated by this procedure, now presented as part of a chain of associations and a series of dreams. This indicates how much more freely the patient is now able to regress and experience her own memories and fantasies.

In reporting the patient's irregular attendance as well as the lack of continuity in the material, the candidate acknowledges her awareness of this pattern—"It does all begin to make more sense." Possibly in response to the previous associations in material focused around phallic competitive issues, the patient now voices and expresses a more sustained level of interest in babies than previously, suggesting the beginning of a new shift in the transference toward the mother as the libidinal object.

The candidate's comment to the supervisor, "this came entirely from her," represents several developments in the candidate's identification as an analyst. She is indirectly indicating her awareness of the importance of suggestion and interpretation in influencing the patient's material during an analytic session. She is also observing the process and her role in it, and is reaffirming her awareness of the importance of spontaneous material from the patient in contrast to suggestions in the form of interpretations. The patient's awareness that there is something more to her absence last week than manifest rationalizations is a sign of the patient's increased self-analytic capacities, her tolerance for awareness of conflict, and her own deepening recognition of attachment to her mother. The candidate makes a transference interpretation of the patient's avoiding disappointment, and the patient begins to cry and to elaborate upon her own role in keeping distant and isolated from both mother and analyst, and recognizes how she is reenacting this in the current relationship with the candidate. This is another manifestation of change in the patient, an increased capacity to accept and appreciate her own role in difficulties she previously has ascribed to others, as well as direct and immediate access to her own affective experience, life, and memories. As part of this increased freedom the patient continues in a more focused and affectively significant way to elaborate and explore the maternal transference as well as to recover memories from her earlier relationship with her mother, at both a preoedipal and a negative oedipal level of organization.

The candidate's uninterrupted presentation of subsequent material is expressive of the patient's increased freedom, and the candidate's continuing effective focus of the patient's material into her current transference reexperience. The patient also displays an increased capacity for self-observation. For the first time she expresses recurrent dreams of bathrooms, and the candidate is able to accept this manifestation of previously unrecognized resistance without criticizing the patient or feeling hurt or disappointed that this material had not previously emerged.

At the end of the session the candidate acknowledges the importance of these dreams, but her suggestion that they represent an important issue is followed by the patient's increased resistance, manifest in her absence the next day. The candidate brings up the issue of fees, indicating her own recognition that this important interaction has not yet been satisfactorily addressed.

In the next session the candidate introduces the issue of the fee but with minimal progress, and the material remains predominantly descriptive. The candidate seeks to interpret into the bathroom dreams, but the patient is unable to make use of it at this time and instead launches into another series of dreams. The patient at this point seems to be complaining and defensive, and seems to be avoiding both the transference and any other manifestation of regression. The candidate is reporting the process material in a relatively uninterrupted flow while the supervisor listens without actively intervening. In retrospect it seems as if the patient's response is a resistance to her movement into anal-urethral issues in the previous sessions, but apparently neither the candidate nor the supervisor recognized it, either in the analytic process or in the supervisory session. The patient indicates her growing feeling of helplessness and of not having enough time.

The candidate interprets into this area of conflict—"I made a statement about the analysis and other things in her life now having to do with time and controls in the bathroom dreams, and not having her work appreciated." Although the candidate's self-assessment is that "it was really not a very specific statement," it was at least a recognition and provided a focus into the area of conflict being avoided. The patient's responses ("it all fits," "we probably don't have enough time to go into it," her laughter, and the immediate somatic urge to go to the bathroom) indicate that the intervention was effective, and the patient continues with a variety of anal memories and associations.

The candidate expresses independent curiosity in questions about the material, indicating interest and awareness in the struggles for anal control, as well as an ability to associate from the patient's anal behavior to her daughter's toilet training. Here she demonstrates a capacity to use her own experience and associative material in connection with the associations and the experiences of the patient. She demonstrates also an empathic ability to recognize that it is important for her own child to "be doing this at her own pace." This awareness helps her tolerate the patient's retention and resistance in the analytic process without urgency and without pushing or forcing the issue. This is in significant contrast to the sense of frustration and irritability she experienced in supervisory session 88.

At this point, more than halfway through the supervisory session, the supervisor for the first time intervenes in a focused and didactic fashion. His initial efforts begin with a summary of the patient's responses to the candidate's previous intervention about the urethral stricture, and are followed by his pointing out the important omitted material in regard to the candidate's having canceled a session shortly after her important interpretation. He follows this with a summary of the patient's general behavior since that cancelation, emphasizing the importance of the patient's fantasy as to why the cancelation occurred. The supervisor summarizes the patient's associations and behavior, at both a macroscopic and a microscopic level, and then proposes a possible explanatory fantasy focused at a phallic level of experience and conflict.

The candidate is able to disagree and maintain her own dynamic and conceptual formulation, marshaling appropriate material to support it. Although the supervisor indicates reasonable openness ("it's possible"), he follows with an explanation of his own formulation and reconstruction of the issues in question, thereby illustrating what lines of evidence he selects as important. In this he relies on general clinical experience and formulations somewhat apart from the immediate material from the patient, thereby demonstrating how an analyst may make use of general clinical theory to understand clinical material that seems relatively idiosyncratic. The candidate reiterates her own formulations, differing from the supervisor's and marshaling what she considers significant clinical support for her ideas. This represents a consolidation and further expression of her clinical development and capacity for independent conceptualization about the material she observes.

The supervisor seems to ignore the candidate's ideas and to push his own, trying to persuade the candidate of his opinion and using the authority of Freud to support it. This attempt to force the candidate to an acceptance of his ideas is poor supervisory technique. The candidate senses the supervisor's pressure and seems to give in to it, and the supervisor continues to rush on, forcing his ideas in an inappropriately forceful way. The candidate seems then to provide new material which allows the supervisor to continue his line of speculation, but it is unclear from the data whether this is the candidate responding to an accurate synthesis by the supervisor, thus allowing the opening of new channels of information, or whether the candidate experiences the supervisor's pressure and then provides the kind of confirmatory material the supervisor seems to be demanding.

The supervisor seems then to force the issue further by pushing ahead to the formulation of an anal pregnancy fantasy. In this and the ensuing material, he seems to be pressuring the candidate to do what he later cautions her not to do to the patient, namely, to lead and direct the associative material without allowing it to unfold spontaneously. The supervisor is demonstrating poor teaching technique, and seems to be taking the case over from the candidate, in terms of both his formulations and his directions.

At the end of the supervisory session the candidate returns to a formulation of the trauma of the urethral stricture, but it is difficult to know how much the candidate is acquiescing to the supervisor's pressure, indicated possibly by her comment, "I wanted to make sure you weren't saying that."

Review of the data suggests that the supervisor is unusually active in pushing his formulations upon the candidate too strongly, and that even if they prove correct he is forcing the candidate in a passive, accepting mold. The candidate is capable partly of maintaining her own position in withstanding this pressure but eventually she seems forced to submit.

Although the supervisor generally uses a fairly active style and teaching technique, this degree of pressure seems unusual, and there is need to inquire as to why it is occurring at this time. It is significant that the supervisor is also the Medical Director of the Institute, and that this supervisory hour is occurring one week in advance of an Institute site visit conducted by the American Psychoanalytic Association. The occasion of the site visit had activated a variety of concerns in the supervisor as well as a number of conflicts among the Institute faculty in regard to their role in the site visit, as well as concerns that the inspection go well and that the visitors approve the Institute program. Not only was there a heightened pressure on the supervisor as Director of the Institute, but he also experienced anxieties and concerns that the program fit an appropriate mold.

It is likely that the supervisor was displacing these issues onto the supervisory situation and the candidate without being consciously aware of doing so. In this sense, the supervisor was responding on the basis of an unconscious transference, displaced from the site visitors and the Institute faculty onto the candidate, in the form of a countertransference response in the supervisory relationship. Although no major and sustained disruption seems to have occurred, it nevertheless created a situation of interference with the optimal learning needs of a candidate. As such it serves to illustrate how extrasupervisory issues and conflicts in the supervisor may contaminate and distort the supervisory process. It is thus similar to the effects noted earlier in regard to the supervisor's illness.

Chapter 12
Supervisory Session 92

Supervisor: Come in. I'm sorry I'm late.

Candidate: Did you get any feedback from the site visitors?

Supervisor: Yes. They were favorably impressed and quite complimentary, indicated they thought we have a good program, the candidates are of high caliber, and the teaching and program are good. They had some suggestions, mostly minor, and those are things we'll discuss over time. It was better than we hoped or expected.

Candidate: They had to have suggestions, that's their job. They certainly seemed to feel that way on Thursday night.

Supervisor: To feel positively?

Candidate: Uh-huh. I kind of went around and felt them out. I didn't say, "How do you feel about us, do you like us?" But there was just a general feeling of goodwill and a sense of "I don't know what everybody is so uptight about, we know you're doing a good job." And if they had had major criticisms, I doubt there would have been that feeling.

Supervisor: That's right. Several of them said they'd enjoyed it and had learned some things.

Candidate: That's nice! So you're all feeling good, I hope. Okay. I got myself straightened out on this, and I want to read some process to you. I got things messed up on a—let's see. She didn't come, she didn't come, she didn't come, she didn't come. She came on a Tuesday, and I got things turned around and made some inappropriate—I think—comments, not-to-the-point comments, and she didn't come Wednesday or Thursday, which collaborated what you've said. She came the next Monday. She couldn't wait to get here. She's been so busy, she doesn't have time—

Supervisor: Now this is when? A week ago?

Candidate: The fourteenth, March fourteenth. She's so busy she doesn't have time to go to the bathroom. She's feeling a real sense of pride in her work that has been missing for a long time, but something's been pulling her down. She felt bad that she wasn't here last week. She felt really terrible Wednesday because Wednesday is her favorite appointment, but she couldn't come. I asked her for the details of that. She told me about her work. She felt she didn't know what to do. She wondered why she couldn't just walk out of her work and say she'd do it tomorrow. She doesn't know why she can't. She thinks they won't believe her, almost like she doesn't, like she doesn't herself. Then she talked about—well, there was a lot of mixed-up feelings this weekend and right now she feels like she doesn't have enough time. Last week was the busiest week in her whole career. She described the cascade of work, and I said something about is her work having the quality of an uncontrollable stream she can't stop? She said yes, it's never been that way before. She has been very proud of her work, but she can't control it and fears that if she stops she won't be able to get it started again.

Frank told her to give up a project, and she just can't do that. Her work fits—you either have nothing or you have so much you can't control it. I said she's been experiencing many aspects of her life this way: her analysis, her work, and money. She then went into a big long thing about their periodic money troubles and how—it wasn't a big long thing, it was just another—well, how everything goes along, how she believes there will never be any more serious trouble again. They'll be able to take a vacation, de-dah de-dah de-dah, and then wham, it all blows up and she's disappointed and wants to get rid of Ted. Then her parents get all hysterical about her troubles and all her mother cares about is her goddamn diet. She is furious with her mother. She talked about visiting her grandmother and how her grandmother has always listened to her. They can talk back and forth. They can have a two-way conversation in which only one thing is being talked about, rather than parallel conversations. Her grandmother is so full of life and so full of joy, and she feels sad at the notion that her grandmother is getting older and is going to die some day. Then she feels real resentful coming in here and having it all come out like this. I made another comment about—Oh, she said, "all rush out," and I said, "A rush and uncontrollable flow again. And I don't fix it." She said yeah. She had made a comment earlier in the session about something to do with her menstrual period. Oh, she was so busy at work she canceled her gynecological appointment because she started menstruating or something. She worries if it stops, I say, and yet she hates it when it rushes out, like it worried her when her menses were not starting. Now that the flow has started, why should she go to the doctor? She laughed; she started laughing in the middle of this. She said, "You got it." She was worried when she didn't pee that she'd never be able to again. She didn't want to go to a doctor about it; she wanted to see to it herself. Why should—

Supervisor: This is her own spontaneous associations to your statement about the menstrual issue?

Candidate: Yeah. She talked about hating the pain. The way she managed pain as a child was to detach herself from her body with the fantasy that she could control anything if she just stepped out of herself, detached herself. Her not having sex anymore reminds her of the vow she made never to masturbate again when she had the urethral stricture. She has been masturbating a lot lately. As a child it used to be the way she would get away from any kind of pain, a way to go someplace where nothing could touch her, where she didn't have to deal with anything or think about any of this crap. The hardest thing she did last week was to call an illustrator and reject a piece of art. She was up all night agonizing about it. She knew she had to do it. She did it and felt better afterward. She couldn't even say why. Then she described this guy that came into her office and presented this thing as if he expected it to be accepted, but it just wasn't right and she just had to tell him no. It was just on a gut level. It reminds her of another event she told me about. I said, I suppose I made some interpretations on Tuesday that just didn't make sense to you. She said yes, she couldn't put her finger on it—those were her words—on why it just didn't feel right. She was afraid she was cutting me down. The illustrator walked into her office and presented this and she didn't like it. She didn't know why. But she had to tell him so, but she couldn't. I said, "Like telling me I'm off base," and she said, "Yes." She feels like she really grew a lot last week, because she looked at her portfolio Saturday and she has really come a long way. She even was eventually able to reject the illustrator. She talked on about that last week. Then I said something about the stresses she talked about. I suggested that all of this had some effect, maybe, on her not being able to come last week. There was this "Maybe," and then there was silence. An obstreperous sort of silence. Then I said, "What's going on?" She said, "I don't like it, I got upset." I asked her to expand on that, what was going on, and then there was an interchange about her acquiescence, agreeing with interpretations just because I said them, resenting it, but being afraid to say, "Hey, you know, stick it." Feeling that the important thing last week was the uncontrollable stream, she feels that she never does enough, and it was all making sense. It was beginning to all make sense. It was all coming together for her, and then I said that. And she never does enough. She couldn't tell me I was wrong. She was afraid of some kind of punishment. It is tied in somehow with urinary pain. She wonders if it happened, the urethral stricture, when she was furious with her mother and didn't want to tell her mother about it because she did not want her mother to know that she had gotten to her.

Supervisor: That she, the mother, had gotten to the patient?

Candidate: Yes, as if the pain was how she had gotten to her.

Supervisor: Like pain is the persecutor, like the mother as persecutor.

Candidate: "It all got pinned on me." This is from the end of the session. She said—I'll put it in the first person because it is easier to follow—"I wonder if it happened when I was furious with my mother and didn't want to tell her because I didn't want her to know that she had gotten to me. And then it all got turned around and pinned on me. That has something to do with why my mother appears so virginal to me. I think that is why I am in such awe of you and my mother." The next day, Tuesday, she canceled twenty minutes into the session. She called my office number. This was a difference in the way she canceled. She will sometimes cancel at five o'clock in the morning by calling my answering service. Sometimes she will call directly into my office with the, at least expressed, feeling that maybe I'll pick up the phone. Then Wednesday she came; she was ten minutes late—a lot of emotional changes, upset. She is really depressed at the way she looks. She has a real feeling of self-hatred. On the other side, she feels vital and real and in control of her ability, directed, and it all does not fit. She does not fit. It's funny, for so long she has ignored the feeling of her body. The feeling of something—she does not know how to get these things in sync. Something has been out of sync for a long time. Now, for the first time, she felt angry about it. Her mother called last night about her gynecological appointment. The patient said she made an appointment to get her hair cut. Her mother and father said, "Oh, I am so glad. You haven't been taking care of yourself. It's not like you." The patient was enraged. "If I had to live with you, I'd be—if you had to live with a mother like me, you'd be like this too." She was very depressed on Tuesday, very resentful of spending so much time at work, resentful of not being able to come for her appointments. She stood outside and waited for Ted until twelve-thirty. Her appointment was for twelve-twenty. He never came. She was depressed.

Supervisor: So she called because Ted didn't show up, or she canceled rather, because Ted didn't show up, not because she didn't want to—

Candidate: Yes, she stood outside and waited for him. She thought about taking a cab. It's really ridiculous for her to think about taking a cab actually. She was so depressed she called—I swear she said she called her mother. Who couldn't talk. The patient should come and visit this week. The patient wanted to get away but wasn't sure she would enjoy herself. The friendship has always been so unsure. I realize at this point that she is talking about this girl friend of hers, not really a girl friend at all. It's a very ambivalent relationship. Then Betty called her very upset last night. No one has ever listened to her, except me. No one has ever extended even that courtesy, and the patient was upset. Betty was cutting and terrible and didn't have time. Then Betty has to talk all evening about how upset she is. Her parents called and Betty called back again. And she realized that she didn't want to go there this weekend. It was not appropriate for her to go visiting this girl in New Orleans. Then she had a dream, after this hullabaloo with her parents and Betty. She had a dream that she and Ted were getting married. And somehow there were two sisters. Harold, who's not married, had a wife who was some kind of sister-in-law, and then a regular sister. Anyway, she said two sisters were talking to her, to the patient. They were mad because Harold thought she was wonderful, and their father thought she was wonderful, and the other sister's husband thought so too. So all the men thought she was wonderful. And they ganged up on her. They didn't think she was so neat. They thought she was a fake and didn't know how she got all those men to worship her. It was like being slapped in the face. She really, genuinely loved them, all of the men, innocently. She was marrying Ted or was married to him, and she loved him, and it was all very clear to her. She loved these other men in an innocent way. She woke up feeling violated, that someone had misunderstood her and hurt her needlessly. That's what she is always afraid of. She's always afraid of it but never expects it, never knowing why it happens when it does. She was silent and then talked about this guy who came into her office from Abbot's for an interview today. It was like rubbing salt in an open wound. She felt invaded. Her place was being invaded. There are idiots running things now. He will probably get hired. She can't stand him. If she really felt secure in herself, she wouldn't care about these things. She can't figure out what's going on. She feels so out of touch. She feels real sensitive emotionally, like exposed nerve endings, and sluggish and slow physically. She feels out of sync with herself. She feels out of kilter more than she ever has before. She feels a lot of anxiety which is not necessary. She means the real world isn't causing it when she says it's not necessary. She feels angry underneath it all, frustrated and scared, like she doesn't know what is going to happen next, like she's waiting for something to happen, like she's waiting to fall out of favor.

Supervisor: Waiting to fall out of what?

Candidate: Out of favor. I said, "Here?" And she said she expects everyone to go away: me, Ted, people at work, to all go away. She feels so angry with her mother right now she can't stand her. Her father just seems like a true idiot, and her mother seems vengeful, out to get her, hard and cold. She has no feeling and no emotion. I said, like the sisters in her dream? She said yes, except that her mother doesn't have the nerve to be open about it. It's coming out in cutting, sarcastic spurts that really cut deep. She was silent for a while, and I asked her what was going on. She said she feels like she casts herself aside somehow. She doesn't like herself very much. No one else likes her, why should she? I played back to her how she was feeling in her body, the feelings of dislocation, and suggested that—oh, and the disdain she was expressing for herself. She was disgusted, awful, terrible, and suggested that she stepped away from herself in order to tolerate some massive feelings or massive humiliation. And I used the story—I don't know if this is a correct thing to do or not—I used a story I happened to know about a little girl who peed on the floor and was made to clean it up in front of her classmates and stand there. And she remembers the incident as being one of her classmates standing around jeering.

Supervisor: That's Arlow's paper on depersonalization (1966).

Candidate: Okay, so it is a real story. I did read it somewhere once. And I used it—I was grasping for words. I knew what I wanted to say and I didn't want to say it in technical language. I wanted something that would give her the meaning of what I was trying to say. And she said, "Yes, that's what it feels like," like now she's standing with the jeerers and she hates to admit it is her. She has a picture. She feels like a broken doll who has become inflated, that person years ago that she envisions as broken. She tried to put it back, the pieces, and then inflate it and became a caricature of that doll. That's what she feels like now, a caricature and very inflated and very broken underneath. I said, "And very reluctant to go back and feel the brokenness." She said yes, she doesn't want to. It was so awful, she had to split herself up. She has felt that way for a long time.

She doesn't want to feel it again but it comes. She doesn't feel like she can do it. She doesn't know why it seems like a thing that she can't do. She will have to do something she doesn't want to do. She will have to say something she doesn't want. It doesn't make any sense. I said, against her will, and she said, yes, against her will. She'll have to do these things here. I said, "Like being tied down on the table again and having something stuck up you," and she said yes, she must do that or live with the pain, like never being able to pee again, live with that inflated body. She feels that same anxiety, the same fear in her chest. She wants to run. She has to either tell me or live with it, and she can't live with it anymore, anymore than she could stand never to pee again, the same kind of wanting to relieve herself of the pressure. She feels the pressure. She wishes she could fix it herself. Everything that we have dealt with so far, here together, seems like nothing compared to this. It has all led up to this, and this is so scary. I said she must have been very scared, both now and as a little girl. I wondered what she thinks they were going to do to her. She laughed and said she could tell me one thing, she never thought they would do what they did, not in her wildest dreams. Even to this day she can't put it together. She expects me to do something awful to her, and she can't imagine in her wildest imagination what it would be. She expects it to catch her off guard, like the two women in her dream, wham bam!! Now it will be very hard to force herself to come to deal with this, to come back again and again. It's like going to the doctor's office. But she came, twenty-five minutes late, to the next session, that's Thursday. She walked into the room, laughed, and then said, "I made it for twenty-five minutes." She laughed about—

Supervisor: Let's stop here a minute. Do you have any reactions about that material yourself?

Candidate: The reactions were kind of—

Supervisor: How do you think this whole thing adds up?

Candidate: Well, I am having trouble with the question.

Supervisor: I'm asking you to guess what's in my mind.

Candidate: Because there's a couple of blatant levels and then there's—I don't feel you're talking about the blatant levels, so I don't know what's in—

Supervisor: No, I think the issue is her masturbation and fantasies she's hiding. She's undergone a regression from the masturbation fantasies, whatever they are, back to this urethral business as a defense against the fantasy that she's damaged herself by her masturbation. Now she alluded to the fact that she'd been masturbating as a child, but she's never gotten into what the fantasies were. She'd been masturbating more recently—

Candidate: She had really gotten into it in terms of being her dad's hostess.

Supervisor: Yeah, well that's on a very, very superficial level. And she's back to masturbating again now, more frequently in recent weeks, but hasn't said anything more about it. Again, why is she masturbating while Ted is still there? Is it she can't stand him? What's going on?

Candidate: She can't let him touch her.

Supervisor: She can't let him touch her. What's going on and why? That's where I think you need to begin. This urethral business is very important.

Candidate: And it's at age four. Finally, the dating has gotten clear. At age three her brother was born and at age four she had the urethral stricture.

Supervisor: The issue then is, I think, that the urethral stricture is the regressive expression of her fantasy that she castrated herself. She used the words "cut" and "cuts deep" and "I'm split in half."

Candidate: Uh-huh.

Supervisor: All these other images have something missing, something cut off, something destroyed, something damaged.

Candidate: And she said at some point now in this material that she thinks that's what they did to her. They castrated her.

Supervisor: That's her defense against her fears that—

Candidate: That she did it.

Supervisor: She did it herself, and she hates herself for it but can't bring herself to face it. So what I'm saying is listen to this, allow her to work it out but keep in your own mind that this is probably a regressive position away from, a retreat from, a more fully developed oedipal constellation that was the focus of her masturbation fantasies.

Candidate: If they happened at the same time, if the urethral stricture was at three and the masturbation fantasies were at four—I mean if the urethral stricture was four and the masturbation fantasies were three or four—then why do you call this regressive? Because it's consolidative? Because it's where the symptoms went to?

Supervisor: The genital is being used less for sex and more for excretion.

Candidate: Okay.

Supervisor: This whole area of her body, the focus now is on urethral, painful—penetration not in a sexual pleasurable way but in a sense of catheterizations, the pain, but also the pee and the flow, coming. It is all experienced not as a sexual-heterosexual, triadic, pleasurable, sensual quality but in a regressive way, like it's halfway between an anal and a sensual-genital point where she used the area for excretory purposes. That's what I meant by regressive.

Candidate: So, then, even the pregnancy fantasies in this material—it doesn't get entirely clear, it gets somewhat explicit that the bladder and the uterus are one, and to urinate is to menstruate or to menstruate is to urinate.

Supervisor: But to menstruate is to urinate.

Candidate: And to hold her urine is to—oh, I asked her if she, well, somehow it got into when her mother was pregnant with Harold. She was talking about how now her face doesn't feel blown up; during this week her whole body felt blown up. Now just her belly feels blown up.

Supervisor: Uh-huh.

Candidate: And that led into some talk about my being pregnant and when her mother's belly blew up and blew down and her wanting to have, in a very general way, not a specific way, but her wanting, her remembering the fantasies of being her dad's hostess and having babies and thinking that she didn't know where babies came from. I said that her mother probably blew up and blew down and there was a baby there, so I thought she probably had some fantasies about where they came from.

Supervisor: But she seems to know—

Candidate: And some notions that she held her urine in an attempt to have a baby, and then stopped being able to pee.

Supervisor: Fine, but also keep in mind the belly blowing up and then blowing down as an expression of erection. The body is the phallus, getting bigger, getting smaller, shrinking, the whole question of her weight, of getting fat, getting thin. These are also, in addition to her oral, in addition to the pregnancy fantasies, fantasies of the body as phallus, alternately the erection and then, afterward, the detumescence.

Candidate: Uh-huh.

Supervisor: And so all this is in together, my point being, is you are going to need to—

Candidate: Watch for it.

Supervisor: Watch for it but also begin to tease it out: "You mentioned the masturbation, but you never mentioned your fantasies." "You mentioned that you are masturbating recently when you can't stand for Ted to touch you, but you haven't talked about what the connections are between these two."

Candidate: Uh-huh.

Supervisor: "You mentioned feeling driven in your body and also that you've been masturbating lately, as if there's no connection in your mind between those two experiences." That kind of an intervention begins now to encourage her to elaborate on and look more introspectively at these preconscious and unconscious kinds of fantasies, especially the masturbation fantasies.

Candidate: She made it for twenty-five minutes. She talked about—

Supervisor: Now this is Thursday?

Candidate: Thursday of last week. She talked about running into her uncle in the elevator and how she doesn't like him. She is so wound up. She thinks she's really upset because it's Thursday and she won't see me until Monday. She feels like a caged lion. She wants out and she can't get out. She feels like she did when she was a little girl. She had to stay in this awful place. At lunch today she hated having to come to the session. Everything is on my terms. She was so frustrated that she couldn't get here any faster. She talked about the traffic jam—why even bother for twenty-five minutes, why not cancel and make it on her terms? She'll walk out of here at one-ten and feel abandoned again. She feels inflated, a massive, heavy helium balloon, ugly. She wants to stand up and shout, "Let me out of here!" There's a real strong part of her now that likes her but hates what she's showing the world. She feels like she sees herself realistically on the one hand and crazily on the other. If she could just get it all into kilter. I said I felt her pulling; I should do something. Rather than say, "You want me to do something about it," I said here she is so inflated and so uncomfortable and wants me to stick a pin in it and fix it. She laughed and said that struck a chord, that's what happened with the urethral stricture and with sex and the neighbor. So she's starting to make these associations but not in detail. With sex and the neighbor it was like having an audience criticize her, more overt than the urethral stricutre, with him standing there looking at her, more overt because the urethral stricture was a fantasy. What her mother thought, what the doctor thought, that was all just in her head. With the neighbor, he expressed himself rather clearly.

Supervisor: Now what was that, he expressed himself?

Candidate: Oh, their bed was banging up against the wall two summers ago and he came and banged on the door and said that he wasn't going to be subjected to their sexual activity.

Supervisor: Uh-huh.

Candidate: And then she got vaginismus after that, and it hasn't gone away since, except little tiny isolated instances, maybe three. With the neighbor, he expressed himself out loud and rather explicitly. With the urethral stricture she really thought her mother knew that she was touching herself. She was certain that the doctor could tell by looking at her. Last night when she left, things felt cleaned out. She felt cleaned out. Now she feels anxious and depressed.

Supervisor: She insinuates she was certain the doctor could tell by looking at her that she's damaged herself.

Candidate: Uh-huh. And the details of that have soon got to be available. Previous times when I've asked her about her—I don't get the idea she is withholding them. It's just not been available to her. And she could just tell how, what—

Supervisor: Has she ever looked at herself in a mirror, at her genitals?

Candidate: I don't know.

Supervisor: That kind of question might be worth asking. "What about yourself when you look; can you tell?" "I've never looked."

Candidate: Uh-huh.

Supervisor: "What's the matter, are you afraid of what you'd see?"

Candidate: Especially since there is so much emphasis on not looking at her whole body, which may just be a global thing.

Supervisor: A global thing and again—

Candidate: A global thing over a specific thing.

Supervisor: Right.

Candidate: She doesn't want—she feels so anxious and depressed. And I made some kind of an intervention. She doesn't want to wait anymore. She's been waiting her whole life to get her body back in shape. She feels real distorted looking. I asked for specifics. She said her face is inflated, her features have sunk back in, all the sparkle and pep is gone. She feels very old, older than her mother. For so many years she felt no one was taking her seriously. Now she realizes that it's her; she doesn't take herself seriously. Everyone else has really been quite empathetic. She's jeering at herself, she's still jeering at herself. It really upset her. She's standing there poking fun at herself. She's not taking herself seriously. It makes her crazy when she thinks about what she looks like. She looks like a joke to herself, a stupid joke. She described in great detail, laughing while she was describing this three-hundred-fifty-pound woman at work who wears too-small stretch pants and bikini underwear that's too small so that you can see the lumps of flesh. She feels she looks like that. Her mother has been telling her she looks like a joke for years. There she was, putting it out again. Her mother always says, "You don't think you look bad, but you really look horrible." She can't even express how mad she is, she feels she never felt that she looked good, even when she was thin. Inside she was never any different than she feels right now. Here I have a blank, so I don't know what she said. Then I said, bearing a resemblance to how she might have felt with her legs spread and them looking at her. She said, so distorted she thought something was wrong. They were looking, they were seeing something wrong. She was afraid and wanted to make it go away. That's how she's been feeling lately. She wants to hide, fix it, lose weight secretly. Her mother keeps saying things to her and keeps triggering her rage. Every time she calls up she asks her about the diet, she says she can't stand it. She wants to say, "Leave me alone." She sounded hysterical. Time was almost up now and she feels terrible. I said that time was almost up and how can I leave her like this? She said all the time she has wanted to talk with her mother about her body and all this stuff, and her mother was never there and never had time. She gets this replaced, critical scrutiny from her mother. I don't know what that means. That's the end of it.

Supervisor: Uh-huh.

Candidate: I presume I'm going to understand more about how her weight and never eating fits into this. Sometimes I think it's some kind of anesthetic, kind of regressive—I'm not saying it's one thing. Sometimes one of the things I hear is like an anesthetic kind of masturbation, just kind of a place that she can go where she doesn't have to think about anything. But other times I hear it as the other things, and her body shape is certainly important to her.

Supervisor: Yeah. And I think what she's doing is she's trying to make restitution for and trying to make her body heal up, the wound in her or the damage she did from her masturbation fantasy. "If I eat more, maybe it will grow?" "If I get fat and big it will be there." There are multiple ways in which she is essentially, in an illusory way, trying to put back the penis that her brother has. The image that she has that she caused it. They know she's damaged. She can't look to see what the damage has been, but she has all of these magical ways in which she's going to repair the damage.

Candidate: By herself.

Supervisor: Well, but how do you get bigger? Kids are told in order to grow up you've got to eat. So she eats more, in order to grow up, grow big. And I think that it means grow a penis.

Candidate: Well, that also. Maybe this is where the anal image of eat more so you can poop fits in.

Supervisor: Right.

Candidate: Which comes occasionally, you know, just sneaks its way in. And also eat so you can grow a stick.

Supervisor: The stick of feces is again a phallic equivalent, which you grow and which you can produce. "If I can produce it there, maybe I can produce it someplace else too." This little girl's mysterious understanding of, observation of—my hunch of what she's saying is that she's seen her father's erection or at least seen his penis large and then small, or maybe her brother's, and that she's seen changes in shape and wondered and been fascinated by it and hopeful that maybe she can get the same thing for herself.

Candidate: Is she likely to remember that or just reconstruct it?

Supervisor: Probably a reconstruction, but this image, for example, of herself as a balloon—my image or my association is of a condom. Did she find some of her father's condoms someplace? Did she blow one up and wonder what it was? Did she and her brother begin to experiment with them? Who knows? But the image that you see with the balloon and when you said put a pin in and prick it, there again I mean the whole imagery is of the same thing, herself as a balloon, herself as a condom, her body as phallus, of being penetrated, the vaginismus—this is more than just the neighbor saying, "I'm not going to be subjected to your sex"—

Candidate: Oh yes, oh yes.

Supervisor: It's fear of penetration and the idea of having a pin—

Candidate: Well, fear of penetration and the idea of having a pin stuck in, but it's also something about being looked at or being—it being public.

Supervisor: Sure. They will know.

Candidate: It's all about them knowing.

Supervisor: That's right.

Candidate: Because she was able to comfortably have sex prior to its being public. Like anything she can do just in her mind is okay.

Supervisor: You see, "Mother and the doctor now know that

I've been masturbating and that I've damaged myself." Or, let's put it differently: "The way they know I've been masturbating is I've done damage to myself." The guilt is not just for the masturbation and the image of damage, the guilt is for the fantasies.

Candidate: Whatever the fantasies were.

Supervisor: The masturbation fantasies. And those, then, are the fantasies you're going to try to get to now, what her current masturbatory fantasies are.

Candidate: Okay, that's the road.

Supervisor: That is a currently viable and active, immediate, affectively experiential way of getting to what the nature of the masturbation is all about. And then you may be able to reconstruct what some of the childhood masturbatory fantasies might have been.

Candidate: Rather than just going and knocking on the same old door again.

Supervisor: Right.

Candidate: What I'm saying is there's another route opening itself.

Supervisor: Exactly. And when she says, "You know, I've been masturbating more in the last few weeks," she's going to have some fantasies and those are what you want to try to get her to explore.

Candidate: Uh-huh.

Supervisor: But you see, to tell you about it is the same as telling Mother and that then brings with it all the disapproval, all the anger, all the pain and persecution, all the being looked at, and then Mother will know what she has been thinking.

Candidate: But with even being interestingly difficult and painful for her to tell me about being dislocated—she said something about how it was very hard to come back now that I knew about—

Supervisor: Hard to come back, what?

Candidate: Now that I knew that, now that I knew how—

Supervisor: That that was how she felt?

Candidate: Yeah, how out of sync, how dislocated she is. And the feeling of exposure in the analysis right now is very alive, very omnipresent, looking at her. And she will tell me and I will see.

Supervisor: Now, she came this Monday and Tuesday?

Candidate: Uh-huh. Well, she came on Tuesday. She didn't come Monday. She came Tuesday and said she's in the midst of this—well, Tuesday was pretty much taken up with her description of this uncontrollable stream at work. But it's pleasurable, she said. There's a pleasure because it doesn't hurt. And when it gushes out, she doesn't want to stop it because it won't start again.

Supervisor: That's a transition, I think, back toward the erotic, sensual, pleasurable elements of masturbation.

Candidate: And it is interesting that it's in this session and at my probing some that there is the beginning of pregnancy fantasies with her bladder filling up and she just doesn't—it feels good when she can just let it go and it doesn't hurt. She said there are different kinds of feelings, she even notices it now. There's when she has to push it out, and there's when it hurts. Now when it hurts is at one extreme; it still does hurt sometimes and she knows it's psychological. She always wonders, is it going to hurt? And then when she has to push it out. And then when it gushes out like natural and she doesn't ever want to stop it. And that's what her work is like right now. She keeps accepting more and more and more work. She is literally working twenty-three hours a day. She worked all weekend, she's producing top-notch work, she's getting all kinds of accolades for it. She's not getting everything done, and her fear is that because she can't keep it all in balance, it's just not possible to keep it all in balance, she will have to start shutting it down. And then it will get closed up again and she won't be able to start again. There's more material but that's the spontaneous kind of stuff that she brought in.

Supervisor: She's equating this with her creative process.

Candidate: Uh-huh.

Supervisor: Her creativity. How much can she let it come out and how much does she have to hold it in and then get plugged up and she can't let it out?

Candidate: Uh-huh.

Supervisor: Again, creativity has many different levels of meaning and fixations, all the way from anal, productive, whatever products she produces, the urethral business, the baby business, and then up to her head and her job and her creativity.

Candidate: Uh-huh.

Supervisor: So these are kinds of equations and fantasy systems that you'll want to begin to interpret her defenses against. She tells you that she's masturbating, but the hard thing is to tell you what her fantasies were, that somehow it's in the fantasies from when she was a child and also it's difficult for her to go back and recapture these. "And even today, you talk about sex with Ted as being so unpleasant, but you don't explain or don't come up with or have any awareness of why it's so unpleasant. There must be some sort of a fantasy, since at other times sex is very pleasant. The fact that it's not now means some fantasy is blocking it, that you're reluctant or it's difficult or it's painful or it's frightening or you don't want me to know." Whatever the interpretive resistance is, to come out with or to directly expose and express what the basic fantasy is.

Candidate: And to let us look at it.

Supervisor: Right. "For me to look at your fantasies is like Mother or the doctor looking at what you have done to yourself. And the fear is of our opinion of what you have done to yourself and what you will be punished for or of what you have been punished for." Okay. See you in a couple of weeks. Bye-bye.

Candidate: Yes, goodbye.

Supervisor's Comments

The candidate's initial question about the site visit may reflect her awareness (preconscious or unconscious) of the supervisor's countertransference responses from the previous session. But the question and the initial interactions between candidate and supervisor also reflect an increasing sense of herself as a colleague sharing an interest in psychoanalytic education and sharing responsibilities for the Institute and its functioning. The supervisor's response accepts and encourages the candidate's functioning as a colleague, and they share a sense of mutual accomplishment as the session begins. Then the candidate spontaneously initiates a return to the supervisory material and her wish to discuss some of the therapeutic process.

She then begins a lengthy narrative of the process material, to which the supervisor listens in a quiet, nonintervening way, with the exception of a few short interventions designed to clarify his understanding of the unfolding material. The material from the patient seems to confirm the supervisor's urethral formulations in the previous supervisory session, and in her interventions the candidate helps the patient elaborate the material at that level. The patient begins to reveal the origins of her defense of depersonalization. The candidate's sophisticated level of function is seen in the way she directs the patient's attention to her own incorrect or ineffective interventions, having recognized the transference references in the patient's manifest material about an artist whose work she rejected. Also evident is the candidate's confidence in herself, her willingness to acknowledge her failure to understand, without defensive self-justification. At the same time it allows the patient to feel more comfortable about her own reluctance to confront the candidate. This interchange helps the patient confront her disappointment in the candidate as well as to voice criticisms and doubts.

In retrospect, the possibility exists that a parallel process had occurred in the previous supervisory session, when the supervisory was "off base" in his interventions, but the candidate had been unable to actively confront that issue during the supervisory hour. At the time, however, the supervisor did not recognize or appreciate this possibility when the focus returned to the patient and the therapeutic process.

The supervisor's remark about pain as the maternal persecutor presents a deep, primitive concept to which the candidate's response is an empathic first-person expression of the patient's conflict ("It all got pinned on me").

As the narrative continues regarding the patient's cancelation, the candidate indicates her capacity to observe subtle differences in the patient's behavior and to recognize their various meanings. She renews the narrative, but the patient's material is predominantly at the level of resistance and avoidance; finally she indicates through a dream the feeling of having been misunderstood and needlessly hurt. The patient continues to complain of the distress and pain she is experiencing, feeling misunderstood and discriminated against, and the candidate recognizes that the patient is referring to the transference ("Here?"). The candidate is then able to follow with an interpretation, demonstrating to the patient how she turns her anger, hurt and shame back upon herself in the form of humiliation.

In her interaction with the patient, the candidate is able to make use of an appropriate case vignette from the psychoanalytic literature (Arlow, 1966), another indication of her capacity to use her associative processes to formulate appropriate interventions based on material not the patient's. The supervisor indirectly supports this by commenting on the authorship of the vignette, and the candidate explains her rationale for using this kind of intervention at an effective and sophisticated level of conceptualization.

The patient responds positively to the candidate's intervention ("Yes, that's what it feels like"), and is able to elaborate upon it. It is possible that the patient's response was suggested relatively directly by the nature of the candidate's vignette, but even so, the elaboration is effective and focused on a major personal trauma. The fact that it was so successful is an indication that the candidate's use of the clinical vignette was probably based on an empathic identification with the patient's distress. Candidate and patient interact at an empathic experiential level, and reconstruct and recall the distress, pain, and helpless difficulty the patient experienced in the urethral dilations and catheterizations.

The supervisor's question interrupts the flow of the candidate's narrative, but he seems to recover and recognize his poor teaching technique by admitting, "I'm asking you to guess what's in my mind." When the candidate indicates that indeed she had been confused by his intervention, he begins actively to explain that his formulation focused on issues of masturbation and fantasies of bodily damage, as well as on resistances against the experience or expression of the details of the masturbatory fantasies.

Supervisor and candidate then begin an active interchange in which they formulate their understanding of the patient and her material. The candidate asks a cogent theoretical question in regard to regression, to which the supervisor responds in an explanatory, clinical-theoretical fashion. The candidate is capable of responding with new material partially confirming the supervisor's formulation.

They continue this interchange in regard to the unconscious dynamic meanings of the patient's material, during the course of which the supervisor introduces a new formulation, the equation of body and phallus, as well as some technical suggestions in regard to the candidate's fostering the emergence of the material in question.

The candidate resumes the narration and demonstrates that the patient is increasingly capable of free-flowing associations organized in a primary process mode, as well as an immediate and direct response to the candidate's transference interpretation about sticking a pin in it ("that struck a chord"). The patient can also associate from early primitive fantasy to current reality and into the transference, as well as back to current interactions outside the analysis. This material also illustrates the development of a neurotic symptom (vaginismus) in a precipitating situation that has specific meaning for the patient associated both to present and to early childhood psychic conflict. It also demonstrates the patient's experience of psychic reality in regard to damaging herself through masturbation, as she again expresses fantasies associated with the doctor looking at her during treatment for the urethral stricture.

Once again the supervisor suggests a line of investigation and intervention which initiates an active interchange ("Has she ever looked at herself in a mirror, at her genitals?").

The patient's material indicates a growing awareness of her active role in the creation and perpetuation of her difficulties. Simultaneously she is able to take distance on her immediate symptomatic experience and to begin to laugh at herself in an appropriate fashion. Once again the candidate demonstrates her increasing technical sophistication by interpreting from the current symptomatic distress to the childhood traumatic experience. The effectiveness of the intervention is confirmed by the patient's further elaboration both of the past and of current associations and material.

The candidate shows she is capable of tolerating doubt and uncertainty in regard to the patient's material without experiencing undue pressure or an immediate need to clarify things. Once again the supervisor suggests a formulation focusing on the patient's fantasies of having damaged herself through masturbation and her various attempts to restore the phallus in an illusory way. Supervisor and candidate then discuss the possible meanings of the patient's symptomatic behavior and material. They continue their formulation in terms of hypothetical primary process fantasies and equations. The candidate then makes an active attempt at learning ("Is she likely to remember that or just reconstruct it?"). Subsequent formulations and attempts at understanding lead candidate and supervisor to focus on technical interventions designed to confirm and develop the formulations being considered, and they alternately take the initiative in discussing the material. The candidate seems pleased that a new line of intervention is becoming clear to her.

She reports how the patient has become increasingly capable not only of observing her own sensual bodily experience and functions, and her associations to them, but of reporting to the candidate with a minimum of withholding or hesitation, all of which indicates further comfort and progress by the patient in the analytic process. These changes reflect increased superego tolerance for her fantasies and wishes; identification with the analytic ideal of open conscious awareness; increased confidence in her own adaptive and consciously controlling ego functions; further distinctions between thought and action; and increased capacity for reality testing and correction of psychic reality and fantasy. The patient also demonstrates a capacity to associate from her bodily functions and symptoms to more abstract and remote attitudes and experiences in regard to her work behavior, and patient and candidate demonstrate the capacity to explore these connections together and to recognize how two very different sets of functions can ultimately share a similar unconscious meaning.

The supervisor's brief comment about creative process elicits an active interest in the candidate, following which the supervisor gives a theoretically couched elaboration of creativity and its various meanings. He is attempting to encourage the candidate to recognize the derivative elaborations of primary process fantasies, and to illustrate how theoretical conceptualizations can be derived from manifest clinical material. The supervisor ends the session with a relatively detailed series of suggested models for therapeutic intervention.

Throughout the session the supervisor has been quite active at conceptual and theoretical levels, as well as offering immediate direct technical suggestions. It may be questioned whether this activity (particularly the suggested interventions) is necessary, as candidate and patient seem to be functioning well together. Candidate and supervisor are enjoying the experience and are interacting with each other in an animated and mutually evocative fashion.

In some ways this illustrates the pleasure and excitement felt by the supervisor who observes the analytic process unfolding in candidate and patient, and who enjoys being part of the learning process. It may be argued, however, that from the candidate's perspective the supervisor is taking too active and directive a role and not permitting or encouraging the candidate's independent formulation and application of technique. However, it might also be argued that the supervisor's level of interest helps the candidate appreciate more fully the richness and multiple layers of meaning the patient's material contains and expresses during this phase of the analysis. Were the candidate left more on her own, she would probably function effectively, but it is probable also that some of the richness of the clinical material might not be fully appreciated, that she would not be alerted to the possible meanings and lines of expression in the patient's material.

To some extent these are questions of teaching style; beyond that the supervisor is trying to encourage in the candidate his own sense of intellectual excitement at listening and associating to the material of a patient deeply immersed in an analytic process. This is an illustration of reaching for the broad educational goals of supervision described in chapter two.

Chapter 13

Supervisory Session 99

Supervisor: How was your summer?

Candidate: Good. I feel the fall grinding up again. The advanced psychotherapy people will just call me?

Supervisor: Yes.

Candidate: Okay. So when I hear from them—

Supervisor: Right.

Candidate: In looking over the material since we last met, I decided I'd like to break it into a couple of pieces and do some of it this time and some of it next time, because it's rich. The last time I saw you I think I had just made the first body-as-penis interpretation, her erect body.

Supervisor: And the rigidity.

Candidate: Uh-huh. And I think at the end of that session—I don't have those notes and I didn't go dig them out—I think at the end of that sessison she got a headache. And you had some thoughts about this headache being an explosion. So the next day she came in and started getting a headache on the way. And I asked her about it. She says she feels so exposed, so aware, it's like eating quickly. It feels like it's preventing sexual feelings, prevents her from feeling good in her body, it makes a heaviness in her chest and then stops all feeling below the chest. She feels very nauseated as she talks. All the way through this session she thinks she's going to throw up on the couch.

Supervisor: Which in the metaphor you're using would be—

Candidate: It could be an ejaculation. Eating fast like a pig, crams it in, feels like she could throw up, has a pain in her chest. She's having fantasies that seem so far off, so far away, of when she felt lean and mean. Seems like she was thin and looked good in her clothes and didn't know it at that time.

Supervisor: Has she actually gained weight?

Candidate: Not any more, but she did gain a lot of weight. She's holding herself back, she feels like she's a car, but she is not in the driver's seat. She's getting more nauseated. She doesn't know which is worse, men or women. Vicki is a tramp, it's disgusting. Vicki is this woman who just had a baby, I think it's the same one, I get Vicki and Sally mixed up. Anyway, they're these two women, both of whom are tramps in her vocabulary, they've slept with a number of men. At least one of whom, and I think both of whom, have new baby boys and are very proud of it in a phallic kind of way, and they're repulsive, trapped, obnoxious, creepy women. How could they sleep with different men, these disgusting repulsive women? Sex is subservient. It's not equal. Both people don't try to make each other happy. It's a taking proposition. These women, they don't want to have sex; she feels sick, she doesn't want to talk about it. She feels really sick, it's making her nauseated. She talked a lot about—I ultimately made a primal scene interpretation, I don't know what I said. In all of her fantasies the woman is on the bottom, is taking. It's disgusting, it infuriates her. She can remember when she found out about sex she wishes the two people could face each other. The thought about having someone on top of her disgusts her, it's awful. When she has had someone on top of her it's not been good. They don't give a damn about her, or her pleasure. They just want to get off. She remembers her father making all these disgusting sounds and she would lie in her bed and wait for it to be over.

Supervisor: So this confirms the primal scene.

Candidate: I thought it did.

Supervisor: Uh-huh.

Candidate: She always had feelings that she wanted to be better at sex than her mother, good in bed and yet still innocent in outward appearance. She wanted to be big and to have control over her pleasure and theirs. She did with Ted, she felt he was a Milquetoast, he was disgusting. Then when he wanted to take control it was awful; she felt guilty, terrible, she wanted to be pleasured and to forget about him but she hated him through that. If you're a man and you moan and groan you're disgusting and weak. If you're a man and you take control you're a goddamn son of a bitch. If you're a woman and you take it you're disgusting, a Milquetoast. Then there are no notes for a long time, and ultimately I made an interpretation. She went on about it, she kept getting sick, more nauseated, and having this terrible headache. And I made an interpretation of her body as a penis and the headache and nausea as an ejaculation. And she said that's why she's so afraid, because it withers and becomes pathetic. She has to keep it going. And that was the end of the session.

Supervisor: That's a very nice confirmation.

Candidate: Of the primal scene?

Supervisor: Of the primal scene, but also of the idea of the body as phallus, the idea that it's withering. Sometimes patients with eating disturbances will have this particular image or fantasy, they're getting bigger and smaller, stretching their clothes and then shrinking. Again, it's erection and detumescence.

Candidate: Yeah, there's a whole lot of that and we won't even get to all the material. But that gets confirmed over and over again. That when her mother was big and fat she was strong, now she's skinny and weak. Her push at work, when she can keep things going on this fast flow, is when she's erect and when it stops it's—

Supervisor: So it seems to be more and more confirmed by the material, so at least you're on the right track.

Candidate: The next day she was ten minutes late. She feels okay when she leaves but almost shy when she comes back, almost embarrassed that she wants to talk about this more. She saw women jogging this morning as she was driving to work, arms and legs real tight, not an ounce of flab. It reminded her of her body as a penis, that's how she wants to be—tight, taut, powerful. Strange dream. This is a period of time that's just replete with real interesting dreams. Sally Jones, who's one of these—Sally and Vicki. Sally Jones and her husband were living in the same apartment complex and the patient walked into their apartment. Theirs was bigger and plusher and she wondered why. Her parents were there and Ted was there. She was trying to get Ted out of town and kept finding more of his clothes and shoes around. She couldn't get them all out. Sally Jones came out, the patient was hiding in a closet, scared, and her mother kept coming and checking on her to see if she was okay. Ted was going through her mother's wallet looking for money, and she asked why he was doing that. She found a rolled-up wad of money in his pants. He said, no, he didn't have money. And she couldn't figure out why he was lying, or if he was lying, or if he didn't know that it was there. In the plush apartment with Sally Jones, and she asked to see the baby, and Sally Jones said, "Why, you've never cared about the baby before." She was then in a group of girls of her sorority, going to get something to eat. That was the end of the dream. The whole thing with Sally Jones and a bigger apartment reminds her of her parents and her brother. She had the one smaller bedroom; her mother had the whole damn house. She was found out about her feelings about her brother. She never cared about him before. She was losing herself behind the girls, hiding behind the drapes and in the closet, miles away from her parents' room. Wanted her mother to come and hide with her. The money, it was as if she didn't trust him or something. I asked her about how the money was, what it looked like. She said, well, it was rolled up in his pants and then she laughed and said, "It's similar to a penis, it's very valuable." And the clothes, she could never get rid of her brother. It feels like so long ago that Ted left. Why does he take more from her mother?

Supervisor: Why does he take?

Candidate: More. He's going through her mother's wallet for money. And I said, "Who owns it and where does it come from?" In this session, and in several of these sessions, it made sense as we were going on, talking on, that we were talking about two things at the same time, penises and bodies and the tangible, the money or whatever else she's talking about.

Supervisor: She's asking a question. "Why did my mother give my brother the penis, not me?"

Candidate: That's right, and that's getting more and more

explicit. Mother gave him one and didn't give her one. This is in response to my saying, "Who owns it, where did it come from?" Mother gave him one and didn't give her one. She had him, he came out of her body. Because he had one she chose to make him big and strong. Father is in the background. A lot of frustration and jealousy, that's how she felt in the dream with that damn wad of money. Here he has this and she has nothing, she thought in the dream. Sally Jones had a plush apartment and Ted had a wad of money and she had nothing. It felt—

Supervisor: Sally Jones somehow is the boy with the penis, as with Vicki, and that's why she's so angry at these two women.

Candidate: Uh-huh. It felt, it's one of them. If felt like when he took the money out of the wallet: "You have no shame, you take and you take and take." She's afraid of leaving her mother like a shriveled-up penis. Like her brother took it. She sees Sally Jones as successful, her plush apartment. She has her penis on. In the Jewish family the boy is the great white hope. Sally Jones did it, she had a boy, she did it on the first try, her mother had to do it on the second try, then she had a miscarriage. It was all one. Then she had to become one to give it back. The patient had to become one to give it back. That's part of her personality.

Supervisor: Give it back, meaning—?

Candidate: There's a fantasy in here which gets more explicit, I think, later, that if she became thin, that her mother needed—

Supervisor: If she became a penis, her mother would want *her*.

Candidate: Yeah, her mother would want her, and part of the weekend trouble is that I am rejecting what she's offering me with her penis-body. And, going away, I need someone else to nourish me. She can't somehow get it across to me.

Supervisor: She would be available, the one that could give it to you. "You're turning me down."

Candidate: But the defect, part of the defectiveness, then, is that she obviously, even if she turns herself into a penis, she can't nourish. She can make herself bigger and bigger and stronger and stronger, but I won't take her up on it. She sees a man's penis like a—it's a wonderful image—as a gasoline pump at a gas station. It feeds the car and then the car drives so long, and then it runs out and needs another gasoline pump. And on the weekends I go to my gas station.

Supervisor: Which is part, then, of the primal scene, where she's listening to Father, waiting for him to get finished filling her mother up.

Candidate: Uh-huh. And where she's furious because she keeps, when Father's traveling, she keeps being there for Mother and offers herself to Mother, but Mother keeps going back to this sniveling idiot, as she eventually describes him. She lost weight when I got fat and pregnant and big. She gained weight when her mother lost weight. When her mother was here last week she said she seemed so little and so pathetic. At some point she was big and strong and her father was weak and pathetic. She had all the money in her purse. When the patient was little he was soft, she laughed, and gentle. Then at some point he became enraged and bigger, bigger than life. After Harold was born he got crazy. She talked about her fantasies and weight loss and said, "Maybe being thin is like having all the parts and not needing anyone. Wow, Jesus Christ, my head just started pounding," and that was literally the end of that other session. I couldn't follow all of it. That was a Thursday session. I got a call on Sunday from my service saying that she had left a message that she had to be at a funeral; she would see me Wednesday.

Supervisor: So ordinarily you see her Monday, Tuesday, Wednesday, Thursday. So that had been the last session.

Candidate: Yeah. So she comes in Wednesday full of the events of the weekend. Thursday night her grandmother had gotten sick. This is the grandmother she loved, and then for four years she hated her and didn't have anything to do with her, and thought she never liked her. And now she realizes again that she loves her. And her main experience with her grandmother's getting sick was that it's damn dangerous to like somebody, because you can lose them, and it's much easier—it's so painful to love someone and so much safer to put it all into inanimate things like work. And while she was visiting her, her mother came up and drove to Peoria. The patient took her there to see the sick grandmother. The grandmother turned out not to be lethally ill, but in the meantime her uncle, whom she was very close to, died. And the mother, I think this is the grandmother's brother who died, and so the mother stayed through the funeral and the father said to the patient, "Well, you better stay for the funeral too, your mother will need to have somebody with her." And she was enraged with her father for dumping the care of her mother on her. While she was at the funeral and all the surrounding events, she met a guy she had necked some with a long time ago. He's recently married and he and his wife have separate bedrooms and his wife said she should never have married him. The patient had fantasies about him, wants to have sex with him. He's married but not really. She also has some fantasies and wishes, and very intensely, about a man at work. She's scared. She would act on them if she had the chance. She knows she would. She feels terribly guilty and ashamed and it feels like a childish guilt. It's so similar to her parents, especially knowing that he and his wife don't sleep together. And she feels awful, as if everything is descending at once and she can't stop it. She talked about the new John Travolta movie and feeling very attracted to John Travolta and feeling that he was somehow familiar, and she described him, feeling that she had known him, and then she realized through a series of events that he looked, he reminded her in the movie of Harold Frank. Her infatuation with Harold Frank came in that period of time right before I had the baby, when she was getting thin, or she had gotten really quite thin. She was really full of herself, sexually very alive and aware, and very in touch with her body. It's all connected with that period, I said, and with your freedom to feel sexual feelings. And she said, "yes and you got disgusted and went off and had another baby." She vowed when she was a little girl that she would be very good; the urethral stricture was a punishment and she was going to be good, no matter what the price was. The next day she has a dream. Woke up with a bad dream. Ted was following her around and she couldn't stop him. He wouldn't stop. He started screaming at her. He said he was living in a building, in that building. And she said she didn't buy that building, and he said, yes, you signed for it. She didn't know that she had done that and she was furious. He wouldn't stop following her and teasing her. The police pulled up, two women and a man. And he took off and they arrested her. She's coming up for trial, the bankruptcy trial, that's part of the day residue. I think it's the following Tuesday and this was a Thursday. They arrested her, he took off. They wouldn't tell her why they arrested her; they took her to a dumpy little house and she demanded her one phone call and called her Uncle Dick, who's her lawyer, and got her aunt in Peoria and her mother. She told them she was calling for Uncle Dick and hung up. And then they told her no more calls and she couldn't find Uncle Dick's number and she asked why was she there and they said because of the property. She felt real trapped. She felt like her mother held the key. She wouldn't talk. She felt like her mother held the key but she wouldn't tell her what to do with it. She felt very abandoned and the feeling of abandonment was so intense. Regarding Ted and the anger at her father for not coming in and being with her mother during the funeral. The teasing, the tormenting, but leaving when it got too hot. The dumpy house made her question whether they were really cops. Then she wondered why she was being arrested, kind of reminds her of the urethral stricture. She finally told her mother what happened, she wanted to be able to take care of herself, she was turned over to someone else, there was no one she could talk with. Her mother was being frivolous on the phone and telling her what they were having for dinner. Amanda turned her in. Amanda was crazy about Ted. (Amanda is the woman they bought a building from; they owe money to Amanda in this bankruptcy. Amanda was crazy about Ted. Amanda is a crazy woman, makes threatening phone calls, runs around in her—she's just an unusual lady.) Anyway, Amanda was crazy about Ted and wanted the patient out of the picture, like her mother turned her in. I asked about the building that she said she didn't know was hers, that Ted was moving into; he kept it from her, he needed it, from her. She racked her brains, what papers did she sign? What made her buy that? How come she owned it? The first thing that comes to her mind is that it could be his penis, but that just doesn't fit quite right. It reminds her of feeling so open and so vulnerable in the relationship. She gave everything, there were parts of him that he didn't give. There were a lot of lies. There were so many things she didn't know and that she didn't want to know. She feels real taken in. She was this stupid trusting person who was really taken in to believing that he would make all these dreams come true. How could he mess up so much? How could anybody mess their life up so much twice? He is so much like her father. He'd listen to any schmoe around but never to her. He'd listen to anyone. Details of her life with Ted. And then she eventually got around to talking about the police people. She is sure about the two women. She's not sure there was a man there. She thinks there was a man. The women were real close. They worked together real well. The man seemed secondary. They were really mean and awful. She felt the reason she was there was that she had trusted someone who had led her down the garden path. She was paying for it because of the jealousy of this old woman. Cinderella and the two stepsisters with a modern twist. And I said that yesterday she was talking about her recently discovered sexual feelings and fantasies and she said she wanted to yell out, "I haven't been sleeping with him, goddamn it." So they would tell Amanda. But somehow the building, there was that building, and she knew that that made her guilty. That's why they were arresting her. She hates talking about these things. It must have to do with penises but she doesn't—it doesn't fit. And I said he's living in the building and she didn't even know she had it, as if it has to do with spaces inside her, her vagina, her bladder, rooms like the rooms in her apartment dreams, with broken bodies. She said, "That feels perfectly right." That infuriates her. With the reality that men aren't so great. All of the time he was living off her in this fertile place. She tried to make him into this man she wanted him to be; it enrages her. Now she goes on, and there's a lot of unnecessary stuff in here, but as she goes on and on I kept thinking that she was molested as a child. Let me just finish this. I didn't say anything, it's just something that keeps, and it may just be that the urethral stricture dilation, that's an invasion and a molestation, but there's always this, this guy is getting off scot-free, and some feeling of being invaded and led down a garden path, and she was taken advantage of and didn't know it. It reminds her of losing her virginity and not knowing it. She's always been angry that she can't feel a man's penis when it's inside of her. She never knows if it's there or not. Even if she feels the pressure, somehow like she has no sensation deep inside, just the clitoris. She has always had the fear that she'd get punctured. She read that if a woman was on top she could get punctured. She likes being on top because she can control the position of the clitoris. She was afraid she'd get broken again, not knowing that the penis was inside of her, not being able to feel that it was there, that there was a space there, not being able to ask. I wondered if this dream—something about fantasy and sexual play when she was young. It feels to be about that, and about being pregnant. In this fantasy he's living inside of her in this dream. He was living in this old building that she didn't know she had. Then she felt trapped and scared. She didn't want to give everything up in the bankruptcy. She didn't want to lose that. Then these women took her away and the whole thing is based on Amanda's jealousy, she adored Ted. Somehow this building, even if she hadn't had sex with him no one would believe it because of this building, it proved something.

Supervisor: Has this come up before, that she's vaginally anesthetic?

Candidate: This was the first time.

Supervisor: That's what I thought.

Candidate: Monday she has a dream that she can't get the door locked. And that's the first of several dreams of being somewhere and feeling that somebody's going to break in and steal something. She can't get the door locked, there aren't enough locks; she can't get the door shut, she can't get safe.

Supervisor: I wonder why, after all this time, this comes out? Why hadn't it come out before?

Candidate: It surprised me.

Supervisor: It surprised me too.

Candidate: And I'm not quite sure what to make of it. I just kind of, didn't make any kind of intervention because I didn't know.

Supervisor: Yeah, sure. I think that one of the things that's happening is that, as this fantasy of being a penis has become conscious after your interpretation of it to her, and after she recognizes how much she has been involved in that image and fantasy in her vomiting as ejaculation, simultaneously, although it's not explicit in the material, she's probably correcting that image. And she's saying, in essence, "I can't do it, it's impossible, I'm whistling Dixie, it's not going to work." So as it doesn't work, and as that line of defense, "Who needs the insides of her body because I'm a penis?" is gone, then comes the acknowledgment—

Candidate: That she's got insides.

Supervisor: "I have to have the insides because that's all I got." And I think, as you mentioned, why was she so outraged at her father's saying to her, "You stay with your mother over the weekend, she needs you." In many ways, what she'd said in the transference to you, and what she'd experienced as a child was: Father goes off on weekends, Mother—I am here—let's get together. Here she has a chance.

Candidate: There's a wonderful confirmatory dream a month from this. She has a wonderful dream, maybe just two or three weeks from this, where she and her father are going to Europe together. She's in the car with him and they stop somewhere. And her father gets out and her mother gets in and her father says, "Surprise, your mother's really here." And she's happy. And either in the dream or in response to the dream, she said, "What I wanted all along really was"—and this was after a whole series of things—"what I wanted all along really was my mother. And because Mother wouldn't have me, I decided to pay her back by taking her man." Just as in response to my vacation or in response to a weekend, she has a fantasy: She gets real interested in some married man at work whose wife is about to have a baby, and she said that it's in response to my absence. If I'm going to reject her then she'll take my husband and let me see how it feels to be left alone. But what she really wanted was her mother, and her father was the substitute in an attempt to get back, which I think is confirmatory of what you're saying.

Supervisor: You see, what I'm saying, then, is that in a sense automatically, as a result of the insight resulting from your interpretations, although it's not explicit in her associations, and you haven't said it explicitly, she's correcting and giving up—

Candidate: The body as a penis has never come up again.

Supervisor: Yeah. Giving up the image of body-as-penis.

Candidate: And she's lost twenty pounds.

Supervisor: That confirms it. She may be talking to herself but not reporting it to you, but the correction factor—suddenly that whole set of behaviors and symptoms and expressions and fantasies is dissolved and the pathogenic effect is gone. Now she can begin to address herself as a woman, with the apparatus of a woman.

Candidate: In fact she comes in, I have on the top of the next page, she comes in dressed nicely, with her nails painted and her hair just cut. It's the first time that I can remember. This was a woman who was immaculately groomed when she first started treatment, and has turned into a real slob. She was immaculately groomed as a little girl, with cute shoes, and now she's coming back looking more as a woman.

Supervisor: So all of this behavior, both behaviorally and associationally, as well as in terms of her fantasy life, has begun to confirm this idea. That has been one of her hang-ups, and now it's gone. It's a pathogenic fantasy system. Now the other, more appropriate lines of development of behavior can occur, including, in a sense, the discovery of her vagina, first through the recognition of its absence, psychologically, and that's what she's getting at. That's why it's just started to come through now, after four years of analysis.

Candidate: Isn't that interesting!

Supervisor: When you have nice, rich, uncontaminated, and responsive affective material like this you can begin to see these kinds of patterns, which you can't see in many other cases because the material is so fragmented. There's such enormous resistances against spontaneous emergence of this kind of material, where you make an intervention and she is able to confirm it and go on with it and it moves—

Candidate: It moves quickly, relatively quickly.

Supervisor: It moves very quickly, and that's why you can see the sequence so much more clearly. And it's worth a written vignette of the effects of that interpretation, the dissolution of the fantasy and the behavioral change. All of which was not explicitly directed by you or alluded to by her. She doesn't come and say, "Look at my beautiful nails"; she just has painted her nails and neither you nor she—you notice it but don't say anything, and she doesn't say anything. But there's a behavioral shift. It's a very nice illustration, in a clinical vignette, of the effectiveness of a properly timed correct interpretation. Its effects are more than just spitting back, "You're right." She may say that too, but then there's a lot of other things that go on as a result of this interpretation, not the least of which is that you accept her. You don't need her to have a penis, or be a penis. So she can begin to accept herself. If you want to write a paper, that's a neat, well-circumscribed little vignette that shows a lot about the analytic process.

Candidate: Even with these crummy notes?

Supervisor: Uh-huh.

Candidate: I had a hard time taking notes during this period because it's a real fast-moving—

Supervisor: Sure.

Candidate: And I'm terrible at making notes afterward, so whatever gets down on the paper during a session, that's what I get.

Supervisor: That's a sad but interesting phenomenon. When the analysis is going at its best you can't capture it. There's no way you can capture that material.

Candidate: And when you do get some of it on paper, it's real hard to capture that sense of talking about three things at the same time and the fact that you know that she knows that you know that you're talking about three things at the same time.

Supervisor: You're in tune.

Candidate: So all the pronouns can get all mixed up and you all know, you know what you're talking about.

Supervisor: That's right.

Candidate: And you know you're talking about Ted and father and brother, all, and it doesn't matter what name you use.

Supervisor: That's right. And it's inevitable. That's one of the sad businesses, because in terms of convincing people about what an analysis is really like, it's so evanescent you can't recapture that moment, and yet it's so clear when it's happening.

Candidate: Uh-huh, uh-huh. I have to leave at four so I have to watch the time. Let me see if I can capture this next session. She called to say, this was a Monday, she came in with her nails painted and her hair cut and everything. She had called earlier to say that she'd be late. Yesterday was a strange day. She was enjoying being alone and then late in the afternoon she got upset. She was upset Friday. Then details of meeting her mother at the airport, then the police came about this bankruptcy—the police keep coming to her house and making her late. But it's interesting that I don't hear very much about it.

Supervisor: Uh-huh.

Candidate: Then more about how she had to take the rap and he got off unscathed, and she can't believe that she hasn't heard from him. She doesn't want to but it's really crazy. I make a comment like again she finds herself in a situation where she feels a man gets off scot-free and she's left holding the bag. She said it fits into her fantasies about her father, that he'd play dumb and innocent with her mother, that she'd be pregnant. She doesn't know why this just popped into her mind, she thinks that she had a fantasy when she was a child that she couldn't get pregnant by her father. She remembers thinking that because he was her father she couldn't get pregnant. And later in life when she and Phil did everything but have intercourse, it never occurred to her that she could get pregnant. It never even occurred to her after she did have intercourse for the first time until about six weeks later, and then she had an absolute hysteria. And I said something about her father being very present for her in her masturbatory fantasies as a child, her hidden spaces of yesterday. She said she can remember one time seeing her father undress, between the second and sixth grade, saw her father undressed and thinking his penis looked like a sea horse. Now this is a woman who always maintains she knew nothing about sex and had never seen an erect penis, or an unerect penis. And I said it must have been erect because it looked like a sea horse. And she said yes, it must have been.

She remembers when she first saw him she couldn't believe—when she first saw a nonerect penis, it looked so weird. Her father's penis looked so huge. It also seems like she believed that you got pregnant when you decided to be. It reminds her of what has happened to her periods. She hasn't menstruated in a long time. She was silent for a while. She feels very vulnerable and very exposed. She feels people can look at her and know what's going on, like her parents could look at her and know that she had lost her virginity. The way she often feels that I know. She knows now that I don't know. She always felt through this whole analysis that I was baiting her, that I really knew everything, just like she really felt that her mother really knew everything after the urethral stricture and was just acting dumb. She really felt I knew everything and whenever I would ask questions or comment about something I was just teasing her, tantalizing her. That's what she referred to. We talked about that before—the way she's felt that I know. But she knows now that I haven't known. She really feels passive and doesn't want to be. I asked her, "Any notion of what it is I would know?" I would know the fantasies about her father and that she hates her brother. He got everything because he was a boy, he was king of the world. She fears that her mother knew that she hated him. She had a dream last night. She was at her grandmother's house with old friends, Roger, whom she had dated, and Harold and her mother. She couldn't get the door locked, she was terrified. Then they came back. Roger was real mean, he said to her—somebody was real mean—he said he wouldn't wait, that she had always made him wait. She was very scared. Her brother took over and tried to protect her. Her mother was very lackadaisical. Fear of being exposed, fear of being entered, almost without any protection.

Supervisor: Is this some of the material that leads you to think there may have been a childhood molestation?

Candidate: Yes, the discovery of this part of her that she didn't know she had, but that somebody else knew she had. The men getting off scot-free. This is the kind of material that—I don't know whether it's her sexual fantasies and wishes together with the urethral dilation, which is itself a sort of molestation. That could be enough.

Supervisor: Well, I'm reacting to the idea she's always thought you knew what had happened or what happens, and that she therefore has a secret, which she assumes you know, which in actuality she never realizes you don't know. Which also may point in that same direction of something happened, Mother should have known but probably didn't.

Candidate: And her fantasy about the urethral stricture was that her mother did know and was punishing her for it. And I asked some questions. I asked does she remember, at one point did she remember, anything about sexual play as a child. But I didn't make any interpretation. I felt on shaky ground, so I just left it.

Supervisor: Yeah, I would not push in that direction or ask that kind of question. It's going to come as a result of eruption or the return from repression. If you try to push for factual information it's just going to activate her resistances, and you may get an answer to your question but it's not going to get you anyplace.

Candidate: Yes.

Supervisor: So I'd back off on that.

Candidate: I did.

Supervisor: And just sit and watch it and see what comes out. At most you might interpret her resistance: "You know, when you think I knew and didn't say anything about it, there must be something that you were hiding from both of us."

Candidate: And all that she'll say is fantasies about her father.

Supervisor: So you've got to wait.

Candidate: And so I just kind of put little feelers out in different directions. I didn't ask a specific question about her father, I just asked kind of a general question like I'd asked about masturbatory fantasies. And in response to that she said she always felt very awkward and didn't want to be seen and would never play doctor with any of the boys, which is the castrated—

Supervisor: Yeah. Well, it's very rich material and it's very nice, you know, and she's obviously back in it, which is different than it was for so long when she wasn't getting there and was missing and skipping. And it also illustrates that even when there's enormous external crises, bankruptcy is on her, she's handling that, so she doesn't bring it into the analysis. It's also a good illustration of how reality is available but she's not using it for resistance; she could but she's not. And the reality is the same as it would be with somebody else who would be using it.

Candidate: Who would be using it, or some other period of time when she's using it.

Supervisor: That's right. Okay. I'll see you then in two weeks.

Candidate: Yes. Thank you.

Supervisor: Sure. Bye-bye.

Supervisor's Comments

After a brief informal interchange, the candidate reverts to the supervisory task, indicating that she has planned how to use this supervisory session and referring to the previous one (which had occurred prior to the summer break) and the material that had been most strikingly focused upon there. Once again she is demonstrating her initiative and responsibility as she participates in the learning alliance. She selects for herself what she considers the most helpful approach to the material she wants to cover. As the candidate resumes the narrative of the patient's material, both candidate and supervisor agree that the central issue is an unconscious intrapsychic fantasy within the patient in which her body is equated with a phallus.

As the candidate presents the material she becomes increasingly but intermittently identified with the patient in her choice of words and form of expression, thereby giving the supervisor an opportunity to experience something of how the patient behaved during the actual session. The candidate's affect and vocal tone are also part of this temporary identification, which is interspersed, however, with commentary. The candidate reverts to her analytic reporting position when she indicates, "I ultimately made a primal scene interpretation."

The patient's material indicates a significantly enhanced capacity to associate freely, with direct and affective experience, and to participate in a sustained analytic process. The candidate's oscillation between direct identification with the role of patient (providing the supervisor a three-dimensional view of the interaction) and an observational, synthesizing, or interpretive position is sometimes known as parallel process. However, in this instance it seems to be more effectively understood as a window by which the supervisor, through the candidate, is afforded a more direct experience of what the analytic process is like.

The supervisor's initial comment, "So this confirms the primal scene," is a demonstration of the importance of data from the patient in the evaluation of hypotheses. Supervisor and candidate had in the past entertained the possibility that the patient had been exposed to overt primal scene experience, but this had never as yet been confirmed through direct recall or reporting of such experience by the patient.

At this time the supervisor's comment is an attempt to demonstrate the importance of data, and the distinction between hypothesis and confirmation that analysts use in assessing the validity of their interventions and interpretations. The candidate's response, "I thought it did," indicates that this attitude has been internalized by the candidate, partly as a result of previous supervisory contact and work.

The candidate's description of her body-as-penis interpretation and the patient's direct and immediate confirmation are both couched in terms of primary process fantasy and experience, and are indications of how far the analytic process between patient and candidate has progressed. They communicate with each other at this level of experience without undue concern, and with apparently mutual understanding and acceptance. Once again the supervisor's emphasis is on confirmation of hypotheses, in regard not only to the primal scene but also to the body-as-phallus fantasy. The candidate indicates that she too has been aware of the repeated confirmations manifest in the patient's material for some time. This capacity to marshal apparently disparate behavior patterns, associations, memories, and experiences and to organize them around a central theme so that they become a more coherent construct, is another form of confirmation, which neither supervisor nor candidate chooses to comment on at this time.

The patient's response to the material the next day is a desire to return to the topic and discuss it further, thereby suggesting again the correct timing and content of the candidate's intervention and the idea that it is compatible with the patient's intrapsychic experience. She moves from there to further associations to the lengthy dream, as well as associating once again to the dream in a spontaneously meaningful way. The patient demonstrates her analytic progress when, in response to a question about what the money looked like, she spontaneously laughs, saying it was similar to a penis. The laughter reflects a quality of tolerance within herself for her own thoughts and fantasies, as well as a capacity to take her distance from them in a self-observing position, and to recognize her own use of symbolic expression in the manifest dream.

The patient's material demonstrates her ability to present primitive fantasies in a direct fashion without hesitation or inhibition, thus reflecting a well-established therapeutic alliance within which the patient feels comfortable in relating her fantasies to the candidate and whereby she is capable of suspending reality testing and undergoing psychic regression with reasonable confidence and without fears of dissolution or disturbing disruptions within herself. These are all indicators that she is curious and psychologically introspective, and is enjoying the analytic experience even though it evokes in her a variety of unpleasurable and frightening affects and memories.

The candidate explains her awareness of the varying levels of communication going on between herself and the patient. She is thus demonstrating both the capacity to communicate with the patient and to observe herself in her analytic work, as well as in supervision. Empathy for the supervisor is evident in her clarifications and anticipations of questions. She thereby shows an ability to move fluidly and spontaneously from one perspective to another, while responding and relating to the analytic material and process.

The supervisor joins the candidate in an active interchange regarding the primitive fantasies being dealt with, and the candidate's focus of the material into the transference is supported by the supervisor's participation in the expression of the fantasy

("If she became a penis, her mother would want *her*"). In this sense one could describe a parallel process occurring between candidate and patient in regard to her fantasies, a process reenacted in the supervisory session between supervisor and candidate. However, the description of this in terms of parallel process adds very little to the meaning to be derived.

The candidate is clearly aware of the implications of the patient's material and is enjoying the experience of observing this material unfold. The supervisor is enjoying the candidate's mastery, and is capable now of enhanced participation in the analytic understanding of the material, including the emergence of the primitive fantasies. This is in contrast to his concerns earlier in the supervision, when instructing the candidate in regard to technique, and the form her interventions should take was given priority. The patient's use of the gasoline pump as a metaphor and the candidate's appreciation of it are indications of the state of the process and of various changes, within both patient and candidate, that have permitted this to emerge as spontaneously and freely as it did. It indicates that the patient is capable of regression in the service of the therapeutic task, and is capable also of separation of fantasy from action; hence she is less anxious about the emergence of this kind of wish or fantasy. It means also that there has been a shift in superego organization so that her own impulses and their expression are less fraught with shame or guilt leading to conflict and hesitation, and that she is capable of observing herself in this activity, as when she develops her own interpretation about being thin, as well as about the conversion symptom of the headache. This material demonstrates the candidate's capacity to be a facilitator and to accept comfortably and without concern or the need to correct, the patient's primitive psychic experience. She is capable of understanding it, while also recognizing that there are elements she is not clear about; she can tolerate the ambiguity.

After a brief excursion into reality the patient returns to intrapsychic issues and conflicts; once again she shows herself capable of further exploration and expression. Both candidate and patient can return to an event that occurred a year and a half ago and to the patient's response to it at that time. They can now analyze the patient's responses to the analyst's pregnancy, responses which were at that time largely inaccessible.

The candidate continues her lengthy narrative in a lively fashion that lets the supervisor follow the flow of the analytic process. Both patient and candidate are capable of sustaining the interaction, the depth and nature of the process fluctuating without undue concern or inhibition on the part of either. The candidate's highly symbolic interpretation is effectively used by the patient and leads to more direct experience and to further associations. The candidate demonstrates her capacity to observe the flow of the material from a macroscopic perspective, to entertain hypotheses, and to search the material for confirmation or validation ("I kept thinking that she was molested as a child"). In addition, the candidate is careful to put off any intervention based on this hypothesis until further confirmation is obtained.

The supervisor shows, through his question in regard to the vaginal anesthesia, that he has internalized a macroscopic overview of the case. As the candiate returns to the narrative, the supervisor considers the fact that this material had not come up previously. Supervisor and candidate share their sense of surprise, and the candidate shows she was capable of tolerating the surprise without a need immediately to intervene.

The supervisor then begins a formulation aimed at elucidating the analytic process and the effects of what is recognized by both candidate and supervisor as an important interpretation of an unconscious core fantasy. Candidate and supervisor then focus on a presumed but silent component of the analytic process, namely, the patient's inner, unverbalized responses to a correct interpretation. The candidate indicates further identification with the supervisor's attitude regarding confirmation by bringing up a dream from subsequent material, noting that it is confirmatory of the interpretation being discussed.

Candidate and supervisor interact in a mutually enjoyable series of interchanges confirming the effects of the body-as-phallus interpretation. The confirmation is convincing in that the changes the interpretation stimulated in the patient's behavior, at various derivative levels, occurred without direct analytic dialogue or focused attention. The candidate expresses her pleasure at learning ("Isn't that interesting!"), and the supervisor uses the opportunity to discuss the process of confirmation through changes in derivative behavior that have not been verbalized or questioned.

The supervisor then shifts to a more scientific focus suggesting that this vignette be used as the basis of a paper. He thereby offers the candidate a model of how clinical material may be generalized beyond the immediate therapeutic process. The candidate's concern about her "crummy notes" leads to a discussion of the evanescent quality of much psychoanalytic experience, of how difficult, if not impossible, it is to capture this, to allow an outsider access to a particular experience and process. The candidate demonstrates her enjoyment of the multiplicity of simultaneously occurring phenomena and a capacity to deal with the process in a comfortable and stimulating way. She describes very sensitively the interaction and level of engagement between patient and analyst when an analysis is going well; each experiences the communication with the other in a deeply personal, idiosyncratic way and yet at the same time at an objective level.

After this disgression the candidate spontaneously returns to the narrative, noting the patient's capacity to sustain an analytic process even in the face of significant life events (a bankruptcy proceeding). The supervisor returns to the candidate's question about childhood molestation and the model of seeking confirmation in the patient's spontaneous associations.

The supervisor's first direct suggestion in regard to the candidate's psychoanalytic technique and handling of material ("I would not push in that direction") reveals that the candidate herself had already recognized the technical issue and corrected it spontaneously.

The supervisory session ends with the supervisor praising the candidate for the way the analysis is progressing. The candidate's need for direct technical advice is minimal, but what she does need is a sounding board for her own ideas. The candidate is clearly enjoying her role as analyst and is heavily identified in it, and the learning alliance is solid and mutually gratifying.

At the same time the patient shows that she is deeply immersed in the psychoanalytic process and is capable not only of sustained psychoanalytic work but also of intrapsychic change leading to dramatic modifications of behavior and of the internal organization of conflict.

Chapter 14
Supervisory Session 100

Candidate: This group of sessions, which is a continuation of where we were last time, the reason I'm dwelling on it, rather than just giving you a thumbnail sketch and going on to the present, is that this all happened just prior to my two-week vacation in August. She was enraged that I was going on vacation. However, her actual experience of my going away was that the minute I was gone she felt free and could enjoy herself. And there had been, like dominoes, a series of changes in her that I think flow from this material. If we can get through this we can then go on to what's happening right now. Changes—like her vaginal anesthesia is gone. She can feel, she's sexually alive, she can enjoy fantasies of a man on top as well as of her being on top. Her vagina feels electric when she's sexually aroused. She hasn't had intercourse with anybody, she's just courting someone in a new way. His moaning moved her and seemed tender, in contrast to her earlier attitude that when a man moans he's a pussy or something. She feels in a controllable whirlwind, as opposed to the uncontrollable flow. Masturbation is not satisfying anymore. She got her menstrual period for the first time in ten months.

Supervisor: The first time in ten months?

Candidate: Yeah, almost a year. She simply can't control or win someone anymore, doesn't have the impulse to win this man she feels attracted to right now. She must take the risk, feels open, vulnerable, scared, a lot of that. None of her accustomed ways of protecting herself against disappointment work, like believing if you do everything right the other person will like you, minimizing her feelings. There's a whole list of them. None of them work and she's not trying them very hard. Many of her old friends seem real neurotic and she doesn't have anything in common with them anymore, friends from before the analysis. She feels whole, like she has all the time in the world as opposed to never having any time. And she has stopped working eighty hours a week. It's just a cascade of—but it doesn't come on me like a flood. You know, like one of these floods? Though I may be flooding you with it, because it's all several weeks' worth written on one little piece of paper.

Supervisor: And what do you attribute all this to?

Candidate: I think it's coming out of this series of sessions, interpretations in this series of sessions, which is why I wanted to go over this material in detail. Because I think there's some unfinished business and also I want to understand for sure what happened. Let's see, she didn't want to come today.

Supervisor: Now this is before your vacation?

Candidate: Yeah, and she knows about it. No, I don't know if she knows about it. No, she doesn't know about my vacation yet. This is before my vacation. This is a Thursday session. It feels like she gets pulled apart, but she didn't want to come today because she feels like she gets pulled together during the course of the week. She isn't going to see me for three days and she's tired of being a big girl. She thought of every possible reason for not coming, but she came anyway. She believes I really care about her and am really interested in her during the week, and if she's good enough I wouldn't leave her on the weekend; she always falls short. She used to feel that way intensely, now it's more that she believes that she uses me up, she drains me and makes me need to go away.

Supervisor: To get away from her?

Candidate: To get filled up. She feels that I find her lacking, that I need someone or something else. She can't fill me up. She remembers the most obvious thing she said, that she's lacking a penis. She doesn't sound real excited about that. She remembers the fantasy about my going away on the weekend with a young man. That was a vivid fantasy, how I went away. But it was a strange young man; she feels it was representative of a boy child. As soon as she got her parents' attention something always happened with Harold and boom, they were gone. I go away on the weekend with a young man to get filled up. She depletes and she has no way to fill me up again. She doesn't know what her early notion of sexual intercourse was, but it's somehow connected with this. Somehow it's a boy or a man and it has to do with the penis. She doesn't know whether the fantasy involves oral sex. It isn't conventional intercourse, because that just doesn't feel right. Oral sex makes more sense in terms of filling me up. Seems irrelevant, a penis in a vagina. It reminds her, a penis reminds her, of a gasoline pump thing that you put in your car. And as I was reading this over, it made me think of anal sex, you put it in the back of your car. But it didn't trigger that at the moment. When the car runs out of gas it stops till it gets more. It was her mother's decision to have another baby and it happened. Dad had to nourish them both. When I was pregnant with a boy, a child, she couldn't lose weight. In the third grade she wrote an autobiography that started, I was supposed to be a boy named Alfred, that's what her father was supposed to have. So then he took better care of her mother during the second pregnancy and they had a boy. This fits with her feelings of not being enough, not being whole. She feels that she was the center of attention, she had gotten to be the center of attention, and it was wonderful. But then her brother was born and suddenly she wasn't enough anymore. Male children are the chosen ones, the great white hope in the Jewish family. When her brother was born she suffered a terrible, terrible shock. It's almost as if her father thought she was okay and so he had a son. An interchange about how on the weekends one of the ways she experiences that time is that I won't accept what she's continually offering me with her penis-body, and she said yes. She has always tried to be everything to her mother, but her father always had more to offer somehow or must have, because her mother kept taking him back and preferring him to her.

Supervisor: So a negative phallic-oedipal constellation.

Candidate: Uh-huh. The mother was always the strong one all those years; her father was a total pussy. She could never forgive her mother for taking him back, he's such a jerk. He's a total schmoe. However, she, the patient, is the total schmoe. She's just standing there, always has to do what her mother says, afraid to jeopardize her position, afraid. And I said, afraid to jeopardize some chance of her ultimate fixing. There was an interchange about this in view of the father being weak and the mother being the powerful one, with power to give and take penises, and fears of alienating me for fear of never getting what she came for. And in that context, somewhere in these sessions, I reminded her of her statement about analysis to begin with, and she felt that everything would work out and she would become happy and get everything she wanted, except something would not remain changed, something would remain unchanged.

Supervisor: But behind this is the fantasy when she came for analysis, that her analysis would give her a penis.

Candidate: Yeah, and that was explicit in this material, is what I'm trying to say. When I said that she said, "I wouldn't get a penis, I wouldn't get fixed." Thursdays remind her of the closing of the bedroom door and the long hall, and she always finds herself on the other end. I made a statement about her feeling left out by her mother and jealous that she preferred Dad, and being enraged, wanting to get back at her for that. I don't know just where this comes from. She said something about having to stay in Mother's good graces, because her mother held the key. Somehow it took Mother, she's not sure how, but somehow it took Mother to get fixed. Sometimes she thinks Dad would—after all, Mother gave Harold a penis. If she tells me how she really feels about me on Thursday, if she knocks my block off, I won't come back on Monday, and there'll be no hope. Sunday evening she gets anxious if she hasn't thought about me all weekend, because maybe I'll be mad and not give her what she wants. Things are falling into place for her, she says. Okay. Monday she has a dream. Monday and Tuesday she has two dreams, which seem to me to be back-to-back dreams. She felt particularly abandoned on Thursday after leaving here. Felt tense. Then things happened. Ted called, details, can't believe how angry she is with him, he's so naive and so self-centered. She told him to stay away. Then the executive from

New York, whom she went to New York with, called, and whom she really can't stand. This is a woman she's competing with for a man. She's nuts. One day she's nice, one day she's mean, the next day she's tough. Thursday after five run-ins with her she was furious. And I referred it into the transference. She said yep, it's too clear. She thinks she told the executive off. She told the executive off and it didn't work and it didn't make her feel any better and that's always a clue to her that it has to do with me and not with what's going on. This woman's there every day and pisses her off every day and she doesn't tell her off every day. And this executive, then she went on to tell me how this female executive is competing with her, jumped right in to compete with her for this man in New York whom they both met. And when they both met him this executive wasn't very interested, but something got started between the patient and the man and the executive jumped right in. That made her feel the rage, and it's rage spilling over from here too, it really got her. Then she and Harold over the weekend went to see their grandmother in Peoria. She feels so terribly vulnerable, this is the one who's always dying, and whom she said she hated for years in order to protect herself from losing her. She felt so very vulnerable loving someone; it hurts. Grandma is going to die, she can't stand it, she wants to turn her back on all of it and not care. Had a dream she died Friday night. It was so real. She woke up and called the hospital. She thinks she has really loved this grandmother this much all along but couldn't stand the intensity of these feelings and has been waiting for the grandmother to die since she was five years old. The grandfather died and grandma was sure she would die any day and would talk about it all the time. The patient remembers that every night when she would go to bed she would pray that her grandmother would still be alive in the morning. She dreamed about, this was the dream, she dreamed about Harold Frank Saturday night. Harold Frank is an old flame during the analysis. Harold Frank is a designer and he had told her that eventually she was going to be working with the top guys and would drop him. And in the dream, he had told her that.

Supervisor: That's reality.

Candidate: Yeah. That's reality, I think. In the dream she was working with the top guys and she had also made a booking for Harold Frank for the same job and hadn't canceled it. He was waiting for her. After the day's work she drove over to Harold Frank's and he was really disappointed and he said this could have really been a big start for them, they could have had a relationship. She remembers in the dream feeling she didn't want a relationship anymore with him. She had, but she didn't want a relationship with him. But because she had disappointed him she had to pursue a relationship with him. It reminds her of being a little girl and wanting her father badly and not being able to have him. And then she grew up and didn't want him anymore, she wanted someone better. That made her feel bad, made her feel guilty, made her afraid in the dream to hurt his feelings. That's what she felt with her father when her father chose Mother over her, that he wants someone better. Tied too with Diane and the guy in New York; he prefers Diane, Diane is better.

Supervisor: Diane is the executive?

Candidate: Yeah. Father chose Mother. I said it was a weekend and I chose someone over her. Now she feels bad, chosen over. She said the hallway felt so long, so very long, she felt so vulnerable; how much loving can hurt her. Then there was a fast-moving interchange about the competitive triangle to get someone better than her father, to pay him back, to get him to pay Mother back, to get Mother, but it was one I couldn't ever replicate.

Supervisor: She's oscillating between a positive and a negative oedipal triangle.

Candidate: Yeah, and with both sets of parents. Talked about her cousin who went—this has to do with this Peoria group. If you're nice to them they think they own you. She pushing herself mercilessly at work, it satisfies some competitive impulses or void in her; by doing more than anybody else she quells her guilt over competition. And there was an interchange about that, about punishing herself for getting something she wants. Oh, she must know about my vacation. An interchange about vacation; she resents it. I pry her open and then I go away. She gets lulled into trusting me and then I go away again. It reminds her of brother needing mother more than the patient does; he's sick, he can't play alone, needs me more. Doesn't want to come back until I come back. Wants to push on and explore more but not until I come back. This was the first session I guess after I told her, anyway it's pretty early on in the talk about vacation. I ask her about fantasies about my going away and she says she's mostly afraid of my retaliation. Oh, the end of this session is confusing. In that interchange about my going on vacation, something happened which was a mistake on my part. She interpreted it as a reprimand for her anger. I think, in fact, countertransference-wise, it was my guilt, and my not wanting to cause her distress and trying to say, "Oh, it won't be that bad." But it was just a fast thing and she was—well, we had to spend some time talking about that. She felt in the interchange between us that I was reprimanding her. She showed a microgram of anger and I was saying I wouldn't stand for that. She feels like she got reprimanded for all her brother's idiocies, she got reprimanded for everything. She always had to play with him, even if she didn't want to. She still has to now; he's living with her right now but she got rid of him. She feels guilty, she felt guilty about how hateful she was to him. She described how angry she is with him now. All of this in response to the mistake I made. So the next day she comes in,-where she's *really* mad at me the next day. The more she thought about this, the madder she got at me. And I was real careful not to relieve her of it. And the madder she got, she was real mad because of my remark, which she interpreted as "Cool it baby, I won't take that crap from you." She would never have been able to tell me that before, that feels good. The madder she got at me the more attracted she became to this married man at work whose wife was pregnant. It felt like to get back at me she'd take my husband. Then an elaboration on this vengeance feeling, and a dream from last night. She's going on a business trip to Europe and she's going to take her father and stay at a house they owned in Europe. At the last minute, they were on their way to the airport and the father got out of the car and her mother got in and said, "Surprise, I'm going with you," and stayed. She had real mixed feelings. She had wanted her father to go but underneath it seems to her that she had really wanted her mother. It's a representation of it all—she wants me exclusively, yet gets mad at me and wants to pay me back and take my husband, to leave me alone as I left her. She described the competition with Diane at work and said she feels that really is at me, but it's harder to direct it here because a lot of stuff out there is good fertile soil. It's also harder to direct at me because she likes me, she doesn't want to alienate me, she doesn't give a shit about Diane and Diane has nothing to give her. She described her brother moving in as just the same as Ted. She's feeling very rebellious but hasn't thrown him out yet. Elaborates on what a jerk he is, how he's just like her father used to be, impatient, unhappy, flies off the handle at the drop of a hat, sits around all day and smokes dope, the great white hope. She wanted him to be a failure and he is, and she feels guilty. She's *really* mad at me. She feels real led on; when I am here I seem so understanding, I egg her on to trust me, then bam, I go on a goddamn vacation and next it will be Christmas. I must have heard this eighty times in this two-week period. It's August already and I'm feeling like I haven't had a vacation in seven years and already it's going to be Christmas and I'm going to take three days off. It reminds her of the summer off I took. Every time she turns around I'm going away. Will she ever get done with all my going away? It's so double-edged; if she misses me that hurts, if she gets angry she feels humiliated. She trusted me, the joke's on her, I'm testing her, making her admit that she can't live without me. When she had the urethral stricture she felt her mother knew that she masturbated, that her mother had a plan, but over the years she came to feel that there was no plan, it's just a total lack of understanding, like I think she's a big girl and I can do whatever I want but she has to be pathetic in order to keep me. One way she is interpreting my vacation is "You're okay, you're doing fine." Father's coming next week for the trial, Mother won't come. It's always at Mother's convenience, just like me. Father is this big dog, he'll always be there, but Mother only when it suits her. The next session, and then I think we can stop and I want to talk a few minutes, is

Wednesday. She feels so lonely, just wanted to get out of work. This is the day she comes at the end of the day, after work. She feels so lonely and depressed. She hasn't felt this way in a long time. She called her grandmother today. She thought of her dying; it's so scary. She feels so vulnerable and exposed and worn out; she felt better when she left here yesterday. Just today is it this. The first time she tried calling her grandmother today, the doctor answered; next her great-aunt answered. And her great-aunt went on about her husband dying. She was so lonely after that phone call that she called her mother. But then she just felt lonelier. She just feels very very sad. Wanted someone to tolerate her sadness with her. She called the guy in New York for business and he was such an ass over the phone. It feels like everything has been stripped. She's tired of having to push herself, she's tired. Has been eating more this week too, hungry. Now her father is coming Monday and she's too tired. And then there's the trial and then I'll be gone for two weeks. She doesn't know how she'll do. She comes here, it's the only thing in her life she looks forward to. She's afraid to admit that, it's the same vulnerability as with her grandmother. She didn't speak to her grandmother for two years, she thought she hated her. An interchange about it's terrifying how much she loves and needs and how sure she is she'll lose and be alone again and she'll be trapped. She's tried so hard with me. She's been so good, and still I go on vacation. She interprets that I don't love her, that she hasn't succeeded in making me love her, that my taking a vacation is proof that I don't love her—that last part I said. She said yes, she really feels that way, she described the situation at work where someone is leaning on her and although she doesn't like this person she's trying to help her. When will somebody ever be there for her? She feels I understand her but still I go on vacation. And then she made this transition: It feels like a tied-together experience (it's a funny phrase) having to do with an erect penis and a deflated penis. She has to be strong and is, and then it vanishes and she's depressed. Has all these screw-the-world fantasies and wants to screw all the married men. It's not really getting back at me; it doesn't feel like that, but at the men. It's fuck you, I don't care about you, screw them and then walk away, want them to want her and then say screw you, I don't need you. "Humiliate them," I said. Yes, see them as sniveling idiots, screw him, have him want her and say that—I don't want you. Humiliate their power. And then she associated to a snotty comment she made to her brother last night which she feels guilty about and I interpret. I made some intervention about her struggling with wishes to castrate.

Supervisor: Castrate the brother?

Candidate: Castrate the brother. That these fantasies, these fuck-you fantasies were real castrative, humiliating fantasies and that seemed to ride right with what she was saying. She feels so depleted, so limp, so exhausted. We both talked about her mind/self/body experience of a flaccid penis, depressed, end of the hall, useless. She would leave them with a totally wanting feeling that she has always had and not knowing what to do about it, slam the door right in their faces, see how they like it. She interprets weekends and vacations as her not measuring up and as her not being a big girl and her not being erect, as her not being able to feed me, multiple interpretations of weekends and my vacations. And then she said now she would just like to go to sleep here and get up when she's ready. She was relaxed. She must remain erect; she has the fear of downtime. She eats to stay erect. Mother seemed so frail when she was thin. This is the next session, but as I re-read this, she was talking about—the uselessness of a flaccid penis and how she has to stay up. And I remembered as I was re-reading this that her father reportedly slept in a chair in the living room for many years and the mother told the patient that he had troubles with impotence, a long time ago. I don't know what this has to do with—it just keeps coming, like that.

Supervisor: "It" meaning what?

Candidate: More material in this vein. In the next session she associates by herself to having bowel movements, sitting on the toilet, trying so hard and being worried that it wouldn't come out. Her mother always wanted to see it, wouldn't believe that she had one, so she didn't want to flush it, wanted to be able to look at it and be sure she had one, and the feces-penis equivalence of it being a piece of her body. Used to worry that pieces of her body would come out. Used to eat so that there would be enough to come out, so that her body wouldn't come out. Feels so tired. She's driven herself mercilessly but is never satisfied, it's never enough, always wants more, better, expects each production to gain her recognition that she is worthwhile. It never lasts, keeps thinking of going to the bathroom; it's weird. We go to the bathroom, it would be such a wonderful accomplishment. Was always questioned about whether she went or not. Then the material that I just told you, her insides would come out. Then she would start worrying about whether she would be able to go the next day. She could never relax. Whenever she has a painful or difficult experience she can only steel herself against it. Moving her bowels and urinating, she described, were both very painful at different periods of her life. It was awful. She thought she would die. To get it started, either of them, at different periods in her life. And I made a statement about the possible fantasy about a penis being the proper equipment to urinate and an erect penis being a full urinating penis, or something having something to do with the proper equipment to do these things. And she said it was a life-and-death issue to her, whether she could pee or poop. Her brother didn't have a care in the world, he did these things all the time. And she remembers being jealous. She didn't want to tell her mother though, and she doesn't understand why. She didn't want to believe that she didn't have the equipment, she didn't understand. She didn't want to call attention to it; maybe her mother wouldn't notice. Then she has another lock dream where she can't keep things out, she can't lock the door enough and somebody's going to come in. And her fears of burglary. I asked her. She said she's always had this thing about locking the door. I asked her what would happen or what she was locking up. She said burglary, somebody would rob her. There's lots of material here that I don't understand, little bits of material I can't put into place, but big themes that I can without much trouble. That last session was a Thursday session. Over the weekend she wanted to talk to me a lot. She was sick of being a big girl and being strong and weathering it all. She overcame it and she was strong, but so much has opened up she can't possibly get through it all in a week. Then I leave with it and she has to deal with it alone, that's how she felt. She had her hair cut and a manicure on Saturday. She was really intimidated by the manicurist and she hated it. She couldn't look at the mirror when her hair was cut. And that's the middle of August, and now she's wearing nail polish. The shifts are so great. Anyway, she couldn't look in the mirror when her hair was cut. She feels grotesque. Last night she had another dream about locks. At her grandmother's house, the whole family was there and the door wouldn't lock. She wanted another lock on there. She feels the same way in her apartment. She doesn't feel quite safe. Then Saturday night she had people for dinner. Someone brought their child and she was furious. He spilled something on the tablecloth. She also wants to have a baby now. She couldn't stand everybody oohing and aahing over this kid, it reminded her of Harold, and then Joan called because she's upset and she had her come over and took care of her. She takes care of everybody, nobody else pays attention to her when she needs it; when she wanted to talk to me I wasn't there. She was thinking about her locks. And she's afraid of a robber, of someone breaking in. She's been thinking about her sexual fantasies of being on top and how weird it is because it always seems she's so much bigger than the man and it reminds her of the reverse in the urethral stricture, of how big the doctor seemed and how little she felt and how scared.

Supervisor: Now you're wondering, how come these changes are taking place?

Candidate: Well, my assumption is that the changes are taking place out of the work that was done in these two weeks—well, in all the time before, but that it's culminating in these two weeks.

Supervisor: And how do you put it together yourself?

Candidate: Some of it I can't put together. I can do isolated things. In addressing her body as a penis, she seems over a period of a couple of weeks to have given that up and she has taken on her female body. She feels that she feels the internal sensations, she's losing weight, she's enjoying being feminine, she's dressing and she's being attracted to men in a different kind of way than she was before. It feels different to her. And I guess I could maybe apply the same thing to her vengeful castration fantasies and wishes. More has gotten expressed in these last two weeks than was ever expressed before, about ways to take vengeance on me, the mother, for rebuffing her, for preferring a man, for not preferring her; ways to take vengeance against the man for having a penis, to castrate them as she feels castrated; some of the ways that very early in the transference, in the analysis, her real obvious positive oedipal father configurations—or some of the positive oedipal is part of the vengeance theme against her mother to pay her mother back. Some of her inhibitions of success and some of the ways she's had to punish herself for her success because it's retaliatory; she wishes to get better than them or pay them back. Part of my problem is that I need to write some things on paper because it seems to me like a bunch of things are coming together here and I can't—it's funny, I think I get perplexed, maybe I just get too concrete, I get perplexed about how, about experiencing herself as a penis. It's *real* clear, I have no problem with the fact that it's *real,* it's just curious to me. And it also seems real clear to me that that was part of her vaginal anesthesia, that she just didn't have a penis, she didn't have any of that equipment, she just got rid of it. It's a fascinating fantasy system or fantasy.

Supervisor: Well, let's put it this way. I think what's going on is the result of the analytic work, the interpretations you've made, particularly this equation of body equals phallus, but it's also determined by the fantasy that the analysis is going to provide her with a penis. For her that was your function. What was the reason you didn't? The reenactment with you, your selfishness, your not letting her have a penis, the negative oedipal configuration of what having a penis would allow her to do, have Mother to herself—these are some of the elements of what you might think of as her core fantasy. With that core fantasy, which probably stemmed from the phallic-oedipal phase and configuration and the birth of her brother, and was reinforced by the urethral stricture, there was then a retrospective investment of earlier phases of development with that level of conflict. So, for example, when she first went through the anal phase she's not such an obsessive-compulsive, but now, having reached a phallic level, she's competitive, body equals phallus, demanding, wanting to castrate, wanting to have her own, manufacturing one, Mother won't give it to me, I'll make it myself, and so on. That configuration, which is phallic and oedipal, is now displaced backward in time onto the anal phase. And even back further, onto the oral phase, sort of an oral-phallic activity. Eating now assumes a phallic quality in terms of "I will eat in order to manufacture a penis." "There's enough inside of me to allow a penis to be made and come out." And then we talked last time about the difference in body size, big versus small, limp versus fat, tension and nontension. These were all different manifestations for erection. But the oral phase has now again regressively been reinterpreted in the light of later development. This is analogous to Freud's case of the Wolf Man. And the primal scene which occurred at eighteen months or something, whenever it was, is then interpreted, from the point of view of a four-year-old, retrospectively. And that, essentially, is what's happening here, which is why this anal material starts to come out now, why oral material starts to come out now, the fantasy that she can manufacture a penis. But the core fantasy is phallic-oedipal. Positive oedipal, negative oedipal. Where is she going to get it from? Get it from Mother, get it from Father. Mother had it. Father has it. Brother has it. She *demands* to have it. These are all configurational elements of that core fantasy. That's why it seems at times so diffuse, so fluctuating, because, and we talked about this before, that core now is experienced by her with multiple derivatives.

Candidate: Well, and that's what seems to me the reason why we see so much change so quickly.

Supervisor: Exactly.

Candidate: And I don't distrust the change, because it seems to me like I don't have any trouble with this material as it is going by. It all seemed to hang together to me, although if asked to explain it I can't always say why; it just seemed to all be of the same stuff, although it was about a wide variety of things. Likewise, I can make a long list of things, and she's constantly noticing them, that are different about her, but it all seems to flow from the same unhooking.

Supervisor: This, in a sense, you see, is the evidence, or let's put it differently: the larger the number of derivatives that either change or are brought up or are mentioned, or are focused on as a result of a particular fantasy being uncovered, the more important that fantasy is. That's number one. Two, the larger the number of things that change without analytic scrutiny, just by themselves, without ever having been talked about, the more important is that fantasy. You and she, I don't imagine, have talked very much about whether or not she's going to wear nail polish, but she comes in wearing it. And it hasn't been the focus of attention. Frequently in analysis if somebody is focusing on "Why don't you wear nail polish, that's a sign that so and so," the patient will start to wear nail polish. That doesn't tell us anything. But when the patient starts to do that independently of its being mentioned here, or she begins to do things differently or walks differently, or she behaves differently, these are signs that a significant change has occurred. And again, the larger the number of derivatives that are modified in that way, the more convincing is the evidence that this was a core fantasy. Another point: the result of exposing this fantasy is, and here she is different from many other patients, that she is simultaneously, and without conscious effort on your part, recognizing and correcting the fantasy. For many patients the analyst must push them, confront them with the reality that this is an unrealistic fantasy, that the body is not *really* a penis.

Candidate: Does this depend on the nature of the fantasy?

Supervisor: Partly the nature of the fantasy, partly the patient's capacity for introspection and reality testing, and also the intensity of the wish and what the analytic process has been right along.

Candidate: Because she sure has done it spontaneously.

Supervisor: But the more she does it spontaneously, again, the more confidence you can have in the correctness of your interpretation. In contrast to, say, a patient who says, "I still want a penis here," and then the analyst says, "You know you can't get one, why don't you accept the fact that you're going to be a feminine woman, you'll be able to have as much enjoyment, as a matter of fact maybe more, as a matter of fact it now seems that women have more sexual fulfillment than men." You correct and try to confront the patient with the reality to get her to give up the fantasy, but here she is doing it automatically, without even mentioning to you that she's doing it. Only through her behavior.

Candidate: Which tells us that we came to and interpreted really important core fantasy material, as opposed to what I might only think is important core fantasy material.

Supervisor: Exactly. By correcting this fantasy herself, by unconsciously or preconsciously recognizing the irrational, by allowing herself and her reality testing to take over, by enjoying and discovering new pleasures in reality in contrast to the maintenance of her fantasy, she is undergoing significant internal structural change and is recognizing herself, and very well, and is correcting what was once a pathogenic distorting fantasy so that ultimately that fantasy will be dissolved. She will really experience the fact, "I'm not defective as I thought I was all these years; I don't need a penis to be happy with myself as I felt all these years."

Candidate: And that's how she's been feeling.

Supervisor: And that becomes the curing process, that the pathogenic source, the source of pathology, the fantasy, unconscious and therefore incorrigible, finally becomes conscious, or preconscious, and is looked at from a current perspective. It loses its pathogenic effects by virtue of reality testing, and a fantasy is corrected which has been a distorting influence all her life. When she finishes her analysis, at least if she were to be an analyst, because this will probably all be sealed over years from now, if she needed to have continuing access to her own internal, unconscious images and conscious recollections of her analysis, she would remember, "I once had that fantasy," and she would remember what its effects were but it would no longer have those effects. In other words, the fantasy would be converted, would not be erased—

Candidate: A memory.

Supervisor: It would be converted to a memory and not an active, distorting influence, dynamically, unconsciously having effects on her behavior. That's the curative process, or it's part of the curative process. In all of this, as she is enjoying her body now, she is finding that she can experience herself in a feminine way and have pleasure from the electricity in her vagina; she's allowing herself to be aware of her inner space and all the other things that are happening, and she is also giving up that old wish to have a penis. It doesn't mean the process is completed.

Candidate: So my stance for the last couple of weeks as she has come back just full of herself, she is so pleased, she has her moments, because life is not—but with new sensations, my feeling has been, this is something she needs to experience, and I don't do very much.

Supervisor: Uh-huh, absolutely.

Candidate: It doesn't seem to require interpretation.

Supervisor: And you would not want to be in a position of, "See what I've done for you." She's done it for herself, with your help.

Candidate: Uh-huh.

Supervisor: You would not want to say, "See, all that time I told you you didn't need a penis," and rub her nose in it, and this is where the countertransference of the analyst can sometimes get in the way. You wouldn't want to be envious of her success. Sometimes the analyst who has not undergone the kind of change that this patient has demonstrated can in some ways be inhibiting; unconsciously, they're enemies of what's happening. "I wish this had happened to me in my analysis." This is a process that is taking place now at a very rapid rate. And it illustrates another concept of the analytic process. Progress is not linear—we talked about this before—progress is geometric.

Candidate: How long we've all worked for this four weeks. (Laughs)

Supervisor: Exactly. This four weeks is not just four weeks.

Candidate: And that came up. She said, "We have worked very hard for this."

Supervisor: Yeah, but it's not four weeks. Everything that has happened up to now has been preparation for this phase of the geometric curve—and soon she will be moving into termination.

Candidate: It feels that way to me, it doesn't feel like she's quite yet in the termination phase.

Supervisor: No, not yet, but she's getting there.

Candidate: It seems like she's getting there.

Supervisor: It's an enormous rate of reorganization and intrapsychic change.

Candidate: It's *very* exciting. I wanted to ask you one other totally unrelated question. In presenting this at case conference I think I would like to start somewhere, just for my own personal reasons, because I would like to write a paper on this, I think I would like to start somewhere slightly back of the beginning of the body-as-penis interpretation thing and move up. My first thought was to start back where I changed the appointment time and she started coming again, but we wouldn't get to this material.

Supervisor: Let's start there.

Supervisor's Comments

The candidate begins with an effective summary of the changes that have taken place in the patient, and demonstrates her ability to synthesize and abstract a useful and integrated picture of the analytic process. She demonstrates also an empathic awareness of the problems of the supervisor—"Although I may be flooding you with it, because it's all several weeks' worth written on one little piece of paper."

When the supervisor asks the candidate what she attributes the changes to, his intention is to help her conceptualize the material she has summarized. The candidate responds with her own plan of how most effectively to use the supervisory session ("also I want to understand for sure what happened").

The candidate then presents in detail the process material of the sessions in question. She does so in a lively and effective fashion, reflecting a significant and sustained analytic process, and the supervisor recognizes that she has no need of technical assistance in conducting the analysis. The candidate shows a capacity to move from the primary analytic data to her own associations and then back to the data in a form somewhat similar to a free-flowing but organized associational sequence ("and as I was reading this over, it made me think of anal sex, you put it in the back of your car. But it didn't trigger at the moment").

The candidate recognizes the transference neurosis and important genetic associations from the patient. The supervisor, for his part, listens quietly, appreciating the candidate's mastery of the material and making only occasional and brief comments that assist in clarifying some of the dynamic meanings. In the material, the patient oscillates between current reality events, transference neurosis, past experience, and fantasies, and the candidate shows a capacity to follow the material and to recognize her own associational processes. She also identifies and comments on her countertransference responses and errors ("countertransference-wise, it was my guilt"), and recognizes the impact of her countertransference-inspired intervention.

As the material continues, the candidate shows a capacity to recognize the importance of the patient's affects, the experience and expression of aggression, and of not doing anything to suppress or inhibit it. The candidate is comfortable allowing the patient's transference-neurosis to be manifestly expressed, and she understands the dynamic process and participates in fostering it with the patient.

It is clear to the supervisor from the process material that the analysis is flowing freely and that the patient has consolidated her capacity for free association and access to more primitive levels of psychic organization and primary process thought and imagery. The candidate empathizes with the patient's experience and intervenes at the patient's level of experience and in her idiom. Throughout all this, the supervisor feels that the analysis is progressing very well, that the candidate's capacity to elicit and participate in the process is superior, and that there is no need for intervention by the supervisor. The candidate also shows an ability to move from specific and idiosyncratic material to a synthesized and summarized presentation of themes ("Then she has another lock dream"). But she is also aware of her own responses to the material, recognizing that in some areas she is having difficulty correlating the data ("There's lots of material here that I don't understand").

After completing, her presentation of the process material, the supervisor returns to the task the candidate had set for this supervisory session: "Now you're wondering, how come these changes are taking place?" The supervisor follows this by inviting the candidate to initiate her own attempt at synthesis and explanation. She makes an attempt to do this, recognizing her own uncertainties and the gaps in her understanding, and by attempting to formulate the process at the level of clinical dynamic theory. The candidate recognizes her own difficulties and indirectly asks for help ("I got perplexed").

The supervisor responds to this with a lengthy and somewhat detailed synthetic formulation, mixing clinical explanation, theoretical abstraction, identification with the patient by describing her possible experience, and an explanation of the analytic process. He includes some clinical psychopathological theory, as well as drawing an analogy to Freud's Wolf Man case, elaborating and emphasizing the importance of the patient's core unconscious fantasies. Part of what the supervisor is doing is demonstrating how the analyst's mental processes fluctuate from one level of formulation to another while listening to the unfolding clinical process and material.

The candidate can appreciate the supervisor's interventions and express her uncertainties, and has also recognized some of the issues raised by the supervisor. The supervisor then participates with the candidate in further formulating the changing derivatives as a result of a modification of core fantasies; in assessing structural change in the analytic process; and in elucidating the curative process in the patient, particularly the correction of primitive and distorted core fantasy systems. When the supervisor says, "when the patient starts to do that independently of its being mentioned here," his language illustrates an empathic identification with the analyst in the analytic process.

This is followed by an active give-and-take between candidate and supervisor in regard to the unfolding process and the nature of cure, expressed in somewhat hypothetical and generalized terms some distance from the specific details of this particular case. There is no need to emphasize technique or issues of the candidate's position vis-à-vis the patient, and the discussion occurs at a conceptual level. The candidate herself returns to an appreciation that her role in the process has been to allow the experience to unfold for both herself and the patient ("this is something she needs to experience, and I don't do very much"). At this point the supervisor resumes an emphasis on technique, tacitly praising the candidate for having avoided potential countertransference responses.

The candidate expresses her appreciation of the mutuality involved in analytic work ("How long we've all worked for this four weeks") and her pleasure at what she is observing and has participated in ("It's very exciting").

The patient is now making rapid progress and undergoing significant intrapsychic reorganization. The analytic process is typical of the late middle phase of a successful treatment experience.

At the very end the candidate shifts to a discussion of how best to present this material at a case conference and anticipates writing a paper. She is now capable of extrapolating from an individual case to different settings and other patients.

The supervisor is pleased with the progress both patient and candidate have made, and is enjoying the supervisory experience. He is now experiencing it less as a teacher-pupil relationship and more as an interactional process between a senior and a junior colleague.

Chapter 15

Supervisory Session 109

Candidate: We need to talk about how, and all those kinds of things, one sets a date; it's coming up a lot. I'm not dealing with it, because (laughs) I wanted to talk with you about it. By this time she must know I see a supervisor on Wednesdays. (Laughing) Interestingly enough, you know this thing that has been going on with this man, Robert? It's finally got clear to me how that's interpretable into the analysis. And that it's been the whole, I don't know the whole, but a significant portion of it has been acted out in the transference. Because her talking—remember last time, the day I saw you? The day before had been his birthday. She worked and worked and worked and made this birthday present which was a work of art for him. A piece of herself she characterized it as. It has teeny tiny imperfections, but she wanted it to be accepted and it was and it was really wonderful. Keep that in mind. It carried tremendous weight, far more than the situation warranted.

Supervisor: For her or for him?

Candidate: For her, for her.

Supervisor: Uh-huh.

Candidate: She stayed up, it was terribly fraught with conflict. She didn't know whether to do it or not to do it. Was he a son of a bitch, did he deserve it? She wanted to do it, but would he respond? She wanted him to respond, that is, to like her. Then she stayed up all night. Oh, and I should tell her whether to do it or not, and the fact that I wouldn't say anything was frustrating. It was dealt with at that point as, does she have my permission to go out again and get a man? Then she stayed up all night the night before his birthday, and she did it. And she did it wrong. And she's capable of doing it right. She says. She spelled his name wrong at one point. She did something else wrong and had to redo the whole thing. It took her twenty-four hours to do a five-hour project. Finally she put it in a cab and sent it to his office and had massive anxiety the rest of the day, that he wouldn't call before she came to her appointment and that I would be able to say I was right. That he wouldn't respond, that he is a son of a bitch. But he did call and he responded so much, in fact—I have a little contamination here because I've heard through the grapevine that he's letting it be known that he gets good work out of her by flattering her. So I have to kind of—it's been an interesting thing to have that in my mind. But he went on and on about how wonderful it was and how he was going to hang it in his house. And she just closed off on this guy. She said she wished she could enjoy it but she couldn't. So that's one thing. Another thing is that she goes on for days, intermittently wondering about this relationship. The characteristics of the relationship are that they are very warm and open with each other when they have occasion to get together over professional business. That he said, whenever it was they first met, that he would not jeopardize the professional relationship with a private one and she is chafing against this. She feels that he really cares about her when she is with him, but then when she goes away from him, she thinks, well, he doesn't do anything. Whenever I picked up on the professional side of the relationship, that she wants something more than the professional, it began to be clearer how many parallels there are from what she wants with him, her frustrations with him, and her frustrations with me. And how the picture was like the analysis. That here she had presented me this magnificent thing. She had done everything I had ever asked her to do; she was more cooperative and wonderful than any patient; and she presented me herself, the most vulnerable and precious parts of her, and what was I going to do with it? I was just not going to do anything. I was going to let her leave me. That she wanted something from me; she wasn't sure what; she didn't want to tell me what because that would spoil it if I gave it to her. That the notion that the way you end analysis is, that when it gets clear you set a date, and then you work toward that date and you end it. It was terribly anticlimactic and infuriating, that after all of this, after everything she's done, that's all that happens. So that was a very satisfying chain of events in the last two weeks.

Supervisor: Satisfying to you?

Candidate: Satisfying to me to see those connections and to be able to bring them in, because I had had a feeling that this thing is carrying so much power out there that it has to be something in the analysis. I haven't, but all the interpretations having to do with whether or not she can have a man, and my jealousy, or I'm prohibiting her—they have only gone so far but they haven't defused the power—

Supervisor: The intensity of the experience.

Candidate: Yeah, but the intensity, for the moment anyway, doesn't seem—well, it's not an every-moment intensity anymore. It's not gone, but some of it—she's not coming in every day with it right there.

Supervisor: Which is what *was* happening before you made the interpretations?

Candidate: Yeah, yeah. All roads led there.

Supervisor: Uh-huh.

Candidate: Yeah, especially as his birthday approached, you know, when she was agonizing about whether to give him a present or not and that I should tell her whether to give him his present and the interpretations about her needing my permission that she accepted. I think this had some validity, but it still didn't defuse it and it still kept coming up, until the interpretation of it being that she does the talking about the picture, that the picture is symbolic of something in the context of all the parallels between the relationship with this man and her relationship with me, and her frustrations and disappointments and her wanting something from me. And then the picture kind of disappeared. She became very sad, depressed, for a while, feeling very good yet at the same time very sad. The analysis didn't give her what she thought it would. The words weren't as important, I don't think, as the affect. She just felt mournful. And then she was furious. This was also, I think, in the context of having to do with Robert as well as me, and how the transference was spilling out there. Another piece of it was she was furious with her grandmother because she hadn't heard from her for a while and she called her up, or her grandmother called her, and she said, "I haven't heard from you in two weeks." Well anyway, it turned out that her grandmother was busy with her cousins for these two weeks. And the patient was furious, and her associations to that were that I was looking at my watch, the next patient will have something better to say, somebody else will need me more, "Come on already, enough of this, you don't need me anymore," and her feeling, her being pissed off at that. Also, another whole chain of feelings and associations, they've all been leading to this, has been her turning her sense that I am throwing her out into a sense of her guilt at wanting to leave me. That she always had the fantasy that if her mother was all of the things she wanted her to be, that she could stay with her forever and that I have come through and been many of the things she wanted her mother to be. I have understood her; I have helped her to grow up and to become herself more, and she still wants to leave me. But as she became an adolescent and started to grow older, her mother also seemed to be getting older and devitalized. She seemed to be vital and she's taking all the goodies from me, and our direct relation, she seemed to feel between her feeling that, and her taking goodies for herself—I thought at one point that I understood better the—maybe it will come back to me—that there was another way to understand the series of dreams where somebody is being bad to her. I don't, at the moment, remember it, maybe it will come back to me. Anyway, the other day she said to me—now, whenever she talks about this man, she most frequently refers it herself into the analysis. Like she didn't see him for a while, she hasn't had a professional reason to get together with him, and wondered if he missed her. And she then said, "I wonder if that has to do with here, will you miss me?" And then feels guilty that somehow, that she doesn't feel that she will miss me all the time like she feels she should. That she wants to leave.

Supervisor: And she's being ungrateful and disloyal.

Candidate: Yeah, yeah, that she's taking the goodies and leaving, that she's become vitalized and alive and how having gotten all that from me, she wants to leave and take it with her.

Supervisor: Take the good part with her, and leave the bad part with you.

Candidate: She knows that she is working out something via Robert when she works it out with me, because when she works it out with me, Robert takes a more manageable form.

Supervisor: These are illustrations, in practice, of her capacity for self-analysis, which is another indicator of change and of readiness to consider setting a termination date.

Candidate: Although I had to do the initial interpreting that Robert was a displacement of the transference.

Supervisor: Uh-huh.

Candidate: Right now she feels okay, this minute. She feels she can leave and it will be okay. She feels she can take at least half of the credit. Oh, we've also been talking about who gets the credit. Am I going to rest on my laurels, am I going to take her success away from her by taking all the credit? Is she going to give me some of the credit? Is she going to give me all the credit in order not to feel guilty for leaving? She can take at least half of the credit, maybe even more. She feels calm and okay. Then she will walk out of here and get crazy. She starts to feel guilty or something. She has thought she was finished a dozen times, when she wasn't. Now she is, and it doesn't feel the same. It's not a thought, it is a feeling. And she has such a mixture of feelings about it. She's not sure how she feels about it, in fact. It's not just a feeling of accomplishment or a hurray, like she thought it would be. It has all kinds of feelings of sadness and loss and guilt. The focus of her life is changing and that makes her feel guilty. Changing from telling me—oh, also, somewhere in this, the end of last week, and I can't remember the context. I suddenly understood something about why she always—my association to whatever she was talking about went to the fact that this lady, every time except once, has told me to have a nice evening or a nice weekend when she leaves. And I have been waiting to understand that, or to be able to talk about it in such a way that will make it understandable. We talked about it three years ago, a long time ago. But something in the way she explained it was that she was taking care of me by doing that. She was reassuring me that she was really okay. She was somehow protecting me, giving me something for the things she had taken. It's still unresolved, she didn't say anything as she left that night. She seemed to leave comfortably. She seemed to find it a curious habit of hers also. So I suspect it will get clearer.

Supervisor: She has noted it herself?

Candidate: Well, yeah, and I haven't said anything about it because a time never came up that I felt like this is what this might be about, so that it would be something other than—this is the lady I told early in the analysis to stop talking to so many people. And she compliantly stopped talking to so many people, but it also then removed that as something we could analyze at that time because she just complied with it. And whatever it was that triggered my associations to—aha! This has to do with her saying, how she says goodbye to me every day. It must have been an appropriate association, because she then picked up on it and said, "Yeah, that is kind of peculiar that I do that every day." And then yesterday, as she left, she said have a nice evening or something, and she said, "There I go again with my—" whatever, so that it will get clearer what that's all about. Yesterday she came in, on time—oh, no. Monday she didn't come. She came in on time on Tuesday. She felt really guilty not coming yesterday. She didn't want to work all weekend. She had premenstrual—she talked about her wanting to talk about how you set a date, but being, wanting, not knowing how to ask me. Who sets it? About wanting to leave all the difficult—oh, another thing that came up in interpreting this business about this man, when she said spontaneously, "I never thought I would get so attached. How the hell will I ever"—to me—"how the hell will I ever get unattached?"

Supervisor: From you?

Candidate: Yeah. And my feeling about it is she is *finally* taking responsibility for this, or starting to. That *she* is attached to me, that *she's* needing to separate from me. Not that I'm throwing her out, not that there's a good job and not that she's ready to leave any minute and I'm holding her, but that she began to have some real sense that she's hanging on and that she is terribly attached. Oh, here it is. There was some interchange yesterday of things that we have seen before, her fantasy that she's leaving me devastated. And I interpreted it and she said, "Yeah, I know. That's not the point. I feel like I'm evading something; I'm evading something." And there were several things like that. Interchange about these things being flat, red herrings, covering up something. Something that she feels she's evading with Robert and with me. With Robert she doesn't want to leave him; she wants to share her life with him. She wants to stop this battle. It's all about wanting to leave. Being all dressed up with no place to go. Waiting for something from me. For me to tell her what day she can go and that it is okay. Keep holding herself back; not afraid to fly anymore. Wants me to tell her it's okay. Wants me to say, "We can set a date." She's afraid to bring it up; she wants to. She's afraid she will stop feeling okay after she stops coming. She's afraid she won't miss me enough, that she will miss me too much. That's why she felt bad yesterday. She didn't miss me. When she didn't come to her appointment she knew it was because she didn't want to come to her appointment. She said that, and she made it impossible for her to come, which she recognized without my help, that she had made it impossible to come. She didn't miss me. She had a good day, and then she got crazy and felt guilty and made herself miserable. She also knew what that was about. I didn't have to say anything. She said that, and it's all tied up with feeling like and being a woman. Those feelings are getting stronger and stronger and she's having a tougher battle keeping them down. The last time she felt really good her mother found all these things wrong with her. That makes her want revenge, and afraid she won't be able to lose weight. I said, "to keep from exploring this revenge," which doesn't make sense; I didn't know what I was doing. Yes, because she wants revenge; she's furious that she spent all these years so fat and so miserable. An interchange about having to admit there's no revenge. She's so attached here. Oh, another thing that had come up recently is her feeling disturbed and angry that I will let her go. That in my responses I seem to be indicating that I would let her go.

Supervisor: That you are not planning to keep your little girl.

Candidate: Yes. That also, I think, was part of a series of responses on my part that have been making her take more and more responsibility for who's hanging on.

Supervisor: For what?

Candidate: Who's hanging on, that *she's* attached—

Supervisor: Uh-huh.

Candidate: And I think for her—and maybe for everybody, I don't know—but for her this date-setting process and then dealing with the date is the detachment process. I think that only so much is going to be able to be dealt with with her, prior to the setting of the date. And my sense of her now is that she is waiting, and she's, well, biding her time is a little, but that she is not going to engage in the final skirmishes until it is necessary. I guess it's part of her.

Supervisor: Uh-huh.

Candidate: She feels guilty because I have helped her so much, have been so good to her, and still she wants to leave, and she won't miss me piercingly every moment and this makes her feel unappreciative. She sat for a while, and she says she feels better and she feels calm. That's real characteristic of this period of time. She can be *so* upset, and then she feels calm. And it feels calm to me. It doesn't feel like a whitewash job.

Supervisor: You don't see her being so upset as histrionic, either? It's genuine, a working through?

Candidate: Oh, yeah. It doesn't feel at all histrionic. The way she used to be is histrionic. No, it feels more like she's fighting a tiger. You know? And then she gets into it and settles down, and it feels real. When she gets to feeling really good she—she was silent after she said she felt better and calm. When she gets to feeling really good, she has to reel herself back in, because she realizes how close she is to really leaving. She never thought it would be this hard. She always thought I would tell her, "Well, you're better, now it's time to go. Goodbye." If she has to tell me, it's a real double-edged sword. That's the end of yesterday's session. Whenever we talked about how the process of terminating an analysis worked, she and I, I said whenever enough of it, of what leaving and finishing means, is worked through, then we'd set a date several months in advance and work some more. And her response now is, "I've had to go through *all this* to get to talking about leaving; *I don't want to go through it for three more months.*" So she has this number three in her head. I mean, it keeps coming two or three, and then it was three. I won't do it, which doesn't sound—I'm not afraid of her leaving; I'm saying I need to talk to you about technically how to proceed.

Supervisor: Now, what you did say to her, though, was several months?

Candidate: Yes, I said several, and I said that on purpose.

Supervisor: Why?

Candidate: Because I didn't want—I had said a couple to people, or other things that can be construed more narrowly, and I didn't know what it would be.

Supervisor: Uh-huh.

Candidate: My feeling is that, about her at that time, and continues to be, well maybe not today, but up until the middle of last week, that if I had said we'll decide on a termination date an hour in advance, she would have said, "Great!"

Supervisor: Absolutely.

Candidate: So that if I gave her enough leeway in terms of, if I didn't make it broad, I said several, in terms of making it broad.

Supervisor: That's cutting it short, is what I'm saying. Several.

Candidate: I know that's what you're saying.

Supervisor: And my guess would be that for her she would probably need about a six-month termination period, which would include, among other things, your summer vacation as a trial separation.

Candidate: It probably won't be that, because six months—well, first of all, I don't exactly take summer vacations for another six months.

Supervisor: It's the beginning of March, roughly, so it'll be September.

Candidate: If a person takes an August vacation.

Supervisor: Yeah, well, the point I was making is, as she says, "How am I ever going to break it off?"

Candidate: What I don't know is how to present it to her without—I don't want to set a date for her.

Supervisor: Uh-huh.

Candidate: And I think she wants me to. I don't know. I think that would be a mistake at this time.

Supervisor: But she needs from you some kind of ballpark figure as to what would be appropriate. She has no way of knowing. And although you may not set the date for her, presumably it would be a joint setting of the date; it's the same as if she says, "Who's going to take the credit?" You get half and she gets half. And ultimately she's going to recognize that neither of you could do it without the other. "I couldn't do it without you and you couldn't do it without me."

Candidate: Uh-huh.

Supervisor: So in a sense it's been a joint venture. So usually one wants to say to the patient something like this: "The process of concluding our work together, the process of terminating the analysis, is likely to stir up a lot of feelings, and I would expect it would take a considerable period of time to resolve it optimally and successfully. The arrangement that usually works best is to set a time, at least six months from the time that we finally do pick as the date, whatever that date may be." And let her chew on that for a while.

Candidate: Okay. That's what I need to hear from you, something—

Supervisor: And when she says, "Yeah, but you said a few weeks ago just several months—"

Candidate: Well, see, to me several months includes six months.

Supervisor: When I was using the term several I was using it loosely.

Candidate: Simply meaning more than a couple.

Supervisor: More than a couple, right. "So that I would say at least a six-month period from the time that we finally do decide to set the termination date would be optimal and would make sure that we have adequate time to look at and deal with whatever inevitable conflicts happen to come up in this period."

Candidate: She has, in the last two weeks, been able to recognize or state like she thought the whole analysis was the point, and now she feels—

Supervisor: She thought what?

Candidate: The whole analysis, the analysis, all of the things she has gone through so far were the point of the analysis.

Supervisor: Uh-huh.

Candidate: And now she's feeling that all of the things she's gone through so far have simply led up to this and that *this* is the point of the analysis.

Supervisor: Uh-huh. And she's right.

Candidate: Yeah, she is.

Supervisor: A really nice awareness that from here on out is where the analysis really resolves the issues. But not without a struggle, which she is telling you. So, I would present it to her that in your perception it should be at least a six-month interval between the time that she decides to pick a date to the time of the end. She will—

Candidate: And that it shouldn't be—if I take a couple of weeks. I never take the whole month of August, but if I take a couple of weeks—

Supervisor: When she says, "Well, when do you think we should terminate?" I would say, sometime in the fall, that would be the optimal time. In other words I wouldn't take six exactly even. "When do you think we can terminate?" "Sometime this fall." "Well, when this fall?" "When would you like?" "Well, I don't know." And so on and she backs away. Say, "Well, why don't we do this? Why don't we tentatively set a date for—" and then presumably you'll have looked this up on a calendar in advance, and say, "Let's tentatively, today—"

Candidate: Would you pick a date for her?

Supervisor: I would have no objection if she doesn't want to. You see, sometimes patients will not, sometimes they will. "Well, all right, I'll pick a date." "Fine, what date would you like to pick?" A patient of mine was terminating his analysis and wanted to know how long I thought it should be. I said it should be at least six months. "Oh," he said, "that's much too long. I was thinking of two." I said two was cutting it very short. "Well, can we compromise?" I said, "Well, it's your analysis. I'm not in a position to insist that you stay longer. I can recommend but you have to make the selection." "Well, I'm going to pick four months." Okay. We looked at the calendar and picked the end of the four-month period. I said, "All right, April twenty-seventh will be our last session." I set it. Then come the reactions to that the next day.

Candidate: Did he keep it?

Supervisor: Yeah, he kept it. But not without a storm and not without a lot of protest, and not without a lot of backing and filling both in terms of "I can't wait until April twenty-seventh, it means going over and over this stuff time and time again, there is nothing new," plus "Why does it have to come so quickly?" and all the anger and all the hurt and "Why aren't you stopping me?"

Candidate: So you're saying that if she, that—

Supervisor: I'm saying that you pick a general date; sometime this fall is about the perfect time.

Candidate: Yeah, but if I say that—

Supervisor: And she says, "Well, that seems like an awfully long time away, why can't we do it sooner?" Well, then you say, "Well, what did you have in mind?" "Well, how about July?" "Well, July might be a little early. And I think there is going to be a lot for us to do between now and whatever the time we set is." "Well, are you saying Thanksgiving?" "It doesn't have to be Thanksgiving, it could be earlier." You don't want it to correspond with some other separation, a holiday, and so on. And then if she says, "Well, I don't know, why don't we look at the calendar—"

Candidate: Or if she says, "I want to be done August first. That's it."

Supervisor: There I would say, "That's pushing it. It would be preferable if" and so on. And if she says, "Well, I'm not going to come after August first," you can say, "Obviously nobody can make you come, but I think in the long run if it were set for the middle of October that would be a preferable arrangement." And then she says, "Well, what day?" Or you might just leave it in the middle of October now and set the actual final date six to eight weeks from now, or two months. Or you might, today, pick out what the final date will be and look it up on the calendar.

Candidate: I have a feeling that this lady is going to need a final date.

Supervisor: Uh-huh.

Candidate: You know, I'm not saying it has to be such—

Supervisor: Yeah, that makes it more concrete.

Candidate: You know, I'm not saying it has to be set today or tomorrow, but there's something that this lady is going to need, a final date to buck against, and once she has that, then I think the real storm is going to start. But I think between now and then, actually between a couple weeks ago and then, we've done some valuable things, but I felt the need of a backboard.

Supervisor: Pick a date, let's say the end of a week in October. The twelfth, the nineteenth, whatever; it will be about seven months from now.

Candidate: It would make it eight months.

Supervisor: Okay, March, April, May, June, July, August, September, and October. Eight months from now. Or you could pick the middle of September, but I wouldn't take much less than that, or I wouldn't encourage much less than that, because she's going to have a long and stormy termination but a very meaningful one. You can begin to see how she's reorganizing and reintegrating herself. A lot of old material is going to come back up again and she needs time to really remember and—

Candidate: Reconsolidate.

Supervisor: Yeah, in a sense, you see, everything up to now has been prologue; in a sense the cure of the neurosis occurs in the resolution, or the *partial* resolution, because it is never complete, of the transference demands, of the transference neurosis.

Candidate: I know this thing with Robert, this has been an intense maternal transference from eight months into the analysis. There was a—remember there was a paternal transference that was a defense against it? And for the most part, there are still, you know, it's obvious that there are still pieces of that. Robert is, it's almost like she—one of the most memorable days of her life was the day her idealization of her dad cracked. She was at college with dad. He had been, and then he became kind of a user of people. She views him as that, a sick kind of user of people, and this guy that she's mixed up with—it's like she's setting herself up to go back to that again. I wonder whether there's a—we haven't seen much of a paternal transference in a long time in this lady, and I just began wondering about it in the last couple of weeks.

Supervisor: Well, it's possible, as you suggested in the earlier material today, that this business with Robert is a displacement from you, and Robert may have some maternal components but he may also become the father with whom she is going to become increasingly disillusioned. You mentioned that you have some extraanalytic information to suggest maybe he's using her.

Candidate: Well, yeah. My office partner's husband is in the same business, and apparently—but not in the same firm or anything—and if he's heard it and she's heard it at parties, it's around, whatever that means. I mean, it's not like they're bosom buddies or something.

Supervisor: Uh-huh.

Candidate: That he has been saying how he really knows how to pull her strings. He gets such good work out of her by—

Supervisor: Well, that illustrates several things.

Candidate: And that, you know, this group of people really think he's a sociopathic son of a bitch. But a very successful sociopath.

Supervisor: Well, that illustrates the compounding and complicating issues of learning about material from somebody else and trying to keep it separate, so that you don't suggest to her or say something which comes from some—

Candidate: Which I've been real careful—

Supervisor: And that can create a certain amount of self-consciousness.

Candidate: Yeah, but it also makes me aware that I'm not to take things at face value, even at this point.

Supervisor: Exactly.

Candidate: And you know this is such a rosy—he's such a rosy-glow man in her view, it should make a person suspicious anyway.

Supervisor: She is presumably, then, again displacing on him some of the idealized father transference images which may have originated with you, and because it's difficult to see and feel here she uses him out there for it. She may very well become more involved with you as the termination process goes forward now, particularly the setting of the termination date.

Candidate: Well, and that's what I'm trying to be conscious of. There was one point a couple of weeks ago when it seemed increasingly clear to me that there was a component of the father transference that wasn't being addressed, and I started to address it, and I began to feel that some vestiges of the maternal transference were a defense against feeling this cross-sex transference with me. And that's difficult or complicated somehow, and it would be easier just to go put it somewhere else now. And it's not always clear to me how to bring it in. It's obviously easier for me to bring the maternal transference in than it is to bring in the paternal transference.

Supervisor: Right. On the other hand, it's possible to make the intervention too, that "even though I am a woman—"

Candidate: That's what I did several weeks ago.

Supervisor: "The feelings that you are having toward me are those that you once had toward your father."

Candidate: That's the kind of thing I did several weeks ago when it seemed clear to me. I said something to that point, that she has for me, it seems, feelings that she has had toward her father, toward men, even though I'm a woman.

Supervisor: Now there are those who say that patients with a woman analyst never experience a genuine father transference.

Candidate: How could men experience the genuine maternal transference with a male analyst?

Supervisor: Well, the presumption being—I don't happen to agree with this, I'm just saying that this is the way it is sometimes presented. I have forgotten who wrote it, but there was an article in the *International Journal of Psycho-Analysis* five or six years ago about just that topic: does a patient ever experience a real father transference with a woman? The article argued no, that this is usually acted out and displaced onto some male figure in the environment and can be interpreted by the woman analyst through the acting out in the environment. I think that is not quite correct. These are significant and at times very intense elements and particularly the fantasy system—the woman analyst as a male. Or at least as a phallic woman who is potent and powerful and so on, and who can destroy and can love and who can protect—all male qualities that would be experienced by the patient. This can also be experienced with you. So I wouldn't buy that and I would keep interpreting this as a defense against a full experience of those feelings here with you. The other thing she will need to do, and a place where the cure really comes, is in the resolution, in the experience of the grief, the mourning, and ultimately the voluntary renunciation. To the extent that she is forced out, to the extent that she is frustrated by, and feels that you are not giving her what she wants, and you are forcing her to let go, to that extent the resolution is relatively incomplete. To the extent that she says, in essence, "There is nothing here for me, I am going to let go because I am going to get more out there. I'm going to let go because I don't want or need this anymore," to that extent the renunciation is voluntary and ultimately the resolution is better.

Candidate: Is better.

Supervisor: Uh-huh. But she'll have to go through a lot of grief and a lot of mourning and a lot of anger, a lot of disappointment, a lot of resentment, and a lot of hopes that maybe it will happen still. And many times patients will retain that fantasy and will specifically have images and fantasies about the last session.

Candidate: It's in a fantasy that she would bring a piece of her art work in on the last day.

Supervisor: Yeah. That's right.

Candidate: That's the kind of thing that I would not be terribly surprised at. She's been threatening to do that for five years, four years, however long it's been. But it would really be—I can't think of the right word—to do in the last session.

Supervisor: But it would be a form of acting out. So when the thought starts to come up you interpret very early so that she doesn't act it out, so that you don't end up in the last session saying, "I'm sorry I can't take it" and offending her, or in the last session taking it and interfering with her full resolution.

Candidate: With her ability to leave. Yeah. Her resolving—

Supervisor: That's right. No, it would allow her to leave but she would be leaving a piece behind.

Candidate: That's what I mean by leaving.

Supervisor: "So you'd never leave."

Candidate: For her to really leave and take herself with her.

Supervisor: And take herself with her. Accept the death, as this is going to be equated with death. Because presumably you and she will never meet again.

Candidate: She's brought that up. "How can we have spent all this time doing these things and then the last day will just come and then I'll just leave, just like any other patient?"

Supervisor: And so all of this is going to take a lot of time to really work over and work through and integrate, but I see every evidence that she is starting to do this already.

Candidate: Do you think that's an appropriate thing to start doing? To start to sever things?

Supervisor: Oh, yeah.

Candidate: I really have been feeling that. For close to a month I've been feeling the need of what I'm calling a backboard, something to push against.

Supervisor: Yeah. And something to make it crystalize into, "This is a reality."

Candidate: That's what I meant by something to push against.

Supervisor: "Not just some day in the future when I grow up."

Candidate: Not a theoretical thing.

Supervisor: That's right. That will accelerate the process, but she will still need a good deal of time.

Candidate: To work it out.

Supervisor: And I wouldn't hesitate if she says, "Ah, you said just a couple of months."

Candidate: No, no, not a couple, a few.

Supervisor: A few. Several.

Candidate: Several. I very carefully did not say a couple. (Laughs)

Supervisor: Okay. Good.

Candidate: Well, it would be easy to say with her, because that's where she's pushing, she's pushing real hard to have me say, "You don't have to do this. You can get out of this without pain."

Supervisor: Uh-huh.

Candidate: It's a bitter pill, and the way she'd react—I'm cramming it down her throat, so that it's real easy to say it's okay. It's like I used to, whenever I'd take a vacation a long time ago, I'd do something to kind of mitigate it. That's why I was so conscious that I was not saying a couple.

Supervisor: Okay, well it's all going along nicely.

Candidate: All right.

Supervisor: Now you are into the interesting termination period.

Candidate: I think I sort of feel it's getting a little like a roller coaster.

Supervisor: Yeah. But you see, if you don't get on it, then the analysis is incomplete. This is where the analysis really is completed.

Candidate: Well, I really want to, and I'll watch for it and we can talk about it next time. Whatever the paternal part is going on is going to be really important. I mean it's not going to be the only important thing, but I think it's easy to let it go out and I want to.

Supervisor: Right. Okay, I'll see you, then, in two weeks.

Candidate: Yes.

Supervisor: Okeydoke.

Supervisor's Comments

Once again the candidate indicates her initiative by suggesting an agenda. She also shows growing sophistication and tolerance regarding both the analytic and the Institute situation by indicating her awareness that the patient must know about the supervisor, and at the same time expresses her growing independence by demonstrating how the patient's relationship with Robert has become clear to her over time and how she was able eventually to find a way to bring this into the transference through direct interpretation.

Additionally, she indicates from her own learning experience how extraneous knowledge from a source other than the patient can serve as a distraction and a contaminant for the analyst ("it's been an interesting thing to have that in my mind"). She then demonstrates how she was able, with considerable skill, to interpret the transference displacement to Robert, and shows a sense of personal satisfaction at having been able to figure out the issues for herself. She indicates that she had recognized the distortion for some time but had been capable of abstaining and waiting for an appropriate opportunity to introduce the interpretation in question.

The interpretation seems for the moment to have reduced the intensity of the experience for the patient ("It's not an every-moment intensity anymore"). The candidate is capable on her own of following the dynamic line and the transference in the patient's material, as well as the patient's spontaneous movement into a termination position. The patient herself recognizes the transference elements and distortions, as well as their origins, and reenacts, as part of the mother transference, her sense of guilt at the thought of leaving the candidate. There are indications of a direct and active analytic process in the patient, inasmuch as she is experiencing the transference without displacement or distortion, and is capable of working with it spontaneously, while the candidate is capable of observing it and of allowing the patient to work on it actively and independently.

The candidate's ease in the supervisory learning situation is illustrated by her recognition that she has repressed some of the material ("I don't, at the moment, remember it"), and she manifests a comfortable sense of acceptance of herself as well as an expectation that the repressed material will be accessible again in the future ("maybe it will come back to me").

The patient herself shows an awareness of her displacement of the transference to Robert ("I wonder if that has to do with here"). The supervisor points out that this suggests significant change in the patient, as well as a newfound capacity for self-analysis; it is therefore time to start considering termination. The patient's capacity to feel that she deserves much of the credit for the success of the analytic experience, as well as her recognition of the previously premature impulses toward termination, are both indicators that the patient is beginning the process of resolving her transference idealization and the transference neurosis in favor of a more objective and reality-oriented perception of herself.

The patient also shows the beginnings of grief and sadness at the loss of the analyst as a real object, as well as of the analyst in the transference; for her part, the analyst is able to develop a dynamic understanding of a behavior pattern which apparently has persisted for several years. She recognizes the limitations in her understanding, however, and expects that it will become clearer in the future. She is able to learn, from her experience with this patient, how to modify her technique as this becomes appropriate. The patient demonstrates growing self-observational capacities, recognizing a pattern of behavior and spontaneously observing herself continuing in its use ("There I go again"). The candidate is capable of observing and allowing the patient's shift to actively assuming responsibility for her own feelings and experience ("she is *finally* taking responsibility for this"), while the patient shows increasing self-awareness and self-analytic capacity, a recognition of the transference and her reactions to it, and an awareness of the internal structural changes taking place as a result of the analytic experience.

A typical pattern of progressive movement followed by regression and neurotic conflict, followed by a return to progress, is evident, all of this oscillating very rapidly. The candidate is able to describe and accept her own confusion ("I didn't know what I was doing") without particular hesitation or inhibition in recognizing and admitting her difficulty.

The candidate shows a capacity to observe and appreciate these volatile progressive and regressive shifts in the patient, as well as to recognize the analytic work being accomplished and the changes taking place toward genuine working through and resolution. She gives evidence of being able to allow the patient the opportunity to accomplish this effectively and to appreciate the extent to which the termination process will be conflicted and painful for the patient. The candidate recognizes her own learning needs, this being the first case she has ever terminated ("I need to talk with you about technically how to proceed"). The supervisor mistakenly assumes the candidate has set too short a time for the termination phase, and there ensues an interchange during which the misunderstanding is clarified; the candidate is able to explain in an active and firm way her reasons for acting as she did.

Following the resolution of this misunderstanding, the supervisor responds to the candidate's learning needs by explaining the rationale for setting the date mutually. He presents a technical model of how this can be accomplished. Candidate and supervisor engage in an active give-and-take with considerable didactic emphasis by the supervisor on the technique and process of termination, including potential interventions which allow the candidate to observe the thinking processes of a senior analyst. The patient herself demonstrates her perception of the importance and dynamic significance of the termination experience. ("she's feeling that all of the things she's gone through so far have simply led up to this and that *this* is the point of the analysis"), and the supervisor confirms this to the candidate ("A really nice awareness").

The supervisor further delineates the termination process, using a clinical vignette to emphasize to the candidate the conflicted nature of the termination experience ("Then came the reactions to that the next day"), and offers various models for intervention. This active consideration of technical options is different from what has gone on in the past year of the supervisory process, and is more reminiscent of interchanges occurring earlier in the supervision. The supervisor recognizes that the candidate has learning needs in regard to the termination phase, that this is her first experience in this arena. The candidate needs a basic orientation from which to work in order to feel comfortable, capable of applying her own individual style to the process in question.

The candidate demonstrates a fairly sophisticated recognition of the patient's needs ("this lady is going to need a final date . . . , to buck against"), and the supervisor encourages her to proceed in a somewhat directive fashion, as well as explaining the very important dynamics in the termination process ("the cure of the neurosis occurs in the resolution, or the *partial* resolution . . . , of the transference neurosis"). He also alerts the candidate to the inevitable regressions and oscillations that will occur, in an attempt to keep her from being surprised or even upset and discouraged when they occur. This anticipatory awareness will allow the candidate more calmly to observe and participate in the termination process. The supervisor is very aware of the fact that this is the candidate's first planned termination, her only other model for this experience being her own analysis.

The candidate next introduces questions regarding the dynamics of the transference and the nature of the experience with Robert, and the supervisor supports her speculations. But at this point he returns to the candidate's comment earlier in the supervisory hour regarding her extraanalytic knowledge of Robert's character. The candidate responds by elaborating on the source and the nature of her information, and the supervisor demonstrates the countertransference issues such information may activate, emphasizing both the technical issues and the transference implications, as well as the patient's displacement.

Candidate and supervisor engage once more in an active discussion regarding the possibility of experiencing a father transference with a woman analyst, and of how these issues might be considered. They discuss also the possibility of the patient's presenting the analyst a gift at the last session and how that would be understood, as well as some of the technical issues it would raise.

Candidate and supervisor have an active interchange at the level of peers in regard to the termination issues, and the candidate indicates one of the artifacts of supervision; for close to a month she has been feeling the need to set a termination date but has artificially waited in order to discuss it with the supervisor. The candidate is again able to learn from her own past experience with this patient ("the way she'd react . . . it's real easy to say it's okay. It's like I used to . . . do") and the supervisor offers direct praise ("well, it's all going along nicely"). His comment regarding the interesting nature of termination elicits the candidate's enthusiasm; she anticipates the next supervisory hour, and what in the meantime she will be looking for in the analysis.

As mentioned earlier, this supervisory hour differs from some of the more recent ones in that the supervisor is more active, didactic, and instructional; he has in some ways reverted to a supervisory style more typical to the early stages of supervision. This is a deliberate response to the learning needs of the candidate, for whom this phase in the analysis represents a new experience. She needs a conceptual as well as a technical model, and the supervisor is deliberately trying to provide both. The assumption is that the candidate's ability to understand the process as it unfolds will allow her to be more comfortable with it and thus to maintain her analytic stance and position more readily, allowing her also to observe the process more comfortably and objectively as it unfolds. The candidate seems to appreciate this and responds in an animated way, and the learning process and alliance are demonstratively active and functional for both participants.

Chapter 16

Supervisory Session 110

Candidate: I'm going to do two sessions from a month ago. And then I'll tell you what happened in between. This is the session from the last day I saw you.

Supervisor: Uh-huh.

Candidate: She came ten minutes late. I think it drags in the beginning but I'll see if I can get into it. Strange day. She described a conference with Robert where she felt totally exposed, like he could look at her and know how she feels. He seemed happy and attentive and made her feel very exposed and very sad. She talked about that more and I noted some parallels to how she feels here with me. She was thinking about that on the way here. She is afraid to show me how attached she has become to me and how much I mean to her and that she really wants to leave here and show me how good she really feels. The feeling from yesterday that she could only feel her best after she leaves here. She feels so on the line. It's new to feel so exposed. She's afraid of the acceptance more than the rejection. I made a comment about her feeling so terribly attached, afraid she'll never get free without a fight. She used to refer to the hatchet, something that would cut it off. No one could ever really like her for herself. Strong parallels with Robert. She was really herself today with Robert. She feels very much herself right now. She was silent for a while. Strange dream last night. I think it would be fun, I don't know, but I don't think I would ever do it, to go back and pull out all this lady's apartment dreams.

Supervisor: Uh-huh. Yeah, that's the kind of thing you do sometimes in retrospect, go back and pick out a specific target and use it as a tracking device to observe how it modifies over the course of time.

Candidate: The apartment dreams have really undergone significant changes, and this is the latest one.

Supervisor: There was a case illustration of that, I've forgotten where, called the Chinese checker game in which somebody did that, but used Chinese checkers as a target or as a flag, and demonstrated over the course of an analysis how the use of the game and its implications and its childhood memories and the way in which it's being used today varied and was modified and became, instead of an aggressive, hostile, murderous act, a sublimated form of competitiveness. You could do that sometime, at your leisure.

Candidate: She had a strange dream last night. She didn't have to move into another apartment. She could stay in her apartment, but she had to live in this ratty old apartment some of the time and couldn't lock the doors and every time she thought she had it locked, someone came in. There was a door through the closet to the outside. She couldn't lock that either. And she thought, her jewelry is here. She must take her jewelry. By being allowed to keep her apartment she is being allowed to keep her life. She was thinking how she could get the movers to take her furniture back to her good apartment. Because she didn't want to be there, even part time.

Supervisor: In the ratty old apartment.

Candidate: Yeah. Here, even though it's only four days a week, she doesn't want to come anymore. She was silent for a while. She was just thinking how hard this is. She felt so good walking in. She feels weepy now. She is going to miss me. She felt real unsure of herself today. Wasn't in control and it was pretty visible. She couldn't help it. The feelings just came pouring out. That's what she feels like now. With Robert in here she feels on the fence. On the one hand, "You don't want him, he's like a snarly growly old bear with a pot belly; he doesn't mean anything to you." But then on the other hand, she really loves this person. She was talking on, and I said I thought she was talking about how she loves me. And then she made a gesture. And a sigh. I don't know, she says, well maybe. It feels so goddamn unattainable. Feels like I care about her as a person, I guess, feels like she is one of those, like it's one of those goddamn areas where she is beating her head against the wall. She doesn't give a fuck, she doesn't want to do this anymore; she just wants to leave, just leave. Another thing that pisses her off, notice that she never said that the first thing pissed her off, is how she was so assertive in August, and now she is this namby-pamby looking at him with doe's eyes. Is it all right to love you? She was assertive in August and acted on her feelings because somehow he didn't matter so much to her. And I said, there's more at stake, like here. Yeah. She was silent for a while. She had been open here about everything, except her feelings about me. She doesn't allow herself to have fantasies about me, and it pisses her off whenever I ask her about them. I said, like it pissed her off when I said that she was talking about loving me. She said "Yes." She does feel so terribly attached to me, she can't figure out how ever to leave. She can't just walk out. She really feels she has to put herself on the line. She feels like she put herself on the line today with Robert, and she's doing that here and she's real afraid. There was an interchange about her apartment dream, equates her analysis with the ratty apartment, that someone might get her jewels, and are those perhaps her feelings for me? People were coming in and out. It's interesting that more details of this dream kept coming out. People kept coming in and out. They were people she knew. They weren't robbers. And they kept saying, let's do this or let's do that, like go out to dinner or have a party or something. And she kept saying, "No, no, I can't do that, I have to, I can't move out until I figure out how to move this furniture out. I can't leave without my furniture." It's got furniture here. I can't, she's very attached to me. Silent for five minutes. Mind is racing. It's funny, it was her old bedroom furniture from when she was a child and she wanted to get rid of it anyway. I'll just go on to the next session, which is Thursday. On time. Looks good. When she went home last night she was really tired. Took a bubble bath, and then went out with Amy. She felt very attractive and vibrant. She looked in the mirror. I mean she *really* looked in the mirror. She never did that before. She couldn't even stand sitting in front of a mirror at the hairdresser's, she would have to close her eyes. But now looks different, looks good. But somehow that in itself upsets her. She got a headache. She had to go home and go to bed. Meanwhile she had a really good time with Amy, they went out to Balaban's. She woke up this morning and felt better. And as she was walking down the hall she got the headache again. She doesn't know how to disengage. She got into this thing, she never thought she would be this involved or that it was going to take this long, and yet now it doesn't seem like long, it seems like fast. In some ways it doesn't seem like long enough. The relationship with Robert is so similar because it's totally professional. She got really angry yesterday when she was talking about him, and I said that she was talking about loving me. Is this just another convenient place to put her feelings about me? She got really pissed. And Ted keeps calling her. He is so, I don't know if these notes are going to convey this but I'll try. Ted keeps calling her, he's so stupid, he's such a whiny baby. She told him she never wanted to talk to him again. She was furious. "Leave me alone." And he just kept whining, so she hung up on him. It infuriated her that he won't leave her alone. It makes her sick. Then she thinks about Robert. Are her feelings real? Is she just acting out her feelings there about me? Does everything have to be tied back to me? Isn't she allowed to have her own feelings? And I said, "Like I'm a whiny baby?" She said yes, that's why she blew up. What is real? She has a real problem with that; she can't believe she is doing this on a Thursday. Jesus, she's telling me off on a Thursday. Why isn't she being smarter than this? She feels like maybe if she gets angry and rants and raves she will be able to get free. I said something about her coming in talking about how attached she is and then how I'm clinging to her. She said that's what Ted is doing. It's different because he is this stupid, weak idiot fool. She never loved him though she tried to make it work, and she believed that she loved him. She questioned her feelings about Robert. It would be so much easier to say she doesn't care, that she doesn't have those feelings and walk away. That's the way it is here, too. That it would be so much easier to say I am clinging and she doesn't like me, than to deal directly with her feelings that she's very attached to me and loves me. She feels she will be punished. She got on the scales again. She felt thin. She looked in the mirror last evening and this morning, and she felt pretty. It scares her to death. She's afraid she'll be punished. Mother will find out. There will be something wrong with her physically. She loves feeling like this. She feels like a woman, because the more feelings she has, the more she wants. But it won't come true. She won't be able to lose weight; something will happen; there will be a punishment. She always thought that the day she weighed one-forty she could walk out of here. Mother always said if she lost weight she would be wonderful. Prince Charming would be hers. And I said that I thought she was having some trouble experiencing me as her father and her mother both at the same time, right now. I don't know if those shifts are coming through to you, between the whiny baby and the attractive feelings that scare her, but it gets clearer. She said that makes sense, because on the one hand she experiences me as being real happy for her, in fact too happy and responsive and somehow very scary. And on the other hand, jealously angry. She wants me to be jealous. She wants her to feel bad. She wants Mother to be jealous, wants her to feel bad, never realized how much she wants vengeance until recently. She gave examples of how her mother tore her down when she was feeling good and attractive. It feels like she's experiencing me as both her mother and her father, back and forth and back and forth, and Robert fits in there somewhere. And then I didn't write notes for a while. I suggested that part of the reason she was taking these feelings out was not just because I'm a woman but because of the secrets. It's an "if I, your mother, know that you want me, your father" type secret. "And I will take vengeance on you and punish you. If I, your father, know that you want me, I will overreact, or overrespond to you."

Supervisor: So you interpreted into the oedipal triad.

Candidate: Yes. And into what I had kept hearing her say, which is she gave Robert a gift and he responded and scared the shit out of her.

Supervisor: That he responded.

Candidate: Yes, yes. And I keep hearing her say that it goes from one side to the other with me. One seems to defend the other. At least the jealous mother right now, which we have seen over and over and over, seems to be defending this overresponsive father position.

Supervisor: Hummm.

Candidate: That makes perfect sense. It makes sense with a professional relation too. It's a protection, a prohibition—no sex here, baby. No response here. But when Robert responded she freaked out. Before the urethral stricture she felt wonderful. She knows she had fantasies about her father. A girl, she was a girl like in August.

Supervisor: The novel?

Candidate: No, in August the month.

Supervisor: I see.

Candidate: She was a girl in August with Robert, free, uninhibited, but now it takes on more serious proportions and connotations, because she knows she's a woman. It was such a pure, spontaneous passion then. Then that was just cut off. Now the relationship is essentially platonic and all the passion is underneath, and she's scared shitless and he is something, I don't know. Even if her father is happy for her, she expanded on that some, and then she said, but there's a hitch in here, because even if he is happy for her he wants her all to himself, all the time, and Mother wants the same thing but it's harder to define. It's with her father now. If she loves me she'll never get free. The dream about another man and feeling obligated to her father. A long time ago, a couple of years ago, she had a dream where she was coming down the stairs to go on a date with another man, and her father and mother were standing there and her father, I can't remember the details of the dream, but she couldn't leave her father; he was in direct competition with this guy. And she felt so overwhelmingly sad in the dream, as she walked over to her father and patted him, and the mother was real happy, and she at the time felt that the mother was promoting this, and in the dream she looked longingly after this guy she thought she was coming down the stairs to see. And that's the dream I think she's referring to, the Harold

Frank dream. It's not only that she can't get free of me, the jealous mother, but can she love me, her father, and get free to have another man? She's really involved with her father. Couldn't handle his response to her picture. Then she went to the office, to his office, or someplace, and her picture was there, standing there, it wasn't hung up yet. And she was furious. He said he would hang it up. Stupid son of a bitch, then flipped to the mother's side. Men are such schmucks. It was real clear that she was aware of these quick shifts in herself.

Supervisor: Uh-huh.

Candidate: This is where her feeling that she has to choose me, her mother, over men comes in. She's screwed whichever way she goes in this mishmash. She found a middle ground today, but she's still entangled in these old things. I said, I don't know why I said, looking for a mover for her furniture, her childhood furniture. She said, yes, the dream feels so significant. God, she feels so much pressure, she feels like it's a weight on her head, not a headache like before but just pressure. This makes such sense. There have been so many times when she's been so afraid, like yesterday and the last couple of weeks, and then when we actually start talking about something it never seems so terrible as it did. Something about her father. And her mother's jealousy. Then, that's Thursday. It turns out Saturday she gets sick as shit. I don't know this for a long time. And she got so sick that she got terrified she was going to die. She had a fever of a hundred and four. She was afraid to take her temperature. When she would take it, she would only let the thermometer go up to a hundred and two, then she would take it out. She felt out of control. Like she's never felt before in her life, she said, except maybe the urethral stricture, except that was a localized area and this was her total body. She felt pulled back by me. Jerked. Like she's on a leash.

Supervisor: As if feeling, "That'll show you?"

Candidate: Yeah, that'll show you. She was someone who never misses work because she's sick. She was out for a whole week. She didn't come to the appointments all week. She canceled Monday, though I canceled it also because I was stuck in a snowdrift. Tuesday I canceled for another reason, I canceled it Monday night, but she said that she was about to cll me, and she sounded horrible, but then she started sounding even worse. Then Wednesday she called and canceled the rest of the week. Saturday I had a death in the family. I called her and canceled for Monday, before I went out of town. And Tuesday, when I saw her, she was still sick. And then I think I was out to lunch Tuesday. For some reason I did not let her investigate enough why she got sick, because it was real curious to her. First of all, she was still feeling terrible and very weak, and in danger, but it didn't get clear to me until much later, that part of what the danger was was that she was feeling so good and here she went out, she remembers going out with Amy and looking in the mirror and feeling attractive and good, and then—

Supervisor: The sickness was a punishment for—

Candidate: She made herself sick, is what she said. And it felt like I was jerking her back, or that if I wasn't jerking her back she was going to jerk herself back. That something is so awful about feeling so good, or so scary about feeling so good, that she had to make herself sick. I don't think I know any more about her getting sick. What happened then, I'm embarrassed to admit it, is that that Tuesday she again commented, three-fourths of the way through the hour, about how do you ever get out of here, how do we wind this down? And I did my spiel about six months, at least six months. It was very badly done in that I didn't adequately understand her state, her post-sickness state, and I didn't adequately understand the implications of this illness yet. Her interpretation was, whenever she was really pushing me to get out I didn't say anything, so then she decided, "Well, I guess I can't leave," and then I jerked her. And then whenever she was sick I did like her mother and the urethral stricture. After they took her to the doctor and she got dilated, they went down to the car and said well now we're going on this trip. It was as if none of it had ever happened. And I was acting the same way. And in actuality I *was* kind of acting the same way. The implications of it all hadn't struck me, and I was a bit out to lunch. So we spent some time with her reacting to that, mostly in terms of timing. Nobody ever does things when she wants them to, they do them on their own schedule, and also that I waited until she wasn't expecting it and then hit her with it.

Supervisor: You've described yourself as out to lunch. Did you give any thoughts to what put you there?

Candidate: Yeah, I had just had a death in the family and just got back to town. I mean, it may have to do with her but I was kind of out to lunch with all my patients the whole day. I had gotten back into town late Monday night. It wasn't a tragic death, it was an expected death, but it was the passing of a whole era.

Supervisor: Uh-huh.

Candidate: And I wasn't very tuned in, in any way. It's also possible that I'm having terminating troubles with her, and that I either don't want to terminate her, or I *do* want to terminate her. I think both of those are true. I didn't seem to be having that trouble the week before. I really felt in touch. Unless there's some major thing you're about to draw my attention to, I really felt more in touch with what was going on before this big break. And I think if the two things hadn't come together, if she had gotten sick and come back I think my attention would have been better, or if we had met until Thursday and then I had a death in the family and gone out of town so the continuity was better. Then I think my attention might have been better.

Supervisor: It's a good rule of thumb that when there has been this kind of a break, or when you have had some sort of an event in your life (it doesn't have to be as dramatic as a death), or when the patient has just recovered from some event, that's a good time not to do—

Candidate: Do anything.

Supervisor: To do anything, yes.

Candidate: Yes. And I think that really another way to understand this, besides all those other ways, is that it had been kind of a hidden agenda.

Supervisor: Yeah, I think so.

Candidate: And she, although she talked on Wednesday and Thursday, the Wednesday and Thursday before this big break, about wanting to get out of here, it hadn't come up as a direct thing. And I was trying not to jump all over her about it, and I didn't, because it didn't feel appropriate to how things were coming up on Wednesday and Thursday.

Supervisor: Uh-huh.

Candidate: And on this day, whatever day it was, it came up more as a direct, but it was inappropriate, my response was inappropriate nonetheless. I mean it would have come up again.

Supervisor: Uh-huh.

Candidate: Maybe ten days from then. Or two weeks. But once done, I didn't know what to do, except to wait for her, how it felt for her and her responses to me.

Supervisor: Now, "once done": you didn't actually say we're going to set a time six months from now or—

Candidate: I just said this is how we do it.

Supervisor: Whenever you decide.

Candidate: Whenever we decide, whenever it's right, we will set a date six months from whatever that time is. She hasn't looked at a calendar since then. She occasionally says, I haven't looked at a calendar yet. And I, I didn't feel any, in fact what I was trying to do was to get this, and again it was badly timed, it was a hidden agenda, trying to get that piece of information across. I wasn't in the mood at that moment to set a date, I wanted to set a frame, which should have been a long time ago. And my sense was that it should have been done sometime back, when she was asking me directly. I felt that there's been an artifact in here of my unsureness of how to do this, that at an appropriate time, when it feels like it would be appropriate, I instead waited to talk with you about it. So that's kind of—

Supervisor: Yeah, that may be a contaminant introduced by the supervisory situation.

Candidate: Well, in a first-case situation of not wanting to jump the gun, wanting to not contaminate it further by mishmash or my wanting to—

Supervisor: Sure.

Candidate: Now she, I think, although we aren't yet back to where we were before, I think we're recovering from that. She's really pulled between "I didn't want to come today" and "If she doesn't want it, I don't want to come." Well, there were two sessions in a row in which I felt we were recovering from that mistake and in both of them she comes in, my memory is that she comes in and says, "Really, I don't want to be here, I just want to stay forever. If I'm only going to be able to be here for six months, then why come?" Some awareness of feeling really sad. Her father may have to have open heart surgery. She loses me and the father at the same time. She can't stand that. Nothing is forever. Her dad's getting old. Feels, noticeably, terrible stormy feelings, doesn't seem to take very much for them to settle down, unlike three years ago when these same stormy feelings would go on and on. All of this is right toward the end of Monday's hour.

Supervisor: This is a recent session?

Candidate: Yes, this is just last Monday. Right toward the end of the hour, three minutes before the end of the hour, she said all of this is bullshit, she doesn't really believe it anymore, about being ugly, unattractive, same old things.

Supervisor: Say it again. What's bullshit, that she—

Candidate: Unattractive, can't look in the mirror, ugly.

Supervisor: That's the bullshit?

Candidate: Yeah, that's bullshit. All of this is bullshit. She doesn't even really believe it. She can't even make herself believe it. She believed it for about five minutes yesterday, just saying that's a big relief. She feels much better having said that. And I said, as she's saying we can't end our work, I said, because she's just the same as when she came in. She laughed and said, "Yup, that's exactly how I felt this weekend." It's easier, and that it's easier to hate than to be sad and to miss me. She laughed, left, and had a good day. Came in the next session, "I don't want to be here." Didn't want to come today, thought of every single reason why not.

Supervisor: This is yesterday's hour.

Candidate: Thought of every single reason why not to, feels strange, she felt so much better when she left yesterday, and as the day wore on she felt good, on top of things, attractive. And last night she felt good, and she went out and she felt good. But she woke up this morning and felt terrible, yuck, "I don't want to go there." And now she feels all shaken up.

And I said something about she felt better yesterday afternoon after saying that some of the shakenupness is bullshit, and what she doesn't want to feel about it is that she feels good and that we will be at the end of our work sometime. "I only expected it to take six months, and now I only have six months." To begin with, after all this time, she feels there will be a real hole in her. She feels there will be a real hole in her life, but that she feels good and accomplished. On the one hand, she doesn't want to let go of her fantasies, she thinks. She was thinking about that on the way over here today. She came here a downtrodden Cinderella, and goddamnit she was supposed to leave a fairy princess and there was a Prince Charming in the lobby waiting for her, and I was the fairy godmother, and it's not that way. And everything won't be perfect. She can't even control her feelings like she used to. This was an unusual session—she was silent for five minutes. I'm sure that you remember that this lady is not the master of silences. She feels really relaxed, she could go to sleep. She was silent for five minutes. Somehow she feels really relaxed and calm and comfortable, and just wants to be quiet. I think she said in there she feels like she should talk, "but I don't want to." Silent for three minutes. It felt like a really comfortable silence, it didn't feel defended. It's really strange how she felt when she walked in, and how she feels now, today, how she felt when she walked in. She feels now that she'll be able to walk out of here sometime and it will be better than okay. She felt so anxious or something when she walked in, she just didn't want to come but she made herself, and now she's here she feels real calm and comfortable and relaxed and somehow like she doesn't have to pretend anymore to herself or to me. She does have mixed feelings, it makes her very very sad. The thought of not coming here. I've been such a big part of her life, but the feeling of getting on with her life is exciting and impending and it keeps pushing her. Yesterday was a very exciting day. She felt very alive and attractive and successful. There were still some remnants of trying to make herself feel bad, but it wasn't working very well. She was silent for five minutes. She also always thought that when she left here she would have everything all figured out, everything in its place, and now she's seeing that that will never ever really happen. She was silent for five more minutes. She feels like she should be talking, that's when she said it, but she doesn't feel like talking. She's aware of such an urge when she opens her mouth, to make things look awful, but they don't feel awful. To point up all the stuff, the bad stuff, and it doesn't feel bad. She was silent for ten minutes. And I've written down here that the last three minutes did not feel so comfortable. I suspect something was stirring, but she was aware of the end of the session. I think that's the first time she's been so—I bet half the session she was silent. And it felt like an accomplishment, in that it really felt like she was contemplating and just letting her mind chew on some stuff.

Supervisor: She was testing the waters, also, to achieve the experience of being accepted without having to perform.

Candidate: Uh-huh. And I didn't say, "What are you thinking during the silence?" I said that that was just really important this time.

Supervisor: It was an important experience for her to have, that's right. The other thing she demonstrates here is how she has now reached a point where she can overcome her own resistance. She didn't want to come, she was reluctant, it was the last place she wanted to be.

Candidate: And she was ten minutes late or somehow late, but she got here.

Supervisor: But ordinarily in the past she would have skipped—

Candidate: Broken the appointment.

Supervisor: She would have skipped, she wouldn't have arrived; she would have had a rationalization, and her car would have broken down, Ted wouldn't have called for her, something would have happened and she would have found a way to avoid coming. So that's another indication of an internal change, the capacity for self-analysis, the capacity to observe herself, recognize a resistance, and overcome it and experience and confront and overcome the anxiety connected with it. Just the same as when she is lying there and she wants to say how terrible things are but she can't because they aren't. It's another indication of the same process.

Candidate: Yes, and resistance is getting smaller too.

Supervisor: Resistances are getting smaller, but also she is able to recognize them and to overcome them and modify the behavior in the face of the resistance. To face the anxiety, whatever it may be, to assume she is going to master it, and go on. All of which are indicators of an internal structural change. And the relatively small descriptor, "I want to say things are shitty but they're really not," implies an enormous amount of internal structural change that has taken place as a result of the whole analytic experience. Now, the main thing will be to focus, to activate the grief, the mourning, and the voluntary renunciation. The more she feels you're kicking her out or forcing her out—

Candidate: That's why I don't want to set a date with this lady. I asked you about that last time, and you said sure, you do with some patients. But I felt for some time that I don't want to set a date, that she needs to do it. I mean, I'd try, and be ridiculous about it, but she always tries to make it seem that someone is kicking her out. She needs to know that she can leave.

Supervisor: Uh-huh.

Candidate: It would be *nice* if she could do it.

Supervisor: Right. Also, you see, her comment, "If I'm going to have to leave in six months I might as well leave now," is an attempt to escape the work of the termination phase.

Candidate: That she doesn't really leave, that's bullshit too.

Supervisor: Right. And she knows it.

Candidate: And that's part of what she's saying is bullshit. It doesn't carry the impact that it did either, three months ago, of, "I'm going to go to Chicago"; in fact she even said at some point in these two sessions, "I don't think I'm going to go to Chicago anymore, or this or that. If I do that sometime it will be nice. But I don't—"

Supervisor: She is not going to use that as an escape.

Candidate: Remember, she used to have to go to Chicago, she used to have to move to Chicago about once every other week about six months ago. I don't know, little technical things. I don't want to be heavy-handed about but I think it needs to be understood eventually—this leaving thing, have a good day, leaving.

Supervisor: Her saying to you, "Have a good day." Uh-huh.

Candidate: "Have a good day, have a good day, have a good weekend, have a good day, see you tomorrow." We talked about it a couple of weeks ago for the first time, and I'm kind of waiting. I don't want to inhibit it by calling attention to it. But I presume that some more ways to understand it will come up and stop it, like other things have stopped. I'm not sure of all that it involves.

Supervisor: What do you think it involves? What formulations or ideas have you had?

Candidate: Well, they're kind of scattered. Some of what it involves is, whatever has gone on making it all right between us.

Supervisor: So it's the undoing of an aggression.

Candidate: Yeah. And an undoing of you know, that she's okay and I don't have to worry, which is also an undoing of an aggression. It just has more steps involved in it when she's depressed. I think it's a holding on. A titular, I'm not sure titular is the right word. I'm a little bit vague, a *token* holding on, a doing obeisance to me kind of, not getting up and walking out but turning and saying something to me. It's kind of the epitome of terminating. It's a little example of what she's going to have to do when she leaves finally, which is get up and walk out and leave me, wherever I'm at, without patting me—

Supervisor: Yeah. Whether you're happy or miserable, it won't matter.

Candidate: Without patting me, without making things okay between us, without holding onto me or allowing me to hold onto her or any of those things, but just leaving. And so I guess it's, as I talk about it, it sounds like something that makes sense would get addressed in this lady in the leaving stages, because it's about leaving.

Supervisor: That's right.

Candidate: Because I have not addressed it all along. I don't think because I've been afraid to address it, so much as it hasn't seemed the right time. It hasn't seemed fruitful; particularly, it hasn't seemed like whatever it involves has come up. And that's just what it involves.

Supervisor: So what you're saying is, you see, in a small symptomatic act you're seeing the same overdetermined, compromised behavior, which is a manifestation of a much larger behavioral process.

Candidate: That is exemplified in that dream of going to her father, I mean that's one of the dreams.

Supervisor: Yes, it's also exemplified in the dream of I'm going to stay in the old apartment for a little bit of the time, even though I've got this beautiful brand new place to go to.

Candidate: Her place, her place. She has to stay in this place but her jewels are in there. This is a fascinating thing. And it wasn't that robbers were going to find out about it; it was that somebody was going to find out. It wasn't that robbers were going to steal her jewels.

Supervisor: They were just going to know about it.

Candidate: And I really think this is the lady—oh, you know what she talks about recently, in this session, is all of the things that she has kept from doctors and how I'm not a doctor. And I said, "Yes I am, and you have kept things from me, too." That she tells me only what she wants to, maybe less and less and less, but that her characteristic style has been you tell a doctor what you want them to know. You take the thermometer out of your mouth when it says a hundred and two, and then when the doctor comes back you stick it back in because you don't want the doctor to know you have a one-hundred-and-four-degree fever. But when she went to the doctor when she was sick this time, she didn't do that. That was a big decision on her part, that she was going to let him see all the symptoms she had, including her temperature. She wasn't going to take the thermometer out of her mouth when the nurse wasn't in the room, because how else could he tell her what to do and how to fix her?

Supervisor: So what she's saying also, in that behavioral shift, is that the capacity for trust is enhanced, is increased, and nobody is really out to hurt her deliberately and sadistically, and she doesn't have to protect herself the way she once fantasied she did. And that she can begin to expect that the person you look to for help is going to respond appropriately. Might help you, not only would not hurt you, but also would help you but won't overwhelm you and won't grab you and suck you in and destroy you or keep you from yourself.

Candidate: Won't do something unexpected or damaging or sadistic.

Supervisor: Yeah. So these, you see, are all generalizations from her experience with you into other relationships. The new sense of basic trust.

Candidate: And her capacity to be silent is a reflection of that too.

Supervisor: Right. And your capacity to tolerate and accept her silence, without demands for performance, essentially strengthens this and allows her to experience it.

Candidate: It was such a relief after all these years. It was genuinely pleasant to just sit there, and it was interesting to just sit there and be silent.

Supervisor: Pleasant for you?

Candidate: Yeah, I mean it wasn't over, I wouldn't choose to do it twelve hours a day, but as opposed to other feelings I've had with her, it was clear that it was a comfortable situation for her, because of the amount of comfort that I felt, and then it was also interesting that in the last minute, or maybe two minutes, there was something disturbing in the air. And I think there really was something disturbing her.

Supervisor: Well, it sounds fine, then. Even though you may have introduced the six-month business in a somewhat clumsy way. Because whenever you did it, however skillfully, it would still have had an effect.

Candidate: The thing I'm sad about is if her getting the flu at that time can be understood in psychodynamic terms of how far out she was coming, I think it would have been easier to see whatever the connections were if I hadn't stumbled in there.

Supervisor: Yeah, that's right, sure.

Candidate: And those connections, you can't recover them easily. We'll just have to wait and see if something happens again, and look at it then.

Supervisor: Or sometime you will be able to reconstruct it. Sometime when she has something like this experience this week. She comes in, she has a good experience with you, she goes out Monday and has a great time, she really feels good, she really feels great. On Tuesday she winds up feeling lousy. That's the psychological equivalent of what happened with the flu.

Candidate: Making her so sick.

Supervisor: So that you can reconstruct it, so to speak, or refer back to it on the basis of her experiences.

Candidate: Other experiences.

Supervisor: Yes. For instance: "This is similar to what happened that time you had the flu, where you were feeling so great and bang, you came down with the flu two days later." Or, rather—

Candidate: Because she's the one who presented it psychodynamically: "People are always around me with the flu and I have never gotten sick. How come I got sick that day?"

Supervisor: Right. So you could ask her, "Do you think this might be what you meant when you were talking about that time when you had the flu?" In other words, it's not lost. It might have been more effectively used, but it's no big deal.

Candidate: That's what I felt today. It was a —

Supervisor: So you come back to it some other way, as a reconstruction maybe, or let her come back to it as a reconstruction, and relate it to some dynamically similar event, which inevitably will occur during the termination process. This is going to be the process now. Feeling great, reintegrating or integrating, reintegrating but in a new way, feeling enormous confidence, getting frightened, the implications of what it means, the fears of leaving you, the fears of the renunciation, the regression and the retreat to helplessness or sickness.

Candidate: Well, and I feel like the father transference, this is the time that the father transference would come up. I don't know why, maybe I'll understand that better as I think about it.

Supervisor: Uh-huh.

Candidate: But maybe, because what it's initially about, its deeper roots, is a turning, a triadic, a turning away from her mother to her father—

Supervisor: From a dyad into a triad.

Candidate: And that that shift was so conflicted for her, so that as she's talking about terminating and as she's leaving me, her mother, she is also turning to me, her father. Then she also has to leave me, her father, but this is where it's the father transference that seems clearer and stronger now than I have heard since the beginning, when it was very definitely a defense against that deeply regressed maternal transference.

Supervisor: Yeah, I think that formulation makes good sense.

Candidate: Thank you.

Supervisor: Okay. I'll see you then in two weeks.

Supervisor's Comments

The candidate again indicates her plans for the supervisory hour, and begins by articulating her own recognition of the importance of the termination phase and process. She introduces the idea that it would be fun to go back and examine all of the patient's "apartment dreams," a move that shows she is aware of the progress reflected in this series of dreams. The supervisor supports her initiative, demonstrating more conceptually the "scientific" use of this kind of marker in reflecting on an analytic experience, and broadening the field by mention of a similar instance.

As the candidate had suggested, the patient's dream and her responses to it are reflections of some of the changes which have occurred as a result of the analytic experience. The patient seems to have moved spontaneously into the termination process, and in a direct, comfortable, and effective way the candidate interprets this into the transference ("talking about how she loves me"). The intervention encourages the patient to experience and express more directly her sense of frustration over abstinence in the transference; this in turn leads to her more deeply experiencing the hostility and aggression she feels in reaction to this frustration, and to being focused into the transference experience. During this interchange the candidate appears comfortable and able to tolerate and work with the patient's negative transference.

The unfolding material demonstrates how both patient and candidate have grown in the course of this analytic experience. The patient's new experience of observing herself pleasurably and comfortably in the mirror is a sign of internal change, both in her self-image and in her superego functions. Pleasure and a positive sense of personal fulfillment are now permitted, as well as a feeling of being attractive and worthwhile—all this in contrast to her previous inhibition based on guilt and shame. She also shows a capacity for self-analytic scrutiny in the termination process and a new ability to deal effectively with Ted, someone toward whom earlier she had felt quite helpless. She recognizes her own residual symptoms, as well as the onset of symptoms in relation to currently activated dynamic transference elements. She is able to express more effectively and confidently her anger and hostility toward the analyst, "even on a Thursday." This last remark is an indication that the degree of object constancy is enhanced, and anxiety in connection with ambivalence reduced. There is a solid recognition of the analyst's commitment, even though negative feelings may be expressed. She has a greater sense of confidence that her ambivalence and aggression will not destroy the relationship, that the analyst will bear up, and that feeling and action are not equivalent.

Interspersed through this material, however, are continuing derivative manifestations of neurotic conflict, particularly fears and fantasies of competition with the mother in the oedipal triad. There is an expectation of punishment for oedipal success or pleasure.

The candidate's development is illustrated by the skill with which she deals with the patient's transference responses, by her direct, meaningful, and appropriate interpretation into the transference neurosis, and by her ability to tolerate and interpret the various affects the patient experiences toward her. Additionally, she shows herself capable of a complex interpretation in which she is simultaneously both father and mother in the transference, and of allowing, encouraging, and explaining to the patient this oscillation of transference experience and the bisexual nature of the transference. That the patient can accept, understand, and elaborate this interpretation is a further indicator of the patient's development and growing capacity to tolerate in conscious awareness experiences, affects, and memories which previously had been the source of intense anxiety and defensive avoidance. The candidate conceptualizes the process at a theoretical level for the patient, who shows she can use this kind of explanation to further work through the issues of her neurosis.

The patient observes and tolerates current manifestations of oedipal experience in her relationship with both her father and her mother, and both patient and candidate show a capacity for free-ranging association in their ability to call up and use in the present context a dream reported several years earlier in the analysis.

The patient shows evidence of having further worked through the conflicted positive and negative oedipal configurations. The candidate's comment that the patient "found a middle ground today but she's still entangled in these old things" indicates a fleeting awareness by the patient of the working through process, followed by a return to previous neurotic adaptations. In her comment, the patient demonstrates a capacity to use this material effectively: "This make such sense."

For a variety of reasons, the meanings of the patient's somatic illness are difficult to conceptualize. The candidate recognizes her own difficulty in coping with the problem ("and then I was out to lunch"), but at least she is capable of recognizing the impact of the disruptions and of her countertransference reactions. The question of whether the illness is primarily a psychological response, expressed somatically, or whether the patient's fantasies and thoughts about the illness are a secondary response in terms of currently activated transference feelings, is difficult to sort out.

The patient's own interpretation, that she had made herself sick, may reflect transference compliance with what she thinks the candidate wants to hear, a need for control (she did it to herself rather than its being done to her), or possibly a denial of the idea of illness. The candidate indicates her awareness of her own difficulties ("I'm embarrassed to admit it.") and of the mechanical way in which she introduced termination issues, not understanding the inappropriateness of dealing with them at this time. In retrospect, the candidate had obviously thought about the issues and had recognized how her countertransference response resulted in a reenactment, in the analytic setting, of a childhood trauma connected with parental attitudes toward the patient's urethral stricture.

The supervisor recognizes that the candidate is aware of her countertransference but that she has not fully analyzed it; his question as to why she was "out to lunch" leads not only to the candidate's elaboration of the death in her immediate family and its implications, but also to the recognition that perhaps she too is having difficulties with termination. The supervisor accepts the candidate's countertransference behavior without criticism, recognizing that she is trying to understand it herself. He seeks to use the experience constructively by emphasizing the "rule of thumb," assuring her that events like this occur in the life of any analyst, and suggesting ways of coping with such situations. The candidate uses this intervention effectively, recognizes the possible technical advantages of the supervisor's suggestions, but then continues to explore her own reactions and self-observations. She feels that supervision may have introduced an artificial inhibition, a point the supervisor confirms and accepts as inevitable in the educational situation.

Both patient and candidate show signs of growth, inasmuch as they prove capable of gradual recovery from the disruptions and the technical error, and the analytic process is resumed without defensive denial of the disruption. In this connection, the patient demonstrates a capacity for self-observation and recognizes that her old neurotic behavior and complaints are no longer appropriate, even though the words and the descriptions remain the same. Candidate and patient interact in ways that permit authentic experience in the patient, leading to the resumption of a comfortable therapeutic alliance.

The patient also shows her growing self-awareness by contrasting her initial perception of analysis with the way she views it now. She recognizes the gains that have been made, as well as the expectations that have been disappointed. The prolonged silences, a new occurrence in the analysis, are another indicator of change. The implications are that the patient is more self-directed; she seems capable of experiencing her own feelings more directly, and of deciding for herself what to do rather than feeling that she must be compliant. She anticipates acceptance even though she fails to do what previously she thought was expected of her. She accepts herself as tolerable and lovable. As part of this she is working over some of the termination affects and experiences, and shows a typical oscillation between progress and regression, as well as the need to experience grief and mourning over the anticipated loss of the analyst and the analysis. The candidate not only tolerates the silence well but, recognizing it as an accomplishment for the patient, responds to it appropriately.

Supervisor and candidate next engage in an active dialogue about the implications of these recent behavior patterns regarding change within the patient. The supervisor attempts to describe to the candidate the kind of detailed clinical observations that permit inferences of intrapsychic structural change. Here clinical phenomenology is integrated with theoretical inferences and deductions to show how analysis effects such change.

The candidate is capable of independent technical decisions with regard to setting a termination date, and supports her belief that the patient should be the one to do it. She then introduces, as a new technical issue, the question of how the patient says goodbye after each session. Here the candidate seems to be functioning at a sophisticated level: she does not want to inhibit the behavior, but rather waits for an opportunity to understand its latent meanings. However, she seems to be requesting from the supervisor an explanation or formula, a request the supervisor frustrates by deflecting the question back to the candidate, asking for her own formulations. The candidate begins to formulate possible meanings of the behavior, which the supervisor indirectly supports. The candidate seems to feel good about this attempt at active learning: "as I talk about it it sounds like something that makes sense." This feeling is directly reinforced by the supervisor, who then expands the focus from the immediate symptomatic act (the patient's saying goodbye) to a broader conceptualization of behavior as a compromise that is reflected in a variety of forms. The candidate makes use of this understanding by extending it to the dream, to which the supervisor responds with a supportive elaboration. The candidate's remark ("this is a fascinating thing") expresses the pleasure she takes in learning.

Another indicator of structural change in the patient is her response to the illness and her allowing the doctor to see how sick she actually was. The supervisor uses this to illustrate once again the implications of manifest behavior with regard to underlying intrapsychic events and shifts induced by the analysis. Such repetition helps the candidate recognize how structural change is assessed in the clinical situation and how behavioral shifts may permit metapsychological and clinical-theoretical inferences with regard to unconscious mental processes. The candidate is able to use this and to recognize that the shift just described with regard to the illness relates to the patient's capacity to remain silent, a point which the supervisor actively reinforces. The candidate is able to elaborate upon her own response to this shift and change in the patient.

The supervisor then offers reassurance and a positive assessment, while at the same time making reference to the technical error the candidate had made. The candidate recognizes her difficulties and the fact that the situation would have been better had the error not been made. While the supervisor confirms this, he also points out that errors are not necessarily irremediable; it may be possible to reconstruct the events in question at a subsequent date through other clinical interventions and experiences. This is an attempt to emphasize to the candidate that no analysis is ever conducted perfectly, that errors and countertransference interferences will always occur. They need not have disastrous consequences, however, particularly if they are recognized and dealt with subsequently.

The supervisor then resumes the discussion of termination issues. Supervisor and candidate work together to elaborate a dynamic line in the transference and a formulation of material the candidate is now observing. The supervisor supports the candidate's formulation directly, and the session ends on a positive note.

Both candidate and supervisor are clearly enjoying their work with each other and the interactions it entails. The progress of the patient in the analytic process has been clarified and better understood.

Chapter 17

Supervisory Session 117

Candidate: We're getting to something interesting, but I didn't bring my notes, so I'll just have to do it from memory. I saw you on a Wednesday. I saw her on Wednesday and Thursday, and I told her Wednesday that I wouldn't see her Monday, Tuesday, or Wednesday of next week. That Wednesday was the Fourth of July and I wasn't working until the day after. Then she asked me if I could start tomorrow's session ten minutes early. I said no. The next day—

Supervisor: Friday or the day after?

Candidate: Thursday, yeah.

Supervisor: The next day from the time you told her.

Candidate: Yeah. It was the end of Wednesday's session, and as she got up I said, "You know, next week I won't see you until the Thursday after the Fourth of July," and she said, "I wanted to ask you if you could see me ten minutes early tomorrow." She knows she is my first patient of the day. I said no. I paused for a minute, because actually I could have seen her ten minutes earlier but I decided I would say no and see what gives. She came in the next day, and felt that it was really insignificant. I think maybe, if I had said yes, it wouldn't have been so insignificant. I did read the next day's notes, but I don't remember them. What then happened was she had a weekend in which she was feeling really good. The only thing that had come out on Wednesday and Thursday was her continued concern at the way she uses her fantasies about this man—not in fantasy, in reality—when she bumps into him. She thinks he is a son of a bitch and she doesn't want anything to do with him.

Supervisor: This is still Robert you're talking about?

Candidate: Yeah. But she continues to fantasize about him. She had a dream in which he was being a son of a bitch and she told him what a son of a bitch he was. He said, "You are right," and started to cry. Then he made up to her and she made up to him. I think this was part of the dream. She invited him over for dinner. He was going to come, and her sole motivation for inviting him over to dinner (and she finally got around to talking about that part of it) was that he would really want her and she could tell him to fuck off; she has a tremendous wish for revenge before she gives up. She will let go of it after she has her revenge, not before. So she has a good weekend, or she starts to have a good weekend. Saturday she has a good day. She feels good, she feels real aware of her body and sexual, and wanting to meet a man and being able to meet a man. Now that's the first time in a long time that she has felt that she wants a man in her life and is able to do something about it. She cleaned up her apartment. She likes it when her apartment is clean. She feels good. Everything. She had tickets to some charity cocktail party at the Veiled Prophet Fair. She asked a girl friend if she wanted to go with her, and they went. She felt that she should ask Jean. I don't know if you remember, Jean is this middle-aged, bitchy, single man-hating woman, and in the last year the patient has realized the implications of her befriending her and didn't want to ask her. She felt a little guilty, but she didn't ask her and instead she asked this girl friend. They had a third ticket, but it went unused because she didn't want to ask Jean. She goes to this party and they are having a good time. They are just about the only young, available, attractive females and there aren't really any available, attractive young men, but they are enjoying wandering around. In the middle of this she starts to throw up. She said she didn't get woozy. She doesn't believe it was alcohol. She thinks she made herself sick. She didn't get woozy, didn't get hot, and didn't have any sense that she was going to throw up; she just started throwing up. She carried on in a kind of strange way. She continued to talk to people and then she'd throw up, continue to talk, throw up. I guess it wasn't bothering her very much. She must not have felt very sick immediately.

Supervisor: And this was actual vomiting?

Candidate: Oh, yes. She said she vomited for about four hours. Then she was dry-heaving. She said it was so awful, ultimately it was so awful she thought she was going to die. Do you remember the time in February when she got sick? It's the same affect, a different physical symptom but the same affect. It was so awful she was going to die. It was so totally out of control. She's convinced—oh, it's also important that she didn't eat on Saturday. Not that she didn't eat anything; she just didn't *over*-eat. She didn't overeat at the party. She had a couple of drinks. So she goes home from this cocktail party and sleeps all night. Well, she didn't sleep much. She dry-heaved all night. She thought she was going to die. She slept off and on Sunday. Somebody asked her to some other brunch. She had already had lunch, but she went and she didn't overeat there. On the way home she started getting a migraine. She's sure she's going to vomit and she's terrified she's going to vomit. I don't exactly remember the sequence of it, but anyway, the only way she knew to not be terrified was to eat; she knew then that it would be better if she ate. So she ate some stuff. And she got to talking about how being fat protects her from getting sick and being thin makes her sick, or to be thin is to be sick and not to be thin is to be vulnerable to getting sick. She talked about—oh, was that the session she was late, forty-five minutes late for this Monday session? I think it was the day she was late. It's one of these days she was forty-five minutes late and she said, "I made it." She got out of a meeting. This wasn't the session. No, she was only ten minutes late. She got out of a meeting and it was definitely the sort of time she would never have come before. And it was definitely as early as she could get out of this thing. Okay. She said the fantasy is that if the eating and staying overweight keeps her from getting sick, it's an endless circle. She can't get out of it, because every time she gets to the point where she wants to do something about it and feels like she can do something about it, she actually gets sick or makes herself sick. It scares her because it's so incredibly powerful. There is the fantasy that not eating or getting thin makes her sick connected to that, and the reason it's so scary is that she has no control over it. It knocks her off her feet. Being overweight symbolizes being in control. The next day—Thursday—is the session I want to have reviewed so I'm going to look at it a little bit. The next day—and there was an error in this in that I probably shouldn't have gone into it the day before a five-day break—she and I talked about that and its implications before the end of the session. We got to talking about—well, maybe if I just read the session. She came in on time; in fact, she was early. She feels depressed, sad, really sad. She wanted to go see Linda Ronstadt at the Muny Opera last night. She asked Jean. She wanted to go yesterday and had tickets, but she didn't want to go by herself and everybody else was busy. Jean really wanted to go someplace afterward, but she didn't want to, so she dropped her off. She knows Jean is mad at her, but fuck her. Yesterday she was really afraid to diet. She had a fear of eating, like she was so crabby. She didn't have time for dinner before going to the concert. She was hungry and afraid she would get sick again. She wouldn't let herself, she won't let herself be what she really is. She gets sad and angry. She's been coming here for five years. Isn't it time she's able to get over this goddamn hump? She feels so frustrated. She feels caught in a web. She's disgusted with work. It's obvious that she shouldn't stay there much longer. She gets angry with herself. Why can't she be happy with what she has? But she isn't. She just wants to be who she is. Her father called this morning, and that irritated the hell out of her and she let him have it. She really likes her apartment and it really reflects her. She really likes to go home now. That makes her sad about moving. She'll never get anything as nice, but it's really okay because she knows she'll get something nice. She just tries to lay that on herself: you'll never get anything as nice again. Her father said, "Your next move must be to Chicago," and she got pissed. He wants to believe that he makes all the decisions. It really pissed her off. There were more details and I said, "A similar thing here." If she moves to Chicago now he'll think he did it; if she loses weight now and is herself now, will I be satisfied that I did it? And she said that's true but that's a known and there's much more right now. She is really scared that she'll get sick and doesn't understand this. There was an interchange about magical thoughts, about being heavy protects her from something and being thin feels horribly vulnerable, physically vulnerable. It has to do with how she sees her mother, too. Her mother wore the pants, was domineering, and she was very, very heavy. Over the years her mother has lost weight, and now she seems so fragile. She seems more fragile than her eighty-year-old grandmother. Her mother is obsessed now. She can't do anything but pay attention to her weight and her clothes. She seems so pathetic. Looking at all these people at the Muny—thin women to her never had any problems, that's how her mother always felt. She always felt awkward with her body, never felt comfortable. There was always something wrong with her body. She would never be attractive to someone. She was fine. Beauty is only partially the outward shell. It's really strange the way she associates different times with her mother and the way she looked and what it meant. She was a lot more powerful when she was heavy. Then she was drained of her power. She looks at Ellie Meyer; she's all bones. She said how excited Ellie was she was going to visit her family. They think—oh, Ellie Meyer said, "Oh, I'm so excited I'm going to see my family. They think I'm wonderful." Ellie Meyer has a bad marriage. She is wonderful. Tears welled up. Why do people let men or anyone beat them down? I said, "As you lose weight, are you telling me that you've been more physically vulnerable in your body?" She said, "Oh, god, yes. Terribly." I said, "So that's what we're talking about, your armor, your fantasy that your flesh protects you." She said yes, she feels so naked, so vulnerable, so without protection and most intensely sexual. That's the worst. She went on some about that, and I made a statement that sexual arousal is a building up of tension, like urine in her bladder and, surrounding the urethral stricture, the pain of being totally consumed, overstimulated, flooded. Massive. Sexual arousal is totally consuming, very stimulating. Again she is dependent on somebody else to relieve it, and that flooding. She said yes, she is dependent upon someone else to relieve it.

Supervisor: She added that?

Candidate: She added that. The fat protects her, keeps her from feeling things so intensely. That's how she felt Saturday night. The sickness was all-consuming. She thought she would die. She has never let herself go sexually. She's afraid she'd feel she would die. She had experienced that. She has experienced that occasionally: physical pleasure until it hurts. She can't stand it anymore. It's true. There was a long silence. She thinks she can connect this analogy into a lot of things. It reminds her of how she feels about work right now, how she has felt. Her job is so easy. It's a safe place to stay right now. She has proven herself. She isn't on the spot, if she goes with the flow. She isn't being acknowledged. I said to be acknowledged and to be challenged is stimulating. She said yes, exactly, and there is no vulnerability to it there. There is just boredom. It's boring but safe. It's the same with her body. It's boring but it's safe. She yearns for stimulation, to be touched, but she's afraid it will kill her. How does she stop this? It's so strong. Understanding helps, but she's afraid that the wanting to go for it won't last. She doesn't know how to say this. I said I think she's saying that the first success she has, the first five pounds, she feels her body more, feels sensations, and this triggers the fear of overstimulation and pain. She said that something will exlode inside her, that she will die, yes. I said we can understand her reluctance to demand more acknowledgment. She said yes.

Supervisor: Understand what?

Candidate: Her reluctance to demand more acknowledgment at work. We've understood that from a number of different vantage points. This is just another aspect of her masochism, and her reluctance to show how angry she has been. It's a focused, intense, building sensation that demands release. She said, "Oh god, you're right. Oh god, I feel so much better." Then she was silent for a while. I don't know what happened in between. I said I felt that her sense of her body as a penis is also, perhaps, a sense of her body as an overly filled bladder, tense, taut, powerful. The awful pain of draining and then it's empty, nothing, you can't feel it anymore, it's all gone. She said yes, that makes even more sense than just her body as a penis. That has always felt like not the whole story. Her bladder was so powerful; it was everything then. It made her so vulnerable and so weak, all the things she never wanted to be. She used that experience to conceptualize a penis. She conceptualizes a penis the same way. It's strange. She feels she's overloaded right now. She wants to understand every little piece of this. She feels—I don't know if she said this or if I just wrote it down—she feels overstimulated. I said, "And then we miss sessions, we miss appointments." She said, "Yeah, but that'll be okay." I said I think it is important because again she has a lot going on that needs another person to help relieve it. There was an interchange about how it could confirm her feeling that to be stimulated is bad. She had a piece of it and she wants to hold onto it. She wants to follow it up. She wants to get hold of it. She wants more. She feels that there she will be again, like after the urethral stricture, trying to understand something. But there was nobody. There was nothing. She was stuck with it, with nowhere else to go, no way to understand it. We've opened this and now she is stuck with it. That was the end of the session. I felt like it was a mistake to go into it at that point, but I also felt like it was suddenly very available. Later she said it was the longest weekend of her life. She took the same days off I did. She realized how much she despised me for doing that to her. She felt she had made so much headway on Tuesday and then there she was. She went to Peoria this weekend and that made her really sad. She feels like such a failure. Then it's interesting, she talks, oh, we have time to do it, she feels like such a failure because she doesn't have a man. What her grandmother really wants more than anything else in the world is to see the patient married. The grandmother is getting older; she isn't going to be around forever. She even felt guilty about Natalie after she had stood up for herself. She said, "No, you can't come." Then she got down there and she wondered. She took a step back. She left here Tuesday and really really wanted to take care of herself, to walk, to eat right. She did okay Tuesday and Wednesday, and then Thursday she just lost it. She didn't do anything she wanted to do. She just sat there, totally immobilized. She feels like a yo-yo; just as she feels better, she pulls back into her old ways. She had an interesting dream Thursday night, another apartment dream, but it wasn't real clear. She was just moving into a neat older building with great potential to be truly wonderful. She really liked it; it was the kind of place she always wanted to live in, but she had only moved half of her furniture in. All these people turned around and were trying to help her, but she wouldn't let herself move the other half of the furniture in. That's how she feels right now. She feels she understands a lot, but she won't let go. She's afraid of the overstimulation. That got real clear. It's really going on, it's really going, active, everything. It's really about going after everything, not maybe getting everything, but experiencing it all. All weekend she fantasized about Robert and wondered why the hell she was doing that. She forced herself to remember all the realistic things about him. He's a son of a bitch, but she couldn't get rid of the fantasies, sexual fantasies, all like that first night last year. He seemed like this wonderful, warm person. He isn't like that. He's a grumpy schmuck, yet she doesn't want to see it. She came home yesterday and was reading the paper. Then she picked up a romance novel and was pissed. She spent four hours reading this romance novel. Is that how she is going to spend her life, in a goddamn romance novel? Immobilized. She feels guilty, but her feelings are stronger than her guilt. She feels disgusted that she spent time with Jean; she didn't enjoy her. Then she refused to go out with her Thursday evening though Jean was pissed off. Wednesday she went to a fabric store to buy some material. She's having a dressmaker make her some clothes. She had a really nice time being with herself. "This is okay," she thought to herself, "but I don't want to do this every day. I don't want to be by myself every day or be with people I don't like." She's sick of Jean; she's sick of her attitude about men. She's an old, bitter lady. She felt a little guilty, but she isn't going to see her anymore. So it wasn't a complete step back, only a half step back. I said something about being immobilized and into fantasy. She said that is a protection. I said, "Against overstimulation?" She said yes, it's just like being fat; you put up this screen. She said fantasizing about Robert prevents her from meeting anybody or doing anything. She keeps hanging onto the fantasy, just like she's hanging onto her fat. I said that on the way here she realized how much she hated me for bringing this up, for doing what I did to her Thursday. She said she hated me because we finally cracked the nut, and then there she was hanging there, angry with me because I asked a lot of probing questions that led her there. It reminded her of the urethral stricture, so much to deal with. It was a massive—then she clouded over, veiled herself. There are so many times in her life—she's done that so many times in her life. It always makes her feel stupid. She has often been in situations of overstimulation and then she blurs it out and gets mad because she says, "Concentrate on this," but she can't. She blurs it out. She makes herself unable to understand things and then feels stupid. I said that one reason she was immobilized this weekend was my following up on those things the day before a long weekend.

Supervisor: Those are the events of your latest session?

Candidate: Yeah. It was overstimulating and then she was left with, she felt, no way to deal with it and blurred it out. When she blurs out things, she's left with nothing. And she said, "Exactly, and I have—" It must have been more exactly. She had another thought this weekend in Peoria. She grew up in a family of secrets. "Don't tell your mother that I said that. Don't tell your father that I said that. Don't tell your grandmother that I said that." She was a nervous wreck trying to remember who to tell what to. She talked about talking with Virginia and commenting about being disappointed in her mother. She commented about being disappointed in her mother and being sad that she had said this to these people. She was disappointed in her mother and sad that she doesn't have the kind of relationship she's always wanted with her mother, and that's just the way it's always going to be. That was a new thing: to say that to someone outside this room. Then she worried: what if someone finds out that she said that? She can remember worrying about things for years. Would her grandmother find out that she said this or that to this or that person? She still has twinges. It's interesting, like reminiscences of it. She gets tired—oh, and then she said I get tired of hearing Ted and what a crook he is. I don't remember the other things she said, but a whole long string of things that she's tired of about this wonderful grandmother. I said that then her grandmother is a disappointment to her too, and she said yes. I said then that I had disappointed her on Thursday by leaving her with all this stuff to handle by herself, and she said what a disappointment her mother is and then described how the grandmother disappoints her. She comes in today and says she's a failure. She said, "Yes, I always do that, don't I?" She talked about how compulsive her grandmother and mother are and how crazy they are about cleaning up. What would they do if there was nothing to clean? She is tired, she's tired of being badgered for not being like they are. She's not like they are and she doesn't want to be like they are. Her grandmother made notes in the middle of the night so that she would remember to bug her in the morning. She would wake up at two in the morning and make little notes and say, "At two o'clock in the morning I thought of this." The things they get in their heads, their expectations. You can never relax there, at either place. There is always something that has to be done. Grandmother promised the dining room set to her years ago. She said, "When you die, I would like your dining room set," and Grandmother said, "You're welcome to it." On this visit she said could somebody, Aunt Edna, Cousin Harriet, have that corner cabinet, and the patient said, "No! It's all part of the dining room set and you said it was mine. I want it all. No!" The grandmother said, "But there are twelve pieces to the dining room set," and the patient said, "I want all twelve of them." She said, "I was very proud of myself," but then said she ends up feeling like she's the failure. It's easier to feel that she's the failure (this is her talking) than to face the ways in which these people and I have failed her. Thinking about the men she has been involved with, she hasn't really loved them. It was control she liked. She hasn't let herself love anyone. She was silent for a long time and sighed. I made a questioning sound, and she said she was thinking about how hard this is, how impatient she is. She has had so much patience in her life. She wants out for a lot of reasons. It's overstimulating. We threaten her protections against her overstimulation, and it's scary. That was the end of that. The next day she feels fat and unattractive. She felt she would throw up as she came in the door. On the way home the day before she wondered if she'd been telling me all the good things that had been happening, like the fact that she did all the Thunder River designing in the United States last year. That's what she did, all of this. The good things. She's so used to presenting all of the negatives in herself as a hopeless schlepp. She talked with her friend on the phone who got a job in Chicago and went there two weeks ago. The friend said, "It's everything we thought it would be. I'm working forty-seven hours a day. I'm paying six hundred for an apartment and it's much smaller than I had for four in St. Louis." And she presents this in a nah-nah way. Then it starts sneaking in that it's very exciting because this girl also said, "It's all what we thought it would be. People up here are so competent. They are really on the ball." She is working with really smart, exciting people and that's worth whatever there is. To leave me is to leave safety and the sorority house, and she doesn't want to move the rest of her furniture. It's scary and stimulating to think of going to Chicago, of making whatever, Chicago, New York, whatever is next. She was able to see that it's not going to Chicago that's scary and stimulating; it's making this internal step that she's trying to make to not blurring herself out, not protecting herself so massively against all stimulation. I mean, she could go to Chicago and continue to do this. But what's exciting is that she's trying to come out from behind all these barriers and it's scary and exciting, and staying in analysis would keep her from having to do that, and staying in St. Louis would keep her from having to do it.

Supervisor: It's like giving up the fat.

Candidate: Yeah, yeah. And the fat is the most readily available evidence of it. It's a palpable example of it. But she was able to come up with a half-dozen more—the way she's dealing at work for instance. She tried to get herself fired at work. She went to work after this Tuesday's session and sat out in the main room with her secretary with her feet up on the desk and talked all day and didn't do any of her work. Her boss walked back and forth, and she didn't do anything. Because if she got herself fired, then she would be forced to do something. To make the decision to come out and do the next thing, to make the decision herself, is disturbing.

Supervisor: The difference between deciding to terminate the treatment and you kicking her out.

Candidate: Or of getting a job precipitously in Chicago, like Ruth. It's funny, because she said, "I can't stay. How can I stand it until October eighteenth? I've got to go to Chicago now. I've got to be looking for jobs now." That's on the one hand. On the other hand, she'll never be ready to leave. At some point in this session I said that it's as if she put the good feelings into wanting to come here today, instead of feeling good about herself. Because she really wanted to come to Tuesday's session. She really wanted to come. She left on Monday, she felt really good, and she really wanted to come to Tuesday's session. But she felt terrible about herself, starting maybe Tuesday morning. She felt really good when she left here yesterday, but she realized that she felt good because she was here. For five days she felt bad. She's afraid that when she leaves there won't be any refuge, no one to understand her like I do. She's afraid of losing that. If she feels good, she will want to leave and she will lose this. She said that the opposite side is if she doesn't want to leave, she won't have to. Somewhere in this context I said that maybe that's why she hates her job. She said yesterday she hated it. It really sounded totally disproportionate. So I said maybe that's why she hated it so much yesterday, because from the way she's talking it's as if she was going to be there forever, not just twelve weeks. The point I'm trying to get to is that I interjected this twelve weeks, and she just hasn't said anything about it yet, but I could feel a startle in the air. To start looking for a job twelve weeks before you're going to move someplace is not unrealistic. She is not as stuck as she is perceiving herself to be. That's what I'm trying to say, except in her fat, in this protection that she's hanging onto, in this terror of being stimulated.

Supervisor: Is she planning to leave?

Candidate: Ultimately.

Supervisor: But not twelve weeks from now.

Candidate: No, but you see, her fantasy is that if she started, because this has happened to several of her friends and because she's so good and because the feedback she gets is that she's good and she's already known in Chicago, her fantasy is that if she started to look for a job, she would have one the following Monday. They would want her to come there as soon as possible, preferably the following Monday. It's happened to two of her friends. They went up and stayed in hotels and worked and moved. In the spring she was threatening to do it; "I'm going to go look for a job in Chicago, and of course I may get one and have to move next week." Now she wants to. She feels that professionally the next thing she has to do is to make a leap to where she is not the most competent person around, to where she is being challenged, to where it is stimulating and where she can make the next growth step she needs to make professionally. To go to New York or Chicago. She has done St. Louis. There is no place else to go in St. Louis. So there's nothing to do but to make that move. She's very excited secretly and lets me know occasionally that she's very excited about that prospect. She's looked into apartments. She's looking around to see what firm she might want to work for. When she is feeling good about herself or isn't so terrified, she's getting her portfolio together.

Supervisor: Now, have you interpreted to her that she's keeping the excitement a secret?

Candidate: Oh yes, oh yes.

Supervisor: And that she—

Candidate: And that's what she—no, no, not the excitement. See that whole notion of excitement has just come up. That she keeps good things a secret has been a persistently interpreted thing, but that she's keeping the excitement a secret is another connected issue. And that's what she was saying.

Supervisor: See, if she goes to Chicago, she's looking forward to it, she's eager and excited, she's now in the big leagues, then she's leaving you back here in the bush league and she's ungrateful and she's taking your strength. You could probably be in the big leagues, but she's going to be taking you and your strength with her and you're going to be left behind.

Candidate: Like her skinny mother.

Supervisor: Like her skinny mother, her frail, skinny mother.

Candidate: That's the image, like her frail, skinny mother.

Supervisor: Or her inept father.

Candidate: Yeah, the father transference is so—oh, and her fantasy that came up last week with the dream about Robert and really goring him was the fantasy that her father's ineptness was due to her successfully venting her vengeance on him. She had made him the weak, hopeless schlemiel that he is, and her glee at having that much power to wipe him out. Oh, yeah. And her parents are moving to Chicago too. I mean they are actually moving. I don't know if they're moving anywhere near her, maybe they're just moving to a suburb. I don't know why they're moving to Chicago.

Supervisor: How does she feel about them moving to Chicago when she's thinking of moving there?

Candidate: Invaded. But she hasn't talked about it a whole lot. When it's come up, it's come up in terms of how much she will be earning—more money than her father has ever made, which won't be a hell of a lot. Her father never really had a lot of money. She's going into the big leagues, but not into the big money yet. But she'll get there, and she knows that she will unless she restrains herself.

Supervisor: The question is really how much of this is being experienced in, but not expressed in, the transference, in terms of her comparison of herself to you, in terms of her capacity—

Candidate: Yeah, it's been a couple of weeks since that's come up, and I think things moved quickly enough that it needs to—

Supervisor: Her capacity to outdo you, to get beyond you, to leave you behind in the dust, to leave you in the bush leagues while she moves off into the majors. She's going to be famous and she's going to owe it all to you, and you're going to be back here, pathetic, and that's going to make it impossible for her to enjoy it because she really gets all of what she's got from you. And if you didn't let her take it or if she didn't steal it from you, if you were more assertive, you wouldn't have let her do this and you'd be the one who was going to Chicago. What I'm trying to get at is—

Candidate: Do you really think that? I think that this whole issue of going without her blanket and that I am right now a part of her blanket is very—is the uppermost issue right now. When I bring up these other things, she says, yeah, but. The same thing she said about one thing I brought up: "Yes, that's true, but that's a known and I know that but there's more to this than that."

Supervisor: And what's the more that she's saying?

Candidate: The whole, the, the exposed feeling, this, all that's encompassed under overstimulation, going without her blanket, me, her fat.

Supervisor: Did you ever—

Candidate: And that's only just been talked about.

Supervisor: Did you ever establish why she vomited at the party?

Candidate: No, that's one of the things that I wanted to talk to you about. When she came in Tuesday, I asked some questions and I tried to get more information to try to see if either of us could make connections about what it was that stimulated the vomiting. She comes in Tuesday and she's all detached and trying to make herself out to be in a terrible situation. Then it sneaks by a little bit later that she's not in any terrible situation but she's all excited about a possible move to Chicago. But she walks in and says, "It's funny, I just thought I was going to vomit." You know, maybe she's cramming stuff down her throat. This number about how pathetic she is—

Supervisor: Yeah, that may be, or maybe she is—

Candidate: Maybe it has something to do with the excitement.

Supervisor: I still suspect, I don't know, but I suspect that she sees this as she is taking something valuable from you. She's either stealing it or she's leaving you; at least, she's leaving you depleted.

Candidate: How does that fit in with the vomiting?

Supervisor: Because the vomiting is the defense against this. She's going to orally incorporate it.

Candidate: Oh, she's taking it in.

Supervisor: She's taking it in and she feels guilty. She feels it's going to hurt her or overstimulate her or she's going to have too much.

Candidate: But she can't take it and be happy with it.

Supervisor: That's right. She's got to spit it back out. She's got to vomit it back out, because it's so bad it's going to ruin this relationship or because she feels guilty—

Candidate: There sure wasn't any notion of that when she was talking about it. There wasn't any notion of anything, except what I was listening to was how she felt leaving Jean out. I asked her about that, and I said, "You know, Jean has been a stand-in for me in your feelings for me a lot. And to leave me, the old, bitter, unfulfilled lady at home while you go out and flirt with all these men. But then you couldn't." She said, "Yeah, I know."

Supervisor: I don't know, but I still suspect—

Candidate: I'm not arguing, I'm just saying—

Supervisor: I would target that symptom as something that needs to be explored, something that is probably related to a specific fantasy in terms of separation and loss or giving up or letting go in the transference.

Candidate: And taking with you.

Supervisor: And taking with you, in contrast to feeling guilty for taking it with you. Taking with you and incorporating it, internalizing it, in contrast to the feeling that you're not supposed to have it.

Candidate: And contrast it, yeah, spewing it back out.

Supervisor: Spewing it back out—

Candidate: Giving it back—

Supervisor: And vomiting it back out.

Candidate: Uh-huh.

Supervisor: We've got to stop here, but I would look for. Or let me put it another way. That particular symptom, I feel as though I'm going to vomit, the exact detailed fantasies that are going on just before she experiences it is what you want to look at. One of them occurred at the party when she was having a good time, where she feels thin, where she is not with Jean, where she's with a girl she likes, where she's anticipating that she and this other girl are the only two people at the party that are young, vibrant, and alive, and presumably somebody's noticing.

Candidate: Everybody was noticing.

Supervisor: And immediately she starts to vomit.

Candidate: And she said she was loving it.

Supervisor: So the vomiting it back out again suggests that—

Candidate: She was taking something in, yeah.

Supervisor: She was taking something in and the vomiting has to spoil it. And the same thing when she's about to come into your session with you; she has the same sensation.

Candidate: Well, no, but you know, that the day before, I know we have to stop, but the day before she said she felt so much better, she did get something from me. Then she wanted to come in the next day because she wanted more of it. She said that in words: "I wanted more." She walks into the session and says she feels like she's going to vomit. She feels guilty for wanting more and what she's taking from me.

Supervisor: Wanting and taking from you leaves you depleted, I think, or because you're not going to want to give it to her or it's got something to do with "Mirror, mirror on the wall," as in "Snow White and the Seven Dwarves," and so on. Now she is the fairest and now you're going to poison her. In some way it's in that ball park and that's where I think you specifically have to get to, because that's where the dissolution, the resolution, and the renunciation of the transference is going on.

Candidate: Uh-huh, good. Thank you.

Supervisor: Okay, Bye-bye.

Candidate: Bye-bye.

Supervisor's Comments

The candidate presents most of this supervisory session from memory without reference to her notes and does so in an active, lively, and reasonably well-organized fashion, which illustrates her overall grasp of the process and of the interaction between herself and the patient. She is not overly concerned that there may be temporary gaps in her memory and account of the material, and she is able to demonstrate how she and the patient together sustain the ongoing psychoanalytic experience. With the exception of a few clarifying remarks there is no particular need for the supervisor to intervene.

The material demonstrates the patient's continuing neurotic behavior patterns, illustrated by her continuing attachment to an inappropriate man in spite of her recognition that the relationship is pathological. At the same time she uses new and more appropriate behavior patterns, illustrated by her reaction to the girl friend she no longer wants to see, as well as her behavior at the party. However, the apparent progress in her behavior elicits conflict, followed by the regressive symptomatic experience of vomiting. This sequence illustrates how at this phase of the analytic process there is considerable fluidity and rapid oscillation in behavior patterns, including a propensity toward defensive retreats. The patient is increasingly aware of the meaning of her own behavior, as seen by her comments in regard to being fat as compared with being thin.

The candidate herself recognizes that she had made a modest technical error in introducing new material just before a prolonged separation. However, what she considers a mistake (her deep symbolic interpretation of the experience of overstimulation) would have been an effective intervention had it been offered during a time of continuing analytic contact. Although it results in the patient having symptomatic and behavioral difficulty during the subsequent separation, the patient nevertheless is able to amend, and somewhat modify toward a more correct solution, the candidate's previous interpretation of the body as penis "that makes even more sense than just her body as a penis. That has always felt like not the whole story."

Both patient and candidate recognize the analyst's importance in relieving the patient from her overstimulation. The interpretation in question had repeated and reenacted some of the original traumatic overstimulation by activating a variety of thoughts, feelings, and fantasies and then leaving the patient "high and dry" during the separation. Even though in some respects this was a reenactment, the patient demonstrates her enhanced ego capacities and analytic progress by being able to withstand it with only moderate disability, and she then is able to describe and report on her perceptions and experience in an appropriate way when the analysis is resumed. The candidate, having openly recognized the technical problem, is able effectively to return to it, acknowledging her role in repeating the trauma, as well as her capacity to tolerate the patient's response of anger and resentment. The candidate uses the incident to help the patient recognize how she turns her aggression back upon herself, and ultimately the untoward effects of the candidate's intervention are alleviated and an important piece of analytic work is accomplished.

In telling her friends about the disappointments she feels toward her mother, the patient manifests a newfound capacity for openness and communication. The behavioral effects of intrapsychic change are evident also in the way she responds to the issue of the grandmother's furniture. She asserts herself and is able to say, "I was very proud of myself."

The candidate again returns to the issue of her "error" and demonstrates to the patient how the transference is being displaced and the aggression turned against herself in a defensive way. She thereby makes effective use of what she had considered an error.

The patient also avails herself of a defensive maneuver typical of the termination phase, namely, hiding her pleasure, enhanced abilities, anticipation, excitement, and other positive experiences from the analyst while at the same time enjoying them. Eventually they become manifest in her spontaneous material, but the withholding bespeaks the anxiety she is experiencing at her new sense of freedom, potential, and ambition. The candidate is comfortably aware of this entire sequence and is able to help the patient cope with it and elaborate on it. These are all typical patient responses to the prospect of termination. The conflicts and anxiety evoked by separation and maturation during the termination process offer the patient a chance to master her reactions. At the same time she expresses a sense of apparently appropriate self-esteem and confidence, as well as the desire for challenge and further growth.

At this point, almost three-fourths of the way through the supervisory session, the supervisor intervenes with his first lengthy comment with regard to the patient's feeling she is robbing the analyst for her own benefit. The candidate comfortably maintains her independent assessment and disagrees with the supervisor's suggestion ("Do you really think that?"). The supervisor continues to push his ideas by focusing on the symptom of vomiting ("Did you ever establish why she vomited at the party?"), to which the candidate responds with new material; she also expresses a generalized, nonspecific idea ("Maybe it has something to do with the excitement"). This is followed by her wondering more actively about the dynamic meaning of the vomiting, to which the supervisor responds with a formulation. Candidate and supervisor interact, with the supervisor indicating his belief that the symptom of vomiting is a manifestation of a specific intrapsychic fantasy and conflict. The candidate continues to have difficulty accepting this.

The supervisor reiterates the general technical precept regarding the importance of uncovering the specific and detailed fantasies behind neurotic symptoms, in this instance the vomiting. After an active interchange the candidate suddenly is able to confirm the hypothesis based upon the patient's "wanting more" from her. The supervisor ends by reiterating his position, using the Snow White story to illustrate the construct. He emphasizes its importance in the resolution of the transference neurosis.

This session shows the candidate's increasing capacity to function independently as an analyst, to recognize her role in the process, and to observe her own technique. The patient shows considerable change, though during this phase she oscillates rapidly between progress and regression, as well as new organization and further resolution of neurotic difficulties. The patient evinces typical termination process conflicts and the ambivalence, grief, and mourning characteristically induced during this phase of the analysis. Candidate and supervisor interact in an animated and collegial way. Although the supervisor makes several suggestions, the candidate for the most part conducts herself independently, and with considerable effectiveness and enjoyment, in both analytic and supervisory processes.

Chapter 18

Supervisory Session 118

Candidate: Ooh, I'm five minutes late. I'm having a problem with punctuality. Well, we made some progress. I was just trying to remember on the way here what precipitated it. She was ranting and raving, railing against the incompetent sons of bitches she works with, and also being real hung up on Robert and how or when to call him. It was toward the end of the session and I had at various times said, "You know, I think this applies to me," and she would say, "Gee, I wish I had something to say. I don't think that at all or I don't feel that at all." I said again but in a little different way that maybe I had just worn her down. I don't know whether it was the different way I said it. I said that I had made mistakes with her—she was railing about some asshole's mistakes—that I had made mistakes and that I hadn't always understood her and that I took a long maternity leave and had handled it in a way that she had really felt was not in her best interest. She got *really* mad, and I was *really* happy. It was close to the end of the session, and when she left she slammed the door. She didn't say anything on her way out. She didn't get mad at me for saying that. Her anger at me finally cracked through. She was openly angry the next day and was able to talk about paying me back and about her impetus to quit. At least once a week she says she understands why people don't finish. She is finding she doesn't want to screw around here until October eighteenth, and it often comes as a little threat or something. Her earlier fantasy, that she never talked about, is that she could really screw me in training. I had to dig for some of this; it didn't just all come out.

Supervisor: Uh-huh.

Candidate: But she *could* really screw me in training. But she said, "I think it's too late for that now." She says, "I think I let it go too long." She has a couple of friends who are in analysis with candidates, one of whom did quit very prematurely, after a relatively long time but obviously very prematurely. Somehow it came out that in the four years she had been in analysis she had increased what she earned by a factor of six. Six times.

Supervisor: This is the other patient?

Candidate: The friend. Yeah, and when her analyst suggested that they increase her fee she just quit. But this friend is leading a life obviously in need of analysis and the patient knows it. She said that it just galled her that any way in which she could get back at me would really just make her suffer. She is aware that to not finish her analysis in an effort to punish me would probably do nothing whatsoever to me but she would be unfinished, and that's too high a price to pay, but she would like to do it anyway. She wants to deny me satisfaction. It galls her that I might take some pleasure in my skill as a therapist. She would like to not appear better until after she terminates. She would like to hold it up so that I wouldn't see it. She doesn't want me to get any professional accolades for having "done a good job." She's the one who did it all, and I'm just riding on her coattails. And that last part is the only thing that was not explicitly said that I think may need to be, but it hasn't come up to be said. It was implied. The session was quite full, and it wasn't until afterward that I thought, "I could have said that, too." It was implied that her hanging onto Robert, to these fantasies of Robert, is a way of punishing me. She is just going to hang on to this sadistic woman-hating man until *after* the bitter end, and thereby keep saying to me, "I'm not better, you haven't made any progress." Since that time I haven't heard anything about him though, so I think that at least some of it got through, although it wasn't explicitly stated. So much was explicitly stated—all of the ways in which she is attempting to punish me and is punishing herself instead. It blew over pretty quickly. She felt almost immediately better.

Supervisor: This is how long ago, this material?

Candidate: Shortly after our last supervisory session. Like maybe within three analytic hours, three or four. I can't find it here.

Supervisor: All right.

Candidate: But I'm only in the second analytic hour. I was reading it in the car. But it was not last week.

Supervisor: Uh-huh.

Candidate: Since that time she has had fluctuations between feeling really good and powerful and independent and talented, attractive enough, spectacular, and old and ugly and dumpy and frumpy and untalented and horrible and all that. At least to some extent she is explicitly aware that when she starts feeling powerful and good these other feelings come in. She has been to see some friends and she feels like she has outgrown everybody. She is having her grandmother's bedroom furniture refinished and is replacing the furniture in her bedroom with it. The furniture in her bedroom now is the furniture she got when she was six or seven years old.

Supervisor: She kept it all this time?

Candidate: And in fact in the last session the major issue was her parents' thought that for sure she should sell it. She wants to just give it away. There is this little tiny part of her that says she should get money for it. And I interpreted that as retribution. I didn't say retribution, but you want some payment before you reconcile, which seemed like an appropriate interpretation at the moment. It seemed to feel right to her, but not to me. She wants to give it to Goodwill.

Supervisor: It may also be an indication of a wish to think it still has value.

Candidate: Well, she is overvaluing it, which I think is also important. Her parents said she should ask four hundred dollars for it, and she said that's way too much. She said, "They think it's got all of this phenomenal value. I couldn't get any more than three hundred." She's twenty-seven. A 20-year-old child's furniture set, painted white, with a lot of pieces, now I don't know what that means. It probably has corner cabinets and two or three dressers and a desk. I've seen those. It may even be a canopy, you know, one of those old white canopy beds that they sold twenty years ago, that was in a wreck when she was twelve, when they moved to wherever it was they moved to when she was twelve, that has paint chipped off of it everywhere. She's not going to get three hundred for it. But she had a dream some time ago, actually there were two dreams about this furniture. About three months ago she had a dream that she lived in this apartment that had a door going into the next apartment and she couldn't quite get it closed, or it was the door going into the hallway that she couldn't quite get closed. It was an okay apartment but she wanted to move. It was time to move, but she couldn't. And there were people offering to help her move. "Fine. Move." But she couldn't figure out how to move her furniture. There was this one bunch of furniture, which I didn't know anything about. I asked her about this furniture, and the funny thing about it was that it was this furniture. I didn't know she still had it at this time. She said it was the furniture she had as a child. I didn't realize she still had it. That came out only a good bit later.

Supervisor: Uh-huh.

Candidate: She kept trying to figure out how to take it with her and to dump it, both at the same time. She didn't want it anymore. She hates this furniture but she couldn't leave it in this apartment. So that was one dream. And then in a dream recently she—I don't remember the rest of the dream, but it was another apartment dream, in which half of her furniture was moved but the other half wasn't, and the half that wasn't was this childhood furniture.

Supervisor: Uh-huh.

Candidate: And I guess it was yesterday that I realized she still has it and that Friday, this coming Friday, the new furniture is coming. She is struggling with how to divest herself of the old furniture. And she laughed when she said this: "When that furniture is gone and the new furniture is here, my apartment really will be finished." She has been aware that when she really starts to feel sad, when she feels powerful and good and happy and then also feels sad, and when she feels that she will miss me but that she can't keep me, that with her growing she has outgrown me, then she will precipitate feeling old and ugly and frumpy and a failure and weak, and she will no longer feel sad.

So that's what's happened. She also said that she realized she doesn't have to move to Chicago on October eighteenth and that in fact it would be a mistake because she has a lot of things to do before she leaves. She has to put her portfolio together. Looking at her portfolio, this is little bits over a number of sessions, looking at her portfolio is like looking at herself. What is there is fine and certainly enough, but it's not as much as she thought.

Supervisor: It's not as much as—

Candidate: As extensive as she thought.

Supervisor: Uh-huh.

Candidate: It's not grandiose. And so she has to put her portfolio together and make some decisions about it. She has to find out some more about places. There are things she needs to do. There are things she needs to wrap up here. There are some projects that it would be worth her professional while to wrap up and this and that. A precipitous move to Chicago would be not acknowledging what leaving me is all about, would be hiding it in some big geographical move.

Supervisor: She comes to this mostly by herself?

Candidate: Yeah.

Supervisor: Or you have to—

Candidate: No, no, she comes to most of it by herself. Sometimes I have to do some what I call digging for things. I don't know that she would have spontaneously told me that she had previously had fantasies about quitting in order to pay me back, unless I had said—well, she came in that day so angry with me and wanting to pay me back, and I said, "Perhaps some of your talking about quitting before you're done is to try and pay me back." She said, "Oh yes," and then it all came out. Then I suggested some other way, which I can't remember, that she was perhaps keeping me from taking pleasure. But that's been where I have made the majority of contributions in that material. One day she came in, this was this week, maybe Monday, she came in and she had a good weekend that had its downs also but she thought she understood. She had a good weekend and she talked about it; I don't know what else she talked about. And then she was silent for the last fifteen minutes of the session. It was a very comfortable silence. She had talked about what was on her mind and looked around and said some new things and then just was silent. And she said that after she left she thought she had been really comfortable in that silence, but then she felt depressed, ugly, fat and terrible, and then she was able to work her way back to yes, she was comfortable with the silence and she felt that we were both letting go. And that's another thing she was mad at, that I would let her go. But if I wouldn't let her go, she would be mad too. There's nothing I could do that she wouldn't be mad at. She was lying on the couch thinking of other things, feeling comfortable and drifting outside the hour, drifting to things in the future, putting things kind of together in her mind, being generally unaware of me, and I didn't say, "What are you thinking?" I didn't pull her back in, and so I was letting her do that, and that made her sad. That this is what's happened, but then she pulled herself back.

Supervisor: She can't even fight you to leave.

Candidate: Yeah. I will tell her today that four weeks from today I start a vacation, not a very long vacation, only two weeks. Monday is the earliest I could have, when I finally knew. Usually I tell people by the beginning of the month, when I pass out bills, and had the dates been set I probably would have told people when I passed out bills at the beginning of July. But it wasn't that clear to me and I didn't want to change it. So then I thought by last Wednesday it was clear what I was going to do anyway. It wasn't that clear what everybody else in my family was going to do, but it was clear what I was doing and so I could have told her, but Wednesday was the first day after all this anger that she felt freed and comfortable. She'd had a good day and a half. She felt problem-free, and I just decided four weeks ahead is long enough and that I was going to let her feel that for a while.

Supervisor: Very wise. Otherwise she would inevitably have said, "You're doing this to get even."

Candidate: Yes. Doing it to get even with her and also that I waited until she had a good day. Because if she feels comfortable and okay, then nobody is going to pay attention to her. I would have confirmed her fantasy that if she's all right I will leave her, and if she's not okay I won't.

Supervisor: That's right.

Candidate: Because I hadn't told her when she was mad at me.

Supervisor: That's very, very good judgment not to have said anything.

Candidate: But I have to say, I mean, I have to say it now.

Supervisor: Sure, sure.

Candidate: Whether she's, you know. I have made a deadline for myself.

Supervisor: Uh-huh.

Candidate: You know, I hate to tell people I'm taking vacations. So I made a deadline for myself that I would do it.

Supervisor: I approve.

Candidate: That except if there are some extraordinary circumstances, so whatever mood she's in today I'll just tell her at the end of the session. Because it's time and she's had some time now after that experience. I think that's what has happened. She's torturing some man at work. She just started to let me know yesterday. I think it may be her boss. I get these guys mixed up; she talks about so many of them. She said, because it made my ears perk up when she started to tell me this, she said she's really rubbing his nose in it. I thought, "Well it isn't over yet." Oh, she had a different time sense. I'm interested in time. I don't know exactly why I'm interested in time, but it always comes to my attention when one of my patient's sense of time changes.

Supervisor: Did you read Arlow's article?

Candidate: I've read some articles. I don't know if—

Supervisor: He has a recent article in the last issue—

Candidate: Yes, I did read it.

Supervisor: About time and the sense of time.

Candidate: Yes. Yeah. In fact, I read it because I saw time.

Supervisor: Yeah, it's his address to the American Psychoanalytic Association (Arlow, 1984). Excellent.

Candidate: I have written up here, "Shift to longitudinal time." I don't know what made me think that. Oh, she was talking about—it's really a pretty long section in this session in which she is talking about what a sense of relief she has that she no longer feels driven to do things immediately. She used to feel that she had to go to singles bars, go and be seen in Balaban's, be dating, even if there was nobody she wanted to date. She was always terrified that she would jump in bed. She could never use any birth control, except the pill, because she would never know whether she would just end up in bed with someone, because the moment—it was like cross-sectional time. I don't know what to call these things.

Supervisor: Uh-huh.

Candidate: I kind of made up terms. She only had up-and-down time. And what she was describing was having a far greater sense of what I call longitudinal time. It comes out in terms of plans about where she is going to move next, professionally. She doesn't have to do it tomorrow or October eighteenth. She can do these things now, and then these things and then that will happen. That's never been possible before for her. She's never been able to enjoy herself sitting in her apartment on an evening because she will probably always be sitting in her apartment every evening the rest of her life, so therefore she better get out and stand around Balaban's and be seen. Now she can feel that in this period of her life she really is enjoying being alone and that some other time she will do something else.

Supervisor: So simultaneously, a sense of continuity in herself longitudinally, in terms of she is the same person who goes all the way back—

Candidate: And all the way forward.

Supervisor: And also a sense of evolution, that she is *not* the same person.

Candidate: Uh-huh.

Supervisor: It is part of the process of renunciation. At one time she was a little girl for whom this furniture was very good, and now she must get rid of the furniture because it is no longer appropriate. She is the same little girl; there is continuity, but she is also different.

Candidate: Uh-huh, and that wanting to sell the furniture does not denounce the little girl.

Supervisor: Right. It doesn't mean that she didn't exist. It doesn't mean that she wasn't important, and it doesn't mean that the furniture wasn't important to her.

Candidate: And it doesn't mean that she doesn't still exist. I mean it doesn't cut off that experience to her, as having been part of her.

Supervisor: Exactly. See, it's the same as in the transference. Her sense of having outgrown you doesn't negate how important you were to her during the height of the analysis, and that is the sense of continuity we hope the patient will ultimately achieve in a comfortable way, because it means an acceptance both of renunciation and loss, as well as continuity, but a retention of images and experiences from earlier life and an awareness of their impact and influence today but a difference in terms of their significance. You don't have to cut yourself off from the past to get away from it; you also can acknowledge that the past *was* there and *still* is there but in a very different form.

Candidate: So her expression—she has been expressing to me, just very recently, that she feels guilty because she feels as if I am becoming less important to her, and I have just acknowledged that I *am* becoming less important. And she feels guilty. For a long time she was okay, she could get away with a lot and have other interests other than me because I was the most important thing in her life. But now I am becoming less and less the most important thing.

Supervisor: So you see, what's happening simultaneously is that she is on the one hand renouncing and giving up her attachment to you in the transference. She's having a positive sense of herself, a sense that she herself is good enough, a sense of having outgrown you, a sense of your being less important. But she is simultaneously acknowledging how important you once were, and this is what ultimately has to happen with parental imagos also. There is an acknowledgment that you don't want to wipe them out, you don't pretend they didn't exist or that they weren't significant. They assume a continuity but a changed awareness of their importance today; a recognition of their impact and how significant they were in one's development, but one has now outgrown and gone beyond the need to have them as continuing parent figures, in the sense of being currently significant. Even though one will never forget them and will always appreciate what their impact has been. James Anthony has a nice toast in which he says—in essence, he toasts the parents of our patients who were good enough parents that the patients could be analyzed.

Candidate: Uh-huh. She has come to have more and more realistic views of her parents now. In talking about her parents moving to Chicago she says she's proud of her father. This is the first time she's been proud of him because he apparently is getting some job—that's why they're moving to Chicago. He got a new job doing something. It's a post-retirement job which will be a good job for him and he's proud of it, and she's pleased that he went out and scrounged it up. He went after it and he sold himself and got it and they are going to go on to a new phase. They are not sitting around waiting to die. They are both retired and have just been getting on each other's nerves.

Supervisor: Uh-huh.

Candidate: And she said that they are neither as—she didn't say this all in one session or as direct or concisely as this—but they are neither as great as she once thought they were or as abysmal as she thought they were. That they did the best they could and they're okay.

Supervisor: Yeah. And you see, that's essentially also the position she will come to vis-à-vis you. You don't have to have been the greatest analyst in the world or have conducted a perfect analysis or never made mistakes, but you were good enough. She got from you what she needed, and she can tolerate and accept your imperfections without it detracting from your plusses.

Candidate: Yeah, and well, that reminds me of another thing you read about in termination papers that she has expressed without my initiating it, because I hadn't even remembered it. She thought that when she left analysis she would be finished, she would be perfect, everything would be tied up, and now she knows she never will be finished and she is most imperfect. There are jobs she has finished and is finishing with her analysis, but the jobs are not done and they may never be done. That was a sizable disillusionment for her and a disappointment, but one that she is adjusting to.

Supervisor: Uh-huh.

Candidate: The imperfectibility, her imperfectness. She's doing funny things that she is aware of. She tells me these things with, it seems like, full understanding of the implications, or at least pretty full understanding. For instance, she had a good weekend but came in on Monday feeling down. Tuesday she told me that part of the reason she felt that way was the dress she had on. It was a dress that she bought when she was with Ted and had no money. She associates it with that period of time and with how she felt about herself and she never wears it. She hasn't worn it for a year and a half. And she said, "But I chose to wear it yesterday after I had such a good weekend."

Supervisor: Uh-huh.

Candidate: Full, powerful. "I put myself back in it," she said. "I went home," after her session apparently, she went home and took the dress off and said, "I would not put it back in my closet. I am done with that dress." So she's doing a fair amount of this.

Supervisor: It's the same symbolism with the dress as it is with the bedroom furniture.

Candidate: Uh-huh. It's the same—an attitude of making herself sick, trying to go back. Yesterday she went to work after the session. She treats Bill Adams like shit. She hates him because he's like her father, she thinks, and she's really, really nasty to him. She talked a good deal about that.

Supervisor: And how does he react to her nastiness?

Candidate: He puts up with her. She says, "I'm surprised that he hasn't fired me." She says, "That's another parallel." I guess I hadn't heard that one. Essentially he puts up with her.

Supervisor: You see, what I'm getting at is this: keep in mind that one swallow doesn't make a summer.

Candidate: Yeah. That perked my ears up and I thought, well, I don't know how you're using that right now. I thought it was not over yet, her tormenting of—

Supervisor: Just because for one or two sessions she really let you have it and was able to torment you—

Candidate: And then felt better—

Supervisor: And then felt better, it doesn't mean that all the aggression, all the resentment, all of the wishes for revenge—

Candidate: That's what I heard when she said she was tormenting Bill Adams.

Supervisor: So the point is to interpret the displacement so that she recognizes it.

Candidate: It was also interesting because this was the session after her quiet session. After feeling quiet and good, then she went home—but I didn't know this yet, this stuff about her dress. She came in the next day in this crappy mood. She didn't want to come. Nah, nah. At the session she really gave it to Bill Adams. He was a son of a bitch and he's such an idiot. She felt depressed and ugly. Her predominant feeling during the quiet was that we were both leaving each other. Then as she walked out she felt really sad, and then went and gave Bill Adams the what-for. She treats him like shit. She hates him. At work she's going crazy. She's not getting anywhere. I said that's a reflection of a lot of worries and a reflection of the feelings here too, slogging through her feelings and hating me. She said, "Yes, that's true." She got her portfolio out and what is there is quality and good, good enough, but it's not as much as she would have thought. She thought she had more to choose from. It's like looking at herself in the mirror.

Supervisor: You see, I would keep in mind that she is sophisticated enough to realize that if she "lets you have it," if she expresses her anger, her hatred for you, you will take pleasure in it. That's another sign of your success.

Candidate: That's interesting, because she has said—it was a long time ago, but she has said periodically over the whole analysis—"I know that if I get mad at you, you will say you are now done."

Supervisor: You will say what?

Candidate: You are now done.

Supervisor: Uh-huh.

Candidate: I won't let you come here anymore.

Supervisor: But also that it will be a sign to you, that you won't be frightened or upset by it.

Candidate: Yeah, that I will take—

Supervisor: You'll be pleased—

Candidate: That I'll be relieved. Wooh!

Supervisor: Yeah, that you will actually be pleased with her and she's not going to give you that satisfaction. So again, it's all tied up with the revenge and the continuing displacement of the anger to Bill Adams. It's something you'd want to interpret so that it gets more focused into the transference, or look for other places where it's being displaced.

Candidate: Displaced, yeah. That's the first time I've heard about how she's treating him.

Supervisor: Uh-huh.

Candidate: We talked about her furniture. She referred to something about it and I wanted to know what was really going on, so I asked her, but what I felt at the end of the session was that whatever is going on with Bill Adams is what comes next.

Supervisor: Uh-huh.

Candidate: I also felt, "Poor son of a bitch." You know, this woman can really let you—I mean she hasn't let me have it, in a way. I am not vulnerable like Bill Adams would be, is what I'm trying to say.

Supervisor: Right.

Candidate: It's part of my job. I expect it.

Supervisor: Not only expect it, but enjoy it when it occurs.

Candidate: Yeah. I may. And with some borderline or psychotic patients that's a different thing. They can rip into you in a way that gets real personal or real—I don't know the word for it, but I know she can really drag somebody over the coals, and I'm sure she's making him feel like a piece of shit.

Supervisor: Uh-huh. And that's another part of the interpretation. "One of the reasons that you're taking it out on Bill is because you can make him feel bad, whereas here you have less trouble making me feel bad."

Candidate: More trouble.

Supervisor: More trouble. "You are less able to make me feel bad. With Bill you can make him feel that it's something personal."

Candidate: Yeah, because what he does is tolerate her and try to do what she wants. He cowers a little bit, at least that's the impression I get.

Supervisor: So that's the interpretation you want to make to her. The reason for the displacement of her anger is that she can get pleasure and fulfillment for her aggression there. She doesn't here. All she gets is more frustration.

Candidate: I've got to remember to tell you when I'm going to be out of town. I don't know if it's next—let me see. I'm going to be . . . This is the twenty-fifth, so let's see, the eighth. I don't see you the twenty-second. I am out of town the twenty-second. I wouldn't normally see you the twenty-ninth anyway, and I will be back on September fifth.

Supervisor: It's just one session?

Candidate: One session. I'm only going to be gone two weeks and hopefully in October I will go away again. I will not do it until after October eighteenth.

Supervisor: Okay. (Laughs) That's a good idea.

Candidate: Well, like my feeling about it is: One, I don't have to do it, I just want a vacation; and two, since I hadn't announced an extended vacation prior to setting the termination date, I have some responsibility to stick in there. She expected a ten-day or two-week vacation in August. I mean, I always do that. So that she expected that. But two, one in July and one in August, or one in August and one in September—I think I can wait until the end of October.

Supervisor: Yeah. I think that's probably wise, because you do want to get this really wrapped up.

Candidate: Yeah, and it just feels like part of my responsibility.

Supervisor: Yeah, and it's important for her to be the one to outgrow you and leave while you are still here in the same old place.

Candidate: And I'm here after she leaves.

Supervisor: After she leaves.

Candidate: Likewise, it is now inconvenient for me to work the hours that I see her, but I decided back in March or April, when she was coming around to setting a date, that it would just have to *be* convenient until she terminated.

Supervisor: Uh-huh.

Candidate: Because of where we are at in this process.

Supervisor: That's part of the analyst's responsibility to the patient. This is another reason that some people, you see, will correlate a termination—

Candidate: I haven't told her it's inconvenient.

Supervisor: No, I know. But some people correlate the termination, for example, at the start of summer vacation and they'll both go off together. In a sense, it's not a horrendous thing, but it does interfere with a full resolution, the analyst being there and it's the patient who leaves. The thought of both going off together detracts from its significance.

Candidate: I am leaving home.

Supervisor: That she is leaving home and home is still here, and it's her growth and not your whim or your departure.

Candidate: Or some mutual—

Supervisor: Or some mutual agreement.

Candidate: Or mutual convenience.

Supervisor: Right, that has caused this separation. That's right. So, fine. That's very, very nice.

Candidate: Okay. Thank you.

Supervisor: Okay, right.

Supervisor's Comments

The candidate initiates the supervisory hour with a description of the progress she feels is being made, and a recognition of how the patient is displacing the transference to various people in her current external situation. She continues her analytic interpretive stance, recognizing that she said it "in a little different way," as well as the possibility that she perhaps had forced the patient into a state of compliance. Nonetheless she expresses pleasure and a sense of progress when the patient finally is able to directly expose and express her aggression and hostility in the transference. The candidate's pleasure probably contains some elements of countertransference condescension and control, but nevertheless implies a recognition by the candidate of the importance of the patient's aggression in the transference, and a sense of relief that the analytic work has finally allowed the patient to reduce the intensity of her defenses and permit the aggression to emerge more directly.

The patient's response of elaborating her self-defeating wish to terminate analysis as a means of gaining revenge on the candidate reflects a typical fantasy occurring as part of the dynamic process in termination. The patient also brings up an issue which had been dormant for some time, namely, her fantasy of being able to interrupt or destroy the candidate's training, and her knowledge that the candidate is receiving credit for the analytic work. She expresses her further recognition that she "let it go too long." Through references to her friend who terminated an analysis prematurely, she expresses a reality-oriented appreciation of the importance of completing her analytic work. Her unwillingness to use adaptive and defensive techniques which would result in her own suffering is an indicator of a reduction in the intensity of her masochistic organization, even though this had not been prominent earlier on. The patient also comes to her own realization that she is using the same type of self-defeating mechanisms in clinging to the sadistic, woman-hating man with whom she has been involved, as a means of frustrating the candidate's therapeutic ambitions for her.

The patient shows that during the termination phase insight into a neurotic pattern or process often leads to shifts in neurotic behavior ("It blew over pretty quickly. She felt almost immediately better."). Also evident is a process, typical of the termination phase, of rapid oscillation between progress, leading to awareness about the changes that have occurred and the independence such changes imply, and anxiety triggering regression to previous neurotic behaviors and experiences. This is followed again by progress and recognition of the pattern involved. The patient's behavior in regard to her childhood bedroom furniture is a symptomatic and neurotic act—her simply having kept it all this time—as well as a defense against analysis, as she has until now not mentioned it to the analyst.

Having made significant progress toward maturation in the analysis, the patient now is spontaneously ready to renounce the attachment represented by the furniture, as well as to appreciate her own recognition of the furniture as a form of neurotic compromise. The residual neurosis is contained in her adherence to her parents' wishes and their needs to continue seeing her as immature and childlike. This comes out in her acceptance of their appraisal of the furniture's value; she makes a show of disagreeing, but her inflated estimate is only slightly lower than theirs. However, the issue does not come up for analytic scrutiny until after the structural meanings of the conflict have been resolved.

This material is another confirmation of change, inasmuch as getting rid of the furniture had not previously been addressed as a symptomatic expression. The same conflict is also manifest in the shifting "apartment dreams" to which the candidate has alluded in previous supervisory hours. The candidate accepts the fact that the patient has withheld this data until now, and tolerates this form of resistance without complaint or implied criticism.

The patient demonstrates her capacity for self-observation by laughing at her recognition, "When that furniture is gone and the new furniture is here, my apartment really will be finished," as well as by the recognition that her affects of sadness (the termination mourning process) are stirred in direct proportion to the extent of her own sense of improvement. Her awareness that she is outgrowing her need for the analyst and that maturation brings separation and loss is balanced by her recognizing, from an adult perspective, that the mourning process requires her to remain in St. Louis at least briefly after the actual termination. She knows not to shortcut or avoid the process of separation and loss through making a geographic move at the same time. This same capacity to observe herself and recognize her limitations as well as her assets, and to tolerate the narcissistic injury such limitations entail, is illustrated by her awareness that the portfolio is not as extensive or grandiose as she had once fantasied, but that it nevertheless is adequate.

The patient is now doing much of the analytic work ("she comes to most of it by herself"); for instance, she analyzes the complex responses and fantasy systems connected with her ability to remain silent on the couch during the analytic session. It is evident here how during the termination process the negative transference, both its experience and its expression, can be even more intense than earlier in the analysis.

The candidate hesitates in telling the supervisor about her delay in informing the patient of an impending vacation. She seems somewhat defensive, and makes a fairly detailed explanation of her behavior, as if expecting criticism. The intrapsychic component for her hesitation, a countertransference reaction, is revealed in her subsequent comment ("you know, I hate to tell people I'm taking vacations"). The supervisor, however, offers immediate praise instead ("I approve"), and emphasizes the appropriateness of the candidate's decision given the circumstances. With this, the candidate comfortably elaborates her recognition that to have announced the vacation immediately after the patient's beginning expression of aggression "would have confirmed her fantasy." The candidate is manifesting some of the same conflict over initiative and independent decision making toward the supervisor as her patient is manifesting in the transference toward herself. The supervisor continues to support the candidate's decision, and the candidate now recognizes (1) that it is essential for her to overcome her countertransference inhibition and (2) that the patient is displacing the transference into her work situation.

The candidate shows an identification with the supervisor, using current clinical data and material to pursue a more scientific and conceptual theme, as in her comments about her awareness of changes in her patients' sense of time. By referring to Arlow's article (1984), the supervisor encourages the candidate's interest and stimulates her to a further elaboration. The supervisor responds to the candidate's interest with speculations of his own, in an attempt to encourage a conceptual framework tying this to the patient's behavior in regard to her self-images and the furniture, as well as the general concept of the shifting importance and significance of object relationships while retaining continuity through memory systems. This material is related by the supervisor to the termination process, and the candidate is able to amplify her impression of the patient's experience of termination and renunciation. The supervisor once more elaborates these issues as they relate to the patient's current experience, seeking to expand them so as to include normal developmental experience as well as termination of a therapeutic process.

This leads the candidate to elaborate on the patient's new perceptions of her parents, which tend to be appropriate and related to current reality, in contrast to the previously fixated persistence of conflicted images and relationships from her childhood. The supervisor points out how a parallel process will occur toward the analyst in the resolution and renunciation of the transference neurosis ("that's essentially also the position she will come to vis-à-vis you"). This leads the candidate to elaborate on the renunciation of narcissistic perfection, expressed by the patient's recognition of the need to give up such hopes. Further evidence of her oscillation between progress and regression, however, is expressed in the symptomatic behavior involving the old dress. She also continues to displace some of her negative transference and aggression to people in her work situation, and the supervisor tries to remind the candidate of the need for repetition to achieve mastery through the process of working through. He emphasizes how the candidate's therapeutic stance tends to frustrate the patient's hope in the expression of her aggression. The fact that the candidate has not yet actively interpreted these displacements leads the supervisor to a more directive instructional stance regarding technique, as part of which he offers a model interpretation. Presenting this model, he makes a parapraxis which the candidate corrects. The supervisor concludes this segment of the interchange by emphasizing again how transference abstinence and the analyst's therapeutic posture leads to transference frustration for the patient. While making the situation safe for the expression of such feelings, such abstinence may also transiently stimulate displacement and acting out in the patient's search for immediate gratification ("She can get pleasure and fulfillment for her aggression there. She doesn't here.").

The candidate then discusses the details of her vacation and its impact on the supervision, as well as her recognition of the importance that there not be any further interruptions with the patient prior to the termination date. Throughout this interchange the candidate demonstrates a sense of appropriate professional responsibility in regard to the welfare of her patient and the safeguarding of the termination process. The candidate's conduct is praised ("I think that's probably wise."), and stands in contrast with her decision several years ago regarding her maternity leave, a decision made without particular regard for the patient's needs or the impact it might have on the analytic process. The supervisor explains why it is appropriate for the patient to be the one actively leaving while the analyst remains, rather than scheduling the termination in such a way as to allow the analyst to leave at the same time, even though the latter might in some ways be more convenient for the analyst. The supervisor ends the session with direct praise.

The material of this session, focused as it is around the termination process, illustrates many of the dynamic and clinical issues that typically arise during this phase of a successful therapy. The supervisor is pleased that for the patient it seems to be an optimal therapeutic experience, accompanied by genuine working through, renunciation, and resolution of the transference neurosis. For the candidate it seems to be a genuine and optimal learning experience and an opportunity for her to observe and effectively participate in a typical termination process. Although such hypotheses are difficult to prove, one must consider whether the supervisor's anticipatory focus and suggestions in session 109 have been effective in helping the candidate tolerate this phase of the analysis.

Chapter 19
Supervisory Session 122

Candidate: (Arriving on crutches) How much aggravation it can cause if it's insulted.

Supervisor: (Laughs) Serious? Or just inconvenient?

Candidate: No, just inconvenient. I dropped a one-hundred-fifty-pound solid core door on my bare toe on a cement floor, broke it in a number of places.

Supervisor: That's not too sharp.

Candidate: But not in any way that anything needs to be done about it or can be done about it, except time.

Supervisor: Gee, that's too bad.

Candidate: And at least I have shoes on today. I haven't been able to wear shoes until now. Well, we had a pivotal day, if I remember correctly, after which she feels she is done with her analysis. I just found the notes on my way here, actually. This was the day after I saw you the last time. Remember, she hadn't come for some days and I didn't know what was going on. All kinds of feelings on the way here today. Her mood swings are tremendous, from feeling normal to feeling depressed, to feeling really good. She feels strange, feels she should be apologetic about not being here the last two days. She just couldn't come. She went into the office at five in the morning on Tuesday to try to be here, and yesterday she was waiting for a work proposal to arrive. She thought she had it all organized so that she could come. The proposal was to get there at four-thirty, but it didn't come till five-fifteen and our appointment is at five-twenty. She was disappointed, she was tired, she just didn't feel like jumping in the car and rushing here for five minutes. She needed to finish her work, though she was disappointed and looked forward to coming. I said so she makes a decision for herself that leaves me out and she feels she should apologize. She said yes, she feels so vulnerable. As long as she has been coming here she's felt protected; she could come here. Now she feels out in the world by herself. She feels there are shits out there, and she has to protect herself from them and navigate in the world. Monday was crazy, something at work, but that's settled down and things will change. They always do, you know. There will always be shits out there. Oh, she's referring to some stuff that's been going on at work that for a while she's felt she just couldn't tolerate for the year she wants to give herself before she makes another major move. And this is a different attitude toward it. Things will change, they always do. There will always be shits out there. But there are okay people and things, too. She's been less frantic about not having a man. She really doesn't want to settle, to marry just to marry, to have a noose around her neck. She was really mad at lunch yesterday. Phil Edwards said, "You know, if you lost a little bit more weight, you could find a man in a minute." And she lit into him. Who does he think he is anyway, to assume that she must find a man, just any man? Grandma is saying, "I hope next year you're married." I said that. She said exactly, she does want a man but only a good relationship. She refuses to get thin to get a man. She refuses to focus on that, getting a man, as the center of her life. She's accepting that nothing—tastes good? Oh, she's accepting that nothing tastes good, that she has no energies these days and she knows it will pass. She is mourning. She feels so sad. She really does.

Supervisor: So, she's alluding to the termination process and the depression and this is not the time to get involved.

Candidate: Yeah. And I said something to the effect that she's being able to accept and feel the sadness and mourning, not frantically trying to cover it up or do something about it. She's not moving to Chicago. She's not finding a man. She's not doing anything about it. And I thought she had said that so clearly. She's accepted she has no energy these days and is depressed and sad. She really feels that way. It's funny. She has such strong feelings of wanting to get a cat, but she doesn't really want to think about it. She doesn't want it to be a substitute for me. It would make her feel better to have a cat, because there would be someone there who needed her. She doesn't know if she'd rather get a cat when she feels good and not as an escape from these sad feelings. She thinks if she got a cat now, she would end up resenting the cat, transferring a lot of her feelings onto it, and that would be rotten. She doesn't want to do that. Even a couple of weeks ago she was thinking of getting a new job. She doesn't want to do that either. She doesn't want to do anything. She just wants to get through this period openly and honestly and be sad, because she is sad and it will pass. There's an interchange about this as a change. She was silent for a while. "God, this is really not easy." She was silent for a while more. It has been so many years, so long. "I grew up here," she says. "I really feel that you know. I had never really thought about what the end would be like until the beginning of this year, and I certainly didn't anticipate it would really, what it would really be like." There was some kind of back-and-forth then about how part of the whole function of her neurosis, but that word wasn't used, was to maintain the fantasy that she would never have to mourn, that she would never lose anything, and to deal with the fact that she could not tolerate mourning and was refusing to. Within that, I don't know if it came up at this point or not, from within that stance, she couldn't ever really allow herself to have anything because she was always in fear of losing it. She had to keep herself in the position of never losing anything, and now she's allowing herself to lose. It's true. It was an interesting timing. She never said anything about it. It was interesting to me and I wrote it down. She said, "It's true," and—we have great soundproofing in our office, but every once in a while something really dramatic will seep through—and there was this anguished wail, a male wail, coming from another office. She was silent for about five minutes. I knew she heard it and it was as if she smiled, and I didn't feel like anything needed to be said. She was silent for about five minutes. "Somehow I feel a lot better." She was silent for about five more minutes. It's really strange. She has a really strong sense about how much she will miss me, but she feels ready to leave. Somehow it's okay. She feels a real sense of peace about it after a couple of weeks of horrible turmoil. She's had such strong feelings of being afraid of the panic, but she doesn't have that sense right now at all. "In fact, I think that this is really the first time that I really felt that I will be okay. I will be and I know it." She was silent for about fifteen minutes. Since then she hasn't been in very much. Analysis has been sort of a past thing. I don't know how to express it. She does a better job of expressing it than I do. She almost drove by my office one day. She was doing something else, she was doing something and she came—she didn't drive by the office, but I will always have been important. I am almost a past. I am almost already past tense.

Supervisor: Uh-huh.

Candidate: I look in that for some kind of defense against her feelings of really needing, but I don't think it is. I think I *have* become the past. The eighteenth of October is her final date.

Supervisor: What does she say about not coming? Why has she not been coming?

Candidate: Well, she's been in L.A. for a while; that's some of the time she hasn't come. A couple of times she hasn't come because, let me see. She came Monday, she didn't come Tuesday. That Monday she just said in essence that she had a good weekend. She feels free and good, and she continues to feel sad; it's bittersweet. Then she didn't come on Tuesday. I don't know if she told me she wasn't going to come on Tuesday or not. Oh, another thing that she said on Monday was she talked about her new ability to relax. She doesn't have to keep herself on all the time. And then she didn't come Tuesday and Wednesday. She really wants to go home tonight, she's so tired. She feels really fine. She got here half an hour early. She left work at four-fifteen. She was so tired she didn't want to come, but she decided she would. She sat in the waiting room and remembered how there were so many times she wanted to memorize every little detail about that waiting room, every little detail of my office. Now, as she sat out there, it didn't matter anymore. It is the most important thing that has ever happened to her in her life, but it's taking its place now.

Supervisor: Referring to the analysis and the whole experience?

Candidate: Yeah, the whole experience. The analysis is the most important thing that's ever happened to her in her life, but it's somehow taking its place. It's not her life anymore.

Supervisor: Uh-huh.

Candidate: She wonders if the other shoe will drop. That's the phrase she uses.

Supervisor: For?

Candidate: If she will fall apart. But somehow she doesn't think so. She will just be sad and she will miss me, but she feels she's finished. That's the predominant feeling from now on. She feels she's finished. Monday when she was here it felt really nice. It was so comfortable. I think Monday she was quiet for about thirty minutes and it was a very comfortable quiet. I think that was the day she could have gone to sleep. It was so nice to be here, to lie here, to let her mind wander, to relax. But it felt also like a luxury she didn't need anymore. She needed to come for so long so desperately, and she doesn't need to anymore. It feels really weird and very natural, both at the same time. It's nice to be here. She feels so accepted and comfortable and relaxed. But at the same time she was anxious to go about her business and do the other things she wanted to do. Then she worked, and it was crazy there. She worked all day and evening. She had a big project due at two p.m. and someone had told her he would help her do it. She had it all arranged, so she hadn't lined up anybody else to do it. And part of the project involved drawing people. You know, she never could draw people, she thought. Well, she knew she could do it. The guy bummed out on her and didn't help her. And she did it, and they were beautiful. They had spontaneity and freshness. The people were fine. The general supervisor, who she worked with before and hated because he is so critical and derogatory, this time made numerous comments about how impressed he was and how good the designs were. It was really neat, because she has felt handicapped over the years about drawing people. It wasn't a high though, or a great realization or a wonderful thing; it was just a confirmation, another assurance. More assurance that she can do it, that she is okay. She feels that way about a lot of things, numerous little things. None of them are big deals, like losing weight. She just can do it, it's not a big deal. She won't be able to come Monday and Tuesday because she has to go to L.A. She tried to bring them here and it's real complicated, but it happened anyway. She tried to arrange it so that she would be in town, but it didn't work, so she's going to be in L.A. She's looking forward to going too, because she's going to work with a nationally known designer she's wanted to work with. She is so tired she can't believe it. I commented that she was talking unusually softly for her. She said she has this fantasy that she will wake up from a trance and the eighteenth will be here. She doesn't even want to come now. She fears she will be punished somehow if she doesn't. She fears she will be punished somehow, that she will wake up and freak out or something, that I will not be there anymore or something. She'll wake up and be jolted. There is the feeling that she has to pay for the fact that she doesn't want to come anymore and that she doesn't need me anymore with that desperate feeling. But it's really fine, because she's fine. But it hasn't been long that she's felt so fine. There was an interchange about her turning from her mother and then getting the urethral stricture, about this movement to separation-individuation and power and autonomy and the urethral stricture coming at that point. And I spontaneously said in a dramatized, witchlike voice, "Ehh hee he he, you thought you didn't need me." And she just howled with laughter. "I didn't see that coming in me." She said, "I'm ready to go. I want to go. It's time to go." As she left on Monday she wanted to say, "Is Thursday soon enough?" but she didn't. She didn't know how to ask me. She feels guilty about it. She has nothing to talk about except that she feels fine and how many times can you say that you feel fine. "God I'm tired." It's a feeling that she has been through a war and the war is over. She just wants to rest. She has never felt so easy with herself that she is who she is and that's okay. There is such a difference in herself. She's not afraid or anxious. She just feels okay. She feels in sync with herself. She is just very tired. I said, as what has been our work has become less important and vital, less a center of her thoughts, does she feel guilty? She said yes, she does. She did need me and it was the most important thing and I was the most important thing, but it feels and I feel like a part of the past.

Supervisor: It feels a part of the past?

Candidate: Part of the past. Something she doesn't think about much anymore. It was interesting, because what came to my mind when I found myself thinking about a lot of things was the kid going away to college in September and everything is all set and it's the first of August. A kid who can go away, for whom it's appropriate to be making this step and it's the first of August. All right, already, you know, September should come. It's part of the past. It is becoming more and more a part of the past. She is who she is and what she is, and she does the best she can; that is something she could never have even conceived of to ask me to give her or to help her with when she started into analysis. That she could feel that way was not her goal. She didn't know it was possible. She does not care what anybody else thinks. She does not have to like everyone else and they don't have to like her. She feels so much freer. It wasn't really a big deal. None of these things was. Everything just seems so natural these days. To say them makes them sound like big deals.

Supervisor: What she says here illustrates something that Karl Menninger (1973) makes a point of in his book on psychoanalytic technique. Patients don't get some of the things they come for, but they also get some things they never dreamed of.

Candidate: They don't know. They don't even know they exist.

Supervisor: And this is a nice illustration of that. She wouldn't even think of it to be a goal and yet now—

Candidate: She just came to have me help her lose weight.

Supervisor: Now that it's here, she feels how very important it is. But, and you know, she comes in order to lose weight and hasn't lost all the weight that she can or should lose.

Candidate: She probably won't ever.

Supervisor: And she may or may not, but that's no longer the major thing to her.

Candidate: It's of little importance to her.

Supervisor: Uh-huh.

Candidate: Ah, she came Thursday. I don't remember very

much about Thursday except more of "I feel good and how many times can I say, 'I feel good'?" She couldn't come Monday or Tuesday because she was in L.A. So those are all the times I think I've seen her.

Supervisor: Uh-huh. So it's not that she's missing in order to dilute or avoid the work of termination.

Candidate: It doesn't feel that way. In fact, it feels like it's an interesting kind of acting out on her part, because for her to be making a choice for herself over pleasing me, and to feel relatively easy about it, is a sign of progress.

Supervisor: Uh-huh.

Candidate: It's more to still be able to express the residual fantasies that somehow I'll get back at her.

Supervisor: Uh-huh.

Candidate: And she isn't making herself sick. There for a while she was getting sick, but right now she's not sick. If she is in trouble she will always work hard, but she also is relaxing. Her work conforms to her experience in an interesting way. She didn't choose work that's relatively steady and all the time hard. A lot of it comes in bunches.

Supervisor: Uh-huh.

Candidate: But then she also doesn't ride herself to socialize or do much on the weekends if she doesn't feel like it. She stays home and knits and watches television or talks on the phone and relaxes. There was an interesting interchange about how she never had been able to relax. That was another thing she never would have conceived of asking for. Downtime was always a negative thing. To relax and be placid was bad and impotent and powerless, to not be on all the time.

Supervisor: Uh-huh.

Candidate: To really experience the pleasures of relaxing is relatively new. So, I don't expect to see her on the eighteenth. I don't expect to see a whole hell of a lot between now and the eighteenth, which isn't very long off.

Supervisor: Two weeks now.

Candidate: I expect I'll see her some. I know she's been toying with the idea of not coming back until the eighteenth. She's mentioned, "What if I didn't?" She didn't exactly ask it directly in a question, but what if she just didn't show up until then? I don't know whether she's sold me a bill of goods, but I don't feel she has. I feel that she's finished and she will come on the eighteenth, but I think she'll come a few times before then. Between now and then we will see bits and pieces of things. She'll come on the eighteenth and however she finishes that session—well, she broke on through to the other side of what she was going to do in this analysis. And now she's in the process of leaving and in a significant way.

Supervisor: Uh-huh.

Candidate: And I'm basically not doing very much of anything. I'm certainly not going to tell her she has to come every time until the eighteenth.

Supervisor: Uh-huh.

Candidate: If I, you know, if I keep listening for it being a defense—

Supervisor: Yes, that's the only thing I'd alert you to. Don't forget that, or don't assume that her resistances may not reactivate between now and then. There may be specific issues she's defending herself against, so listen for that. But you don't intrude them or force them in or insist that she is covering something over. But you want to listen and make sure it's in the material rather than just assume, a priori, that it must be so.

Candidate: Stuff has been in the material. All I'm saying is I don't think it would be helpful and I'm not comfortable with a priori assumptions that whatever this is it's a defensive behavior. I keep finding myself searching avidly for it, for signs I can read as defensive, that I can reflect back to her, but I feel like I can't without those signs. I can't say, essentially, "You're just being defensive."

Supervisor: Uh-huh.

Candidate: Also, this feeling that I'm having. She really *has* done a lot of mourning and she really will continue to, I think. So I can't really say you're not wanting to work, not without more evidence, without some hard evidence. You just don't want to come because you don't want to mourn and you don't want to be sad or you're afraid of, you know.

Supervisor: Yes, that's what I mean by not pushing it on the a priori assumption that it has to be there. It may be, but you listen for it and want to get the data first. And if it *is* there, then you wouldn't hesitate to interpret it.

Candidate: No, and it's not hard to interpret things at this stage of the analysis.

Supervisor: Uh-huh. But there are instances in which a brand new piece of material may come up in the last few sessions or even the last session or two of a long therapy. Sometimes it's an attempt to sort of continue it, but other times, because it's finally just about over, you want to get it done.

Candidate: To bring it up?

Supervisor: Just before you finish.

Candidate: Or maybe because it has to do with finishing.

Supervisor: Exactly, because it has to do with finishing. I was leaving my office one time and a patient of mine in her last session was aware that the pictures were gone and it reminded her of the time when her father had died and her mother had gone to clean out the father's office; the books had been packed and the pictures were off the walls. It was a re-creation of that last moment in her father's office which had never come up during the course of the analysis. So those kinds of things can sometimes occur at the very, very end.

Candidate: I don't mean to imply that I've gone to sleep, but only that I feel easier about it.

Supervisor: Uh-huh. Good.

Candidate: And I no longer feel that there is such a terrible struggle going on at the moment, as I once did.

Supervisor: You mean because you feel differently about it or because—

Candidate: No, because *she* feels differently. She was hanging on with one hand and pushing away with the other. I didn't realize how strongly until she said it after it was over. She was sure she wouldn't be able to survive without me but wanted to get away from me at the same time, horribly sad and frightened and not wanting those feelings, and depressed, and yet super happy that she was getting away from me. In other words, this constant, whatever.

Supervisor: Uh-huh.

Candidate: But also she's beginning to leave me in a more real way than she had previously been able to, so that whether or not she comes for the next however many days, I don't feel as uncomfortable as I did, because I wanted her to be able to reach that point. Before when she was, when I hadn't seen her for a couple of days and I said to you, "Well, if she doesn't come to the end of the analysis," I just wanted that to be able to have happened and it gives me a more—*me,* as the analyst—a more finished feeling.

Supervisor: Yes. One important element is her acceptance of the sadness and the depression and the lack of energy and the lack of interest, simultaneously coupled with, "But I know it is going to pass when this is over and I just need to go through it and live through it now."

Candidate: Yeah. And it is not going to pass on the eighteenth.

Supervisor: That's right. It's not going to pass on the eighteenth, and also it will eventually pass and then "I'll do all the things I'm capable of doing."

Candidate: Uh-huh. And this is the woman who hated her grandmother so she didn't have to deal with the fact that she was dying.

Supervisor: You mean she cooked up the hate in order—

Candidate: Oh, yeah. Yeah. She didn't talk to her, hated her, painted to me only a negative picture. I mean, they're all qualities her grandmother has, but she ignored for herself and in the analysis for a very long time any of the things about her grandmother that she would deeply miss. All because her grandmother was old and was dying. And there are many other ways in which she refused to be sad, that was just a real obvious one, one that started to break down. She went and saw her grandmother and remembered that she really loved her. Anyway, that's where it's at. I have anxieties of my own, I guess, anxieties about the last day, which I think just reflects my own separation problems. The fact that I'm losing her, too, that I won't know how she does.

Supervisor: Yes. There's a reciprocal mourning process that the analyst has to do, particularly if it's been a particularly important, significant experience in your life. And this having been your first case, that's very likely.

Candidate: Well, and since I was in analysis myself for a considerable period of this analysis, and we not infrequently in the first couple of years had some parallel stuff going on, I had to deal with some of these same things. And it's a rite of passage.

Supervisor: Uh-huh.

Candidate: And there are all kinds of things that personally for me—

Supervisor: That's right. What do you think that last day is going to be like?

Candidate: I don't know. It seems to me I have thought about it, but it will be kind of like that, well, like the last session I read to you. One of these sessions, but what I can't figure out is she has stopped saying, "Have a good day. Have a good evening. Have a good weekend." Now she just says, "I'll see you tomorrow." She usually says something like that at the door.

Supervisor: Something that says it's going to go on. I'll be here tomorrow. I'll see you tomorrow.

Candidate: Yes. And for some reason I have been fixated on that. It feels to me like it's a, you know, like what do you say when you say goodbye?

Supervisor: Uh-huh.

Candidate: I can feel the pressures in me to muddy it up. You know, I don't know if that language communicates, I—

Supervisor: Muddy it up how?

Candidate: Muddy it up. Like my own analyst said to me, and I at the time both felt good about it and felt complimented, and I felt, "God, you can't let go, can you?" My own analyst said to me, shook my hand and said "Good luck" or something and "You're such a good person." Something like that, and I felt, besides feeling that somebody who has seen that much of you thinks you're a nice person, that's nice, but, and that's an obvious thing, but the other side of my feelings, which continued for some time, was: "You can't let go. Can't you let go? Let go of it."

Supervisor: Uh-huh.

Candidate: And, in fact, I had a considerable fight with him in the last months of analysis, because it was very important to get him to admit on some level, in some way, I can't remember how, but I was happy, I was satisfied with getting him to admit that he was having trouble letting go, too. Yes, it seems like to me I was admitting that I was having trouble letting go, that I was ready to leave home, but that he was blaming his trouble in letting go on me and saying it was all my ambivalence. And I said, "There are two people in this room, goddamn it, and it has involved *us* for these years, both of us. And it's still involving both of us, and you can't squiggle out of this." And I felt like that continued and that's what comes to my mind when you say, "What do you mean, muddy the water?" I think that muddied up the water.

Supervisor: Yeah. It does. That's right. The reason I asked, one of the reasons anyway, is that Ralph Greenson toward the end of his life came to a new technical approach to termination, and he's someone I've admired in the past as a therapist. But in the last three or four sessions he would sit patients up, face to face, and I think that's a dreadful mistake. It implies that there has been an enormous difficulty in resolving the transference. It implies that the analyst doesn't believe the patient can do it without feedback from reality, and all that.

Candidate: I don't think I could, as a patient, I don't think I could have done that.

Supervisor: Well, he did and—

Candidate: There is an enormous message.

Supervisor: Yeah. That's right. There's an enormous message that goes with it, and the same, I might say, even with these gratuitous remarks toward the end.

Candidate: Have a good life, good luck—

Supervisor: Well, have a good life, good luck, that's fine. But "I enjoyed working with you," or "You were a very rewarding patient," or "It's really been important to me to have had you as a patient"—gratuitous remarks like that, which sound so nice and which the patient latches onto as rewards, so to speak, or as reinforcing, or as "It's so nice to have somebody say it," but at the same time they tend to betray a countertransference and to—

Candidate: Muddy the waters.

Supervisor: Muddy the waters. That's right. It's not a clear, real resolution.

Candidate: So that I can recognize, I think, I recognize my own—that I will miss her as a patient, that I have enjoyed the patient.

Supervisor: Uh-huh.

Candidate: And that I've learned a lot.

Supervisor: Uh-hum.

Candidate: I have more a feeling of where my analyst was coming from when he did that. In fact, I think I probably could have said at the time where he was coming from, but now I'm identifying with him, though I don't want to act on it.

Supervisor: Sure.

Candidate: It took me, I would say it took me a year and a half of extra work, to consolidate a separation, despite this feeling that every time I—and I'm not—despite this feeling of, well, the continued, "Come on, let go. It's okay. Let go already!"

Supervisor: Uh-huh.

Candidate: You know, and it took, it took—and I think I would have had to work on other things probably. I think the work goes on and on and on. But I—

Supervisor: Uh-huh.

Candidate: There is no necessity. There is no need for me to add—

Supervisor: Right.

Candidate: From the inside of me.

Supervisor: Another thing one of my other teachers used to say to patients at the end was, "The door is always open."

Candidate: You can come back. I'll still be here.

Supervisor: Exactly. I'll still be here waiting for you. Here it is again.

Candidate: Here's the road of crumbs. (Laughs)

Supervisor: Gratuitous, inappropriate, infantilizing, and regression- inducing, as well as a denial that it's he who doesn't want to separate.

Candidate: And how, and, yes it really is an insult and infantilizing.

Supervisor: Uh-huh.

Candidate: It really says, one, you can't get along without me—

Supervisor: You can't get along without me.

Candidate: One, you can't get along without me, but two, you're not a big enough boy or girl to figure out that you could come back. Christ, how many years have we worked together and you can't figure out you could come back if you wanted to come back?

Supervisor: Exactly, exactly.

Candidate: You know, what kind of an idiotic—

Supervisor: But these things are usually rationalizations of the analyst's reluctance to let go.

Candidate: Yeah. You know, there is a story called "Little Bear." I'll tell it to you real fast. Little Bear's visit to Grandmother, that's maybe five chapters long. In one of the chapters Grandmother is telling Little Bear a story about Little Bear's mom when Little Bear's mom was little. His mom, Mama Bear, found a bird that had fallen out of its nest. She said, "Oh, where is your nest?" And the bird said, "Up there." She looked up there for the blue jays' nest and it was a haze, she couldn't find it and said, "You can come and live with me." She said she would make a nest for the bird and she did. Then the bird said, "Put me by the window so I can see outside." Mama Bear did but said, "It's nice here too." Then the bird learned to fly and he flew around the house. That was fun, but then one day he was really sad. Mama Bear said, "We'll sing a song," but the bird said, "I cannot. My heart is sad." Mama Bear said, "Well, fly around the house," and he said, "I cannot. My heart is sad." So Mama Bear took him out and set him on the ground outside and said, "You can fly away." The bird flew up in the air and he came back and said, "It is not because I don't love you, but I must."

Supervisor: Uh-huh.

Candidate: The bird said, "But I must fly away," and Mama Bear said, "Fly away." Then the story ends with Little Bear saying, "And he came back every year with his children and his children's children and his children's children's children, didn't he Grandma?" The grandmother says, "Yeah, there's one right now." Little Bear says, "I would have let him go too." And that's what comes to my mind.

Supervisor: Sure, sure.

Candidate: And to say any of those other things is to muddy that up.

Supervisor: That's right. The analyst does have to be aware of the countertransference.

Candidate: The analyst is a person too.

Supervisor: Absolutely. Okay, well, I'll see you in two weeks.

Candidate: Yeah. And I will be walking entirely on my own steam, I hope.

Supervisor: Well, I hope so.

Candidate: I hope.

Supervisor: Was it displaced? The fracture?

Candidate: Oh, no. Just fractured in several places.

Supervisor: That's too bad. Well, I hope it gets better.

Candidate: But it's not—yeah, well it will.

Supervisor: It's just aggravating.

Candidate: Okay. Goodbye.

Supervisor's Comments

The session begins with a bit of informal interaction in regard to the candidate's broken toe, but she spontaneously begins to focus on the analytic material and the supervisory process. She describes the patient's drifting moods and her own recognition that there had been a specific turning point ("we had a pivotal day"). She is increasingly comfortable coming to supervision without special preparation ("I just found the notes on my way here, actually."). In describing the patient's increasing freedom and capacity to make decisions for herself, the candidate shows herself capable of tolerating, without narcissistic injury, the patient's increased independence.

The patient's material suggests an increasing capacity to tolerate frustration, disappointment, and the realities of other people's behavior without undue distress and without interpreting that behavior as necessarily reflecting upon herself, something she might have done earlier in the analytic experience. The patient adopts an essentially positive and optimistic viewpoint, with an enhanced sense of confidence in herself and her priorities. She shows an ability to accept her unmarried status without undue pressures for action, and to tolerate the experience of grief and mourning with regard to the termination; she recognizes that these feelings will eventually subside and she will experience renewed energies. The candidate indicates her appreciation of the patient's capacity to tolerate the termination affects.

In her thoughts about getting herself a cat the patient is expressing her wish to replace the analyst and thereby avoid grief, as well as insight into her motivations and a recognition that to do so would not in the long run be in her best interests. In this material the patient's tolerance of separation and loss, and the accompanying affects, is significantly more mature than in the past. Throughout this section the patient is describing a process and dynamics typical of termination; she recognizes both her difficulty in renunciation and her enhanced ability to tolerate her affective experiences. For her part, the candidate allows the patient these experiences without inappropriate attempts to reassure her or to reduce the intensity of her affective responses. The candidate views this period, quite correctly, as pivotal with regard to the patient's termination experience; she recognizes and accepts the patient's decathexis of the analysis and of herself as analyst, and acknowledges the patient's experience of the analysis as now essentially over, a thing of the past.

The supervisor is still considering the possibility that the patient's absences may be a form of resistance to the full experience of transference affect; his question ("What does she say about not coming?") is an attempt to alert the candidate to this possibility without suggesting that this is actually the case. The candidate's explanation of the patient's absences seems appropriate and suggests minimal resistance, while her description of the patient's behavior in the waiting room presents an earlier and no longer active facet of the process of internalization—the patient's former desires to memorize all the details of that room in order to retain the analyst internally.

In this material the patient shows how resolution of the transference neurosis is experienced as a gradual process of decathexis, with retention of the memories of its previous significance, but also a recognition of the shifting cathexis and an increasing tolerance of the resolution that is occurring. Her affective life is increasingly focused outside the analysis, as the analyst is becoming a less significant figure in her present life experience.

An interesting derivative change as a result of the analytic process is the patient's newly established capacity to draw the human figure. This seems the result of a change in the patient's awareness and acceptance of the human body, and of her own femininity. This change is itself the result of a resolution of conflict occurring in the middle phase of the analysis. The issue is now expressed in her ability to carry out a sublimated function which previously had been inhibited and blocked by conflict. Her ability to accept this new capacity without undue excitement but with quiet confirmation and pleasure is another sign of the extent to which this change is a function of conflict resolution and structural change.

At the same time the patient shows some persistent elements of the transference neurosis, inasmuch as she continues to fear punishment or disruption as the result of her "disloyalty" to the analyst-mother in renouncing her attachments. The analyst's interpretive response is a spontaneous, animated, role-playing exaggeration ("ehh hee he he, you thought you didn't need me"), and the patient's howling laughter at this is a sign of their genuinely direct and affective interaction.

The patient's sense of comfort and self-composure, and the candidate's analogy to the adolescent leaving for college, indicate how both participants are comfortable in the termination. The patient indicates, as an unexpected gain from the analytic experience, a sense of comfort within herself, of natural freedom. The supervisor stresses the importance of such changes in his distinction between what a patient expects going into treatment and what he may in fact achieve, however inconceivable it might have been when the treatment began. Supervisor and candidate discuss this further in regard to the patient's narrow presenting complaints regarding her weight. She still needs to lose some, and while this may still be an issue for her, its importance in her psychic life is sharply reduced; the presumption is that when she has completed the mourning process she will be able to lose weight without undue difficulty.

The supervisor returns to the issue of the patient's absences by concurring with the candidate's understanding that these are a reflection of maturation and shifting cathexis rather than resistance and avoidance of the process of termination. The candidate's remark that "it's an interesting kind of acting out on her part, . . . a sign of progress," demonstrates her ability to use the context of behavior as a way of establishing meaning.

The patient's description of her newfound capacity to be alone and to experience a state of relaxation offers further evidence of the degree to which significant structural change has occurred, but the candidate is able to maintain an objective position and to consider whether the patient has "sold me a bill of goods." She continues her search for manifestations of resistance and defense.

The supervisor's response supports the candidate's position of listening for but not insisting upon the presence of defenses, and there is an interchange in which they communicate effectively around this issue. Here the candidate shows her sophistication and her ability to stick to the material of the analysis rather than to base her interpretations on a priori formulations. The supervisor provides support for these ideas, while also reminding the candidate, through a vignette from his own experience, that surprises and new material may emerge even this late in the analysis.

The candidate describes her shifting perceptions of the patient's state in regard to the termination process and her own increasing comfort. Candidate and supervisor engage as peers in a give-and-take in which each is actively participant and responsive to the remarks of the other. The candidate shows she has resolved her countertransference concerns regarding the adequacy of the termination experience, and the supervisor attempts to synthesize and support this with his comments about the patient's capacity to tolerate mourning. This new capacity is contrasted with her previous avoidance of such a process in her relationship with her grandmother.

The candidate brings up the issue of her own mourning

process, a complement to the patient's experience. The supervisor rather abruptly and probably unnecessarily intervenes to support the candidate. He explains the reciprocal process the analyst experiences during termination. This is possibly the supervisor's response to the termination of his own experience with the candidate, and a sign of his investment in the analytic process.

The candidate is able to elaborate on her countertransference awareness, and this eventually leads to expression of her concern that she might identify with her own analyst in the final parting, recognizing that this would be an unwanted and unnecessary complication. She is able to recognize her analyst's shortcomings and to voice her criticism of his technique in regard to termination. She is able also to benefit from her own experience as an analysand in her current role as analyst. The supervisor broadens the issue by criticizing a technique used by Ralph Greenson, whereby patient and analyst sit face to face the last few sessions. The candidate concurs, and they discuss the implications of such departures from optimal abstinence during termination.

The candidate's fable about "Little Bear" is a nice illustration of the degree to which she can appreciate the dynamics, growth, maturation, and separation entailed in the termination process, and the session ends somewhat the way it began, with a return to the current reality of the candidate's broken toe.

This material illustrates clearly some of the affective and experiential elements prominent in termination and in resolution of the transference neurosis. For her part, the candidate shows a sophistication and an ability to accept this new level of function in the patient without interference. She has a clear grasp of the dynamics of termination for both patient and analyst. The supervisor is pleased with the progress made by both, and at this point there is little need for him to intervene with regard to the candidate's technique. Rather, he lends himself to supporting the candidate's initiative and her experience of this final phase of the analytic process.

Chapter 20

Supervisory Session 123

Candidate: Well, I actually read the notes this time. I think it's more of the same, but let me look at it a moment. It's hard, it's sad. She feels good. The fantasy is that I will not be able to tolerate her independence and will be angry—not devastated—but angry that she does not care about me exclusively anymore, that she doesn't care about me or our work very much anymore, that she has outgrown me. She had a very good week. She was good, it was a solid, successful, feels-good-about-herself week. And then she went to Los Angeles and it turned out she wasn't able to come to her Monday appointment, not because she was going to Los Angeles, but because she had a real early morning meeting that was set by a client. She had no say in it. Some of these meetings she has no say about and they involve ten or fifteen people. It's the people with the money who determine the time. It was like an eight a.m. meeting and her appointment is at eight-thirty. At noon she was leaving for Los Angeles. At six or seven in the morning she got a call informing her that the meeting was canceled, so she could have called me and told me, which she hasn't done the whole way through the analysis. She's never called and said, "Well, I really could make this appointment." But she felt that since there were only two or three weeks left she maybe ought to, but didn't want to. She thought she ought to but she didn't call me and tell me she could make it. She went about her business. She had a good day. By that afternoon she was feeling really guilty. She went to Los Angeles and had a good trip. She had kind of been glad she was going to L.A. because she was going to get to work with this female designer she has wanted to work with and wanted to get to know better; she did and had a really good time. She came back from L.A. and by the time she got into my office was feeling, had decided, that her life was stupid. "I'm fat and ugly, irretrievable." It seemed that those feelings came in response to having made the decision that no, she didn't want to come on Monday morning. She'd already told me she wasn't going to come, that she had other things to do that she cared about more, and she felt that would be unacceptable to me. Eventually I interpreted it as a fantasy and a wish that I would not be able to tolerate her independence. I mean I first interpreted it as a fantasy. Hidden in there was something that she is holding on to, this view of me, this notion that I will be enraged and then reel her back in somehow. And I've suggested that hidden in this holding on to the fantasy is some kind of wish that I do not want her to be independent.

Supervisor: Well, now, have you gone into what her fantasies are as to *why* you would be angry and *why* you don't want her to be independent?

Candidate: Numerous times. I will not be able to tolerate not being the center of her attention, the same way as she was not able to tolerate not being the center of her mother's attention. I would feel discarded, replaced, displaced, unnecessary, unappreciated. The only way she can show me that she appreciates me and what we've done for the last five years is to have allegiance to me. If she turns to other things and leaves me behind, then I will feel unappreciated and she will have over me the power that was over her initially, when she felt so irrelevant and so determined to make herself irreplaceable to everybody. She feels if I am not irreplaceable to her that I will get angry eventually.

Supervisor: This is because you don't have anybody else in your life or—

Candidate: Because I have to—

Supervisor: You want her as your lover?

Candidate: Because I have to be the center.

Supervisor: Because you have to be the center.

Candidate: Uh-huh. Also, I'm going to replace her with another patient who needs me. Since she doesn't need me anymore, I will replace her with somebody who does. So that's been one theme that winds its way in and out. It has been for months. It just came up again. She never has been able to elaborate particularly that I don't have anybody else in my life, not for a long time anyway. Several years ago she talked like that. I was depressed and abandoned and my husband treated me badly. She doesn't seem to be in touch with those kinds of thoughts now. I guess I could put them there in the light, but for the most part it's even dystonic, the notion that I won't be able to tolerate her independence. She's sick of making herself appear to be needy. She says she has the notion that unless she needs me desperately right up until the last minute, that's the only kind of departure that's tolerable. A tearing, ripping away from me. Then she can be free if she doesn't acknowledge to me that she is free ahead of time. If she doesn't acknowledge to me that she's leaving because she wants to, because she's ready to, then I won't be abandoned by her. There has been a lot of that as she struggles with having—oh, and she paid my bill on the day that she came in after the Monday that she didn't come and then went to L.A. Then she came in and paid my bill, which had been overdue. And we talked about the fact that she did two contradictory things. She came in and said, "I need you and I'm fat and I'm ugly and I'm just as terrible as I was when I first came into analysis." She paid me off and—two sessions run together in my mind. Then she had a dream. Oh, and I had pursued her some about the payment of the bill. I nagged her. She has always been so unwilling to talk about money and what the meaning of paying has been. So I was aware of pursuing her some. She has this dream that night, that Ted came back, and she's going to have to pay him off to get rid of him. It's a wonderful dream (laughs) and rather than say to him directly, "I don't want you anymore. You are irrelevant in my life. Get the fuck out," she is considering paying him off to get rid of him. And it is she who interprets that: rather than feeling comfortable and saying to me, "I have grown out of you and this is over," and leaving, instead she pays me off with symptoms and money. She said it is important for her to pay her bill, because she'll be shuck of me that way. She said that for a long time she thought she would leave me a piece of artwork on her last day. I didn't bring this up. I had brought it up some months ago, when you and I talked about it. But I think it comes up spontaneously in that session. For a long time she thought she wanted to do that, and now she just realizes she doesn't want to leave any tiny little piece of her here for me. It's all *hers* and she wants to take it all with her and she doesn't want to pacify me. She doesn't want to, but she feels cautious about that. Oh, in the second session, it's not very long for a change, she had a really bad dream all last night. She dreamed that Ted came back and wouldn't leave her alone. He kept pursuing her and pursuing her. He was pathetic. She kept saying, "Leave me alone. Leave me alone." She felt if she gave him money he would leave. But she didn't want to give him money. She felt she was running away from him rather than dealing with it and saying, "I just don't want to see you anymore." It wasn't like it was when they got back together and she was wavering inside whether she wanted him or didn't want him. It wasn't that way. There was no wavering inside of her as to whether she wanted to be with him or not. There was just a wavering on how to deal with him and how to get away from him. It reminds her of here. "I want to leave. I want to leave, the way I felt yesterday, but I thought it would be easier to leave depressed and feeling bad than to just leave and say goodbye. Rather than confronting that I didn't want to see him anymore, I was running away instead. Even at the end with him I was begging him to leave me alone, rather than just saying, 'It's over.' Actually, the last time I talked to him on the phone I said, 'I don't want to talk to you anymore. Goodbye.' And I hung up." And I said, "You're walking out of here on the last day and saying goodbye, feeling good, but you still have conflicts about that." She said, "I felt really drained when I left here yesterday and went home. Another part of that dream that keeps coming to mind is the money. I brought you that check yesterday and you kept asking me about it and in the dream I felt I had to pay him off." I said, "And did you also feel, perhaps, that I was pursuing you yesterday?" She said, "Yep, and boy I hate it when you do that, not just about money, but when you do that, when you keep after me about something. I just can't stand it. The whole thing is strange." And then there was something about the August bill. I hadn't carried the balance with it. She went back and saw the August bill and thought she must have paid me. Then she went back in her checkbook and figured out that she hadn't paid me, and she paid me for it. She was the accurate one, she wrote an accurate check. She had lost track at times. "It ties into a lot of things. I really want to be an adult and accept responsibilities." At some point in here I said something about I wonder if the dream is a clue to one part of what paying me, what her paying me, has meant to her. To pay Ted in the dream meant to be free. "Not all along it hasn't meant that, but it does now. Now that's right. What you said yesterday, when I write that final check, that's it. And I want it. It feels good." It's here that I said something about the holding on in her dream and in her image of me, or me and Ted, that I will hold on to her, that I cannot tolerate her leaving. She said, "I can't really understand what I'm afraid of. In the way of thinking, being saddled with you forever is preferable to being unlovable." Oh, that was in the session before this. What finally was said was that what she was finally going to have from me before this analysis would end was that I would love her. She said that makes something make sense that she hasn't talked about, that with these feelings of burgeoning independence she feels independent of me. At the same time she feels terribly unlovable and they always come together, whereas out in her life she feels attractive and lovable and okay and feeling that she was going to wrest that lovability, she was going to wrest my loving her from me by needing me and needing me. Then when I finally loved her, then she would be able to leave me. Then there was some interchange about getting a penis from me as being a, what do I say? A consolidation, a concretization, a symbol.

Supervisor: Then a part of her wish that you need her is the idea that she is lovable to you. That you want her.

Candidate: Uh-huh. "Saddled with you forever is preferable to being unlovable." If I don't—

Supervisor: If you let her go without any great squawks, without any great objections, without any great feeling about it, to her it means that you never cared for her.

Candidate: "If I don't treat this situation right, prolong my need for you, I'll be cast out and be unlovable. But the other side is real scary too. In fact, it's more scary. The feeling that I am really lovable, that is, vulnerable, filled with my needs, that's scary."

Supervisor: Her own needs?

Candidate: Uh-huh. "There is a vulnerability in there with knowing that I am lovable and capable of forming a relationship." Somehow, she said, that's tied in with her believing that "if I don't need and want you, my punishment will be there will never be anybody else. It suits me to believe that."

Supervisor: Uh-huh.

Candidate: Then I say it sounds like she is feeling lovable and able to form relationships with people. She said, "Oh, yes, a very strong sense of that, only here, and showing you that I can leave you and form a relationship with someone else." She was silent for twenty minutes. Then she talks about being in L.A. again. She comes back. Then she has this fight at the office, which I have some trouble understanding, and I have to cast around a little bit to understand if she is displacing some, if really she is angry with me. But she is finally able to convince me and I think she's right, I don't know. It's this way: Eventually she has a fight at the office in which for the first time she stands up for herself more appropriately and is appropriately angry and says, "This I don't have to put up with, this shit. I am not going to stand around and wait for you people to appreciate me and love me and take care of me. I'm going to take my wares and go somewhere else. Whenever it suits me." At first she felt she had to leave the next day. Then she figured out that she didn't have to leave the next day, she just had to find someplace where she felt her position was more in balance with what she had to offer. At the same time, she said another part of this that is hard is that her recognition is that she's only twenty-seven, or however old she is, and that she's had six years of experience in the field and that for someone with six years of experience in the field she has a magnificent portfolio. But it's nowhere near what it will be in twenty years; she has a lot to learn and there are other people who know more than she does. But she does not have to be treated in the unappreciative ways she feels she's being treated. She doesn't have to hang around being better and better and better and hoping that she will finally get appreciated. Eventually that was interpreted in terms of she's going to leave whether or not I ever love her.

Supervisor: Good!

Candidate: And that was it.

Supervisor: But these trips to Los Angeles—she's really in the big time now?

Candidate: Well, she's in the St. Louis big time. The next move she is going to have to make—she's always said Chicago, but I think it's very possible that she'll make a move to Los Angeles. I don't think that's occurred to her yet.

Supervisor: Uh-huh.

Candidate: Designing on a big scale. She is, she can't really go any further in St. Louis, I don't think. Especially since she is so incredibly unwilling to "kiss ass," as she puts it.

Supervisor: Uh-huh.

Candidate: She is young and she doesn't want to pay her dues for twenty years to get somewhere. I think she's going to have to get into a bigger firm where she won't be the best she knows. But she certainly is in as big a time as she could be.

Supervisor: Yeah.

Candidate: But it's, it's a significant decision for her. It's interesting, one of the things I don't think I've told you, a theme that kind of got worked out, I think, before I saw you last, was her profession, her choice of profession. One of the characteristics of her profession is that nothing's ever finished. Nothing is ever settled and you've never made it. I mean you do a project and another project and you build your portfolio and you become somebody, but nothing is ever the same. This woman has always expressed that she wants finally to get into a position where everything will always be the same. She should have been a CPA. Oh, nothing is ever the same. She was then able to—we were talking about something else in terms of her aspiration to take these chaotic situations and make them conform to this fantasy that sometime nothing will change and everything will be the same. She said, "I think it's pretty suspicious that I choose a profession which is by its very nature chaotic and which is by its very nature something I can never make be steady and be the same. And then I've been beating my head up against the wall for all these years insisting that it slow down and be the same and at the same time taking great pleasure out of the speed and the chaos of it." So that was it. It was an interesting expansion of her self-understanding. She recognized that her old fantasy was that she would find a house and a job and a man and she would never have to change jobs. So she said it was pretty funny because never, until you own your own corporation, do you not have to change jobs in this field, in the kind of work that she does. You work upward in the best firm in Podunk, then you move to St. Louis and move up in the best firm in St. Louis, and then you move to Chicago and to New York. And by then you're eighty or you own your own design company. But for her to be able to approach this particular fight—the one after she returned from L.A.—it wasn't a blow-up. Now, she's had fights before where she has gone in and blown her lid at something. And it was a step for her to be able to do that and say, "I don't have to take this shit," blah blah blah. But this time it was more of a holding of a line. And it extends for a couple of weeks, and she essentially says, not in words but in behavior, "I am not going to put up with this, and if you don't like it, that's too bad." But she's not saying it snottily or angrily. And she's saying it to me. It's an extension of what she's saying to me, that "I am not going to keep bringing you more and more work and more and more work so that you will love me. I am not going to stay up all night. I am not going to pretend that I am depressed anymore." She said that what you see is what you get. She also decided to get a cat. She did not want to get a cat for any of the wrong reasons. She didn't want to get a cat because it's like she equates getting a cat with having a baby. That you are, one, vulnerable to loss and, two, imperfect because nobody knows how to perfectly raise a kitten, always knowing how to do exactly the right thing, when to call the vet, when not to call the vet. You might make a mistake and you can't pretend otherwise, she can't pretend otherwise, and so that kind of imperfection she wasn't willing to come up against.

In her words, she wanted to be taken care of. She didn't want to have to take care of anybody else and be in a situation where she was the grown-up or the caretaker. The pet owner was intolerable to her because it reminded her of all the needs she had and was not getting met. Later she didn't want to replace me with a cat. She didn't want to, in the same way that she didn't want to move to Chicago in order to pretend that the termination of the analysis wasn't important. At this point she said it doesn't feel like a replacement, it feels like a step in the right direction. It feels like she is able to say that she and life are both imperfect. She decided to get a cat one day. It didn't feel like a replacement of me; she thought about that a good deal. The next day, Robert's cat, whom she knew for seven years and was terribly fond of, died. She thought for sure that that would change her mind. She was very sad but it didn't have anything to do with her cat. Her cat would sometime die too, and she would deal with that whenever it happened. She was pleased that that was her response, but she didn't predict that that would be her response. I don't know if she had gotten a cat. She didn't say. Also, getting a cat at this point is something else. It's saying she's the grown-up person and can fulfill her own needs. If she needs to have something there when she comes home to talk to and to pet and take care of, she can get a cat. She doesn't have to go stand in singles bars in the hope that Prince Charming will come and pick her up and take care of her. She can acknowledge her needs and find a way to fill them. Maybe imperfectly but fill them nonetheless. She feels comfortable, self-sufficient, able to love. "I can get an animal and really love it now. Always before it was too much like having a child. I still feel that way about it, but that doesn't feel bad anymore. I do feel funny, like having a baby and not knowing how to diaper it, awkward, strange. The whole maternal scenario is very foreign to me. It has previously been so distasteful. It isn't anymore. It's just foreign, strange, funny. I am so glad. I thought I would change my mind when such and such a cat died." And that's another interesting theme that weaves its way through all of this. "I thought I'd change my mind when Robert's cat died. I loved that cat. But somehow it doesn't matter. It's very sad and I miss that cat, but I'm still going to get one of my own. I have an important meeting this afternoon after I leave here. I decided to use another photographer besides Robert. I'm not going to put all my eggs in one basket. I feel sad but I feel grateful. I don't want someone who cannot commit and can't give and can't love. It's the end of a whole period of my life and that's sad. It's funny, but that's sad. That's it, the ending. But I really don't want a person like that. I will always have feelings for Robert, but he too is becoming a part of the past. I went through a phase a couple of months ago where I wanted to be touched and to be made love to; now I feel that I don't want to be touched. I want to be left alone. It's like I've been through a war. It's been unbearable at times, but now it's okay and I want to enjoy being by myself. I don't feel I'm isolating myself. I'm not describing this very well. I just don't want to be touched by just anybody. It doesn't feel at all negative or bad; in fact, it feels very good.

Supervisor: She doesn't have to be touched for the sake of being touched.

Candidate: Yes. I said a couple of months ago she had an explosion of body hunger that was almost indiscriminate. She said, "Yeah, it was. The wish to be touched, to be made love to, almost anyone would have done." And now, I said, she is more able to contain and hold herself, and to allow herself to be touched if there is someone around she wants to be touched by. She said, "That is exactly how I feel. I can contain myself. I am whole unto myself. I had dinner with my mother last night and I said something like that to her. I said something about it to my mother, and my mother said again, for the nine hundredth time, some insinuation that I am frigid or have trouble with sex." This has been a constant theme. "Mother is always saying, 'Well, I know you've had trouble with boys too,' intimating again that I am frigid. And I said for the very first time, 'You have intimated over the years, Mother, that I have sexual problems, that I am frigid, and I want you to know that I'm really, really okay. You don't have to worry. That's an area in which I am really okay.' And it felt really good to say that after all these years. Right up front. I had more fun with my mother last night than I have had for years. Then I had dinner at some time or other where Suzanne, a real yentl, was. She's adopted. Real neurotic and unhappy. She's spouting off about treatment and how she's never found the final answer, some b.s. that I don't really understand. I said there is no final answer. There is no pot of gold. There is only acceptance. Suzanne said, 'Yes, *yes,* acceptance is resolution and resolution is acceptance,' and all of that bullshit. I was sad for her. She doesn't know and doesn't understand a damn thing. Our work has meant so much to me. I feel so lucky. I was sitting across from this alcoholic woman who said, 'Gee, did you have a nose job?' I said, 'No, no nose job, no braces, no girdle,' and the woman said, 'Gee, it's hard to believe you're Jewish, you're so cute.' It reminded me of Joe Fowler and all that superficial stuff that will always be there. But I could just smile and turn and talk to someone else. I'm leaving these people behind." And then I said, "I've stopped struggling with them to get recognition from them, to make them understand, to get in touch, to bring them out with me." Another thing she's been trying to do, to fix them so they can come with her. "It's so nice not to feel guilty about that. I just don't want to see them anymore. I don't care. I don't feel guilty." She was silent for five minutes. So it feels good. It feels good. She came Monday. There have been a lot of silences, but by and large they have been comfortable silences and I have left them absolutely alone. If she needs me to nudge her now, she's not going to have me next week, so she—oh, do we have time for this? She came in and told me this big long thing about the finality of this fight at work. And I kept seeing connections with her work and I brought them in—the whole theme of recognition and wanting recognition from me. This was the point at which she was saying, "I will not work harder to get recognition. If you don't want to give it to me, then stick it." And finally she said, "That's it exactly. You have such a way of cutting through all the bullshit for me, cutting through it fast. I can do it, you know, but I'm much slower at it. I'll miss that in you." I said, "Yes," and then she said, "Do you know what I mean?" I said, "I believe so, but I believe you are also saying that if I would be more quiet, more patient, keep my mouth shut, you would come to the same conclusion, that you can do it by yourself." She howled with laughter and said, "Yep, yep." That interchange felt good.

Supervisor: Uh-huh.

Candidate: Both in some ways my nudging her and her being able to—she didn't tell me to be quiet, but she didn't need to, either. She could tolerate my intrusiveness without getting particularly defensive about it but also accept that I was recognizing that she can do it by herself. Now, she came on Monday, she didn't come—no, she came. Mostly what she talked about was that she can't believe it's the last week. It feels good, it's sad, it feels strange, mostly strange. She went to a party over the weekend where she felt like she was walking through her past. All of these people whom she has been involved with in her neuroticness all these years, and she felt she was seeing herself at different ages and stages. She didn't get drunk. She went home. She was cordial to the people. She didn't feel she had much to say to most of them. She went home, had a good night's sleep, got up, cleaned her apartment, and had a good relaxed weekend. She doesn't feel an urgency to get out of St. Louis instantly anymore. It's funny, she said; this is the last thing she said. It's funny. She was thinking yesterday about her perceptions throughout our work and her expectations. She really expected that I would wave that magic wand and everything would happen magically and she would not have to do anything. Like the weight. That it was just going to melt off magically and disappear. It's really hilarious that she really did think that at one time. She was silent for twenty-five minutes. She didn't come the next day. She has an appointment tonight and I don't know if she will come. I suspect she will. She usually comes for her Wednesday appointments. She canceled Tuesday at seven that morning, so I suspect I'll hear about it.

Supervisor: Well, it's very nice material. It shows the extent of the change. It's an interesting change inasmuch as most of it has been intrapsychic. The external observer probably wouldn't see that much change in her.

Candidate: Oh, I don't think that's true, because people have said to her how fantastic she looks. This is a woman who used to—she's tall and imposing, which I am not. But she was ingratiating and took little steps like this—

Supervisor: You mean people have noted the change in her behavior?

Candidate: Oh, yes. She has a smile from here to here, and now she is tall and stately and forceful and direct, not in an ingratiating way. And people have said—I mean, she is like an advertisement for psychoanalysis.

Supervisor: Good.

Candidate: But not in her performance. Her performance, as far as talking, you know, to someone who is unable to do anything and then goes—she's like just stopped apologizing for who she is.

Supervisor: Uh-huh.

Candidate: And people have commented that she—I can't remember the comments, but over—

Supervisor: Well, I would suggest that we perhaps meet one more time two weeks from today, just sort of go over the whole sweep of the case.

Candidate: Okay, and then when I get to writing it up, I'm going to call you up and come in another couple of times. . . .

Supervisor: Sure, okay. I'll see you in two weeks then.

Candidate: Yes.

Supervisor: All right. Goodbye.

Supervisor's Comments

The candidate immediately launches into an appropriately summarized account of the patient's material. It is expressed in a lively form, and demonstrates the partial resolution of the transference neurosis as evidenced by the patient's increasing decathexis of the analyst. This is seen in her decision not to come for the session even though her meeting had been canceled, and also in her talk of having outgrown the analyst. At the same time, however, the persistence of the transference neurosis is shown by the patient's fantasy that the analyst will be unable to tolerate the patient's independence, and will experience anger and rejection; this is followed by a sense of guilt for having avoided the analytic session and also by regression to self-deprecatory feelings and experience ("I'm fat and ugly, irretrievable."). The candidate demonstrates her awareness of the meanings of the material as well as the existence of the unconscious wish hidden in these fantasies.

In response to the supervisor's question, the candidate elaborates on the meaning of these underlying fantasies and on the continuing transference experience of the patient. The supervisor's questions were meant to encourage the candidate to look for the hidden fantasies behind the patient's continuing transference, but this clearly was unnecessary, as the candidate has already considered these issues.

The patient's fantasies with regard to being replaced by another patient are typical during this phase of the analytic process, and the candidate draws on the full course of the analysis to recognize how fantasies which had been significant and manifest several years ago have now been modified as part of the transference resolution. The persistence of other elements in the transference neurosis is seen in the patient's fantasies of termination as a tearing away, as something that cannot be acknowledged in advance.

The candidate recognizes that the patient's contradictory behavior—regressing to self-deprecation—while paying off the overdue bill is a sign of development and maturation. The candidate is herself aware of her countertransference behavior in pursuing the patient too actively in regard to the payment and its meanings, an issue which subsequently is expressed in the dream about paying off the former boyfriend. The patient shows progress in her capacity to interpret her dreams, as well as resolution of her fantasy that she would leave a piece of herself with the analyst in the form of a piece of art. She also recognizes, with considerable insight, her own wish to avoid the distress of leaving.

The candidate is comfortable in acknowledging that she had pressured the patient with regard to money, and appreciates that the patient is able to criticize the candidate and her technique in an appropriate and constructive manner. At the same time the patient shows a more mature attitude in her handling of the money situation and in assuming adult responsibility generally. These are derivative manifestations of significant intrapsychic change.

The patient once again demonstrates the rapid oscillation between progress and regression which is typical of this phase of the analysis; she describes herself as on the one hand being more independent and not needing to be loved, while on the other she continues to wish and demand that the analyst love her.

The patient also exhibits in her description of the fight at the office, a new and healthy capacity for self-assertion, for standing up for herself and setting limits. Her recognition of the realities of the situation, of her needs, desires, and limitations, and of what she hopes to accomplish, is further evidence of structural change.

The supervisor's question ("she's really in the big time now?") is an appreciation of the patient's progress, and shows his pleasure at seeing the effects of a successful analytic and supervisory experience. His countertransference is manifested by pride in the patient's achievement and narcissistic gratification both for himself as supervisor and for the candidate as analyst. As such it is gratuitous.

The candidate announces in a comfortable and confident fashion that she and the patient had worked out the theme of the patient's choice of profession and its various neurotic determinants. The patient provides self-analytic scrutiny of the same issue, and the candidate is able to enjoy both the patient's growing self-awareness and her capacity to be firm without being explosive or angry, to look out for her own interests in the business situation and in the transference.

The search for a substitute object is common during the termination process, and is illustrated here by the patient's desire to get a cat. Her ability to accept the death of her friend's cat and to acknowledge that eventually this will happen to her if she gets one are further indications of intrapsychic change. The patient herself reflects pleasure and some degree of surprise at this newfound capacity.

The patient's self-awareness and self-analytic skills are evident in her recognition of the various meanings of her wish for a cat. It might satisfy some of her own needs, though incompletely. It also involves a major shift in her images and fantasies about having a baby and being responsible for it. It expresses her newfound capacity to search for appropriate and need-fulfilling objects, as well as to regulate patterns of tension without the frantic and indiscriminate impulses that characterized her responses to tension in the past.

Another sign of significant intrapsychic change is the patient's ability to interact with her mother in a candid and more age-appropriate fashion, without undue anxiety and with a new sense of pleasure. A related phenomenon is her capacity to tolerate the neurotic behavior of others. She recognizes their shortcomings but has no major affective response and feels no need to change them. This attitude is also reflected in the treatment relationship, in the interaction about the candidate's having been too active. The patient demonstrates her easy acceptance of her criticism of the candidate, as well as tolerance for the candidate's intrusiveness. Both parties enjoy the interchange, another sign of the resolution of the transference neurosis.

The patient is able to take some distance from herself with regard to her neurotic fantasy of the candidate magically curing her; she recognizes the appropriateness of that thought at the beginning of her analysis, and can amusedly contemplate it now that she is in the process of termination.

The supervisor's comments about the change being predominantly intrapsychic is immediately challenged by the candidate, who demonstrates conclusively that the supervisor has not appreciated the extent to which these changes are reflected in the patient's manifest behavior. Both supervisor and candidate are capable of tolerating his failure to appreciate the externally visible nature of the change without undue defensiveness or disappointment. This is in some ways parallel to the situation that has developed between candidate and patient. The patient is capable of tolerating the candidate's less than optimal interventions without undue distress or anxiety.

Throughout this session the supervisor has said relatively

little and the candidate has proceeded predominantly on her own, presenting the clinical data, analyzing and commenting upon it, and placing it in a useful and appropriate perspective. The supervisor is pleased to observe the candidate's growth as an analyst and her increasing independence. This is a parallel to the candidate's enjoyment of the patient's independence, maturation, and ability to separate herself from the transference attachment to the analyst.

The patient's clinical material is an excellent illustration of the process of grief, mourning, and renunciation of transference demands as occurs during the termination phase of a well-conducted and successful analysis. The resolution has not yet been completed and will still require weeks or months of further self-analytic work following the last session. But the material documents how much change has occurred and that the patient now seems equipped, psychologically and emotionally, to carry on the resolution once she leaves the analytic situation.

Chapter 21
Supervisory Session 124

Candidate: Well, it's done.

Supervisor: Good.

Candidate: In the next-to-last session she came in, I was just re-reading that session, she came in bouncing and happy and excited and then after she was on the couch for a while she got anxious and uncomfortable. She didn't want to be there, and that was the session I told you a little bit about, where she had the feeling that she had a prom dress on and I was going to make her take it off so I could make it all over again. And then thoughts about it having never really been her analysis, that it was a candidate analysis.

Supervisor: And this had come up before but not as directly as this?

Candidate: No, it has come up before and come up directly. It's one of the things that followed her throughout the analysis, and I don't know how it could have been undone, how it could have been worked through so that it was no longer a factor. When she was being evaluated, I don't know if I told you this recently or not, when she was being evaluated to be a control case she saw Dr. B., who didn't think she should be a control case. He wrote in his evaluation that he didn't think she was analyzable as someone's first or second case because she was so voracious; the candidate would be in a voracious period in the training analysis, and trying to deal at the same time with this voracious woman would be—well, I was on the, whatchacallit, Clinic Committee with him, and it turns out that that happened.

Supervisor: It turns out that what?

Candidate: He had a control case who was voracious when he was voracious, and it was a disastrous, horrible experience. So I understand better where he was coming from. I couldn't understand when I first read this, it scared me. I haven't read it recently so I don't know how strongly it was stated, but it scared me. I saw her and I thought, "What's the problem? This lady's not crazy." I don't know if he was trying to get rid of her or if he was trying to test her or if he was trying to set up what actually happened when he said to her, "You really want to be a control case, don't you, you really want to be a clinic patient because you can't afford analysis any other way?" And she said, "Yes." And he said, and this is according to her, "Everything else you've ever gotten in your life that you've wanted, after you've gotten it you haven't wanted it and thrown it away. How are we to know that having expended all this effort and assigned you to one of our candidates that you'll stick? Because the way you get to be a control case is you're a case for one of our candidates and we only want people who," well, her interpretation of it was, "suit our purposes." Whatever was actually said I'm sure I'll never know. But that was her interpretation of it. "And we don't think, I don't think, you'll stick."

Supervisor: He said that?

Candidate: She was enraged. That came up every six months through the whole five years. "That goddamn Dr. B., the only reason I'm still here is because I want to prove him wrong." And her feeling on this next-to-last day was that I could still pull that card out somehow. I could say I was the one who was more important to the clinic, to the process that had accepted her, for the reason she was paying a small fee that she could afford. I was the one who was more important and she had to suit my purposes to be analyzable through the clinic. Now, I don't know how that could have been analyzed away. I might ultimately have told her, "You know I already have enough hours; I don't need you anymore." But that's not analyzing. It seems to me that that's an iatrogenic, whatever. I mean it's built into the system.

Supervisor: It's built into the system, yes. It's the same thing.

Candidate: And that that's something we talked about from time to time, we talked about it and the fact that it had never felt like—I kept saying to her from time to time, "You're acting as if this isn't your own analysis." So it's not that it never got brought up before, but on this next-to-last day it was as if she could talk about it even more, and talk about how she really feels satisfied with herself. And that this is what she wanted. Although she didn't know that this was what she wanted out of analysis. This is what, if she could have known, this is what she would have wanted out of analysis. She knows she's not perfect. She knows she has things yet to do and will have for the rest of her life, but she was forever concerned that she wouldn't be perfect enough for me to be satisfied with her and I would try to keep her for my purposes. Because I wanted to have a perfect patient, a perfect product of my own to be able to say, "See what a great doctor I am, what a great job I've done." And that whole thing just added to what she brought into the analysis, this long train of not wanting her mother to take credit for her growing up, if she lost weight her mother would say, "Ah, I take such pleasure in it." If she did a good job in the analysis for herself it would be for me, I would take it as mine.

Supervisor: So what—

Candidate: She's going to have to authenticate it for herself after the analysis ends. Excuse me. Go ahead.

Supervisor: Well, what it can lead to is a recognition that in any relationship of any meaning, both participants get something out of it. Nobody does anything for nothing. And yet both can get something without interfering with the other guy.

Candidate: I feel that what she was finally able to say, and I haven't read all of this day's notes, so I don't know if it's true, but I feel that it is, is that she was finally able to say, "I got what I came here for. And even if you ask to have the prom dress back you can't get it. I'm not going to do it. But I'm real nervous, because you keep asking me these questions, and I keep expecting you to say aha, there's this whole body of stuff we don't perfectly understand yet. And then I'll have to fight you."

Supervisor: Because of your wish to keep her.

Candidate: Yeah, and that what she really felt was that she had gotten something for herself. And she wanted that to be enough for me. And the next day she came in, the next day is real short. She came in and she was just well, she just felt good. I think that that talking about it helped.

Supervisor: Was she able to see that it was her transference expectation that you were going to want the dress back?

Candidate: She was able to see that, but she was also able to tell me, and I think I was able to acknowledge, not in detail like I'm going to say it just now, that she being my first case, I wanted to wrap everything up, understand everything and that that behavior of mine added to her anxiety. That sometimes when I wasn't willing to let well enough alone, when she's happy with whatever understanding we have, I have to tie up six little loose ends and that then makes her nervous. That I'm not going to have a perfect enough understanding to suit me. Because those things really were to suit me, they weren't to suit her. And I think that my acknowledgment, by just saying, "I think that sometimes in the last several months when I would try to reach a more perfect understanding of something, or tie up some loose ends that it must have, the way you interpreted that was that I wasn't happy with the understanding we had of it and that I wanted a more perfect product. I wanted to do a better and better job for me."

Supervisor: Very nice.

Candidate: So Thursday she came in bouncing, smiling, late, a few minutes late. She got really good when she left last night. She was so happy. And then, well, she feels good and content. That was the overwhelming feeling, that she felt content. She was silent. The whole session was silent. It's weird, she thinks about how long it's been and it seems like yesterday. Long silence. Strange she feels so comfortable. See, yesterday she didn't feel comfortable being quiet. And then today she did again. Her mind is full, and she feels perhaps she should say something. But there aren't any words. Or the words don't do it justice. And besides I probably know anyway how she feels. And anyway it doesn't matter. It's not that it doesn't matter, it's not necessary.

Supervisor: Uh-huh.

Candidate: Long silence. I said, "It's a lot we have done together, a lot we've come through." And she said, "God, yes." It's hard for her to believe that in so many ways she will be grateful to me for the rest of her life. And proud of herself. Long silence. "It makes me smile," she said, "when I think of all the times and these years that I really thought that I was finished. Or very close to being finished. You never know till you get there. And I could never have known or understood this, that these were the kinds of feelings that would make me happy. I would have thought that it was impossible. That this kind of freedom, this amazing sense of freedom, I had no conception of. Finally it is okay to be myself. And that was inconceivable. It's wonderful. And it's a relief to not have such unrealistic expectations that I used to have of myself. That alone is like the burden of the world coming off my shoulders." She was thinking this morning of how part of what seems so—well, she keeps looking back and shaking her head and smiling at her expectations of what she would get. She thought she would walk out of here and never be anxious or sad or unhappy or lonely. And it's almost funny, that at this minute she would be poised, perfect, happy, not anxious. It makes her smile. She was silent. It's strange. She feels sad that it's not that overwhelming unbearable sense of loss. She was silent for a long time. God, when she thinks of all the times she has lain here and looked out that window, it's amazing. She was silent for a long time. That was the end of the hour. I said, "It's time," and stood up, and she got up and went to the door and she turned around there and said, "I'll never forget you as long as I live." And I said, "Goodbye." And she walked out.

Supervisor: Uh-huh.

Candidate: And uh, I (deep sigh) felt at the time and for the few minutes afterward that I thought it was a really important reply to say, that that was the opening that I had to say, "And I won't forget you, ah, you've been, it's been such a pleasure working for you," or that was the opening I had, and to end—and that was also her last, her last, and I also handed her the bill, her final bill. That was her, I don't know how to say it, her offering to me. She was still handing me an offering of some kind on her way out the door.

Supervisor: Yes, I would say it's probably a multiple-function thing. It's an offering, it is also a testing—are you going to snatch it all back again? As you suggest—

Candidate: Well, am I going to accept the offering?

Supervisor: Are you going to accept it? Also, was this more your analysis than hers? That's also contained in that. Are you going to somehow engulf her, are you going to invite her to have some sort of an ongoing relationship with you? These are all testing devices that she has condensed into that one expression.

Candidate: It was extremely, indescribably powerful. Even the process of my saying goodbye, it felt like it reverberated across the room.

Supervisor: Uh-huh.

Candidate: Not, well, and in her response to that, which was nonverbal, and then she turned and went down the hall.

Supervisor: Uh-huh.

Candidate: My sense of it was, she would digest that. And that it wasn't particularly comfortable at that moment, but that over the long run it would be more comfortable than anything else I might have had a passing impulse to do.

Supervisor: Yes, the analyst who says, "It's been a great pleasure working with you" or "I enjoyed" or "I appreciate working with you" or—

Candidate: Well, the opening was sure there.

Supervisor: "I think we've really done a lot together."

Candidate: And in some ways I was a little tiny bit quicker, just in the kind of verbal dance that people do with each other, in timing those things. I think I said goodbye more quickly than I might the next time. Only because the opening was so broad in which to throw myself.

Supervisor: That's right.

Candidate: Ah, and I, in essence, went like this (gestures) and I felt the next instant that it will never be, I hope, but I don't think it will, that it will never be that hard or that awkward again.

Supervisor: Uh-huh.

Candidate: Because it was the right thing to do.

Supervisor: Yes.

Candidate: And awkward is not quite the right word. But I didn't have any doubt that I was going to do anything else. But it was real clear that she was putting out the plate.

Supervisor: Yeah.

Candidate: And it's like when somebody reaches out to shake your hand, and you don't shake it.

Supervisor: Right. Right.

Candidate: Which is interesting, because that just reminded me of something else that happened that I had forgotten about. As she passed me, I stood up and as she passed me she embraced me and I did not push her away. But I did not embrace her back.

Supervisor: Uh-huh. Absolutely.

Candidate: But I didn't feel like this (gestures) either.

Supervisor: No, to flinch or push her away—

Candidate: You know, I didn't feel like a stiff. And in fact I kind of felt for her. But I didn't hug her in return, and then she got to the door and she, she said that and I said goodbye.

Supervisor: Uh-huh.

Candidate: So there were two plates that she was offering.

Supervisor: Uh-huh. Yeah. That's right and that's a very appropriate way—to flinch, to pull back, to say, "get your hands off me"—

Candidate: Or to even get stiff.

Supervisor: To stiffen, that's right, would not be appropriate. But what she illustrates is a point Karl Menninger (1973) makes in his book on the technique of psychoanalysis. Patients do not get what they came for, but they get something much better.

Candidate: Yeah. She illustrates that and talks about it at great length. She also went to buy the kitten and decided not to. That was the next-to-last session.

Supervisor: That's right. When and if she wants a kitten she can get one in six weeks or six months or six years from now. She doesn't have to have it right now.

Candidate: She said she had gone Wednesday afternoon to get the kitten, or Wednesday morning or Tuesday night. Anyway, I heard about it on Wednesday evening. She went to get the kitten and the only one she liked—now this was at the Humane Society, there's probably seven million kittens, so I'm sure she probably could have liked some other one—but he was only four weeks old and you can't have them declawed until they are six weeks old. So for two weeks, well, she said she saw this creature intent on destroying her nice new furniture. Which I thought was kind of a nice way to put it. And then she had planned to take Thursday and Friday off and what she wanted to do was go to movies. Thursday was her last session. She wanted to go to movies because she's been so busy recently, she loves movies, and she's so busy recently she hasn't been able to go to the movies she's wanted to, so she was just going to go to the movies and go out to dinner with someone. And then she thought if she got this kitten who was intent on destroying her house she wouldn't be able to go to the movies, so screw it, she's not getting it right now.

Supervisor: Uh-huh.

Candidate: But it felt like a lock on her freedom. She was just getting free. And what I said at that point is, "You're just getting rid of me." And she laughed and said "Yeah, yeah, I'm just getting free, I don't need to do this."

Supervisor: Uh-huh.

Candidate: So I was—

Supervisor: Well, what did you learn from the case?

Candidate: (Laughs) I'm sure I can't tell you that yet, in a sentence.

Supervisor: No, I mean, as you sort of think back over the whole experience, what has it meant for you and to you?

Candidate: I had a supervisory session this morning with the psychotherapy group, and one of the people was presenting a good hour in an adequate therapy; it's not a mess. And as I was listening it was like transparencies of all of the hours we have spent together, putting them together in a pile, because he was right here and what I found myself talking about was probably what you would have found yourself talking about, or some reflection of it, with me. Which is where this fits in it in the whole picture. It was a very gratifying hour, a very positive transference, and there is going to be hell to pay if this case continues, eventually. As there was hell to pay in this one. And I was surprised at myself, it was fun. I was surprised that I was able to reach some comprehension of what was happening in the moment in the case, but then also pull back and say, "Hey, this is only one little piece of this whole picture, and what's your understanding of where it's coming from and where it's going?" And in a way that must have been helpful, because he thanked me for it afterward. But that wasn't the point so much, as my own thinking process. I had a dream, and this is not in answer to your question, this is me bouncing off the walls. I had a dream recently. I was putting, I can't remember the exactness, but I can remember my interpretation of it. It was that now I am very quickly in a position to put somebody in analysis without a supervisor. Not a control case.

Supervisor: Uh-huh.

Candidate: And it was an anxiety trip. I was looking for you. (Laughs) "Where is my supervisor?" Besides a better understanding of the developmental process and how people get neurotic, the most valuable thing I think I've learned from the process of this case at the moment, and I may say something different next week from last week, is both to tolerate and to take advantage of what I frequently experience in my mind as transparencies. I one time made a map of the cradle of civilization in the Near East, the Middle East, from the dawn of time until the modern age, and there wasn't any way to make a map of it, so I made a land map and then I made like fifteen transparencies, and I frequently find myself thinking about that map because it's like all the transparencies are down all the time. And I can see through them. And not to be anxious when that happens, but to be able to take advantage of it. It's kind of a loose association (laughs).

Supervisor: Uh-huh.

Candidate: In my head, that has to do with using lots of sensations and thoughts and all of what the patient is saying, all at the same time. It's still not very fluid.

Supervisor: Well, I would say that you could think of this in some respects as a paradigm of a relatively uneventful, uncontaminated, minimal-parameters but effective classical analysis.

Candidate: That's nice.

Supervisor: That what has happened, as you suggest, is the unfolding of the whole series of layers and levels of meaning. That even though one can see from, say, the first session or two that lowest transparency, there is no urgency to get there right away. And to jump through all those other transparencies is not going to do you any good and would be a mistake.

Candidate: Uh-huh.

Supervisor: There's a process that has its own timetable.

Candidate: Well, and that it's a process of infinite, in some ways unmanageable complexity, that I will never fully master.

Supervisor: That's right.

Candidate: The complexity of a particular person. All the details on all the transparencies are not going to be available to me, but they don't have to be.

Supervisor: That's the important thing.

Candidate: Or they may be available and I may not know how to put them all together. Or they may go together in seventeen different ways at different times and they may all be valid.

Supervisor: That's right.

Candidate: And that it doesn't wrap up in a neat package, in which, you know, it doesn't wrap up in that same internally, wonderfully, internally consistent way in which there are no loose ends, in which you understand everything.

Supervisor: That's right. And that's an important thing to appreciate, to enjoy and not feel bad about. That you should be unable to wrap it all up or come to one comprehensive formulation that somehow encompasses everything.

Candidate: When cases are written up they sound like that, you know, because you can't, you just cannot capture easily, except possibly in some long diatribe, the infinite complexity and all of the things that you aren't wrapping up. You know, you write a paper because you wrapped something up. So when you read about cases they sound like—

Supervisor: Yeah, and then the other thing I think you can see here is that even though there was the business of the interruption for your pregnancy, even though there was the business of her job changes, of the struggle about how often she was coming, sometimes once a week, sometimes twice a week, sometimes missing a whole week.

Candidate: I would hate to even go back and tabulate and admit to how many sessions she missed. (Laughs)

Supervisor: That's also a good illustration of why it's important to charge the patient for missed sessions.

Candidate: Yeah.

Supervisor: It's also important to recognize, however, that maintaining an analytic posture vis-à-vis that behavior is the only appropriate position to be in. And not to try to manipulate or artificially influence or demand or set deadlines or expectations to try to change the behavior.

Candidate: Something else—

Supervisor: That would be a parameter. You see, to say "You get here or else" would be a major parameter.

Candidate: Oh, like the guy, who is it, who was here? It begins with an *s*. I have a brain like a sieve. He was here on the site visit and wrote up a case where he told the kid he had to stop smoking marijuana.

Supervisor: That was John S.

Candidate: That's it. And that's a parameter. Huh. Something else I—wait a minute, it just slipped my mind—oh yeah, something I've learned in this case, in the process of this case, which is probably just part of the process evolving in me, is to be curious. I guess I was before, but I think I have a much more highly developed sense of curiosity now, or of not actually wrapping things up, leaving them open. You know how sometimes you can say, "Aha, that's because of that. Now I know why; it's because of *x*" You wrap it up. And that curiosity extends over to me, and not being embarrassed with myself anymore, or ashamed of what my reactions are. I was reminded of this by your talking about how many times this patient has been absent, and how mad I eventually got, and how when we talked about it, how helpless I realized I was feeling and how I felt like I had the tools to help her but she wouldn't let me. And that led to an understanding that made it possible to interpret what was going on, that made it possible to make the next steps, and if I hadn't had that reaction, if I somehow had managed to anesthetize my reactor enough that I hadn't had that reaction, I would have had one less piece of information.

Supervisor: Uh-huh.

Candidate: Ahhh, and that's been freeing, too. That if I find myself doing peculiar things or having peculiar thoughts it's not because I'm a bad person or dirty or something. It's that something's going on that it's worthwhile being curious about.

Supervisor: Yeah, and to maintain also an ability always to be surprised. Never to figure, "I know it all now."

Candidate: Yes, I guess that's what I mean by not wrapping things up.

Supervisor: Uh-huh.

Candidate: Because at one time M.S. was talking about how everything, there's papers in every case, or something. I don't know exactly what he said, but that's the conclusion I drew, that he says there's papers everywhere.

Supervisor: He what?

Candidate: He sees papers everywhere. In every case there is a paper to be written.

Supervisor: Oh, you mean a write-up.

Candidate: Yeah, yeah. There is a paper to be written. There's a paper in every case. And at the time I thought I could not comprehend what he was talking about. But now I understand. I'm not saying that I would see a paper to write on every case. But there are far more surprises and interesting things, things that I didn't understand before, that this particular patient put together. Just questions, that's the thing I call curiosity.

Supervisor: Uh-huh.

Candidate: I would think this work would become undoably boring without that. Curiosity. Without that quality of surprise and curiosity.

Supervisor: That's right. And the other thing, of course, is that your capacity, your technical skills, your ability to work with this kind of material doesn't get established once and for all and then stop there. It's a continually evolving process.

Candidate: That is continually interesting or challenging.

Supervisor: Yeah. Which is different from internal medicine where you give a certain dosage of digitalis or—

Candidate: Whatever, nitro something or other. I don't even know what those things are.

Supervisor: The treatment is essentially prescribed and it becomes a very dull routine and every case is virtually the same, with very few or only minor variations. Also there is an evolutionary process in the interaction between the patient and the analyst, and each of them shifts and changes in that interaction over the duration of an analysis. So that you can feel and understand and say things at the end of the analysis that you couldn't possibly have said or thought or felt, and certainly not have presented to the patient, at the beginning.

Candidate: It's been an incredibly significant process, and I was so struck by those notes that you sent me because it was so exciting to see the evolutionary process at work.

Supervisor: Uh-huh.

Candidate: To see a piece of it from a different angle. You know, from the angle of you and me and my development, and me and the patient and her development. And my development, this kind of lets you see the—I can't think of another word besides evolutionary.

Supervisor: Uh-huh.

Candidate: Growth over time. It's very exciting.

Supervisor: Well, that brings me to the proposition I have for you. Which is as you know, intermittently I've made these tape recordings.

Candidate: Uh-huh.

Supervisor: And I have a contract with a publisher to publish a book on this, to intermittently show the development from the very beginning up to the end of the case. I've not mentioned it before because I wanted this to be a natural and uncontaminated experience. But what we have are a series of varying intervals, sometimes three months, sometimes a year difference between them, and in these intermittent glimpses one can observe enormous changes that don't come out if you try to chart them from one session to another.

Candidate: Uh-huh.

Supervisor: It's never been done before. The data have never been available. And it could illustrate both the analytic process and the changes in both the patient and the supervisory process.

Candidate: The development of an analyst.

Supervisor: Development of an analyst. So what I'm asking is two things. One, would you be willing to have me publish that? And two, would you be willing to write a chapter yourself on what the experience was like from your perspective, having read over all of the data?

Candidate: I think it's very exciting. I—

Supervisor: Have you read Wallerstein's book, *Becoming A Psychoanalyst* (1981)?

Candidate: Not entirely. I've read parts of it.

Supervisor: Well, look it up, because Howard Schevrin was the candidate involved, and he has two chapters in it.

Candidate: It's rather overwhelming, I didn't feel like reading it. (Laughs) I read some extensive reviews of it.

Supervisor: Well, yeah. But just read those two chapters anyhow because—

Candidate: The ones that—

Supervisor: Well, they're really, there are a number of chapters. I wouldn't read the others, ah, but I would read the ones that Schlessinger wrote, because he was the supervisor.

Candidate: Yeah.

Supervisor: And the ones that Schevrin wrote, because he was the candidate being supervised. His interpretation and Schlessinger's interpretation were quite different.

Candidate: Yeah, but see, you must have let me know somehow, because I figured that that's what your proposition was. I mean, I know you didn't sit here and tell me, but—

Supervisor: No, anyway, after I sent you that recording.

Candidate: Well, after I knew you were doing that and I knew you were taping a number of your supervisory things, but when I got to thinking about it, I realized you had done the recorded analysis and that it stands to reason.

Supervisor: I think it's, it's—as I read and re-read some of these sessions, and I'm going through them and editing them now, so I'm changing names and identifications, and so on—I see it's really a very exciting progression, that demonstrates an enormous amount about the analysis, about the patient-analyst interaction, about learning, about identifications. All kinds of things get demonstrated here. So I think it's going to be a significant contribution because it's never been done before.

Candidate: Who is the publisher?

Supervisor: International Universities Press is publishing it. And so what I'd like to do is run off a copy for you. I have copies of all my discussions and descriptions and I'll give you those, but also then the originals of the actual transcripts.

Candidate: Then that'll be the format? It sounds like then, it would be the—

Supervisor: The format would be the transcription of the supervisory hour followed by the supervisor's comments.

Candidate: I see.

Supervisor: It comes to about fifteen supervisory sessions, but spaced across—that's the trouble with the Wallerstein book, it was the first fifteen supervisory hours and that was it. No other data used. And most of the data to the book, most of the discussion of the supervision, occurred around the fifth supervisory hour.

Candidate: I was still trying to find out where the bathroom was by the fifth supervisory hour. (Laughs)

Supervisor: Plus it was the supervisor's account and recollection, dictated after the session.

Candidate: Untaped. Uh-huh.

Supervisor: Of a—

Candidate: Very intricate process.

Supervisor: Of a memory. It's a very intricate process and cannot be captured except—I mean even this just doesn't capture all of it. But nevertheless, I think it might be a good project for you, having looked over this data, to present it from your perspective: what it was like both in the analysis and in the supervision, picking out as you go along whatever things you want.

Candidate: Uh-huh.

Supervisor: And make it a thirty or thirty-five page paper. From the candidate's perspective, which I think is going to be very important.

Candidate: What kind of time frame are you talking about?

Supervisor: Well, the contract calls for March eighty-five, but if we're a little late it's not too big a deal. The other thing that's going to be a complication, not a complication but another element, is that, and it relates again to this business about her being a supervised case, is whether or not to get the patient's permission. We have two problems here. I don't think anybody would identify her as the case. But conceivably she might somehow identify herself.

Candidate: Uh-huh.

Supervisor: So it's a problem. If you ask the patient's permission you put a burden on the patient; if you don't, you end up vulnerable to violation of her privacy. So even if no one else could recognize who she was, the fact is she could recognize herself. So I would think probably what we would best do is have me, as a representative of the Institute, rather than you, write to her and ask her permission.

Candidate: Yes. I think if I were to write to her it would continue this notion that it wasn't her analysis, that I was using her.

Supervisor: That's what I was trying to say. So I think it would be appropriate for me, in some official capacity, or maybe the director in his official capacity, to write and give a brief portrayal of what the project is, so that she can give a reasonably informed consent, but not necessarily giving all the details.

Candidate: Uh-huh.

Supervisor: Which is what I did with my first case that was in the book. (Dewald, 1972)

Candidate: Was that after it was finished?

Supervisor: After it was finished, right. I don't do it right away. Because the termination phase is too much—

Candidate: Well, yeah, I don't even know if she'll pay her final bill, but I think I should wait for a while.

Supervisor: Definitely.

Candidate: I expect she will, but I suspect she will wait a few weeks.

Supervisor: Okay, well, I'll get that material to you sometime in the next few weeks and then you can think about it.

Candidate: I wanted to also say that one of these days, probably by the middle of spring, I ought to graduate.

Supervisor: Uh-huh.

Candidate: Well, if I do this chapter for this book it may be more like June before I graduate, because I have to write up my cases. And I think sometime, whenever a space becomes available, and I don't know how to, I don't know what the routine of this is, I think that sometime I would like to be officed here.

Supervisor: Be officed here? Uh-huh.

Candidate: Yeah, in this building, and I just thought I would mention that, because I think there's probably a waiting list of people or something.

Supervisor: Well, the usual—

Candidate: I suspect you have to graduate.

Supervisor: I don't know whether there is a waiting list or not, but by and large people should graduate, should have graduated.

Candidate: Yeah, I just got a letter today saying that I—

Supervisor: Then their counselor—how many supervisory hours do you have?

Candidate: I don't have two hundred yet.

Supervisor: How many have you got?

Candidate: That's what's holding me up. A hundred seventy-eight.

Supervisor: That's all?

Candidate: Yeah, really one eighty-two, as of the end of October.

Supervisor: Well, we had about what—a hundred and twenty? What about your second case?

Candidate: My second case went fifty-three hours supervised. Yeah, and he quit.

Supervisor: That's one-seventy, and then the patient quit, so it's one-seventy.

Candidate: Yeah, and then my third case, which is real erratic. I've only seen my supervisor twelve times.

Supervisor: That's where the delay is then.

Candidate: Well, also in the second case. You know if my second case had flown, if I was still seeing my second case, I'd be over it today.

Supervisor: Fifty-three hours was what? A year and a half?

Candidate: No, more than that, but I don't remember. But I need only eighteen more hours and I've a fourth case starting. So I figure by June I'll have eighteen more hours somehow or other. Twist my supervisor's arm and make him see me every week for a while.

Supervisor: Sure, I would. Absolutely.

Candidate: So anyway, you were about to tell me what the—

Supervisor: The procedure usually is to—what I would do is I would write a letter to the director of the Institute saying you're interested in arranging to office here when and if an opening or opportunity develops, and you would like your name put on the waiting list. And do it right now.

Candidate: Oh, do it right now?

Supervisor: Sure.

Candidate: Okay, and say that I should graduate in the spring?

Supervisor: Expect to graduate in June or by June and in the meantime you'd like your name on a waiting list for any openings that might—

Candidate: That wouldn't be impertinent? Okay, I will do that.

Supervisor: But as of now I don't think anybody's planning to move out.

Candidate: I don't expect there to be any openings for the present. I would expect it might be another five years.

Supervisor: It might, but you never know, somebody drops dead or somebody decides to move out or somebody retires from practice, or whatever.

Candidate: And you don't know when something like that is going to happen.

Supervisor: No, you never know.

Candidate: I don't know, I mean I'm just signing a new three- or five-year contract in February. I'm not standing at the door huffing and puffing.

Supervisor: No, I wouldn't.

Candidate: All I'm saying is that in my long range planning I would consider that a reasonable—

Supervisor: Yeah, sure.

Candidate: It would be good for me, I think.

Supervisor: Now what M. had to do, he had to take the office here and retain his lease in his old place.

Candidate: I think I would have to sublet. And I have a very desirable office situation. Several people have asked me about it over the years, so I think I could.

Supervisor: That can be done. That'll be good. It's very appropriate. So I would, yeah, but write him and tell him that you're interested.

Candidate: That's what I wanted to know from you, is whether that would—

Supervisor: Would he please put your name on the list.

Candidate: Okay. Thank you.

Supervisor: Sure. Good luck now.

Candidate: And you're going to send me that stuff?

Supervisor: I'll send it as soon as I can get it copied.

Candidate: Okay. And I'll be in touch with you.

Supervisor: Fine. Good. Bye-bye.

Supervisor's Comments

The description of the patient's fears that the clinic and training situation meant that the analysis had not really been her own raises a number of issues. It shows how things said in an early diagnostic evaluation may have a continuing impact on an analytic process, even to the very end of the treatment experience. It shows also that certain significant factors may be inherent in a treatment setting and situation, and may not be analyzable in the sense of being eliminated as active foci of anxiety and resistance; they persist even though subjected to analytic scrutiny. The candidate demonstrates her tolerance of this irreducible complication, her recognition of possible distortion by the patient, and her own independent judgment of the diagnostic analyst's formulations.

In spite of these inherent limitations and resistances the patient seems to have accomplished more than she set out to do, and to have achieved significant awareness and tolerance of how the structure of the analytic situation has impacted upon her. The candidate accepts the realities of the patient's perceptions and the limitations imposed on the outcome. This is supported by the supervisor's explanation as well as the candidate's understanding of the patient's position and recognition of the degree to which the patient is now capable of self-sustained and self-initiated behavior. Both patient and candidate can comfortably acknowledge the candidate's countertransference needs and responses. The supervisor's comment, "Very nice," serves as immediate reinforcement for the candidate's behavior in coping with these potentially difficult issues.

The patient's experience of her silence during the last session and the candidate's reporting of that material indicate the significant resolution of transference distortions, and a capacity on both their parts to reflect upon and accept the work they have done and the experience they have had together.

The patient recognizes that the freedom she has achieved and the changes she has undergone were beyond her comprehension when she began the analysis, and is capable of tolerating imperfections in herself and of recognizing that many issues require continuing work. She demonstrates reasonable equanimity at the final loss of the analyst after this session.

The candidate's description of their actual parting at the end of the session shows sophistication and sensitivity in her understanding of the material and of the patient's needs, and illustrates her capacity to respond in an appropriately analytic way. The supervisor provides immediate support for this interaction, and the candidate continues to elaborate her recognition of the intensity and meaningfulness condensed in the final experience of saying goodbye.

Following these interchanges about the departure the candidate is apparently reassured sufficiently to permit the return from repression of her memory that the patient had embraced her during the leave-taking. Her spontaneous reaction to it is immediately supported by the supervisor. He knows this has been a totally new experience for the candidate and he wants her to feel comfortable in it. This enables her to elaborate further the experience and its implications both for her and for the patient.

In the candidate's description of the patient's decision not to get a cat at this time she demonstrates awareness of the patient's progress; and the patient herself expresses an appropriate capacity to recognize reality, to tolerate separation from the candidate without immediate recourse to a substitute object, and ultimately to arrive at a comfortable decision after considering the factors involved.

The supervisor's broad question ("What did you learn from the case?") is an impossible one but is designed to focus the candidate's attention away from the immediate clinical material toward a macroscopic view of what the experience has meant to her. The candidate's response shows her in her role as a supervisor of psychotherapists as she integrates her experience through the use of a personalized metaphor; she shows a sophistication with regard to the therapeutic process, as well as an appreciation of her changed status. Simultaneously she expresses (with some amusement) a mildly regressive yearning to retain the relationship with the supervisor ("Where is my supervisor?").

But she is able to continue her metaphor and to take the kind of position the supervisor had hoped for; she reflects upon such features of the analyst's role as tolerance of ambiguity and uncertainty and the capacity to recognize complexity. The supervisor supports her with his own formulation with regard to the nature of the overall analytic process. The candidate is able to elaborate on this formulation herself, and the discussion continues on a colleague-to-colleague level.

The supervisor returns to the clinical situation and reinforces the importance of an analytic posture vis-à-vis the patient's acting out with regard to absences from the analysis. The candidate expresses her appreciation of the importance of a continuing sense of analytic curiosity as well as the importance of acknowledging and working with her own countertransference responses and reactions (see session 88). It is probable that the generally comfortable and tolerant atmosphere throughout the supervision regarding the analyst's countertransference has contributed to this development within the candidate. She is able at this point to recognize the parallel process occurring between the patient and herself and herself and the supervisor.

This leads to a discussion of the present study and the supervisor's interest in having the candidate participate with him. The candidate indicates her previous recognition of the existence of some kind of project. Her awareness of her own learning process is humorously demonstrated in her comment, "I was still trying to find out where the bathroom was by the fifth supervisory hour."

Candidate and supervisor then discuss some of the administrative details regarding the candidate's progress in the Institute, as well as the candidate's desire someday to have her office in the Institute building. The supervisor accepts this in a matter-of-fact way and encourages the candidate's perception of herself as worthy of such consideration; he deemphasizes the candidate's initial doubts ("That wouldn't be impertinent?").

It is on this note, as colleagues discussing reality issues important to both of them, that the supervisory experience comes to a close.

Chapter 22
Contribution

Mary M. Dick, M. D.

In this chapter I will explore aspects of my experience as the supervisee in the supervisory process described and discussed in this book. First I would like to address the study itself and describe how this chapter came to be.

The supervision was already well under way and the learning alliance established when Dr. Dewald told me that he was interested in further studying the supervisory process and asked if I would object to his taping some of our sessions. It is significant that this discussion took place the first time I saw him during his recovery from a sudden and very severe illness which could conceivably have caused permanent intellectual as well as physical disability. I had been relieved to see that although he was obviously not completely recovered, he was functioning well and had found a project in which to involve himself. I felt that this was an important step in the process of recovery. I believed that he was intermittently recording sessions with various supervisees and that he would perhaps write a paper using excerpts from the various supervisory processes.

These two fantasies, that the taping was a vehicle for my supervisor's recovery and that I was one among several being studied, protected me from feeling too exposed or self-conscious. Sometimes it was apparent that a session was being taped, as when the recorder was on the desk between us. At other times it was on the bookcase and I could not tell for certain that it was running. At one point, when the tape recorder had not been visible for months, I was surprised to see it on the desk again. I had assumed that either the study had been completed or my supervisor, who was now back at his work full time, had lost interest in it.

Immediately after the termination of my patient's analysis, Dr. Dewald told me in detail about this study and suggested I make a contribution to it. He gave me the typed transcripts of the recorded supervisory sessions along with a copy of his analysis of each session. I found it extremely difficult to read this material, and it was several months before I could fully understand why.

Initially I felt somewhat anxious and self-conscious reading the transcripts, as I had felt on other occasions when listening to myself on tape or watching myself on videotape. I felt somewhat exposed and narcissistically vulnerable to humiliation. This had been my first analytic case, and I had made errors, been awkward, and had not always understood clearly what was going on. The case, however, had gone well and I had learned a lot in the process. I believed my supervisor would not publish anything that would be seriously embarrassing to me, so I resolved to set aside these feelings of exposure.

I read some of the transcripts and my supervisor's discussions. I felt anxious and exposed in a different way. I felt it would have been less anxiety-provoking had I seemed even more inept in the transcripts, and had my supervisor been more critical of me in his discussions. I had to come to terms with this anxiety of narcissistic gratification before I could read further.

I felt exposed also in writing of my experience in the supervision. I spent some time reading the literature regarding supervision in psychoanalytic training and composing didactic discussions of the process. Since early in my training, however, I had believed that there was not enough raw clinical data in the psychoanalytic literature. In this context, a detailed description of my personal experience as the supervisee in this case is raw clinical data. This view allayed these feelings of exposure.

Finally I was able to approach the task at hand without significant interference from these anxieties. I read and re-read the transcripts, immersing myself in the experience. I set aside a day to write a draft. Everything I wrote seemed somehow false. I was perplexed. When I wrote of my solid trust in and evolving freedom with my supervisor, it seemed facile and shallow. I kept wanting to describe him as rigid, dogmatic, dictatorial. I knew he was not. I kept wanting to say I had lied to him, fooled him. I knew I had not. I felt angry and vindictive. I re-read transcripts. I kept being vaguely bothered by an image of him as rigid and dictatorial. Something was not making sense. At the height of my confusion I literally could not figure out what year the analysis had ended.

In this state I read and re-read portions of the transcripts. Suddenly I became conscious of an experience I had had of my supervisor of which previously I had been unaware. The confusion cleared immediately and I began to laugh. This unconscious transference to my supervisor had been the source of the feeling of falseness when I had tried to describe my experience. Exploring this unconscious transference allowed me to see and understand the analytic and the supervisory processes more fully. In the following pages I will describe my experience as a psychoanalytic candidate in supervision with my first psychoanalytic case. I will try both to describe the experiences of which I was most conscious at the time and to elucidate the concurrent transference experience of which I became fully conscious only recently.

I had always found it particularly difficult to be a beginner. If this was unavoidable, I preferred to master a skill privately. As a child I disliked being clumsy in sports and avoided participating in them. Twenty years later I hung in the back of the group in the operating room, never wanting to be chosen to "learn by doing." I preferred at least to appear to know what I was doing.

Therefore, it was with particular anxiety that I approached my first supervised case as a psychoanalytic candidate. I was still in the midst of my own personal analysis with much work yet to do. I felt relatively comfortable being a psychoanalytic patient. I "knew how" to do that. I did not "know how" to be a psychoanalyst. I knew as a psychotherapist I tended to talk too much and be too supportive. I worried about how to act and what to say. In the year prior to beginning my first case I had read a great deal of theory, which at that point seemed quite removed from "real" experience with people. I felt I was still trying to learn the language of psychoanalysis. I knew that every highly technical field has a highly condensed language of its own, in which single words and short phrases refer to complex concepts that are foreign to the beginner, and that the process of mastering that language was really the process of mastering the conceptual frame and theory of the field.

The mastery of the language of psychoanalysis is further complicated by what Ekstein (1969), in discussing supervision in psychoanalysis, calls "blind spots": "the not yet analyzed part of himself, the lack of continuity within [the candidate], his lack of awareness of his own unconscious reactions . . . [that] make it impossible for him to see the material of the patient fully" (p. 325).

A very memorable example of this kind of blindness interfering with my ability to master the language of psychoanalysis was my persistent inability to comprehend the concept of transitional phenomena in any but the most concrete terms until the subtle transitional object quality of my own behavior during my analyst's vacations was adequately recognized and interpreted. I had read and re-read Winnicott's "Transitional Object's and Transitional Phenomena" (1953), and it was still unfathomable. My colleagues discussed it as if they understood it. I felt ignorant. Perhaps I was not bright enough to be an analyst. Shortly after my own transitional phenomena were addressed in my analysis I had occasion to re-read this article and was suprised to find it clearly written and comprehensible.

I had this experience again and again throughout my training until ultimately I came to recognize this kind of difficulty in understanding (which for me is signaled by a persistently concrete approach to something) as a sign not of intellectual deficiency or of the obscurity or complexity of the issue at hand, but of some conflict of mine being remobilized and demanding attention. However, as I approached my first case such hard-won insight was still to be gained, and I struggled blindly, without understanding the blindness, with metapsychology and the theory of psychoanalytic treatment. I felt unprepared for this first case. At the same time I was eager to get started, for in the supervisory process I hoped to learn things more relevant to doing psychoanalysis than it had seemed I could from didactic courses.

I was relieved to find that my supervisor was someone I had had for a psychotherapy supervisor as a resident, with whom I had enjoyed working and from whom I felt I could learn. I admired him. He would help me. In retrospect I realize I idealized him. He is an articulate, well-published, nationally known psychoanalyst. He was also the medical director of the institute where I was a candidate. I had the fleeting grandiose fantasy that he had chosen me to supervise because I had a particular aptitude to be a psychoanalyst. While this fantasy initially helped mitigate my anxiety over being a beginner, having to learn by doing and exposing my efforts to scrutiny, it too quickly proved to be a burden in that I felt I had to prove myself worthy of such fantasied attention from such an idealized figure. I had to take process notes during sessions because I knew I would not write down the details of my ignorance and ineptitude if I waited until later. I was embarrassed by my blind spots and by my lack of knowledge, information, and skill. I felt anything I had to say regarding how I understood a particular interchange would be far too elementary or not complete enough.

These feelings made it difficult for me to appreciate the truly benevolent and encouraging behavior of my supervisor, and intensified the effects of criticism. The patience that he afforded me in this regard, his willingness to describe to me repeatedly what he heard in the clinical material and how he understood it, gave me time to recognize and work through some of these blocks to the very comfortable learning alliance that in time developed. However, as I approached this first patient my concern about being adequate in the eyes of my supervisor still loomed large. In retrospect I believe the regression I was then experiencing in my personal analysis had intensified my fears of being found inadequate. I remember feeling generally quite vulnerable, woundable, without my accustomed protections. "Because of the regression taking place during the training analysis [the candidate] meets psychoanalytic material in a very different way and, again, analogous to the child, goes through a process where at first he will primarily learn and work for love, a need for acceptance . . ." (Ekstein, 1969, p. 324).

It is also interesting to note, however, since from this distance I cannot distinguish my feelings prior to the beginning of the supervised analysis from those in the early months, that my first patient came into analysis with a terrible fear that she would be found inadequate by me.

In my first contacts with the woman who was to be my first case I felt stiff, formal, and unnatural. I was self-conscious and worried about making a mistake, saying the wrong thing, talking too much. Several years later she described her initial experience of me as cold and wooden, inscrutable. In my anxiety I both overvalued and at the same time frequently failed to see and understand the impact and significance of everything I said and did. For instance, in the early weeks of the analysis, some workmen began to hammer very loudly in the next office on the wall next to my couch. It disturbed my train of thought, made it difficult for me to hear, and seemed to be disturbing the patient. It was my job to provide an "analytic atmosphere." I excused myself, left the office, and told the workmen in no uncertain terms that they were disturbing me in my work. They stopped. I walked back into my office with, I am sure, an obvious look of satisfaction. I had reestablished the "analytic atmosphere." I was surprised when my supervisor questioned my action and suggested that the incident might have fortified my patient's primitive superego and that I should watch for it to come up again later. He was, of course, right.

Supervisory sessions in this early phase were difficult. I forced myself to take detailed process notes and to review them before sessions. My supervisor's insistence that we follow the process in detail, as painful as it was, in time allowed me to begin to relax. *He* did not seem perturbed by my inexperience. I realized I was having, and I continued for some time to have, difficulties typical of a candidate in training. In addition to the anxieties mentioned above, I felt guilty for being a beginner. I believed that someone more experienced could "help" my patient faster and "cause" her less anguish. These feelings made it particularly difficult for me to address my patient's feelings and fantasies about her being a clinic patient and my being in training (see supervisory session 42). I felt guilty for charging her to see me because I was learning from her, using her. Sometimes I forgot to give her the bill, and I did not "notice" when she was a couple of months late paying. When I did attempt to address her manner of paying her bill (early in the analysis she paid me the very next day and once asked for permission to pay me by the fifteenth of the month), I tended to accept concretely her rationalized explanations. Obviously my feelings of inadequacy and guilt hampered my ability to effectively investigate these issues with my patient.

I also felt guilty because I knew I was uneven in my approach to my patient. I now understand that I was still in the process of identifying with different teachers and had not yet consolidated an identity of my own as an analyst. Unevenness occurred as I shifted from one identification to another. It occurred also because I sometimes became so enchanted with a recently understood theoretical construct or new personal insight that for a day or so I would see all of my patients through the prism of that single construct or insight. In time I learned to be suspicious of my vision when I felt suddenly brilliant or enlightened, or when I found myself wanting to make the same interpretation to several patients on the same day. I felt guilty for how the process of my learning must be affecting my patient. My guilt interfered with my freedom to investigate what her experience might be in that regard. When I became pregnant one year into the analysis, I felt guilty because I was acutely aware that my pregnancy and maternity leave would repeat in the analysis some of what had been so traumatic in this woman's childhood. I was so constantly nauseated in the early months of my pregnancy that I had occasion to worry about how I should behave as an analyst were I to throw up in my waste basket. I was embarrassed and felt guilty because of my preoccupation with my pregnancy.

All of these feelings made it very difficult to sort out my patient's material. Was she or was she not preconsciously aware of my pregnancy? As I recently re-read supervisory sessions 42 and 43 it was inconceivable to me that I had not at the time recognized more acutely my patient's preconscious awareness of my pregnancy. The canceled sessions referred to in this material were sessions I canceled for genetic counseling and amniocentesis. I believe this is yet another problem typical of inexperienced analysts in training. As an analyst it takes skill and experience to keep one's view within an analytic process relatively steady despite major personal life events ("falling in love," pregnancy, death of a loved one, divorce, etc.). Not only did I feel guilty for becoming pregnant in the middle of this woman's analysis, and for being preoccupied with my pregnancy; I was aware also that the intensity of my own feelings in response to this long-awaited pregnancy were "crowding the field," making it difficult for me to hear my patient. Later in my training, I was better able to sort through these feelings, so that when faced with the death of a member of my family, I was able without guilt to cancel my patients' appointments to allow myself the time I needed. When I returned to work my mourning did not seem to distort my capacity to listen to and hear my patients. Or perhaps I was more aware of its distorting influence and could better "correct" for it.

At least in part as a function of my inexperience, lack of confidence, blind spots, and idealization of my supervisor, I at times accepted and applied too concretely my supervisor's constructs and suggestions. At that time my conscious experience was that it was difficult for me to ascertain whether I was uncomfortable with a suggested construct or interpretation because it was not quite right or because I had unresolved conflicts in that area. Very late in the analysis my patient described that in the early years of the analysis she had periodically felt that I was "not quite in sync" with her and that at times I was trying to cram my theories down her throat. Her compliance was not addressed and analyzed until late in the analysis.

Once I became comfortable with my supervisor, and once the learning alliance had been established, I continued to feel a subtle caution of which I was only periodically fully conscious. The pervasiveness and power of this caution did not become clear to me until I read the transcripts of these supervisory sessions. I realized then that I had had at least two simultaneous experiences of my supervisor, one conscious and one preconscious, which fluctuated in intensity and which I acted out, both inside and outside the supervisory situation, to a greater or lesser degree at different times. These two experiences intermingled in the way the transference and the "reality relationship" or therapeutic alliance do in an analysis, with the difference that the learning alliance and reality relationship in my supervision were fortified by a previous relationship, by many contacts and interchanges outside the supervisory frame, and by our joint focus on the task of teaching and learning the technique of psychoanalytic treatment.

My conscious experience is the simplest to address. It was what made the learning alliance possible. I had previously found and continued to find my supervisor to be an energetic teacher who was usually patient and tactful. He had never humiliated me for my ignorance, and when he pointed out mistakes or countertransference problems it was with an attitude that made me feel that such blunders and blindnesses were to be expected and could be corrected or worked through. His energetic willingness to "teach"—to review psychoanalytic concepts, to describe psychoanalytic technique and the rationale behind his recommendations, and to delineate his thought processes in response to case material at whatever level of complexity I could manage at the time—usually made me feel that in time I would understand and that I could learn.

This is not to say that he was perfect. Sometimes he seemed distracted or preoccupied. Sometimes he talked way over my head. At times he would go off on tangents that did not seem very relevant to the clinical material. Occasionally he seemed not to listen to me and would seem to be forcing his ideas on me. Sometimes I felt that I knew some of the reasons for his lapses.

Two notable examples are included in the transcripts published here. The first time I saw him after his sudden and very severe illness, I went to his home. I was glad to see him. Everyone at the institute knew how dangerously ill he had been. I had been naturally concerned about him. Although I had not really felt ready to be on my own, the case had gone well while he had been sick and I had had the conscious feeling of "minding the store"—the analysis, the patient and myself—until he could return. I had not contacted him, because I had felt he had enough to do to recover and cope with having been so sick. I was not surprised when in that first supervisory session he was not as sensitive and in tune as he had usually been. I had had relatively recent personal experience with the narcissistic withdrawal that comes with serious illness, and I had not even been critically ill.

Another "lapse" that I felt I understood when it happened was in session 91. I had wanted to talk with my supervisor that day because I was having difficulty understanding the shifts in the analytic process. I had found him more dogmatic and less sensitive than usual. Everyone at the institute was aware of the tension engendered by the upcoming site visit. There was also a general awareness among candidates of a power struggle among the institute faculty. I remember mentioning the experience within a day or so to a colleague who was also in supervision with him; we agreed that our supervisor must be uptight about the site visit. These interchanges and the others like them had for me then, and continue to have, more of the flavor of the reality relationship of the learning alliance than do the experiences I will try to describe next.

There was another way in which I experienced my supervisor which was ephemerally conscious, elusive yet subtly pervasive. I believe this second experience of my supervisor, of which I have only recently become fully conscious, will be most visible if we divide the supervision simplistically into two parts: before and after I was able to see and interpret the false self defenses in my patient. In the earlier period, although I was usually able to work fairly openly with my supervisor, I often thought of him as rigid, dogmatic, and judgmental, someone I needed to be careful to please. I occasionally described him as such to colleagues. Like all transference phenomena, it does not bear up under scrutiny, but I substantiated this preconscious view with fragments of experience ripped out of the contextual frame that would ordinarily have made them comprehensible. I will describe two of these fragments. In both of these situations, especially the first, which did not involve me personally, I had consciously felt that I had understood the dynamics of the situation at the time and had dismissed it. The preconscious memory fragment remained, substantiating my view of my supervisor as a dogmatic, potentially explosive, unpredictable man to be "handled with care."

At the time I began my training, self psychology was beginning to be read and widely discussed. There were the inevitable ideological splits in the faculty. My supervisor was a vocal and articulate critic of self psychology. At a Society meeting where a presentation from a self psychological stance had been made, there had been the kind of heated discussion that tends to intensify polarization, and my supervisor had made what seemed to me to be a passionate statement criticizing some vital aspect of the theory. His face had been red and the veins in his neck had stood out. This memory fragment, of him speaking heatedly with flushed face and bulging neck veins, remained long after the actual event had been dismissed. The second fragment came from an interchange in the supervisory situation. Quite early in the supervision I had tried to talk about possible self psychological issues in my case. I felt that my supervisor had cut me off, saying with striking emphasis (in my memory-fantasy he was sometimes even shouting), "This is not a narcissistic personality disorder!"

Another manifestation of this transference was the way I experienced my own need to identify with this supervisor. I had approached psychoanalytic training with some reservation: jokingly, I said I had an allergy to dogma. Even prior to the beginning of this supervision I had begun to identify with my supervisor, as I had to a greater or lesser extent with other faculty members I admired. I was conscious of the conflict between the need to identify and the threat that that need posed to my previously established sense of self, which included my allergy to dogma of almost any kind. Intuitively I understood that the forging of my identity as an analyst would involve a profound revision of my sense of self. I was periodically aware of internal struggles in this regard: my periodic resistance to the process; later, confusion over the multiplicity of identifications; and, ultimately, the struggle to sort through the many identifications to establish a coherent personal identity of myself as an analyst. For a period of time early in this supervision, I felt that this process of identification was being forced on me against my will. Although my reality experience told me otherwise, I felt I was expected to become a reflection of my supervisor, that he required total allegiance. If I had other allegiances and identifications, for instance, if I considered views other than those of "classical theory," it would not be tolerated. When I chose for my second supervisor someone who seemed to be a proponent of a more self psychological approach, I felt almost as if I should do it surreptitiously. I remember telling my second supervisor that I had chosen him because I felt I needed a contrast to help me find myself as an analyst. Still, I felt sneaky, and more disloyal and cautious than the situation warranted.

So, simultaneous with the reality relationship of the learning alliance, which I have described above as generally very positive and open, I had a preconscious transference to my supervisor that required that I protect myself from him. Only once that I remember was I truly conscious of this transference. Sometime early in the supervision I realized that I was terrified of my supervisor. This did not make sense to me because I had known him previously and had had such positive experiences with him. I felt that my terror was "crazy" and forced myself to discuss it with him in the next supervisory session. He did not seem surprised or disturbed but said that we could see that I had the same transference to him that my patient had to me. I was relieved that he responded in such an accepting way; at the same time, I felt he was telling me that this was for me to deal with in my personal analysis. Had I become conscious of the distortion again I would again have forced myself to discuss it with him. I did not.

As I write this, it is almost inconceivable that I was then so unaware of vast discrepancies and inconsistencies. This feeling of incredulity reminds me of how I felt in my personal analysis when a distortion was revealed and made conscious. So, under the influence of this transference, although I felt generally open with my supervisor, I was also cautious. Some thoughts I did not discuss with him. If I had thought about something in detail but did not know if it was "safe" to discuss it with him, I would ask a question about it, try to get him to talk about it first. If it then seemed safe, I would go on and elaborate my thoughts. This transference subtly interfered with my authenticity and therefore made it difficult for me to accept without reservation my supervisor's positive evaluation of me. He did not, after all, really know me. Because of the distorting effect of this transference, the view that I could give my supervisor of the analysis through me was subtly and ever so slightly "false," not false in fact but subtly "off."

My supervisor viewed the analysis through me and told me what he saw. Sometimes his constructs seemed slightly "off" to me, but I did not know how or why. Sometimes we would discuss it. Sometimes I would decide that I must be suffering from blind spots. Occasionally I would simply submit, perhaps because of the pressure of this transference. Sometimes I was able to set the construct in question aside until there was more data available, but sometimes I immediately applied it, frequently too concretely, to my case. At times, even though I had been consciously aware that my supervisor and I were not communicating and had decided therefore to set his suggestions aside until we were in better communication, I would find myself blurting out one of his interpretations in an analytic session with my patient. Perhaps the same forces were at work when I found myself blurting out things that had made sense in a supervisory session but which I had determined to wait until an appropriate time to introduce (for example, the dream in session 43). In such instances, I found my behavior perplexing.

In the second year of the supervised analysis I presented the case in a continuous case conference. I began to listen to and hear my patient more independently of the vision of her I had developed with my supervisor, which I now realize was restricted by the distortions in my transference. I became acutely aware of my patient's lack of personal authenticity. I re-read material on the false self. I felt that perhaps a false self defense was part of the source of an uneasiness I had been having about the case but had been unable to articulate. The uneasiness was part of the reason I had been anxious to present the case in a continuous case conference. I set about trying to interpret this defense. It was an important characterological defense for my patient, and the interpretation of it led to a deepening of the analytic process in which she became significantly more authentic. For instance, she would now bring her unhappy, disheveled self to a session after a migraine headache, when previously she would have stayed home until she was more presentable (supervisory session 87).

Because the case conference leader and my supervisor were known to have ideological differences, I presented this material to my supervisor rather cautiously (session 87). I was not sure if I would "get in trouble." I presented the clinical data and was encouraged by my supervisor's "Good." I went on to describe my *tentative* thoughts regarding a false self defense, ultimately saying, "I've never talked with you about false self and don't really know what you think about the concept, or even what I think about it yet." My supervisor did not seem perturbed and I elaborated further. I still, however, had to ask some direct questions regarding false self. These questions and the interchange that followed were multidetermined.

As I tried to sort through my various teachers' and supervisors' biases, I often went over the same construct with several of them individually, searching for my own orientation. I had learned a lot from this supervisor and had found it particularly helpful to try to articulate my thoughts with him because of his willingness to grapple with clinical and metapsychological issues and because of the clarity with which he expressed himself. In addition, however, I remember feeling distinctly relieved: that he was taking this all in stride, was not exploding. I now realize that this served to correct the transference distortion. I felt free to further elucidate my thoughts. I see now that in the following supervisory session (88) I was more spontaneous and authentic.

The freedom I felt in that session to "let off steam," to allow my supervisor to see how frustrated and angry I was with my patient's habit of "flooding" me with rich material and then skipping sessions so that the material could never be effectively understood or interpreted, allowed my supervisor to see and to help me to see how my patient was experiencing her analysis as a reenactment of the traumatic urethral stricture. I had previously discussed with him my patient's frequent cancelations. We had understood this behavior in various ways. However, the new understanding that began to evolve with my spontaneous, unrestricted expression of my frustration and anger allowed me to make interpretations that precipitated major progress in the analysis.

In retrospect it seems that once I had adequately interpreted the false self defense in my patient, the preconscious distorting transference I had had to my supervisor, although not suddenly eliminated, became significantly less powerful in my interchanges with him. From this distance I cannot detect whether I expressed it in other ways. I am aware that after the working through of the false self defense in my patient's analysis I gained a greater, more substantial feeling of confidence in my evolving clinical judgment, and in my growing ability to use myself, my knowledge, my senses, to understand my patients. The pleasure and satisfaction I had always derived from my work deepened. By the fourth year of the analysis, during a break in the supervision of several months, I was able spontaneously and independently to use my total experience of my patient to understand and interpret what in time were verified to be core experiences and fantasies (body as phallus and primal scene exposure). My pleasure and my sense of growth and accomplishment are obvious in the transcripts of the next supervisory sessions, six weeks later, during which I reported the events to my supervisor (sessions 99 and 100).

In order to try to describe a distortion in my experience of my supervisor, I have artificially divided the supervised analysis and the supervision into two segments, with the interpretation of the false self defense as the watershed. While perhaps facilitating elucidation of this distorting transference, this division carries with it the risk of retrospectively distorting the process, by making it seem that the change in me was more sudden and dramatic than in reality it was. This is the same distortion that occurs when clinical data is condensed to background and highlight a specific interchange in a complex analytic process. It is easy to lose sight of the fact that focusing on one aspect of a process retrospectively distorts the actual import of that aspect in the total situation as well as subtly distorting the overall shape of the experience.

Were transcripts of all the supervisory sessions available, it would likely be easier to reconstruct the actual evolution of the development that ultimately allowed me to see and interpret the false self defense and to overcome the power of the distorting transference to my supervisor. And perhaps it would be somewhat easier to identify the multitude of factors (my personal analysis, which I had terminated some six months previously; this supervision and others; experience in classes, in case conferences, and with other patients; etc.) involved in that development. However, it would never be possible to know with certainty the relative importance of each of these factors and the intricacies of their interrelatedness. This is part of the nature of psychoanalytic data. It is never possible to encompass and understand the implications of all the material, and the process of the selection and organization of data to be analyzed at any one time always introduces biases and distortions. But despite this inherent difficulty we must continue to view data from various vantage points, remembering always the effect that the vantage point itself has on the shape of the data and therefore on the conclusions that might be drawn.

As I have reviewed my experience in this first supervision, the parallelism of the two processes—the analysis and the supervision—is striking. Retrospectively, it seems to have been pervasive. There is the conspicuous parallel between my patient's false self and my own subtly restricted expression with my supervisor prior to my interpretation of my patient's false self defense. The increased freedom I felt and evidenced subsequent to this interpretation further substantiates the parallel. Two equally obvious and concrete examples of this parallelism follow.

My patient expected me to find her inadequate. One of the ways she experienced me (in the paternal transference) was as unpredictable, explosive, dangerous. The image of her father in a rage with red face and bulging neck veins came frequently to her mind. She had learned to attune her behavior to her perceptions of her father and his expectations (supervisory session 87). The similarity between this image and the memory fragment of my supervisor with red face and bulging neck veins is obvious. And of course I used the latter to buttress my preconscious belief that my supervisor was dangerous and explosive.

In the dyadic maternal transference my patient felt I required her total allegiance. She was frightened to show me important and positive aspects of her life outside of me. I would be angry, feel hurt, feel she did not appreciate me. Perhaps I would attack her, most assuredly I would withdraw myself from her, act as if she did not exist. The similarity between this experience and my concerns regarding allegiance to my supervisor and his theoretical orientation is apparent.

These are concrete examples of a pervasive parallelism that became evident as I re-read the supervisory transcripts and reflected on my experience. In one way it was as if psychological forces in my patient resounded on the strings of my psychological structure, just as intense infrasonic vibrations from elsewhere can elicit sound from the strings of an otherwise silent piano. It is, however, far more complex. It was as if the tune already being played by the vibrations from a multitude of forces (the supervision etc.) was subtly distorted by unconscious aspects of my patient's transference to me, so that in retrospect it seemed to have been an echo of that transference.

Ekstein and Wallerstein (1958) pointed out a relationship between the problems a student therapist has learning in supervision and the problems the patient has in the therapy being supervised. Where the "problems about learning" in the supervision parallel the problems in the therapy being supervised, an analysis of the difficulties in the supervision can provide further understanding of the therapeutic process and thereby effect movement in the therapy. According to this model, resistances the supervisee has to learning in supervision (e.g., my unconscious transference to my supervisor) could, if explored, prove to be a mirror in which aspects of the therapeutic process might be viewed.

It is obviously an oversimplification to consider all learning difficulties a supervisee might have to be only the mirror image of aspects of the patient-therapist relationship. Resistances to learning are expressions of the individual character and ego defenses of the student. The role of student itself and how the individual supervisee experiences and responds to that role, the role of teacher and how the individual supervisor experiences and responds to it, the way these two individuals interact and their roles intermesh, as well as the context in which the supervision takes place, are all crucial determinants of the shape of the supervisory process. For instance, as Bromberg (1982) asserts, a supervisee needs to assume a stance from which he might learn from his supervisor without feeling humiliated at his lack of knowledge. He suggests that this stance requires that the student be respectful of his supervisor and his supervisor's views.

> Part of the respectfulness is tied to respecting the supervisor's own self esteem needs coming from his felt competetence as a supervisor . . . the supervisor's natural investment in his own expertise. So the student will in various ways tend to unconsciously leave out or minimize in his relationship with his supervisor, the most pronounced qualities in himself which may be there when he feels in the role of the authority. . . . If someone needs to minimize some aspect of his identity to keep it out of a particular type of relationship, he will, as Issacharoff says, present himself in the relationship as someone minus that quality when he is in danger of that aspect being too clearly exposed. [Bromberg, 1982, pp. 107–108]

Perhaps the unconscious experience I had of my supervisor was simply an outgrowth of my role as a student. Early in the supervision I was conscious of feeling that my supervisor was the master craftsman from whom I, the neophyte, might learn the craft: There were times I consciously went beyond respect and deferred to his judgment. This was especially true early in the experience, at times when I felt serious doubt as to my own view of the therapeutic process, whether because of lack of knowledge, blind spots, countertransference, or personal turmoil. Perhaps the entire unconscious "false self transference" could be understood as an outgrowth of my initial disavowal of my own evolving authority. Such a disavowal would also certainly constitute a "problem about learning" in supervision as defined by Ekstein and Wallerstein (1958), and in this case there does seem to have been a parallel between the analysis and the supervision. There is obviously no one way to account for the emergence of what appears to be a parallel process in a psychoanalytic supervision. The relationship between supervisor and candidate is enormously complex and cannot be encompassed by a single theoretical explanation.

Without fully understanding the multitude of forces that lead to the development of parallel process in supervision, I have found myself considering the implications of parallelism for the teaching and learning of psychoanalysis. Using transcripts of taped supervisory sessions, Caligor (1981) documents an instance of parallelism between a therapy and a supervision in which the supervisor became aware of his participation in parallel process while listening to the tapes of the supervisory sessions in a study group. He then effectively addressed the problem that had developed in the supervision. This is an example of the focal utilization of the parallel process in order to understand and resolve a difficulty in the supervisory relationship. In the period of time in which I was most influenced by my unconscious transference to my supervisor, I was not aware of my behavior, nor was I conscious in any useful way that there was some subtle difficulty in the supervisory relationship. I assume, since he did not confront me with the difficulty, that my supervisor was likewise unaware of it. The supervision and the analysis seemed both to be progressing well.

In order to use a parallel process systematically in the understanding of a case, the process would have to be more constantly available for scrutiny. This would require that the supervisee be able to expose and investigate the process in great detail with the supervisor, who would also be the object of the distortions. The supervisor would have to encourage such exposure and be likewise open to self-disclosure. This would be particularly difficult in an early supervised case, while the supervisee is still engaged in a personal analysis and in the subordinate role of student.

In the interests of further improving my skills as an analyst, I in time developed the capacity to examine and expose some of my own inner process without paralyzing embarrassment and shame. By the time this capacity had evolved I had terminated my personal analysis and had developed an identity as an analyst that allowed me to use myself and my process as a tool of my trade. An identity as an analyst seems vital to being able to use one's own process openly. I believe that my graduation from the Institute freed me further in this regard: I was then truly a junior colleague, more a free agent, and no longer a student vulnerable and subservient to institutional politics and loyalties. Graduation strengthened my identity as an analyst in my own right. Although I had felt really quite free in supervision late in my training, this freedom was increased by graduation and the formal acceptance of me as a junior colleague by the Institute faculty. I feel that supervision that demanded use of the parallel process early in my training, within the context of a program where I knew I was being constantly evaluated, and also while I was still engaged in my personal analysis, would have been extremely difficult if not impossible. It must also be remembered that parallel process is by its nature not fully conscious.

I have described aspects of my experience as a psychoanalytic candidate in supervision with my first analytic case. This supervision was one part of the larger process of becoming a psychoanalyst. In ways that I did not fully understand until much later, my personal analysis and the didactic instruction were background work, the initial essentials required in the process of becoming a psychoanalyst. Ornstein (1967) once wrote, "consider personal analysis and courses in theory and technique as preparatory for the actual learning how to analyze"

(p. 29). I do not want to underestimate the importance of a personal analysis and assiduous reading, because both are necessary to the process, but it was to a large extent through psychoanalytic supervision that I became a psychoanalyst.

Psychoanalytic supervision has on occasion been described as a kind of master-apprentice relationship. Many skills are learned and taught in this manner. Some involve the use of a tool external to oneself, such as those used by tool and die makers. In some, one's body is the instrument to be mastered, as in gymnastics. Many skills obviously require the integration of several abilities. A tool and die maker must develop manual dexterity and integrate manual and visual skills with a rudimentary understanding of the workings of the machine. Some skills require intellectual agility and "learning to think" in a new way. Many skills involve learning to hear or see, and integrating the sensory percept with intellectual knowledge or previous experience. For instance, to track wild game numerous sensory percepts and previously acquired knowledge and experience must be integrated. To teach a complex skill like tracking, the master must impart his knowledge of animal habits and patterns. He must also attempt to show the student what he hears, sees, smells, and senses, and how he integrates these percepts with his knowledge and experience and thereby reaches conclusions and makes decisions. He cannot actually show the apprentice the state of mind, the particular state of acute alertness, required for him to notice the sensory details, nor can he project this state of mind and his highly developed sensitivities into the student so that the student might see what he has not been seeing and hear what he has not been hearing. The master can persistently delineate his percepts for the student while the student begins to build up a body of experience tracking with the master and then begins to hear and see for himself.

During training, the psychoanalytic candidate must integrate various kinds of knowledge, percepts, and experiences. Ideally, in a personal analysis the student analyst gains an emotional and intellectual familiarity with his own psychic conflicts and at least in part resolves them. He also develops the skills and sensitivities necessary to continue self-exploration and analysis after the termination of his formal analysis. In didactic classes and through reading, the student gains an intellectual familiarity with the theoretical constructs on which psychoanalytic treatment is based. He may even understand them. But it is in supervision and in case conferences that these different kinds of knowledge are integrated. Until the beginning of case conferences and the first supervised analytic case, the two bodies of experience, understanding, and knowledge (from the personal analysis and from didactic classes) are quite disparate. One hears and reads that the analyst uses himself as an instrument, but it is in supervision that

> there emerges the recognition that hour after hour, day after day, the analyst is confronted not only with a demand upon his knowledge but with the fact that all facets of his own personality structure—from the more superficial 'habits' and the ingrained characterological peculiarities to the depth of his instinctual strivings become part of the process of psychoanalysis. [Ornstein, 1967, pp. 454–455]

In addition to the most obvious integration, of experience in personal analysis with experience in classes and with patients, the student must integrate different kinds of knowledge and thought—the more intuitive with the more didactic, primary process with secondary process. Like the master tracker of wild game, my supervisor freely described to me his perceptions as he listened to the case material I presented. He detailed the ways in which he analyzed or understood these percepts. He tried to allow me to see how his mind worked, which was enormously helpful to me in these integrative tasks.

Not only must the candidate master and then integrate the experience and knowledge gained from didactic classes, personal analysis, and clinical work; he must also develop the capacity to enter into, manage, and utilize the state of controlled regression employed by a psychoanalyst in analytic work with patients. Balter, Lothane, and Spencer (1980) describe the "analyzing instrument" (a term coined by Isakower and expanded by these authors):

> The analyzing instrument has two constituents: a voluntary

> and controlled, situation-specific and goal specific regressed state of mind in the analysand and a near identical one of the same nature in the analyst. These parts function together through mutual evocative communication, leading to the elucidation of the analysand's unconscious fantasy-memory constellations. [p. 474]

In this model, the student analyst must develop the capacity to enter into a particular state of mind (described as a subsystem in the analyst's ego by Balter and his colleagues) which corresponds to the state of mind of the analysand during free association: a regression of ego functions facilitated by the analysand's attention to his own psychical perceptions and his suspension of critical attitudes and purposeful reflection, and limited by the task of verbalizing to the analyst. Analogously, the analyst must attend to the analysand's communications and to his own internal perceptions with uncritical, evenly suspended attention.

> The voluntary suspension of critical activity, in and of itself, induces a regression in ego functioning. *Thus such a regression must also be assumed to occur in the analyst during the functioning of the analyzing instrument, i.e., in his subsystem in the ego.* It should be noted, however, that the regression in the analyst is limited because, and to the extent that, he attends to the task of understanding the analysand's verbal communications. . . . There will result in the analyst's subsystem a regression that is easily shifted according to the vicissitudes of his or her attention, but that is also relatively stable and controlled. [Balter, Lothane, and Spencer, 1980, p. 485; italics in original]

The student analyst must develop the capacity to enter into and work from within this very special state of mind. This is an enormously complex task, and there is considerable difference of opinion among psychoanalytic educators as to how supervisors might best facilitate the development of this skill in student analysts.

My supervisor periodically talked about the controlled regression on the part of the analyst and stated that the analyst must listen with "evenly suspended" or "evenly hovering" attention. I heard the words and understood the theory. It was a long time, however, until I truly understood, experientially, what the words meant. How does one effectively communicate the functioning of the analyzing instrument to a beginner? Perhaps, just as the master tracker cannot instill in his apprentice his own state of mind and automatic attention to particular details, but must wait, watch for, and then encourage the development in the student of the required acute alertness and sensitivity, so the supervising analyst must watch, wait, and encourage. My supervisor's active approval and encouragement when I began to develop the capacity to enter into the fluid state of mind required for the functioning of the analyzing instrument, his nonjudgmental patience as I tried to learn to balance the forces that allow and yet control the regression, reinforced and thereby facilitated the further development of this state of mind and my struggle to learn to work within it.

In this chapter I have described some aspects of my experience as a psychoanalytic candidate in supervision with my first analytic case and the part that supervision played for me in the larger process of psychoanalytic education. The description is obviously not comprehensive and is entirely personal and therefore idiosyncratic in detail. No two supervisees, supervisors, or supervisory processes are alike, just as no two analyses are alike. Clinical research in psychoanalysis is based on the explication and investigation of individual psychoanalytic processes. Similarly, this material, from a single supervisory process, might be useful in furthering the investigation and understanding of supervision and psychoanalytic education.

Chapter 23

Synthesis and Summary

The concept of a process implies the unfolding of an interaction or relationship over time, with observable change and progressive direction to the behaviors in question. The juxtaposition in this volume of early and late sessions from a lengthy supervision permits the observation of significant changes occurring in the relationship between candidate and patient in the psychoanalytic situation, and between supervisor and candidate in the supervision.

In addition, the candidate has provided an articulate and vivid description of her own experiences and recollections of the supervisory process. Her candor and ability to express herself attest her sensitivity and personal development as a psychoanalyst, as well as a capacity for effective self-analysis against her own resistances. Though written retrospectively, her account provides ample illustration of her private experiences, thoughts, associations, and perceptions in relation to the interactional phenomena that occurred between herself and the supervisor, as well as their latent meanings. This is analogous to the experience of the patient in the analytic situation, where a variety of thoughts and meanings remain private and are not always shared verbally with the analyst.

The intensity of her experience of various transference and reality phenomena involving the supervisor stands in sharp contrast to her observable behavior. The supervisor had on many occasions recognized the candidate's anxiety, particularly in the earlier phases and while the candidate was still in her own personal analysis. It must be noted, however, that this candidate's overt anxiety and other manifestations of restricted or inhibited behavior were not significantly greater than those occurring in other candidates at the same level of training. The supervisor expects every candidate to present a variety of learning needs and blind spots due to cognitive and experiential limitations, as well as affectively toned countertransference responses to the patient and transference responses to the supervisor (see Chapter 2). Only if these difficulties persist and learning becomes stalled, however, do these issues need to be addressed directly. The candidate is used as his own control and the assessment of progress is made on the basis of continued learning and sustained development toward the goal of functioning effectively in the role of psychoanalyst.

Psychoanalytic treatment and psychoanalytic supervision are evolving processes which though significantly different have certain features in common. Both situations involve considerable repetition and redundancy. The analyst must be willing to explore and work through much of the same material with the patient again and again, in the anticipation that with repetition the patient's awareness and capacity for more direct and full experience and expression, as well as mastery of the particular conflicts involved, will be enhanced. This process typically involves deepening awareness in the patient, followed by resistance, retreat, and avoidance of progress as anxiety is mobilized, and then a return to awareness, deeper recognition, and further working through as the patient achieves new insights and mastery of the issues.

A parallel situation exists in supervision. The candidate's learning needs require repeated explanations of technical and theoretical concepts. The supervisor must go over the same material with the candidate until a degree of comfortable mastery has been achieved, and must be willing to subordinate his own interests and level of function to the candidate's learning needs.

The analyst empathically immerses himself in the experiential and therapeutic needs of the patient, recognizing that the patient's experience and understanding may be significantly less developed than his own; but he must also appreciate the patient's needs for active awareness, understanding, and mastery if therapeutic progress is to occur. Similarly, the supervisor immerses himself in the learning needs and limitations of the candidate, recognizing the discrepancy between their levels of experience.

The candidate's presentation emphasizes striking similarities between her own intrapsychic experiences in the supervision and that of her patient in the analytic process. Much of this parallel process she did not consciously recognize during the actual educational experience; it became clear only in retrospect, after she had read and re-read the transcriptions. It was largely imperceptible to her supervisor as well. His basis of evaluation was a comparison of the candidate with other students he had had in supervision with their first case. On that scale the candidate seemed to be progressing rapidly. Although aware of the idealization manifest in the candidate's behavior, the supervisor adhered to the pedagogical principle that it is best to acknowledge and accept the existence of transference reactions in candidates as part of the expected evolution in supervision; these phenomena need be consciously and deliberately addressed only if there is evidence of significant interference with the learning alliance or the candidate's analytic work.

There are times when the candidate in the supervisory situation manifestly relates to the supervisor in ways which recreate the candidate's experience with the patient. This concept of parallel process may allow the supervisor access to the affective tone and experience of the analytic situation. It is a function of the candidate's empathic identification with the patient in the presentation of material to the supervisor; the candidate thereby responds unconsciously in the nondirective supervisory situation in behavioral patterns imitating those of the patient toward the analyst.

The supervisor, in turn identifying empathically with the candidate in the analytic setting, may thereby become aware of the feeling states, reactions, and behavioral processes and patterns the candidate had experienced vis-à-vis the patient. While on some occasions this mode of understanding and access to data may be available and useful, it is difficult to assume that it is a constant phenomenon. The supervisor's ability to discern when a parallel process is occurring becomes a limiting factor here, and the temptation to assume it as constant must be resisted.

In both the analytic and the supervisory relationships there are few absolute standards of comparison or evaluation. There are some general expectations of how a patient in analysis might react, as well as how the candidate in a supervisory situation might behave. However, there are significant individual differences and for the most part patients and candidates must be used as their own controls in determining progress.

Modification of behavior in patient or candidate occurs in a spiraling fashion, by which the same phenomena are approached repetitively but at increasingly deeper and more manifestly open and free levels of experience. In the treatment setting the patient is compared to his previous level of communication and function, and progress is assessed, both macro- and microscopically, by comparing the individual's status at one point in time with regard to a variable with his status at some previous time with regard to the same variable. A similar comparison serves the supervisor in evaluating the candidate's progress toward increasing independence and capacity to function as an analyst. In the supervisor's comments here, the same words are used at different stages to describe the candidate's progress, but the meaning and implication of these words is in part defined by the context in which the description occurs and the advancing baseline from which the candidate's responses and behavior are being observed.

Another significant aspect of this form of learning is the necessity for the supervisor to avoid "overloading" the candidate. This involves a process of selection by which the supervisor chooses what he considers the candidate's more important learning needs at a specific time, while deliberately ignoring or minimizing other issues. Much like an analyst preparing an interpretation in the treatment setting, the supervisor selects from the material presented by the candidate those aspects in the supervisory process that are most prominent and readily accessible. This approach is particularly important early in the supervisory experience, when problems of great complexity may be more than the candidate can reasonably be expected to master. As the supervisory experience evolves and experience and knowledge accumulate, new and more complex issues and phenomena may be addressed.

An illustration of this would be the candidate's finally being able to bring up the issue of the "false self." The candidate had repeatedly experienced the safety of the supervisory situation through conscious and preconscious episodes of self-exposure without humiliation. Preconscious correction and working through of the candidate's transference to the supervisor had already begun. As emphasized in the candidate's report, access to consciousness for both participants regarding this transference is restricted, and the ability to expose and acknowledge such reactions during the supervision is a function of the candidate's progress. It was not until a sufficient degree of acceptance and resolution of the transference had been achieved that the candidate could, in retrospect, acknowledge the intensity of her responses. In the absence of any disruptive phenomenology, the supervisor had no way of detecting these transference reactions.

The likelihood is that even had the supervisor been aware of the existence and intensity of the candidate's inhibition, its interpretation to the candidate might well have constituted an "overload," having the same effect as a correct but premature interpretation in a treatment setting; resistances might have been heightened and genuine experience and working through would have been unlikely. It is probable that in the analytic setting the patient, too, had her own timetable for exposure and mastery of these issues. She too needed sufficient experience and working through of transference distortions before the issue could be meaningfully interpreted to her.

Another aspect of the supervisory process is the gradual shift in the supervisor's behavior as the relationship unfolds. In the data presented in this study there is a demonstrable change in the supervisor's behavior as he observes and responds to the learning needs of the candidate. In the earlier phases he serves as an active model, revealing his thought processes and making direct suggestions as to interventions the candidate may find useful. The supervisor frequently makes specific recommendations, offering several options but serving a somewhat directive function. As the analysis progresses and the candidate demonstrates increasing mastery of the technical and theoretical aspects of the analytic situation, the supervisor becomes less actively directive and serves more as a sounding board and facilitator for the candidate's attempts at understanding and technical intervention.

An interesting illustration of these complexities in the supervisory interaction is the candidate's perception and response to the supervisor's statement, "This is not a narcissistic personality disorder" (Chapter 22). This incident had occurred relatively early in the supervision, and the supervisor's perception was that the candidate was becoming concerned that her patient might be "sicker" than initially thought; the experience of presenting the case seemed to be creating unnecessary confusion at a time when she was not in a position to cope with it. The supervisor's intention in his remark was to reassure the candidate as to the essential analyzability of the patient without invoking parameters. The candidate's transference experience of the intervention as a dogmatic command illustrates the endless possibilities for missed communication in the supervisory experience.

The supervisor has deliberately presented himself as a model for the candidate to emulate through partial identification with his attitudes and behavior. But simultaneously there is the anticipation that the candidate will select only those aspects of the supervisor's model that fit with and subserve the candidate's own learning needs and personality. These ultimately will be combined with identifications arising out of other learning experiences, and the candidate will develop his own composite but personal therapeutic style. The supervisor actively presents a model, but he should not anticipate or insist that the candidate follow it completely or exclusively. Tolerating the candidate's independence and decisions not to accept his suggestions may at times involve narcissistic injury to the supervisor, who must be able to tolerate such responses for the sake of the candidate's ultimate independence and development of an idiosyncratic therapeutic style and capacity for understanding.

Throughout this lengthy supervisory relationship the supervisor demonstrates a commitment to the candidate's well-being and learning needs (parallel to the expected commitment of the candidate as analyst to the welfare and therapeutic needs of the patient). Some of the attendant experiences result in unconscious identifications that are not specifically the focus of attention for candidate and supervisor. Additionally, the supervisor, through his behavior and attitude, demonstrates a scientific curiosity, as well as a willingness to move from one level of conceptualization to another, thus broadening the candidate's approach to the understanding of the patient and the patient's material. By drawing comparisons to other clinical data, by references either to the literature or to other cases, the supervisor seeks to enhance the candidate's awareness of the broader implications of the specific clinical experience.

Most of the success of the supervisor's pedagogic activities is dependent on the innate and acquired talents of the candidate. These may at times limit the effectiveness of the teaching, the rate at which it can take place, and the satisfaction and sense of generative fulfillment available to the supervisor. Similarly, supervisors vary widely in their teaching skills, style, and capacity to relate to the needs or personality of the candidate. Happily, in the instance documented here, candidate and supervisor demonstrate a relatively "good fit." In closing it is perhaps appropriate to emphasize once again the multitude of variables in any long-term therapeutic or supervisory situation, and to reiterate that such an undertaking is a creative enterprise in which each participant is influenced and limited by the input and responsiveness of the other.

References

Arlow, J. A. (1963), Conflict, regression, and symptom formation. *Internat. J. Psycho-Anal.* 44:12–22.

——— (1966), Depersonalization and derealization. In: *Psychoanalysis: A General Psychology*, ed. R. M. Lowenstein, L. M. Newman, M. Schur, & A. J. Solnit. New York: International Universities Press, pp. 456–478.

——— (1984), Disturbances in the sense of time. *Psychoanal. Quart.* 53:13–37.

Balter, L., Lothane, A., & Spencer, J. H., Jr. (1980), On the analyzing instrument. *Psychoanal. Quart.* 49:474–503.

Bromberg, P. (1982), The supervisory process and parallel process. *Contemp. Psychoanal.* 18:92–111.

Caligor, L. (1981), Parallel and reciprocal processes in psychoanalytic supervision. *Contemp. Psychoanal.* 17:1–27.

Dewald, P. (1972), *The Psychoanalytic Process.* New York: Basic Books.

——— (1980), Handling of resistance in adult psychoanalysis. *Internat. J. Psycho-Anal.* 61:61–70.

Dorpat, T. L. (1973), Panel: Research on the therapeutic process in psychoanalysis. *J. Am. Psychoanal. Assn.* 21:168–181.

Ekstein, R. (1969), Concerning the teaching and learning of psychoanalysis. J. *Amer. Psychoanal. Assn.* 17:312–332.

——— Wallerstein, R. S. (1958), *The Teaching and Learning of Psychotherapy.* New York: International Universities Press, 1972.

Fleming, J., & Benedek, T. (1966), *Psychoanalytic Supervision.* New York: International Universities Press, 1983.

Gill, M. M., & Hoffman, I. (1982), Analysis of Transference, Vol. II. *Psychological Issues,* Monogr. 54. New York: International Universities Press.

Greenacre, P. (1975), On reconstruction. *J. Amer. Psychoanal. Assn.* 23:693–712.

Hurn, H. T. (1973), Panel: On the fate of the transference after the termination of the analysis. *J. Amer. Psychoanal. Assn.*, 21:182–192.

Kubie, L. (1958), Research into the process of supervision in psychoanalysis. *Psychoanal. Quart.* 27:226–236.

Luborsky, L., & Auerback, A. (1969), The symptom context method. *J. Amer. Psychoanal. Assn.* 17:68–99.

Menninger, K. A., & Holzman, P. S. (1973), *Theory of Psychoanalytic Technique.* New York: Basic Books.

Ornstein, P. (1967), Selected problems in learning how to analyze. *Internat. J. Psycho-Anal.* 48:448–461.

Pfeffer, A. (1961), Follow-up study of a satisfactory psychoanalysis. *J. Amer. Psychoanal. Assn.* 9:698–718.

Pollock, G. H. (1977), The mourning process and creative organizational change. *J. Amer. Psychoanal. Assn.*, 25:3–34.

Ross, N. (1960), Rivalry with the product. *J. Amer. Psychoanal. Assn.* 8:450–463.
Schlesinger, N., & Robbins, F. (1974), Assessment and follow-up in psychoanalysis. *J. Amer. Psychoanal. Assn.*, 22:524–567.
Schuster, D. B., Sandt, J. J., & Thaler, O. F. (1972), *Clinical Supervision of the Psychiatric Resident.* New York: Brunner/Mazel.
Tyler, R. (1974), *Coper Commission I: The Tripartite System of Psychoanalytic Education.* New York: American Psychoanalytic Association.
Wallerstein, R. S., Ed. (1981), *Becoming a Psychoanalyst.* New York: International Universities Press.
——— Sampson, H. (1971), Issues in research in the psychoanalytic process. *Internat. J. Psycho-Anal.*, 52:11–50.
Winnicott, D. W. (1953), Transitional objects and transitional phenomena. *Internat. J. Psycho-Anal.* 34:89–97.

Index

Active summary by candidate, 9-10
Adolescent ego and sexual developmental models, 122-123
Affective responses
  awareness of, 114
  of candidate, 205
  of supervisor, 24, 26
Aggression
  in transference, 23, 383-384
  undoing of, 338
Alliance
  learning. *See* Learning alliance
  therapeutic, patient evaluation and, 44
Ambivalence
  anxiety and, 343
  toward brother, 113
  of supervisor in final supervisory phase, 26
  termination process and. *See* Termination
American Psychoanalytic Association requirements, 12
Anal conflicts, 223-224, 229
Analysis. *See also* Analyst; Analytic process
  conceptual frame and theory of, 451
  decathexis of, 405, 421
  extraneous knowledge from source other than patient in, 314, 319
  language of, 451
  new material emerging late in, 398, 407
  suitability for, 4
  supervision of. *See also* Supervisor; Supervision
    conceptualization and goals of, 11
    nature of, 2-5
  termination phase of, 25-26
  therapeutic regression in, 14-15, 113, 276
  thinking process of, 23-24, 206
Analyst. *See also* Analysis; Analytic development
  clinical theory used for idiosyncratic material by, 230
  curiosity of, 436, 446
  departure of, 71
  grief and sadness at loss of, 320
  identity as, 12, 467
  major personal life events and, 455
  oscillating between microscopic and macroscopic observation, 181, 186
  reciprocal mourning process and, 399-400, 407-408
  role and function of, 12
  substitute object for, 433, 446
Analytic curiosity of candidate, 229, 436, 446
Analytic development, 114. *See also* Candidate
  awareness of, 209-210
  middle supervisory phase, 24
Analytic process. *See also* Analysis
  description of, 58-59, 71-72
  development of, 114
  macroscopic view of, 21, 162, 181, 186, 277
  significant and extensive deepening of, 160
  structural change in, 299
Analytic work in termination process, 385-386. *See also*
Termination
Analyzing instrument, 469-470
Anger
  candidate expression of, 462
  guilt and, 68-70
Anxiety
  ambivalence and, 343
  candidate, 472
  of narcissistic gratification, 449
  separation and maturation during termination process and, 367

Apprentice, 2, 16, 468
Arlow, J. A., 239, 252, 375, 386
Audio-recorded transcriptions of supervisory sessions, 1, 7-8
Auerback, A., 5

Balter, L., 469, 470
Becoming a Psychoanalyst, 2
Beginning supervisory phase, 18-21
Behavior
- modification of, 475
- rapid oscillation in, 366

Benedek, T., 1, 18
Blind spots, 451, 455
Body equated with phallus, 253, 259, 273, 274, 292, 462
Bromberg, P., 465

Caligor, L., 466
Candidate. *See also* Student
- active dialogue of supervisor and, 186
- active planning and initiative in educational experience by, 75, 89-90
- affect intensity of, 205
- analytic curiosity of, 229, 436, 446
- anxiety of, 472
- awareness of levels of communication, 275
- changes in, during training, 468
- changes in relationship between patient and, 472
- confidence in self, 251
- constructive interchanges with supervisor, 117-118
- countertransference outcome, 445. *See also* Countertransference
- empathic experiential level interactions, 139, 239-240, 252
- evaluation problems and, 25
- excitement in learning process, 209
- first six-month summary of, 38-45
- guilty feelings of, 454
- helping to conceptualize analytic interaction, 58-62, 71-72
- identification with supervisor, 386, 458-459
- increasing sophistication of, 140
- independence of, 386, 425
  - conceptualizations and, 230
  - curiosity and, 229
- initiative of, 386
- interpretive stance of, 140
- learning needs of, 474
  - supervisor indicating, 116
- macroscopic perspective, 21, 162, 181, 186, 277
- major personal life events, 455. *See also* Candidate, pregnancy of
- observation of own interventions, 81-83, 90
- organized associational sequence, 298
- overloading of, 475-476
- pregnancy of, 132-134, 140, 158-159, 277, 454
- progress in development of, 15
- second case in analysis, 88-89, 93
- sense of being colleague, 12, 250, 300
- substitute object for, 433, 446
- summary and synthesis capacities and, 141, 297
- talents of, 478
- technical error by, 347, 366-367
- termination and, 406, 407. *See also* Termination
  - parting with patient at, 430-432, 445
  - professional responsibility in, 388
- tolerance of doubt and uncertainty, 254
- transference to supervisor, 15, 21-23, 450, 457-460
- uncertainty of, 73-74, 90
- understanding and dealing with conflicts and aggression, 73

Change
- in candidate during training, 468
- in derivative behavior, confirmation through, 277-278
- process of, 14
- in relationship between candidate and patient, 472
- in roles in final supervisory phase, 25

Clinic care as issue to patient, 426-427, 444-445
Clinical material
- correlation of theory and, 21
- generalization of, 208, 278

Clinical process, responsibility for, 9, 24
Clinical theory
- as guide for checking formulations, 139-140
- idiosyncratic material and, 230

Colleagues, sense of, 12, 250, 300
Commitment of supervisor, 478
Competitive reactions, 23, 113

Concept of false self, 172-173, 184, 461, 462, 463, 466
Conceptual frame and theory of psychoanalysis, 451
Confirmation process in derivative behavior, 277-278
Conflicts
  ability to carry out sublimated function and, 406
  final supervisory phase, 26
  in giving and receiving, 60-62, 72
  termination process and, 367, 368. *See also* Termination
Constructive criticism, 17, 117-118
Content, interpretations of resistance and, 152, 164
Controlled regression, 469-471
Countertransference, 90, 205
  acknowledging and working with, 445, 446
  beginning supervisory phase, 19-20
  emphasis on manifest material and, 111, 117
  intervention inspired by, 298
  middle supervisory phase, 21-22
  opening channels of association and, 196-198, 207-208
  patient evaluation and, 44
  personal disruption and, 332-334, 344-345
  supervision goals and, 12
  supervisor and, 423
  termination phase and, 345, 399-400, 407-408, 422-423
Creativity, scientific, 27
Curative process in patient, 295-296, 299

Dahl, 5
Decathexis, 405, 421
Decision making, independent, 386
Defenses
  depersonalization, 239, 251
  termination phase and, 367, 407
  varieties of, 167-169, 182
Dependency
  resistance to, 43-44
  transference to supervisors and, 23
  wishes, 43
Depersonalization, 239, 251
Derivative behavior, changes in, 277-278
Description of patient, 29-30
Diagnostic evaluation as issue to patient, 426-427, 444-445
Displacement, transferences by, 305, 315, 319, 322, 383; *See also* Transference
Distractions of supervisor, 457
Dreams
  analysis of, 162
  as reflections of changes, 342
  shifting levels of communication and, 114
  termination phase and, 412, 422
Dyadic maternal transference, 464
Dyadic relationship, 148-149, 162
Dynamics
  of technical interventions, 24
  of termination, 408. *See also* Termination

Education
  awareness of progress in, 209-210
  master-apprentice, 2, 16
  psychoanalysis and, 2-5
    analytic therapeutic regression in, 14-15, 113, 276
  responsibility for student needs in, 9, 24
Education committee, 27
Educational principles of supervisory process, 15-17
Effective intervention, strategies for, 140
Effective learning, 16-17
Ego defenses, 137-138
Ekstein, R., 1, 464, 466
Empathic experience, 139, 239-240, 252
Evaluation, 475
  candidate progress
    problems in, 25; reports of, 27-28
  patient, 29-53. *See also* Patient evaluation and routine
  reports
Expectations in beginning supervisory phase, 18
Experiential form of learning, 20-21
Expression of frustration and anger by candidate, 462

False self concept, 172-173, 184, 461
Fantasies
  acceptance of, without guilt and shame, 160-161
  of bodily damage, 253
  homosexual transference, 174, 185
  modification of core, 292-296, 299
  neurotic symptoms and, 368

oral incorporative, 148-151
termination phase and, 410-411, 421-422
Father transference response, 86-87, 92
woman analyst and, 315-316, 322
Fearful reactions, transference and, 23
Feedback, 17
Fees, issue of, 217-218, 228
Final supervisory phase, 25-27
Fleming, J., 1, 18
Free association capacity, 71
Frustration, expression of candidate, 462

Genetic associations, 298
Gill, M. M., 5
Giving, conflicts of receiving and, 60-62, 72
Goals
of learning, 16
of supervision, 11-13
Greenacre, P., 208-209
Greenson, R., 401, 408
Grief
final supervisory phase, 26
at loss of analyst, 320
termination process and, 368
Growth of analytic functions in middle supervisory phase, 24, 114
Guilt
anger and, 68-70
candidate and feelings of, 454

Hoffman, I., 5
Homosexual transference fantasies, 174, 185

Idealization of supervisor, 452, 455
Identification with supervisor, 386, 458-459
Identity as analyst, 12, 467
Illness of supervisor, 70, 74, 457
Independence
candidate, 21, 25-26, 386
curiosity and, 229, 436, 446
patient, 404
Inferential constructions, 105-109, 115
Initial psychoanalytic evaluation, 35-45
candidate first six-month summary and, 38-45
disposition and, 38
Initiative, candidate, 75, 89-90, 386
Inquiry, scientific, 27
Interpretation
of content or resistances, 152, 164
generalized and specific, 73
mental processes in, 23-24
of resistances, 138-139, 152, 164
supervisor model of, 156, 165, 208, 387, 477-478
Interrelation of intrapsychic experience with reality situations, 88, 92-93
Interrupted observations in studies of supervision, 7-8
Intervention
strategies for effective, 140
supervisor model of, 156, 165, 208, 387, 477-478
technical, dynamic understanding of, 24
Intrapsychic change, signs of significant, 424
Intrapsychic experience, reality situations and, 88, 92-93
Intrapsychic processes, patient capacity to tolerate, 160
Intrapsychic reorganization, 297, 300

Knapp, 5

Language of psychoanalysis, 451
Learning
candidate excitement in, 209
collaborative nature of teaching and, 206. *See also* Learning alliance
distinctions between teaching and, 16
effective, 16-17
experiential form of, 20-21
goals of, 16
selection of, 116, 474, 475-476
and teaching of basic principles, 163
Learning alliance, 19
candidate view of, 455-456
evidences of, 93-94
indicators of well-established, 115
solid and mutually gratifying, 278
Learning needs of candidate, 116, 474. *See also* Learning
Longitudinal time, 375-376
Loss, patient tolerance of, 404-405
Lothane, A., 469
Luborsky, L., 5

Macroscopic perspective, 21, 162, 181, 186, 277
Major personal life events of analyst, 455;

See also Pregnancy of candidate
Masochistic organization, 384
Master-apprentice relationship, 2, 16, 468
Masturbation issues, 241, 252-253
Maternal dependency state, 44
Maternal persecutor, pain as, 236, 251
Maternal transference, dyadic, 464
Maturation
process of, 14
in termination process, 367
Menninger, K., 395, 432
Microscopic issues, 21, 181, 186
Middle supervisory phase, 21-25
Models of interpretation and intervention, 156, 165, 208, 387
Modification of behavior, 475
Mother
interactions with, termination phase and, 424
patient dependence on, 44
as persecutor, pain and, 236, 251
transference and
dyadic, 464
separation-individuation phase in, 58-59
Motivation in beginning supervisory phase, 20
Mourning
final supervisory phase, 26
reciprocal, analyst and, 399-400, 407-408
termination process and, 368
Multiple function principle, 208

Narcissistic gratification, anxiety of, 449
Negative transference, 342, 386, 387
Neurosis, transference, 298
analyst functions in patient experience of, 156-157, 165
regressive, 159-160, 161, 162
renunciation of, 388
resolution of, 320, 388, 405-406, 408, 421
Neurotic behavior. *See also* Neurosis, transference
fantasies behind, 368
reactivation of, 15
shifts in, 384-385
Notes, clinical presentation and, 5, 6

Object, substitute, 433, 446
Objectivity in termination phase, candidate, 407
Observations, oscillating between microscopic and macroscopic, 181, 186
Observers in treatment setting, 4-5
Oedipal conflicts, 45, 90. *See also* Phallic competitiveness issues
transference to supervisor and, 23
triadic organization in, 120-122, 137, 139
Oral incorporative fantasy, 148-151
Ornstein, P., 467
Overloading of candidate, 475-476

Pain as maternal persecutor, 236, 251
Parallel process, 6, 274, 276, 446, 463-467, 474-475
Passive reactions, transference to supervisors and, 23
Patient
choice of profession, 423
curative process in, 295-296, 299
evaluation of. *See* Patient evaluation and routine reports
independence of, 404, 425
levels of communication between candidate and, 239-240, 252, 275
relationship between therapist and, 4, 472
structural change in, 346-347
suitability of, 4
sustaining analytic process in face of significant life events, 278
termination of. *See* Termination
therapeutic needs of, 473
tolerance of separation and loss, 404-405
unanalyzable, 24-25
Patient evaluation and routine reports, 29-53
background information in, 32-34
candidate first six-month summary in, 38-45
description of patient in, 29-30
initial psychoanalytic evaluation in, 35-45
disposition in, 38
presenting problems in, 30-32
sexual information in, 34-35
supervisor routine reports in, 45-53
Persecutor, maternal, 236, 251
Personal identity as psychoanalyst, 12, 467
Phallic competitiveness issues, 212-217, 227. *See also* Oedipal conflicts
Phallus, body as, 253, 259, 273, 274, 292,

462
Philosophy
supervisor, 8-9
teaching-learning situation, 25
Planning of educational experience, 75, 89-90
Practice, effective learning and, 17
Pregnancy of candidate, 132-134, 140, 158-159, 277, 454
Preoedipal state, 44
Presentation of clinical material, 6
Primal scene, 259, 274, 462
Procedures in beginning supervisory phase, 20
Process
of confirmation through derivative behavior, 277-278
of maturation and change, 14
parallel, 6, 274, 276, 446, 463-467, 474-475
Process material versus active summary, 5-6, 9-10
Profession, patient choice of, 423
Psychic reality acceptance, 165
Psychoanalysis. *See* Analysis
Psychoanalyst. *See* Analyst

Reality
intrapsychic experience and, 88, 92-93
of patient's perceptions, 445
Receiving, conflict of giving and, 60-62, 72
Reciprocal mourning process, 399-400, 407-408
Records, 4-5, 6. *See also* Reports
Redundancy, 473
Reenactment, transference, 128-131, 139, 198-199, 206
Regression
controlled, 469-471
patient evaluation and, 44
potential for, 15
therapeutic
deepening and intensifying, 113
psychoanalytic educational process and, 14-15, 276
termination phase and, 423
in training analysis, 452-453
Regressive transference, 159-160, 161, 162
to supervisor, 22-23
Reinforcement of behavior, 17
Relationships
between candidate
and institute, 27-28
and patient, changes in, 472
with colleagues, 12, 250
between patient and therapist, 4
Repetition, 473
Reports, 4-5, 6, 27-28
routine, 29-53. *See also* Patient evaluation and routine reports
Resistance, 68
to dependency, 43-44
explanatory interventions in nature of, 175, 184
interpretation of, 138-139, 152, 164
varieties of, 167-169, 182
withheld data and, 385
Responsibility
for clinical process, 9, 24
for educational needs of student, 9, 24
Rewards for success, 17
"Rivalry with the Product," 176
Role
of psychoanalyst, 12
of student, 465-466
of supervisor, 9, 12
in final supervisory phase, 25
of teacher, 465
Role model, 16
Ross, N., 176, 185

Sadness at loss of analyst, 320
Sampson, H., 5
Sandt, J. J., 2
Schuster, D. B., 2
Scientific creativity and inquiry, 27
Secondary thinking process, 58-62, 71, 113
Selection of learning, 475-476
Self-analysis
supervision goals and, 12
termination process and, 343
Self-defeating mechanisms, realization of, 384
Self-deprecation in termination phase, 422
Self-observation capacity, 228, 385
Sense of basic trust, 340
Separation
analysis and, 71
and loss, 58-62, 71-72
patient's toleration of, 404-405

termination process, conflicts and anxiety and, 367. *See also* Termination
Separation-individuation phase in mother transference, 58-59
Sexuality issues, 212-217, 227
Silences, prolonged, 335-336, 346
Skills of supervisor, teaching, 478
Spencer, J. H., Jr., 469
Strategies for effective intervention, 140
Student. *See also* Candidate
capacity to learn, 3
clinical presentation by, 6
reporting of interactions by, 4-5, 6. *See also* Reports
responsibility for educational needs of, 9, 24
role of, 465-466
Studies of supervisory process, 1-2, 7-8
Style, supervisor teaching, 478
Subjective experience, affective and, 114
Substitute object for analyst, 433, 446
termination phase and, 416-417, 423-424
Summaries
candidate first six-month, 38-45
capacity for, 141
supervisor, 45-53
Superego
shift in organization of, 276
tolerance of, for fantasies and wishes, 254
Supervision. *See also* Supervisor
aspects of, 11-28
education principles in, 15-17
goals in, 11-13
institute and, 27-28
unconscious aspects of unfolding process in, 13-15
audiotape recordings of, 1, 7-8
candidate feelings in early stage of, 453-454
common elements in, 3
cumulative effects of changes in, 166
goals of, 11-13
interrupted observations in studies of, 7-8
phases of, 18-27
psychoanalytic
conceptualization of, 11
nature of, 2-5
reporting of interactions in, 4-5
studies of, 1-2
Supervisor. *See also* Supervision
active dialogue of candidate and, 186
active role of, 255
affective responses of, 24
ambivalence and conflict of, in final supervisory phase, 26
candidate identification with, 386, 458-459
candidate transference to, 15, 21-23, 450, 457-460
clarifying dynamic understanding of material, 163
collegial interaction and, 12, 250, 300
commitment of, 478
constructive criticism of, 17, 117-118
countertransference and, 423
demonstration of sequence of thought process, 206
directive role of, 255
displacement of personal issues and, 231-232
distractions of, 457
formulations of, 105-109, 115
helping candidate cope with uncertainty, 91
idealization of, 452, 455
identification with, 386, 458-459
illness of, 70, 74, 457
as model, 156, 165, 208, 387, 477-478
new, 15
philosophy of, 8-9
regressive transference to, 22-23
reports of, 45-53
role of, 9, 465
shift in behavior of, 323, 476-477
skills of, 478
style of, 255-256, 478
suggestions of, for interpretations and interventions, 85, 91-92, 255
summary of patient responses by, 225-226, 229-230
talents of, 3
teaching style of, 255-256
timing and frequency of interventions by, 113-118
transference of, 232
as transference object, 15, 21-23, 450, 457-460
withdrawal of, in final supervisory phase, 25
Synthesis, capacity for, 141

Talents
  of candidate, 478
  of supervisor, 3
Teacher, role of, 465. *See also* Supervisor
Teaching. *See also* Supervision
  collaborative nature of learning and, 206. *See also* Learning alliance
  distinctions between learning and, 16
  and learning of basic principles, 163
  philosophical issue in, 25
  psychoanalysis and, 2-5. *See also* Candidate
  skills, style, and capacity of, 478
  style of, 255-256, 478
Technical aspects in beginning supervisory phase, 20
Technical interventions
  dynamic understanding of, 24
  resolving problems in, 91-92
  supervision goals and, 11
Termination, 25-26, 311-313, 320-321
  affective and experiential elements in, 408
  candidate description of parting at, 430-432, 445
  comfort of patient and candidate in, 406
  conflicts and, 367, 368
  countertransference and, 399-400, 407-408
  defenses and, 367, 407
  dynamics of, 408
  objectivity of candidate and, 407
  patient self-analytic scrutiny in, 343
  rapid oscillation between progress and regression in, 423
  search for substitute object and, 416-417, 423-424
  significance of object relationships in, 386-387
  spontaneous movement to, 306-310, 319
  structural change in, 423
Thaler, O.F., 2
Theory
  correlation of clinical observation and, 21
  of psychoanalysis, 451
Therapeutic alliance, patient evaluation and, 44
Therapeutic needs of patient, 473
Therapeutic regression, 14-15, 113, 276
Therapeutic techniques, desire to learn, 20
Therapist, relationship between patient and, 4. *See also* Analyst
Thinking process of analysis, 23-24, 206
Training, candidate. *See* Candidate; Supervisor
Training analysis, 450, 463, 467-468
  regression in, 452-453
Training situation as issue to patient, 426-427, 444-445
Transcriptions, audio-recorded, 1, 7-8
Transference, 305, 315, 319, 322, 383. *See also* Transference neurosis
  aggression in, 383-384
  bisexual nature of, 343-344
  dynamics of, 73
  father, 86-87, 92
    woman analyst and, 315-316, 322
  fearful reaction and, 23
  homosexual fantasies and, 174, 185
  mother
    dyadic, 464
    libidinal object, 227-228
    separation-individuation phase in, 58-59
  negative, 342, 386, 387
  oscillation of, 343-344
  patient evaluation and, 44
  primitive distortion in, 177-178, 185-186
    correction of, 161, 461
  recognition of importance of, 83-84, 90
  reenactment, 128-131, 139, 198-199, 206
  resolution of idealization in, 320
  splitting of, 190, 205
  of supervisor, 232
  to supervisor, 15, 21-23, 450, 457-460
  tolerance of wishes but renunciation of gratification, 185
Transference abstinence, 387
Transference displacement, 305, 315, 319, 322, 383
Transference distortions, 177-178, 185-186
  correction of, 461
Transference neurosis, 298
  analyst functions in patient, 156-157, 165
  regressive, 159-160, 161, 162
  renunciation of, 388
  resolution of, 320, 388, 405-406, 408,

421
Transitional phenomena concept, 451
Treatment setting and situation as issue to patient, 426-427, 444-445
Triadic oedipal organization, 120-122, 137, 139
Trust, sense of basic, 340
Tyler, R., 15, 16

Unanalyzable patient, 24-25
Uncertainty of candidate, 73-74, 90
Unconscious aspects of unfolding process, 13-15
Undoing of aggression, 338

Vomiting, 363-365, 368

Wallerstein, R. S., 1, 2, 5, 439, 464, 466
Weaning process, 26. *See also* Termination
Winnicott, D. W., 451
Wishes, guilt and shame and, 160-161
Withdrawal of supervisor in final supervisory phase, 25
Working through in middle supervisory phase, 24